The Image of Antiquity

THE IMAGE OF ANTIQUITY

Ancient Britain and the Romantic Imagination

Sam Smiles

Published for The Paul Mellon Centre for Studies in British Art
by
Yale University Press
New Haven and London
1994

Set in Linotron Garamond Book by Best-set Typesetter Ltd., Hong Kong
Printed and bound in Great Britain by The Bath Press, Avon

Library of Congress Cataloging-in-Publication Data
Smiles, Samuel.
    The image of antiquity : ancient Britain and the romantic
imagination / Samuel Smiles.
      p. cm.
    Includes bibliographical references and index.
    1. Great Britain—History—To 449—Historiography. 2. Man.
Prehistoric—Great Britain—Historiography. 3. Celts—Great
Britain—Historiography. 4. Druids and Druidism—Historiography.
5. Romanticism—Great Britain. 6. Great Britain—Antiquities.
7. Britons—Historiography. 8. Great Britain—In art. 9. Art.
British. I. Title.
   DA135.S63   1994
938.1′0072—dc20   94-9935
                                                                      CIP

ISBN 0 300 05814 4

CONTENTS

Acknowledgements   vii
Photographic Acknowledgements   viii
Preface   ix

1   The Domain of Antiquity   1
2   The Past and its Meanings   8
3   Northern Heroes and National Identity   26
4   The Bards of Britain   46
5   The Druids   75
6   Ancestors and Others: The Origins of England   113
7   The Image of the Briton   129
8   The Megalithic Landscape   165
9   Garden Design and the Prehistoric Past   194
10 Conclusion   218

Notes   222
Select Bibliography   238
Index   248

To Stephanie

ACKNOWLEDGEMENTS

I owe a debt of thanks to Howard Leathlean, Peter Howard and David Jacques for their close reading of a draft version of Chapter 9 and to Steve Daniels and Pyrs Gryffudd for letting me loose on unsuspecting audiences at Geography conferences held at Nottingham in 1990 and Swansea in 1992. I would also like to thank Hilary Carey, Jos Hackforth-Jones, Professor George Henderson, John O'Brien, Michael Pidgley and Jeanne Sheehy for their help and advice. Thanks too to Professor Michael Kitson and the anonymous reader for Yale University Press whose well-judged comments made this a much better book than it would otherwise have been. Eileen Harris, Malcolm Jones, Philip Ward-Jackson and Urszula Szulakowska helped me secure photographs; Ingeborg Davies and Edith Southwell ably translated the technical language of German rights and reproduction. The staff of Exeter Central Reference Library, The Devon and Exeter Institution, and the Exeter Faculty of Art Library were more than helpful in securing antiquarian and other texts. I have received prompt and informative replies from a number of regional libraries, museums and galleries in the U.K. and it is only lack of space that stops me listing them all.

I was the grateful recipient of a Visiting Fellowship at the Yale Center for British Art in November 1987, and the support and encouragement I received there were of immense importance in advancing my research. I am also obliged to the Exeter Faculty of Art's research committee for remitting some of my professional duties in the Summer Term, 1992. The Paul Mellon Centre for Studies in British Art and my faculty's research committee supplied financial assistance for photography.

At Yale University Press, John Nicoll was patience itself waiting for the manuscript to emerge and Mary Carruthers was a sympathetic and thorough editor in all matters of preparation for publication.

My biggest thanks of all are to Stephanie for indulging me in my Druidic delusions over the last five years and for steadfastly believing in the worth of this project no matter how bizarre it seemed to others. Catherine and Fergus put up with their father's strange behaviour and showed a real interest in rummaging through files and typing interesting additions to the text while my back was turned.

PHOTOGRAPHIC ACKNOWLEDGEMENTS

Grateful acknowledgement is made to the following institutions and persons for the provision of photographs and permission to reproduce:

ACL, Bruxelles 13; The Visitors of the Ashmolean Museum, Oxford 59, 100, 105; The British Library 19, 38, 39, 40, 63, 87, 88, 89, 91, 115, 128; The Trustees of the British Museum 18, 24, 25, 36, 43, 44, 45, 46, 47, 84, 113; The Chatsworth Settlement Trustees 37; Christies's Images 74; The Cleveland Museum of Art, Cornelia Blakemore Warner Fund and Delia E Holden Fund, 78.20 52; Conway Library, Courtauld Institute of Art 6, 7, 78, 79, 85, 96; AC Cooper 21, 110, 123; Courtauld Institute of Art 37, 102; Dublin Castle 53, 54; Exeter Central Library 41; Ferens Art Gallery: Hull City Museums and Art Gallerires (UK) 73; The Guildhall Art Gallery: Corporation of London 81; The Huntington Library and Art Gallery 106; Laurent Sully Jaulmes. Paris 35; Malcolm Jones 127; Kungl. Akademien for de Fria Konsterna (The Royal Academy of Fine Arts), Stockholm 118; Kunsthalle, Bremen 9; Laing Art Gallery, Newcastle upon Tyne (Tyne and Wear Museums) 22; The Frances Lehman Loeb Art Center, Vassar College, Poughkeepsie, New York, Gift of Matthew Vassar 111; Maidstone Museum and Art Gallery 122; C Manchester City Art Galleries 104; Manchester Public Libraries, Local Studies Unit 80; Bildarchiv Foto Marburg 11; Musée des Arts Decoratifs, Paris 35; Paul Mellon Centre for Studies in British Art, Photo Archive 50, 122; Tony Mosley 125; National Galerei, Staatliche Museen zu Berlin, Preussischer Kulturbesitz Kupferstichkabinett, Sammlung der Zeichungen und Drukgraphik 10; National Gallery of Scotland, Edinburgh 31; National Museum of Wales 17; The National Trust 76, 78, 79, 102; Godfrey New 81; Norfolk Museums Service (Norwich Castle Museum); 114; Stephanie Pratt 121; Antonia Reeve 109; The British Architectural Library, RIBA, London 123; The Royal Collection © Her Majesty Queen Elizabeth II 4; Royal Scottish Academy 109; Salisbury and South Wiltshire Museum 48; Somerset County Council Local History Library 126; Sotheby's 55; Staatliche Kunstsammlungen Dresden, Gemaldgalerei Neue Meister 12; Statens Museum for Kunst, Copenhagen 5; The Governors of Stowe School 85; Lord Swinton 125; Tate Gallery 23, 27, 32, 34; Tiroler Landesmuseum Ferdinandeum, Innsbruck 8; Mandy Trafford 60, 62; University of Michigan Museum of Art, Ann Arbor 112; Courtesy of The Board of Trustees of the Victoria and Albert Museum 57, 71, 86, 95, 99, 103, 107, 116, 117; Courtesy of The Lewis Walpole Library, Yale University 14, 15, 16; 30; Wiltshire Archaeological and Natural History Society Museum 98, 101, 120; Wycombe District Council 50; Yale Center for British Art, Paul Mellon Collection 1, 2, 3, 20, 26, 28, 29, 33, 42, 49, 51, 65, 66, 68, 82, 83, 92, 119

We live in depressing times. When I started work on this project I had no inkling that European and other nationalisms were merely sleeping, capable of rising to sometimes tragic prominence as old racial and cultural divisions were opened up anew. The fragmentation of the former U.S.S.R. into a looser grouping of republics and nationalist enclaves, the emergence of newly democratic countries in eastern Europe and the disintegration of Yugoslavia have all been accompanied by ethnic and national tensions as historically sanctioned borders and boundaries have been thrown into doubt. Here, in the last days of the 1992 British general election the prime minister, John Major, made an extraordinary appeal to the British electorate to wake up and ensure the safety of the Union, as Scottish nationalism became a central election issue and promised to erase a chapter in British history which hitherto had seemed to be written in stone. As these examples indicate, the identity of a country, of a nation, of a people is an unfinished process and the definitional clarity promised by a world atlas is certainly an illusion. The investigation of origins and the writing of an acceptable history are manifestly part of this continuing search for national identity; we construct lineages to keep ourselves afloat in the choppy waters of indeterminacy and anonymity which threaten to swamp a sense of self.

I believe that the archaic history of Britain, as it was imagined between 1750 and 1850, is a telling example of such a search. It shows how evidence about the past could be collected, debated and organised to produce an image of antiquity appropriate for current interests and needs. I have chosen to characterise this activity as 'romantic' not only because the era that opens with the publication of Thomas Gray's *The Bard* in 1757 and closes with the death of J.M.W. Turner in 1851 encompasses the rise and decline of a cultural orientation which we might call romantic without doing unseemly violence to the term, but also because the habit of mind I wish to investigate, in its imaginative projection into the past, can be detected in neo-classical and realist guises as well; it is 'romantic' in so far as it can be differentiated from the 'scientific' methodologies of archaeology and historiography and the professionalisation of their research as those disciplines developed in the later nineteenth century.

In examining this imaginative approach to antiquity I intend to offer a synoptic review of a phenomenon manifested in many different contexts and to demonstrate how these several manifestations can be profitably studied as parts of an interrelated whole. Necessarily, therefore, no item is studied here in exhaustive detail but features instead as a contributing agent within the wider picture. Similarly, I have tried to avoid the privileging of any one category of evidence over another, such that historiography, the history of ideas, the development of archaeology and antiquarianism, the production of literature, paintings, sculpture, engravings and garden design all contribute in some measure to the wider narrative as it unfolds. If the plastic arts loom larger in this study than might be otherwise expected it is because I believe that they provide a succinct visual distillation of the currents of thought and feeling that surrounded their making and that they were and are productive of meaning themselves, perhaps supremely so when considering the general public's understanding of prehistoric and proto-historic Britain.

This study would have been inconceivable without the many distinguished contributions to the subject of antiquarianism made by Stuart Piggott; without his work, it is fair to say, this whole area would not exist as a focus for contemporary concern. Professor Piggott, of course, writes from a background in archaeology and as far as I am aware, this present book represents the first published attempt by a non-archaeologist to examine in some detail the romantic representation of archaic British history. As such it is a work of synthesis, trying to bring together areas of study which are often kept very far apart today as areas of separate intellectual endeavour. My debt to the writings of authorities in other fields is therefore profound and I have relied heavily on secondary sources outside my own discipline, the history of art, as the notes and bibliography will attest. I beg the pardon of specialists for those all too frequent occasions when my over-simplification of complex issues will set their teeth on edge, but to keep my word length within reasonable bounds a certain amount of condensation was necessary. What I have saved in secondary exposition I have attempted to repay in the provision of quotation and illustration. As its title emphasises, this study aims to examine the *image* of antiquity and I believe that it is in the texture of verbal and visual language, in their rhetoric so to speak, that such an image is constituted. Meaning, in other words, is validated in the performance as much as in the content of these representations, and while I do not necessarily believe that the past can speak for itself, there are significant advantages in letting a variety of different voices be heard within the confines of one book.

Chapter One

THE DOMAIN OF ANTIQUITY

We tend to avoid using the words 'Ancient Britons' these days if we want to refer to the Iron Age Celts whom the Romans encountered. It is a vague expression suitable only for knock-about history, the world of Astérix this side of the Channel, or a reminder of the inadequacies of earlier historical knowledge. So asking the question 'who were the Ancient Britons?' in the 1990s seems a strange thing to do. Yet the question would not have seemed odd at all in the period covered by this book and it would have been answered by scrutinising classical sources and by drawing inferences from megalithic sites and other relics of antiquity.[1] Now this curiosity about ancient Britain, almost from its inception in the sixteenth century, was also associated with the further question of the relationship between these primitive Britons and contemporary British life, what insights they might provide about the nation's origins, character and destiny; and the answers furnished by scholars and antiquarians were often ideologically motivated. To ask 'who were the Ancient Britons?' today is therefore to ask a question about the historical imagination of eighteenth- and nineteenth-century antiquarians, writers and artists. What purposes did their several constructions of Ancient Britain serve, how were the aborigines of the British Isles conceived and on what terms did they enter works of history, literature and art?

Apologists for prehistoric Celtic Britain championed the simplicity of primitive life and the heroic defence of British liberty against Roman aggression; critics emphasised the brutishness, cruelty and cultural insignificance of that era. Writing in 1771, Robert Henry summed up the debate in his *History of Great Britain*:

There will probably be as great a diversity of opinions about the enjoyments as about the virtues of the ancient Britons. The enthusiastical admirers of antiquity will be delighted with that ease, freedom, and independency which they enjoyed; the healthful plainness and simplicity in which they lived; and the rural sports and amusements in which they spent their time. To such readers Britannia, in this period, will appear another Arcadia, peopled with happy shepherds and shepherdesses, tending their flocks and herds in peace, free from all cares and pains but those of love; and making the hills and dales resound with their melodious songs; never reflecting on the many wants and inconveniences to which the swains and nymphs were exposed, by their ignorance or very imperfect knowledge of the most useful arts. On the other hand, those who are enchanted with the opulence, magnificence, and refinements of modern times, will view, with contempt and pity, the humble cottages, the mean dress, the coarse and scanty fare, and the rustic gambols of the ancient Britons: not considering that nature is satisfied with little, and that if they did not possess, neither did they feel the want of the admired enjoyments of the present age.[2]

Henry's account, biased towards the Britons and easy with the idea of some primitive Arcadia, can be usefully contrasted with a much more sombre view of primitive life published exactly one hundred years later. Charles Darwin's thesis about human evolution in *The Descent of Man* (1871) was ushered before a public grown used to the idea of racial hierarchies, the 'atrocities' of 'savage' peoples and a whole cluster of imperialist and progressivist beliefs which helped construct a highly critical view of 'primitive' cultures. In defending his conclusions about the ancestry of mankind Darwin voiced a detestation of the savage which must have been widely shared if his argument in this passage was to succeed.

He who has seen a savage in his native land will not feel much shame if forced to acknowledge that the blood of some more humble creature flows in his veins. For my own part I would as soon be descended from that heroic little monkey who braved its dreaded enemy in order to save the life of its keeper . . . as from a savage who delights to torture his enemies, offers up bloody sacrifices, practises infanticide without remorse, treats his wives like slaves, knows no decency, and is haunted by the grossest superstitions.[3]

But Darwin, as he well knew, was descended from both and whereas the ancestral monkey lay in the almost unimaginable past, the cruel, ignorant savage was merely finite generations away. Who indeed would wish to be descended from such a progenitor? And if the Ancient Britons were the earliest inhabitants of these islands which picture was more accurate – were they gentle pastoralists or sadistic brutes? In short was the British savage noble or ignoble? The answer to this conundrum was of more than scholarly interest precisely because the question of national identity might be addressed by examining national history, even that of the remote past. In reviewing the varying constructions of Ancient Britain, ranging from disavowal and suppression to celebration and espousal, we are, of course, witnesses of a process of self-validation, where present concerns are projected into the past to produce the desired image of antiquity. The past, in other words, was never simply there, to be examined with greater and greater understanding, but was always in the process of being formed. Much of the debate surrounding the primaeval era was of a highly specialised nature, the concern of a small number of antiquarians, but a more general understanding of ancient Britain was available outside this narrow world. Creative literature and the visual arts helped to promote the idea of British antiquity among the public at large and to define what it meant for that audience. They helped to constitute the definitive appearance of archaic Britain while responding to the often contradictory arguments advanced about it and are crucial witnesses of the perception of the remote past, a distillation of antiquarian thought as it percolated into general consciousness.[4]

This is a book, then, about perceptions of the past, perceptions held by a variety of individuals over a hundred year span. Some of these perceptions are characteristic of widely held opinions in society at any one time, others are representative of factional interest, idiosyncracy, even monomania; all of them jostle for position in the articulation of the past. In examining this material we will be looking at competing representations of prehistoric Britain, at the elaboration of an image of the past to serve the needs of particular groups of people in a period of rapid change. Recent developments in literary theory have demonstrated how texts (whether 'literary' or 'scientific' in form and function) mediate between experience and reality, in fact may constitute the only reality we can ever know. The construction of an image of antiquity should be seen as an analagous process, whereby literary, archaeological and iconic representations of the remote past come to stand for archaic Britain. The past 'itself', if such a concept is still coherent in European thought of the 1990s, is not at issue here.[5]

Nevertheless, whatever wariness we might now have concerning the transparency of archaeological interpretation and whatever suspicions we might entertain that our current thinking about prehistoric and Iron Age Britain will itself come to look partial and ideologically motivated a hundred years hence, it is still true that our picture of the past is strikingly different from what it was in the eighteenth and nineteenth centuries. To avoid confusion, it is as well that I set out some of the salient differences between these pictures. Our elaborate prehistory, the product of painstaking fieldwork and excavation, radio-carbon dating and highly organised intellectual enquiry, benefits most evidently from the availability of an expanded chronological field, but until relatively late in the nineteenth century there was no reliable method to distinguish artefacts within an extensive chronological frame. The word 'prehistoric' itself was only coined as late as 1851.[6] As a result, it is fair to say that before the 1830s, to make a rough approximation, for the majority of antiquarians as well as the general public, all prehistoric monuments in Britain were the creation of one aboriginal people, the Celts, whose Druidic priesthood had built stone circles like Stonehenge, who buried their dead in tumuli and whose culture had been described by classical authors.

This highly condensed account of British prehistory was justified by Biblical authority. By the mid eighteenth century over seventy Biblical chronologies existed, giving a range of dates for the creation of the world, from 5,400 BC to 3,964 BC. Of these, perhaps the most well known was Bishop Ussher's, first published in 1650 and included in the Authorised Version of the Bible from 1701. This gave the date of the Creation as 4,004 BC, with Noah's Flood as 2,448 BC.[7] If, as was commonly believed in antiquarian circles, the Ancient Britons were the descendants of Japhet's son Gomer, whose people took two or three centuries to travel from Asia Minor to Britain, their settlement here could scarcely have been much earlier than 2,000 BC and certainly not before 2,400 BC. Theories concerning the origins of the Ancient Britons might stretch and twist these chronologies (the antiquarian William Stukeley, for example, showed an Ancient British iron bridle '5,000 years old' to the Society of Antiquaries in 1759)[8] but they were constrained by the matrix of scriptural authority. Until that authority was circumvented the time-frame for prehistory was necessarily extremely limited, with the period from the remotest British antiquity imaginable to the coming of the Romans squeezed into about eighty generations; but with no means at the antiquarian's disposal of recognising or understanding the sequence of different cultures in British prehistory even this abbreviated time-scale would seem to have given ample time for

Celtic peoples to have settled these islands, built megalithic structures and hill forts and developed the culture described by Caesar, Tacitus and other classical writers. In the case of Stonehenge, for instance, most accounts before the 1850s placed it no earlier than 500 BC. Thus, taking examples at random, Stukeley, offering one of the more archaic chronologies, had dated Stonehenge to *c*.460 BC and Avebury to *c*.1,859 BC., making it coeval with Abraham. A more conservative view can be found in John Hassell's remarks, quoted in Chapter Eight, whose 'seventeen hundred years or more' for the age of Stonehenge would place its origins about fifty years before the Claudian invasion, while the 'twice ten hundred winters' of an anonymous poem of the 1820s would give a rhetorically dictated date of approximately 180 BC. Only Henry Browne, the megalithic model maker, dissented wildly from this consensus, preferring an antediluvian date since he believed Stonehenge to have been erected by Adam in commemoration of the Fall.[9] We can assume, then, that Sharon Turner's confident assertion of chronology in *The History of the Anglo-Saxons* (1799–1805) is a fair representation of intelligent opinion before Lyellian and other geological theories were in play.

> That there has been some catastrophe, like an universal deluge, to which all authentic history must be posterior, is now becoming the belief of the most scientific geologists . . . But the only ancient record, which connects a rational chronology with the revolution of physical nature – the Genesis of Moses – has authorised our best chronologers to place it about 2,348 years before the Christian aera. This period is, therefore, the limit of all credible antiquity.[10]

The recognition of a far longer British prehistory than had been envisaged in eighteenth-century thought is one of the salient features which distinguishes the later nineteenth- and twentieth-centuries' archaeology from their antiquarian predecessors. The steady undermining of Biblical chronology by scientific theory is, of course, a feature of the late eighteenth and nineteenth centuries and would have profound implications for the study of prehistory in the vastly extended time-scale it made available. Buffon's *Epochs of Nature* (1778), for example, suggested that the creation of the earth had taken 75,000 years, with the world as we know it and humanity itself in existence for 6,000–8,000 years.[11] The origins of the earth were being productively debated by late eighteenth-century geologists with speculation divided into three main groups: Neptunists who held that rocks were precipitated out of an originally aqueous earth; Vulcanists who believed volcanoes to be the source of rocks such as basalt; and Plutonists who believed in the subterranean igneous origins of basalt and granite. All of these theories relied, to a greater or lesser extent, on a time-frame of immeasurable extent to explain the geological record. In Britain, James Hutton's *Theory of the Earth* (1788) was the most influential Plutonist account of the earth and, especially in John Playfair's *Illustrations of the Huttonian Theory* (1802), it became very widely known. Although opposed within geological circles by rival theorists, and without by exponents of the Mosaic account of Creation, Hutton's belief in regular processes over huge expanses of time prepared the intellectual ground for Lyell's work of the 1830s.[12] Geology as a scientific discipline may be said to have publicly arrived with the establishment in 1807 of the Geological Society of London and throughout the nineteenth century the publication of geological research was a key determinant in the formation of widely held beliefs concerning the world and its chronology. Charles Lyell's epoch-making *Principles of Geology*, published from 1830 to 1833, was of seminal importance in substantiating a new time-frame within which to situate the origins of the world and man's rise to civilisation. He took Hutton's supposition 'that the operations of nature are equable and steady' as a guiding maxim, the subtitle of *Principles of Geology* being *An Attempt to Explain the Former Changes of the Earth's Surface by Reference to Causes now in Operation*. When volume I was reviewed in 1832 the term 'Uniformitarianism' was coined to express this concept. Uniformitarianism was mainly challenged as a theory by so-called 'Catastrophism', the view that successive creations had been utterly destroyed and the earth restocked on each occasion, with the last catastrophe being that flood recorded in the Old Testament. Thus both schools of thought could envisage a long history for the earth and explain the fossil record but Catastrophists were still restricted to Biblical chronology for the history of mankind itself.[13]

That question indeed remained wide open. Increasingly, the material evidence of human culture suggested a progressive model of development over a very long time span. Stone axes had been known since the Renaissance and were recognised as such by numerous scholars from the late sixteenth century onwards. But stone technology did not threaten a Biblical time-frame, especially when travel accounts of the Americas indicated quite clearly that such technology was still in use among savage peoples. From the beginning of the nineteenth century, however, sporadic discoveries of stone implements in conjunction with the bones of extinct animals suggested a radical rethinking of human history. In 1800 John Frere submitted 'An Account of Flint Weapons discovered at Hoxne in Suffolk' to *Archaeologia*. His conclusion was startling.

> They are, I think, evidently weapons of war, fabricated and used by a people who had not the use of metals . . . the situation in which these weapons were found may tempt us to refer them to a very remote period indeed, even beyond that of the modern world.[14]

If Frere's report failed to ignite interest at the time it was, perhaps, because its conclusions were almost inconceivable in 1800, but similar speculations arising from research by a number of excavators in England, France and Belgium began to be published in the 1820s and 1830s. Independently, Danish archaeologists elaborated a prehistory divided into technological phases. In 1836 C.J. Thomsen classified the artefacts of the Museum of Northern Antiquities in Copenhagen in a tripartite division of stone, bronze and iron and this division of human culture was promulgated by his successor J.J.A. Worsaae in his *Primeval Antiquities of Denmark* (1843; English translation 1849). Thomsen's Three Age system implied a long prehistory ante-dating classical accounts of barbarians armed with iron weapons and so offered to extend the history of mankind further back in time than Mosaic chronology allowed. This conceptual map of prehistory, when combined with the excavation of geological levels containing tools alongside the remains of extinct species would push the origins of human settlement into more and more remote periods. In 1859, a year marked in any case by the publication of Darwin's *Origin of Species*, official acceptance of these new archaeological theories was won. William Pengelly completed his excavations on behalf of the British Association at Windmill Hill Cave, Brixham, demonstrating beyond reasonable doubt the existence of flint tools alongside extinct species in undisturbed strata. At the same time a British delegation from the Royal Society visited the French archaeologist Jacques Boucher de Perthes at Abbéville and confirmed the theories of prehistoric man he had advanced in *De la Création: Essai sur l'Origine et la Progression des Êtres* (1838) and in his work in progress *Antiquités Celtiques et Antédiluviennes* (1847–65).[15]

By the 1850s, then, most Victorians would have been aware of the huge sweep of geological time, whose slow workings were increasingly able to explain the fossil record more effectively than the narrow time-frame derived from strict biblical exegesis. As Ruskin wrote to his friend Henry Acland in 1851, 'If only the Geologists would let me alone, I could do very well, but those dreadful Hammers. I hear the clink of them at the end of every cadence of the Bible verses.'[16] The immediate result of this enlarged time-scale for British prehistory was that antiquities no longer had to find their historical position within the rather narrow compass left to them between the Biblical Flood and the coming of the Romans. Robert Vaughan's *Revolutions in English History* (1859), for example, was already making use of the Danish Three Age system, referring to Stone and Bronze Age peoples preceding the Iron Age Celts described by Caesar.[17]

Our view of prehistoric Britain today is often strikingly different, of course, from that of the eighteenth and nineteenth centuries, so different in fact that we tend to look on the previous 250 years of research as a progressive clarification of what had started out as a hopelessly confused picture. The slow development of new concepts of time is a paradigm of this sort of steady and patient re-orientation of fundamental beliefs. Even if this achievement progressed sometimes by fits and starts, with many an errant theory retarding genuine gains in knowledge, it can nevertheless be stated with some confidence that we know more about prehistory and have better grounds for trusting our information than previous generations. If we compare the state of knowledge in the late eighteenth century with its equivalent in the late twentieth century the realm of prehistory could scarcely be more different. For us, the commonly accepted view is that *homo erectus* hominids may have arrived in Britain about 350,000 years ago, setting up temporary camps to hunt animals in the tundra south of the ice sheets which covered most of the country. Nomadic bands came and went as the ice retreated, was succeeded by warmer interglacial periods, and returned again. The remains of more advanced human-type cultures, the Neanderthals, have been dated in Britain from about 70,000 BC, to be replaced in their turn by *homo sapiens sapiens* some time about 35,000 BC. From about 12,000 BC (the end of the Paleolithic era) the ice retreated for the last time, sea levels began to rise and around about 7,500 BC the land bridge joining Britain to the continent was submerged. This Mesolithic era, marked by a more sophisticated stone tool technology, comes to a close about 4,500 BC as Neolithic farming practices are introduced, animals domesticated and forests cleared. Metal working, first in copper and gold, from about 2,500 BC, then in bronze, from about 2,200 BC, is introduced and the Bronze Age runs until the coming of new technology, the Iron Age, in about 800 BC. Within this picture, the visible remains of prehistoric Britain are chiefly produced in the Neolithic and early

6

Bronze Age periods: the causewayed camps and long barrows are dated between approximately 4,300 and 3,000 BC, chambered tombs between 4,100 and 2,700 BC, Avebury to about 2,500 BC, the various sequences of building and remodelling at Stonehenge between 3,100 and 1,100 BC and stone circles in general between 3,500 and 1,700 BC. The Iron Age Celts described in classical accounts, their bards and their Druid priests had nothing whatever to do with the construction of these monuments, whose purposes were very probably as enigmatic to them as they were to later antiquarians.

In the late twentieth century we find it useful to draw a distinction between prehistory and the proto-historic world of the Celtic Iron Age because we have the means to discriminate between such widely differentiated cultures. Such distinctions could have no meaning for the artists, antiquarians and others whose attitudes to the past are examined in this book. In attempting to demonstrate the complex weave of the web of prehistory in the period 1750–1850 I have followed that era's usage and thus ignored our customary discriminations between periods, cultures and technologies. 'Genuine' prehistoric monuments, the exploits of real and semi-mythical Celtic leaders living between 55 BC and the third century AD, Druids, even mediaeval bards contributed to the image of antiquity as it was researched, debated and presented in eighteenth- and nineteenth-century Britain. The resultant images of the past, constituted in a variety of different forms under the impress of different intellectual and ideological pressures, function like myth where what is important is not how 'true' it is, how well it matches reality scientifically described, but how effective it is, how well it enables its adherents to comprehend and make the best use of a given world. In outlining this my intention is not to mock the researches of the past, but to demonstrate their coherence within the larger epistemic contexts of the age.

If I have succeeded in this, the conclusion that follows as regards our own picture of the past can only be a humble one. Notwithstanding the achievements of archaeology today we too are inevitably the creatures and captives of mentalities we only dimly perceive. In an extreme view, the world scientifically described is fundamentally as mythic a construction as any other and gains its meaning from the manipulation of a particular set of symbolic exchanges every bit as arbitrary as the tenets of Egyptian religion, mediaeval Scholasticism or the beliefs of the Dakota people. Further, our contemporary scepticism concerning truth and progress, our sympathy for 'unscientific' or intuitive knowledge is itself specific to the modalities of late twentieth-century Western culture, our very recognition of the provisionality of knowledge is itself provisional. There is no escape from this dizzying regress, but our awareness of the predicament, our willingness to recognise that there are varieties of truth gives us good reason to put progressivist histories of archaeology into abeyance for a moment and attempt instead to investigate the poetics of prehistory.

Chapter Two

THE PAST AND ITS MEANINGS

The study of ancient Britain underwent a wholesale transformation between 1750 and 1850, from a peripheral antiquarian pursuit to recognition as a central concern for antiquarianism and for the increasingly professional academic discipline of archaeology. This transformation was not merely a change in status for the investigation of prehistoric and Iron Age Britain, from indifference and neglect to interest and attention; it was also a reflection of the way in which antiquarianism itself developed into a variety of practices, some amateur and some professional. There is, thus, a double development to consider, the development of prehistory as a subject worthy of study and the development of methodologies and institutions which underwrote that study. Crudely speaking we can examine these changes as a two-stage process. First, in the later eighteenth century antiquarian research moves in from the margins to compete with traditional historiography in establishing and evaluating the prehistory of these islands then, losing ground before the more rigorous development of archaeological method in the nineteenth century, antiquarianism survives as an increasingly amateur approach to the past, kept alive notably as the animating spark in the approaches to ancient Britain adopted by the creative arts. From the viewpoint of a twentieth-century archaeologist this development might be seen as the steady victory of method over conjecture, with professional archaeology finally and thankfully purged of the excesses associated with antiquarian enthusiasm; but such a teleological approach, concerned chiefly to distinguish fruitful from futile learning, is of limited use in attempting to explain how the archaic past was visualised and what purposes that visualisation served. The rights and wrongs of particular theories are not at issue in this book; what is at issue is the way in which ancient Britain was fought over by competing ideologies, was in fact the creation of these special interests.

In 1788 the Scottish historian and geographer John Pinkerton published in the *Gentleman's Magazine* a series of twelve *Letters to the People of Great Britain, on the Cultivation of their National History*. His purpose was to encourage serious investigation of the earliest history of these islands and especially the publication of the oldest authentic manuscripts which might secure the foundations for a British historiography. Early British history needed to be rescued from neglect, not merely for the sake of historical completeness but as a patriotic duty. As Pinkerton robustly declared in his first letter,

> The history of Greece and Rome all seek for in the fountains: and why should not the history of Great Britain obtain even greater attention from every native? As

the study of our history has declined, true patriotism has declined; and to attempt its revival may, it is hoped, be regarded as a service both to patriotism and to literature.[1]

The shameful neglect of early British history was, in short, a national disgrace and many were open to Pinkerton's strictures: the patrons who would not encourage pre-Conquest historical research, the historians who eschewed its prosecution, the universities who failed to promote it, and the antiquarians whose uncritical approach trivialised it. The central message of his appeal helps to remind us of the urgency surrounding historical debate in this period. '. . . next to the glory of national arms, is that of national history; without which the greatest actions are as if they had never been.'[2] Manifestly, any state cut off from its history is thereby deprived of a vital part of its cultural, social and political identity. Pinkerton's proselytising on behalf of early history indicates how Dark Age and early mediaeval Britain had been overlooked, but his advocacy of under-utilised manuscript sources demonstrates equally how that neglect might be remedied. Even if the period was of scant concern to the eighteenth-century historian, at least the materials were at hand to study it with tolerable accuracy.

Historical investigation of prehistoric, or preliterate Britain, on the other hand, was another matter entirely. For eighteenth-century historians the 'problem' of archaic British history lay in two related areas: one methodological and one cultural. In the former case they had to grapple with a lack of authoritative evidence and the existence of spurious or unreliable accounts in its place; in the latter a complex of assumptions about cultural inheritance divided the prehistoric world from the Saxon settlement. Thus, even assuming that an English historian had decided to tackle archaic Britain, why should he or his English reading public have been interested in such a history, why should they have felt any connection with the aboriginal Celts, a people whose culture had apparently been suppressed by the Romans and subsequently extirpated by their own Saxon ancestors?

If our putative historian wished to demolish such a stereotypical view of Celtic Britain and its fate and wanted to demonstrate instead the mixed inheritance of his eighteenth-century contemporaries, where were the materials that would allow him to do so? To work only with reliable information meant restricting historical sources to classical accounts of the Celtic peoples, most of which were written between the first century BC and the fourth century AD. Such a limited body of evidence would inevitably restrict what could be said. Yet to attempt a fuller picture, allowing a British history coeval with even the classical past was to lapse into the worst kinds of speculative writing. Pseudo-histories, such as Geoffrey of Monmouth's *History of the Kings of Britain* (c.1136) had been famously attacked in Polydore Vergil's *Anglica Historia* (1534) and were by now almost totally discredited. The colourful founding myths of Britain, adequate enough for the late mediaeval imagination, had given way in the early modern period to the realisation that pre-Roman Britain was likely to have borne closer resemblance to contemporary primitive cultures than the magnificent spectacle Geoffrey had related.[3] The Romans, alas, controlled the authentic evidence and to venture beyond them was to abandon history for the world of myth and legend. Pinkerton himself was scathing about the retention of such fabulous material by recent Irish historians.

While the other European nations confess their barbarism till the Greeks and Romans imparted civilization, those weak writers contend for the use of letters, and of civilization, in Ireland, at an early period: so that, by their accounts, to the two civilized nations known to the learned, we must add a third; and Greece, Rome, and Ireland, must form an odd trio. Hence the Irish history is never mentioned but with laughter . . .[4]

How then was the earliest period of British history to be treated? For the historians the answer seemed clear-cut: if no reputable evidence survived then the historian should not attempt to supply it. In the introduction to his *History of Scotland* (1759), William Robertson, Historiographer Royal for Scotland, declared,

The first ages of the Scotch history are dark and fabulous. Nations, as well as men, arrive at maturity by degrees, and the events, which happened during their infancy or early youth, cannot be recollected, and deserve not to be remembered. The gross ignorance, which anciently covered all the North of Europe, the continual migrations of its inhabitants, and the frequent and destructive revolutions which these occasioned, render it impossible to give any authentic account of the origin of the different kingdoms now established there. Everything beyond that short period, to which well attested annals reach, is obscure; an immense space is left to invention to occupy, each nation, with a vanity inseparable from human nature, hath filled that void with events calculated to display its own antiquity, and lustre. And history, which ought to record truth and to teach wisdom, often sets out with retailing fictions and absurdities.[5]

Furthermore, the archaic society that might have been brought within a less scrupulous historian's purview did not easily lend itself to the historiographic project of the eighteenth century. Whether Whig or Tory, historians were concerned to study the past as an exemplum for the present age, especially in terms of constitutional development; but few points of contact could be established with a culture whose every feature, insofar as it could be discerned at all, seemed to be removed from eighteenth-century experience.[6] In his *Letters on the Study and Use of History* (1752) Lord Bolingbroke claimed that it was mere antiquarianism to study a period before its political circumstances were similar enough to the present to be relevant, a statement which boded ill for pre-Roman history especially insofar as many historians, if looking for constitutional relevance in the period before Magna Carta, were only prepared to trace the descent of English law and politics from the 'original' constitution of the Saxon settlement.[7] It was a similar reluctance to deal with the archaic past that propelled David Hume to begin his *History of England* (1754–62) with merely a brief review of 'the state of the inhabitants as it appeared to the Romans on their invasion of this country'. Hume based his account on accredited classical authorities and, like his friend and fellow historian Robertson, emphatically eschewed the pre-Roman history of Britain:

The curiosity, entertained by all civilised nations, of enquiring into the exploits and adventures of their ancestors, commonly excites a regret that the history of remote ages should always be so much involved in obscurity, uncertainty and contradiction. Ingenious men, possessed of leisure, are apt to push their researches beyond the period in which literary monuments are framed or preserved; without reflecting, that the history of past events is immediately lost or disfigured when entrusted to memory and oral tradition, and that the adventures of barbarous nations, even if they were recorded, could afford little or no entertainment to men born in a more cultivated age. The convulsions of a civilized state usually compose the most instructive and most interesting part of its history; but the sudden, violent, and unprepared revolutions incident to barbarians, are so much guided by caprice, and terminate so often in cruelty, that they disgust us by the uniformity of their appearance; and it is rather fortunate for letters that they are buried in silence and oblivion.[8]

This historiographical difficulty affected all those involved in dealing with the past, and that included artists. For artists participated in the presentation of the prehistoric past as illustrators, history painters, topographers and designers and their attitude to their subject matter is manifestly a part of the larger debate. Artists and designers caught up in this methodological stand-off would often have to nail their colours to the mast. Joseph Strutt's *Honda Angel-Cynnan* (1774–5), for example, one of the earliest English books devoted to a history of costume, makes a virtue of its accurate representations of dress and thus follows the historians' strictures in abandoning the pre-Roman period.

> Every one who is conversant in the early parts of the British History, must be acquainted with the doubtfulness and uncertainty of it; and with how little fairness, much less truth and justice, any of the peculiar customs of the Britons can be truly set forth before the landing of Julius Caesar.[9]

We need to remember, however, the extent to which antiquarian study might be inflected by wider social concerns, such that similar sounding sentiments mask quite different attitudes to the past. For example, Strutt's warning against conjecture in the study of the past was echoed some thirteen years later in the observations included in the address to Lord Charlemont which opens Joseph Cooper Walker's *Dress of the Ancient and Modern Irish* (1788), but Walker's project was informed by a wider political dimension lacking in the sedate world of English antiquarianism.

> However ardent I have been in the pursuit of information, I seldom ventured beyond the Christian Age, awed by the settled gloom that clouded the preceeding ages, but I would not have it inferred from this confession, that I consider the pagan ages of Ireland as wrapped in impenetrable obscurity. Disguised by prejudice or tortured into deformity by enthusiasm, Irish history, for some ages, hath worn a forbidding aspect; but touched by the Ithurielan spear, I do not despair of seeing her start up in an engaging form.[10]

The origins of Walker's studies were that of a writer working in an Ireland recently become prosperous and legislatively independent of England with the so-called Grattan's Parliament of 1782–1800. Like other Irish historians writing in the second half of the eighteenth century, such as Charles O'Conor, Charles Vallancey and Sylvester O'Halloran, Walker's attitude to the past was coloured by a pride in remote origins. Irish historiography had been recruited by the Catholic Committee in the 1750s to give a non-colonial view of the past and so aid the drive for emancipation.[11] Charles O'Conor, one of the main propogandists for the committee and a notable Gaelic scholar published *Dissertations on the Antient History of Ireland* in 1753; it can be argued that it was this work in particular which did much to dignify archaic Ireland as worthy of study and to present it as the appropriate prologue to the history of an independent nation, and that O'Conor's example stimulated like-minded antiquarians to continue the endeavour. For an Irish antiquarian in the 1780s, then, the penetration of that 'settled gloom' was almost a patriotic duty while Grattan's declaration still rang in his ears: 'Ireland is now a nation. In that character I hail her and bowing down in her august presence I say *Esto perpetua*.'[12]

In contrast, most eighteenth century English writers on archaic Britain were not usually motivated by an explicitly political patriotism to examine the remote past; they had no need to assert distinctiveness from a stronger and imperial power and, as a result, could accept with relative disinterest the dearth of attested evidence about primitive Britain. Notwithstanding their methodological justification, the historiographic scruples expressed by Strutt and others were also aided and abetted by a certain historical complacency.

Yet, as Hume hinted, 'ingenious men, possessed of leisure' were quite capable of rushing in where historians feared to tread, and it is with such writers that the exploration of Britain's archaic past begins.[13] Their indefatigable researches into archaeology, etymology, folk-lore, anthropology, ethnology, heroic literature, comparative religion and much else besides generated an enormous literature containing material evidence, conjecture, lucky guesses, hypotheses and theories whose sheer bulk, capacity for creative speculation and depth of scholarly knowledge forced Hume's 'cultivated age' to acknowledge Britain's archaic past as a constituent part of its history. Indeed, it was precisely because the new scholarly rigour of Enlightenment histories separated demonstrable fact from hazy speculation that the prehistoric past was left open to other methodologies, framed by different historiographic concerns. Thus when Robertson claimed that the earliest period of Scottish history was 'the region of pure fable and conjecture, and ought to be totally neglected, or be abandoned to the industry and credulity of antiquarians' he was both signalling the limits of orthodox historical scholarship and challenging antiquarians to provide an intelligible historiography of their own.[14] The challenge was accepted by Charles O'Conor, among others, who countered it explicitly in the preface to the second edition of his *Dissertations on the Antient History of Ireland* (1765).

> . . . the idea lately propogated, that the Records of these Northern Countries, before the Resurrection of Letters in the Sixteenth Century, are not worthy of Attention, cannot be supported. It is a Strain of Affectation, and one of those Paradoxes, which, by degrading the Judgements of a great Genius, keeps inferior Abilities in Countenance.[15]

Thus far, it may appear that a fairly clear demarcation line separated the protagonists in all of these historiographical debates but what may have been relatively distinct in the mid eighteenth century was blurred by its close and we need to avoid the temptation of dividing up all eighteenth-century historians into hard-headed Augustans contemptuous of archaic history, on the one hand, and Celtic antiquarians keen to promote their enthusiasms, on the other. To take one example, Pinkerton, as we should expect, was resolutely antagonistic to antiquarian fancy and uncritical historiography, as witnessed by his remarks on Irish historiography quoted above. He strongly believed that early British history could only be put on a firm footing if a rigorous, scholarly investigation of the earliest manuscript sources was undertaken.

> In antiquities particularly, the number of visionary works which have appeared in Great Britain, sufficiently evinces the necessity of mental energy, solid and accurate ratiocination, reliance upon, and submission to, ancient authorities; and a high contempt of conjecture, loose assertion, fanciful prejudices, and all the family of dreams. A cold German, whose erudition is boundless, who collects the most minute facts, and who has not even fancy enough to form one conjecture, is worth a thousand ingenious dabblers, whose light is a mere *ignis fatuus*, and only dazzles to mislead . . .[16]

We should note, however, that Pinkerton's wish to study archaic Britain rigorously was more than just a methodological concern. Alongside his disdain for the fantasy worlds dreamed up by credulous antiquarians, Pinkerton was equally opposed to Hume's and specifically Bolingbroke's lofty dismissals of the earliest British history. In refusing even to tackle the period, historians like these had little to offer, for their historiography provided no understanding of origins, of national character and thus of national potential. In this there was a great deal of special pleading; as we shall see, Pinkerton was an enthusiastic advocate of Saxon England (and could write violent abuse of the Celtic nations in consequence) and had been encouraged by Gibbon to assemble and edit a collection of the earliest national chronicles, a project which was repeatedly frustrated.[17] Nevertheless, his argument with Augustan historiographers turns on his belief in an organic development for a nation, rooted in a particular race and culture, as opposed to their more transcendant belief in the unvarying nature of mankind (or at least civilised mankind). Pinkerton's historiography is, in other words, much closer to that of the romantics.

> . . . it is impossible to have any real knowledge of the modern history of any country without beginning the study at its fountains, in ancient events and manners. One might as well think of building a house by beginning at the garrets. Nay more, the foundation is not only to be begun at the proper place; but, as every part of the superstructure ultimately rests upon the foundation, this radical part must be examined with far more care and attention than any of the rest.[18]

Antiquarians interested in Britain's archaic, pre-Saxon past were in a more difficult position than others, running the risk much more dangerously of what Pinkerton stigmatised as 'conjecture, loose assertion, fanciful prejudices, and all the family of dreams'. Nevertheless, they justified their study by using two major arguments. The first appealed to national pride and historical self-knowledge, insisting, like Pinkerton, that an awareness of one's own country's primitive remains was of educational benefit and that ignorance of it was to be deplored. William Borlase's preface to his *Observations on the Antiquities of Cornwall* (1754) is typical of this approach.

It is the usual observation of Foreigners, that the English Travellers are too little acquainted with their own Country; and so far this may be true, that Englishmen (otherwise well qualified to appear in the world) go abroad in quest of the rarities of other countries, before they know sufficiently what their own contains; it must be likewise acknowledged that, when these foreign tours have been completed, and Gentlemen return captivated with the Medals, Statues, Pictures, and Architecture, of Greece and Italy, they have seldom any relish for the ruder products of Ancient Britain.[19]

The second line of defence was more complex, at least in implication, for it sought to assuage the worries of historians by disentangling scholarly antiquarian research from the wilder flights of fancy taken by some enthusiasts. The antiquarian James Douglas was confident that such a liaison with historical rectitude could be achieved: 'If the study of antiquity be undertaken in the cause of History it will rescue itself from a reproach indiscriminately and fastidiously bestowed on works which have been deemed frivolous.'[20] Douglas seems to have intended to distinguish a serious and 'historical' antiquarian investigation of the remote past from the empty conjecture, obsession with trivia and collection of cabinets of curiosities which typified many people's ideas of antiquarian pursuits. This image of the antiquarian was not necessarily wide of the mark; a review of some of the miscellaneous papers read at early meetings of the Society of Antiquaries provides a telling witness of the whimsicality that bedevilled antiquarianism in this period. In calling for study 'in the cause of History' Douglas was promoting a line of enquiry that could aid the literary endeavours of historians with the results of fieldwork and excavation. So too William Borlase put forward an optimistic if not totally cogent case for antiquarian speculation, disciplined by observation and fieldwork, whose conjectures would be historically valid:

In treating of the superstition, and rock monuments of the Druids, I may seem too conjectural to those, who will make no allowancies for the deficiencies of history, nor be satisfied with anything but evident truths; but where there is no certainty to be obtained, probabilities must suffice; and conjectures are no faults, but when they are either advanced as real truths, or too copiously pursued, or peremptorily insisted upon as decisive. In subjects of such distant ages, where history will so often withdraw her taper, conjecture may sometimes strike a new light, and the truths of Antiquity be more effectually pursued, than when people will not venture to guess at all. One conjecture may move the veil, another partly remove it, and a third, happier still, borrowing light and strength from what went before, may wholly disclose what we want to know.[21]

The pre-literate Ancient British could thus be admitted to history via their material remains even in the absence of supporting texts. It would not be the kind of history recognised by Hume and Robertson, it might even offend Pinkerton's demands for 'solid and accurate ratiocination' but it would be more than 'fictions and absurdities'.

Yet, worthy as Borlase's and Douglas's intentions were, they faced a further major problem with regard to the material condition and quality of the remains they championed so ably. As Borlase acknowledged, once exposed to classical culture few Englishmen had 'any relish for the ruder products of Ancient Britain'. The promulgation of an alternative to classical taste was beginning to emerge in this period with the spread of interest in mediaeval antiquities, but even when dealing with art and architecture of such technical refinement as the Gothic it was by no means easy to encourage a widespread re-evaluation of the art of the Middle Ages.[22] To attempt to interest virtuosi and connoisseurs in cromlechs, kistvaens, flint tools, stone circles and hill forts was of infinitely greater difficulty. Horace Walpole, by no means unsympathetic to the lure of bardic literature and 'Druidical' remains, summed up this problem in a caustic appraisal of the Society of Antiquaries.

> The antiquarians will be as ridiculous as they used to be; and since it is impossible to infuse taste into them, they will be as dry and dull as their predecessors. One may revive what perished, but it will perish again, if more life is not breathed into it than it enjoyed originally. . . . Their Saxon and Danish discoveries are not worth more than monuments of the Hottentots; and for Roman remains in Britain, they are upon a foot with what ideas we should get of Inigo Jones, if somebody was to publish views of huts and houses that our officers run up at Senegal and Goree. . . . I have no curiosity to know how awkward and clumsy men have been in the dawn of arts or in their decay. [23]

Walpole's references to Hottentots and colonial outposts is revealing for it underlines the quickly established realisation that 'primitive' peoples encountered on voyages of discovery and in the process of colonial settlement probably possessed a similar material culture to that of the earliest inhabitants of Britain. A progressive historiography allowed comforting distinctions to be drawn between primitive peoples and contemporary European culture, such that the distance between the savage and the civilised state was indicative of the latter's superiority. It was equally evident that the longer a state had been civilised the greater its status as a developed culture might be and this placed British history in an invidious position when compared to Biblical or classical chronologies, both of which stretched far back into the ancient past. Given that the British people made a late entry into world history after centuries of unrecorded barbarism, it may be that the primitive life of the Ancient Britons was uncomfortably close, too recent to allow a disinterested scrutiny of such a culture to flourish. If these were ancestors, they were scarcely ancestors of whom one might be proud and it is not too far fetched to talk in terms of embarrassment when reviewing some of the reactions to primitive remains. British chauvinism may have scorned many features of contemporary European life, confident of Britain's current military and economic power, but when it came to the celebration of ancestors pagan Britain was no match for Periclean Athens or Augustan Rome.

The chances for public interest in the archaic past were, therefore, seemingly slim. As we have seen, a combination of negative factors seemed to rule out any serious recuperation of Britain's remotest past: good historical evidence was lacking, the material record was technically and artistically inferior to that of classical antiquity, and the Ancient British themselves were a possibly unwelcome reminder of the primitive beginnings of British society. That such an unpromising situation would be transformed by the close of the eighteenth century can be largely attributed to the rise of primitivism as a fashionable commodity within European thought.[24] The celebration of autochthonous culture, free of the mannered artificiality and corrupt lifestyle of so-called civilisation, is a feature of the later eighteenth century, a subversive spring welling up first and most notably in the writings of Rousseau and broadening into a flood of interest and enthusiasm for the innocent, the uncorrupted and the uncivilised.

In Britain, the very factors that had proved so damaging in attempting to recapture the archaic past could now be used to construct a primitivist account. Lack of evidence allowed more room for unqualifiable invention, the inferior quality of remains hinted at a simple society living closer to nature than the over-sophisticated classical world, and the identification of Ancient Britons with contemporary savages now proved a positive advantage. The Celtic revival that began in the mid eighteenth century was the most tangible result of this altered mental climate and the expansion of interest in archaic languages, literature, customs, music, building, costume, religion and social organisation increased steadily as the century wore on. Inevitably, much of this material was indeed the 'fictions and absurdities' which historians like Robertson deplored, but more serious scholars, working systematically with new methods and techniques were beginning to lay secure foundations for a genuine British prehistory where the high scholarly standards of the seventeenth-century antiquaries would be matched again after nearly a century of seemingly 'frivolous' enquiry.[25] Archaeology, comparative ethnology and linguistics are but three of the academic disciplines which may be said to have gestated during the second half of the eighteenth century. Thus, even the most cursory review of the eighteenth century intellectual field reveals a ferment of activity from the middle of the century whose focus of inquiry was the elucidation of the archaic past in Britain. In 1751 the Society of Antiquaries (firmly established from 1717) received their royal charter, a symbol of the increasing respect antiquarian studies attracted.[26] In that same year the London Welsh established the Honourable Society of Cymmrodorion for the study and promulgation of ancient British language, customs and society.[27] The Highland Society was established for similar purposes in 1778, followed by the Society of Antiquaries of Scotland in 1780.[28] In Ireland, the Dublin Society, established in 1731 was the main early forum for historical investigation of the past. At the prompting of Charles Vallancey a select committee of antiquarians was set up in 1772 to inquire into 'the antient state of arts, literature and antiquities' but enthusiasm diminished and the initiative passed to informal groups of Dublin intellectuals in the late 1770s. These fledgling attempts were consolidated with the foundation of the Royal Irish Academy in 1785, promoting the study of Irish antiquities through its library, museum and published *Transactions*.[29]

In all of these developments a crucial place was reserved for the study of language. The survival of the Ancient British tongue in the Gaelic speaking communities of the British Isles provided a tantalising link between the present and the remotest past and language was recorded and studied for whatever clues it might provide. David Jones's 1706 translation of Paul Yves Pezron's *Antiquités de la Nation des Celtes* (1703) was followed in 1707 by Edward Lhuyd's *Archaeologia Britannica* and these two works may be said to have demonstrated the importance of linguistic and philological study for investigating the past, stimulating academic discussion of the historical origins of contemporary European languages and their

1 Thomas Rowlandson after Julius Caesar Ibbetson and John Smith, hand-coloured etching, frontispiece to Edward Jones, *The Bardic Museum*, London 1802. Yale Center for British Art, Paul Mellon Collection.

speakers. Once the antiquity of Celtic languages was recognised the related investigation of the living tradition of Celtic poetry and music was capable of opening a window on to the remote past of Britain. Such studies bore their first popular fruits with Evan Evans's *Some Specimens of the Poetry of the Antient Welsh Bards* (1764), whose publication complemented Bishop Percy's 1765 collection of mediaeval English lyrics, *Reliques of Ancient English Poetry*, but also went beyond it in demonstrating the longevity of the Welsh poetic tradition. Evans's investigations prompted others to follow his lead with the 1780s seeing the publication of three important Celtic revival texts: Edward Jones's *Musical and Poetical Relicks of the Welsh Bards* (1784), Joseph Cooper Walker's *Historical Memoirs of the Irish Bards* (1786) and Charlotte Brooke's *Reliques of Irish Poetry* (1789).

The same quickening of interest in the archaic past can be detected in literature. Later eighteenth-century poetry championed the British resistance to Rome, while two of the leaders of this resistance, Caractacus and Boadicea, were frequently picked out as examples of heroic patriotism. William Mason's verse drama *Caractacus* (1759) and William Cowper's poem *Boadicea* (1782) are typical examples of this celebration of the Celtic past. Macpherson's *Ossian* cycle of the 1760s successfully united both strands of thought, linguistic and imaginative, by publishing 'translations' of Gaelic folk poetry whose subject matter was the heroic culture of the aboriginal Scots. This desire to recapture the archaic past was, perhaps, nowhere more tangible than in the recovery of its music; the 1742 publication of John Parry and Evan Williams's *Antient British Music* allowed the last strains of a seemingly ancient tradition to linger in the fashionable drawing rooms of London.[30] In Ireland a related interest in the popular song and its supposed archaic roots can be detected in works such as Edward Bunting's *The Ancient Music of Ireland* (1796), Thomas Moore's *Irish Melodies* (1808) and James Hardiman's *Irish Minstrelsy* (1831). Ibbetson's frontispiece to Edward Jones's *Bardic Museum* (1802) (Plate 1) captures the spirit of many of these publications, with the harpist in his mountain fastness providing a living link to the archaic past of Britain while passing on this tradition to the next generation.

The role of the artist in helping to construct the image of the primaeval era was of critical importance. In a period when rigid divisions did not exist between archaeological draughtsmen and topographical artists, when imaginative reconstructions of the past could be found in painting, literature and the learned speculations of antiquarians, when histories of England, Scotland, Wales and Ireland were embellished with 'historical' engravings and when patriotic patrons wished to assemble paintings illustrating their national history, in such circumstances it is evident that the visual arts had a large part to play in forming and reforming the period's visualisation of the past. As we shall see throughout this study, when involved with archaic subject matter the artist's position in relation to the wider historiographic realm was reciprocal, both absorbing current concerns and participating in them. So, while Gray's *Bard* (1757) has rightly been seen as the mainspring of the Celtic revival, it is also true to say that a steadily proliferating corpus of images helped promote the idea of the archaic past as a discrete entity with observable and differentiating characteristics.

The beginnings of this corpus were modest enough. As historical and pseudo-historical researches burgeoned in the eighteenth century, so the need grew to improve the quality and the extent of the data on which they were based. In its attention to specific visible remains John Leland's mid sixteenth-century *Itinerary* (published 1710–12) had demonstrated the method to be followed. Detailed description of the relics of the past would provide the information on which a surer investigation of archaic history and society could be established. William Camden's *Britannia* provides a useful example of how this kind of research developed. First published in Latin in 1586, subsequent English editions of the *Britannia* grew in size and importance and, from 1607, included illustrations. Edmund Gibson's revised edition of 1695 was itself augmented in 1722 to include the latest antiquarian research, and Richard Gough's 1789 revision (republished in 1809) had developed Camden's pioneering volume into a massive work of antiquarian scholarship.[31] Surveys and questionnaires to local antiquaries were useful techniques in assembling such data, while the Society of Antiquaries itself, together with the journal *Archaeologia* (first published in 1770), provided a forum for the exchange of information.

The need to record this evidence necessarily involved antiquarians with artistic representation. Many seventeenth-century scholars had been amateur artists of some ability but increased standards of visual accuracy militated against all but the most proficient eighteenth-century antiquaries illustrating their researches themselves.[32] This was especially true insofar as a taxonomic ordering of visible antiquities could offer useful data for historical conclusions. Classical antiquities and ethnographic information were increasingly the subject of ambitious artistic record and expeditions to sites of importance overseas were being organised by the Society of Dilettanti and the Royal Society. Within Britain similar investigations held an obvious attraction for the Society of Antiquaries, especially with regard to mediaeval architecture, and Richard Gough drew attention to the neglect of such studies in 1768.

We penetrate the wilds of Europe, and the desarts of Asia and Africa, for the remains of Grecian, Roman and earlier architecture, while no artist offers himself a candidate for fame in preserving those of our forefathers in their own country.[33]

It took a further sixteen years before such a candidate, in the person of John Carter, was appointed as draughtsman to the society to provide drawings of the most interesting objects shown at meetings and later to record architecture for publication as engravings. These last may be said to represent one of the Society of Antiquaries' chief contributions to the preservation of British antiquities, being printed on specially commissioned paper to a high standard and setting new objectives for topographical publications. Although Carter himself was not initially elected to the society, a significant number of better known artists joined it in the 1790s and afterwards.[34] Most of these were members for instruction and amusement only, we must assume, rather than participants in antiquarian research; only Charles Alfred Stothard and Samuel Prout among them may be said to have enjoyed a reputation for the depiction of antiquities.

Jeremiah Milles's presidential address of 1781 had indicated how artists might profit from an association with antiquarian study.

> The relation which the Society of Antiquaries bears to the [Royal] Academy . . . is no less certain . . . History, Science and Art may claim an equal share in the Attention and Labour of the Antiquary . . . from the judicious investigation of ancient Science, and Art, a more general and useful field of knowledge is opened to the modern Artist. The most valuable Hints for the Direction of his Studies are to be collected from the works of Antiquaries, and the Repositories of Arts have been enriched with a variety of necessary Information from the same source.[35]

Milles's stress on necessary information was indeed an important aspect of the relationship between antiquarianism and art and saw its most tangible expression in illustrated books on historical costume, architecture and design whose research provided valuable detail for history painters increasingly preoccupied with accurate renditions of the past. These included Thomas Jefferys's *Collection of the Dresses of Different Nations* (1757–72), Joseph Strutt's *Honda-Angel Cynnan* (1774–6) and *A Complete View of the Dress and Habits of the People of England* (1796–9), Joseph Cooper Walker's *The Dress of the Ancient and Modern Irish* (1788), Francis Grose's *Treatise on Ancient Armour and Weapons* (1786) and their nineteenth-century descendants James Planché's *History of British Costume* (1834) and Frederick William Fairholt's *Costume in England* (1846). While the antiquarian value of these studies was based on their authors' first-hand observation of the artistic record of the period in question, obvious gains in historical accuracy and the avoidance of anachronisms could be achieved.[36] It was perhaps inevitable that an attempt would be made to admit the dress and customs of the Ancient Britons as equally deserving of study and the publication of Samuel Rush Meyrick and Charles Hamilton Smith's *Costume of the Original Inhabitants of the British Islands* in 1815 is the first and most substantial costume book to attempt such a project (Plate 2). Its appearance within this antiquarian domain of study indicates the extent to which historical scruples had been outflanked by the early nineteenth century. The design of the book adds to its specious authority: it shares,

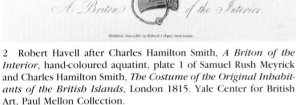

2 Robert Havell after Charles Hamilton Smith, *A Briton of the Interior*, hand-coloured aquatint, plate 1 of Samuel Rush Meyrick and Charles Hamilton Smith, *The Costume of the Original Inhabitants of the British Islands*, London 1815. Yale Center for British Art, Paul Mellon Collection.

3 *Habit of an antient Britain*, hand-coloured etching, plate 177 of Thomas Jefferys, *A Collection of the Dresses of Different Nations*, IV, London 1772. Yale Center for British Art, Paul Mellon Collection.

or so it seems, the concerns for accuracy and documentation of Jefferys and Strutt and uses the same de luxe standards of presentation to offer a convincing simulacrum of the past. Yet the very detail of its plates can only conceal momentarily the much narrower base of research on which this 'evidence' is based; indeed there is a sense in which the illustrations are more convincing than the documentation they rest on. Speculation rather than demonstration is often and inevitably the impetus behind the illustrations but their tangible presence, their ability to evoke the world of Ancient Britain in a concrete visualisation, gives these illusions a seeming accuracy and a corporeal presence which helps to substantiate the ghostly Britons of antiquarian fascination. As a result the interplay between text and illustration helps consolidate an image of the Ancient Briton more securely than either on their own could achieve. An impoverished literary and archaeological record is enriched by means of visual material simply filling in the gaps, quite literally fleshing out the image of the Briton.

In providing an emphatic picture of the prehistoric past Meyrick and Smith offer a paradigm of the relationship between art and prehistory in this period. Their depiction of Ancient Britons encapsulates the dangers of antiquarian speculation warned against by Hume and others; for, by blurring the distinction between documented fact and creative interpretation, their illustrations begin to acquire the status of demonstration themselves. This effect is further reinforced by the provision of a believable context for the figures, who inhabit an uncluttered landscape containing some significant worked feature such as a hillfort, dolmen or primitive structure, whose relationship to the figures is implied as being self-evident. This often spurious detail is a direct response to the use made by Strutt of mediaeval miniatures to show how costumes fitted into the society of their time and contrasts markedly with the earlier, more emblematic presentation of costume as seen in Jefferys's *Collection* (Plate 3). Jefferys offers his readers specimens of Ancient Britons without any further embellishment of historical context. The explanatory text directs the reader to the sources of these illustrations in other histories or accounts, in this case John Speed's *History of Great Britaine* (1611) (Plate 64). From an epistemological point of view, therefore, Jefferys's presentation is static and one dimensional; the figures are presented as generic examples in a dehistoricised environment and no improvement on Speed's interpretation is offered. Meyrick and Smith, on the other hand, consciously avoid past illustrations of Ancient Britons, implying that their figures are based on sounder knowledge, itself signified in the 'historical' context of a seemingly appropriate landscape and accoutrements. Knowledge here is manifestly progressive and two dimensional, able to situate its object in time and space. These Britons are pungent, living beings inhabiting a real physical world.

Such a presentation is indicative of the ways in which antiquarian research was beginning to offer an alternative to the eighteenth-century historical tradition that had been so hostile to ancient British studies. This book, profusely illustrated with aquatints by Robert Havell, was an expensive commodity whose commercial success demanded an interested readership. The fact that Meyrick and Smith were confident of its appeal is a testament to the changed status of archaic and Dark-Age history in the public mind now that antiquarian research, drawing on fieldwork as well as classical texts, had illuminated the obscurity disdained as impenetrable by Hume, Robertson and others. Admittedly these studies still lacked the crucial dynamic of history, a sequence of attested events only becoming possible after Roman records began, and so were restricted to the delineation of static cultural achievement rather than narrative history; nevertheless the picture of archaic Britain revealed through antiquarian pursuits did seem to be clearer. The mists of speculation, fancy and legend were not to roll away (if indeed they ever can) until well into the nineteenth century, but already the remote past had become a possible site for legitimate enquiry.

In detailing the impact of visual presentation in helping to substantiate this enquiry we are brought into contact with a key feature of this period: the extent to which the artistic record helped to establish the image of the prehistoric past in the public's mind. That this should be so may seem surprising, especially when we review the limited interplay between art and antiquarianism in the 1750s and the modest project outlined by Milles of artists using antiquarian data. Tame topographical or antiquarian drawings of antiquities on the one hand and more accurate costumes for a 'Landing of Julius Caesar' on the other would perhaps have remained the standard pattern throughout this period were it not for more widespread changes in British culture. The move away from the cultivated aesthetic of the earlier eighteenth century towards a greater concern with the intuitive and the natural, exemplified most strikingly in Romantic art, helped provide a context less inimical to the monuments of ancient Britain. As part of their wider interest in man's direct experience of natural forces, artists and writers began to explore wild landscapes and the poetry of ruins. Their enthusiasms found a ready subject in the shattered remains of a primitive culture whose most visible sites tended to be spectacularly sited in remote and unpeopled country. The prehistoric landscape becomes a recognisable sub-category within the landscape painting of this period and is intimately bound up with the Romantics' interest in primal experience. The last quarter of the eighteenth century also saw a steady growth in tourism within the British Isles. Improved communications and better facilities for travellers meant that more areas of the kingdom were opened up for leisured enjoyment. This tendency was accelerated by the outbreak of war with France in 1793 which made continental travel much more difficult for the next twenty years. The rise in popularity of the Lake District, Wales and the Wye valley, Scotland and the West Country as picturesque destinations is well known and within this larger picture the popularity of archaeological remains begins to alter too.[37]

Borlase's demands for interest in British antiquity as well as classical remains was answered through necessity. Travel guides to these areas tended increasingly to provide the tourist with a succinct digest of relevant antiquarian theories and often included a small engraving of any substantial remains as part of the area's notable curiosities. Perhaps inevitably, such information tended to lag behind the development of what we might hesitantly call 'true' archaeology in the nineteenth century and the material in guide books was often closer to the antiquarian speculation of an earlier generation. The Victorian archaeologist's demand for accurate plans and surveys based on excavation and fieldwork developed along a different path from the images of prehistoric antiquities and their creators to be found in guide books, in illustrated histories and on the walls of the London exhibition rooms.

As a result, just as the eighteenth century had seen a conflict of approach between historians and antiquarians, so the nineteenth century would see a similar conflict between archaeologists and the icons of popular history. The debate over the past – what it was, how it should be approached, the audience (popular or scholarly) to be addressed – became increasingly complex throughout this period and, especially in the later nineteenth century, participation in it would involve choosing sides to a degree that would have seemed quite extreme even to the antiquarians and historians of the eighteenth and early nineteenth centuries.

In both cases it would be fair to say that a more rigorous scholarly methodology attempted to separate itself from what we might call the poetics of its own area of study; as though it were possible to distil the quintessence of the investigative method out of the flux of more general enquiry. Although we shall have many occasions to scrutinise the growth of more 'scientific' approaches to Britain's archaic past, it was to the poetics of that enquiry that artists made their main contribution. Indeed, in prolonging the speculative and romantic approaches of eighteenth-century thought into the nineteenth century, artists helped to construct an image of the prehistoric past whose legacy is with us still. This involvement in the historiography of ancient Britain proved a two-edged sword; on the one hand artists' interpretation of the archaic past and its remains helped establish a nonprofessional interest in the subject and an audience for the discoveries of nine-teenth-century archaeology, but on the other their creative restitution of that past proved so compelling that it began to dominate the public imagination. In the archaeological nest the innocent egg of illustration had hatched into the cuckoo of imaginative reconstruction. When the satirical novelist Thomas Love Peacock criticised the poets of his day for turning their backs on progress, his comments could as well have been applied to the literary and artistic antiquarianism of the nineteenth century as it threatened to perpetuate outmoded attitudes to the past in an increasingly professional intellectual world.

> A poet in our times is a semi-barbarian in a civilized community. His ideas, thoughts, feelings, associations, are all with barbarous manners, obsolete cus-toms, and exploded superstitions . . . While the historian and the philosopher are advancing in, and accelerating, the progress of knowledge, the poet is wallowing in the rubbish of departed ignorance, and raking up the ashes of dead savages to find gew-gaws and rattles for the grown babies of the age.[38]

In this debate we can detect the shadows of larger issues within the intellectual life of this period. Broadly speaking, the dispute between the historians and the antiquarians would not be resolved until the late nineteenth century and can be seen as part of a wider phenomenon: the emergence of 'scientific' practice within intellectual disciplines, demanding an emphasis on verifiable and documented facts rather than abstract theory or reliance on authority, the growing separation of professional history from the world of letters, and the categorisation of intellectual labour into discrete genera and species with different criteria and emphases. The development of academic disciplines within the Victorian period from a broad humanism to something approaching their current professional identities repre-sents the working out of these larger issues. As Philippa Levine has shown, by the late nineteenth century archaeologists and historians tended increasingly to be trained professionals, supported by university departments;[39] but the early years of the century inherited the less institutionalised world of eighteenth-century schol-arship whose lack of demarcation between academic disciplines allowed antiquar-ian study to straddle history and archaeology. The nineteenth century also saw the growth of local archaeological and antiquarian societies – from four in 1839 to over fifty by the mid 1860s–whose semi-institutional status acted as a bridge between eighteenth-century amateur scholarly endeavour and the development of archaeol-ogy as a professional discipline in the late nineteenth century.[40] Increasingly, however, the professionalisation of history from the 1850s and of archaeology from the 1880s squeezed out antiquarian study as the province of the amateur and parochial enthusiast. Yet, the emergence of a professional historical practice, while it may have marginalised the amateur antiquarian, did not necessarily domi-nate the field in society as a whole. Antiquarianism survived outside academic institutions as an essentially literary approach to the past, in contradistinction to the 'scientific' rigour of late nineteenth-century historiography and archaeology. Henry Thomas Buckle's *History of Civilization in England* (1857) contains an implicit attack on antiquarianism in its general introduction: his enthusiasm for the new historiography of mid nineteenth-century England is opposed to the retro-grade antiquarianism it sought to replace. Buckle's identification of 'reverence for antiquity' and 'poetic sentiment for the remote and unknown' as features of such retrograde writing provides a succinct definition of the antiquarian impulse:

> Of all the various ways in which the imagination has distorted truth, there is none that has worked so much harm as an exaggerated respect for past ages. This reverence for antiquity is repugnant to every maxim of reason, and is merely the indulgence of a poetic sentiment in favour of the remote and unknown. It is, therefore, natural that, in periods when the intellect was comparatively speaking inert, this sentiment should have been far stronger than it now is; and there can be little doubt that it will continue to grow weaker, and that in the same proportion the feeling of progress will gain ground; so that veneration of the past, will be succeeded by hope for the future.[41]

One final consideration needs to be borne in mind. As Levine has shown, whatever their disagreements over method, nineteenth-century antiquarians shared with historians that tendency to confirm their middle-class readership's belief in historical continuity and in social progress; they were capable at the local and national levels of mobilising a sense of historical genealogy, provincial pride and cultural distinction of considerable importance in a world where the pressures of industrialisation were uprooting communities, engendering social mobility and upsetting the settled values vested in the old aristocratic and agricultural orders. Not the least attractive feature of antiquarian investigation was its reverence for the past, its provision of a wider frame, a slower rhythm to set against the worrying changes and frantic pace of contemporary existence. The slow and stately march of British history from its primitive origins to the destiny still to come was, for some, infinitely preferable to the frenetic tempo of the present day. In a period of rapid social transformation, the long reach of the antiquarian imagination could transcend present unease to deposit its grateful reader in a world of high antiquity where party faction, economic change and class struggle had no place; or, rather, seemed to have no place. We might want to argue, indeed, that one of the very features which had made ancient Britain inadmissable for Augustan historians like Bolingbroke, Hume and Robertson, that is, its irrelevance for the comprehension of present day society, was precisely its attraction for those living in a more volatile age. Yet it would be wrong to conclude from this that the study of British antiquity was an 'irrelevant' or disinterested pursuit, immune from the pressures of widespread societal change and development, isolated from intellectual debate and social questions. No matter that the study of archaic Britain might have offered, to the inattentive reader, something close to the untroubled picture outlined above; in truth, the world of antiquarian scholarship was buffetted by a gale of competing theories whose often bitter formulation ruffled the still waters of inquiry. Some, like Pinkerton, were openly combative, calling attention to the contentious issues that swarmed around the subject; others attempted to maintain a scholarly distance. None, however, could escape the fact that they created their images of ancient Britain within a wider context whose outlines are, perhaps, clearer to us than they were to the participants themselves. Sir Richard Colt Hoare's famous introduction to his *Ancient History of Wiltshire* (1810–12) stated 'We speak from facts, not theory', but for us today Colt Hoare is of interest not only for his exhaustive fieldwork and excavation but also for his theories, particularly his understandable belief that his empiricism gave him the basis to make such a claim. To fly from present realities to archaic Britain may have seemed like an innocent occupation, but the writers and readers, the artists and spectators of this constructed world could not but carry with them the realities and the prejudices of their own era, just as we carry ours with us today.

Chapter Three

NORTHERN HEROES AND NATIONAL IDENTITY

The interplay between antiquarianism, historiography and the arts in producing an image of primaeval culture was not, of course, restricted to Britain and we can get some idea of the wider context in which the British past was explored by observing this same process at work in other countries of northern Europe. The situation in Britain was, arguably, more complex than elsewhere and threw up a richer and more sustained debate about cultural origins but it was not unique. It is valuable, too, to remember that works of art celebrating Boadicea and Caractacus, megalithic garden design and patriotic celebration of primaeval ancestors were not some weird eccentricity of the British but part of a readily intelligible and influential current in European thought. From at least the seventeenth century similar investigations and debates are discernible in all those countries bordering the North Sea, each of them seeking to celebrate and clarify their national identities. More generally, in the Romantic period in particular, many countries used mythical and archaic material to elaborate a sense of distinctness, of identity. These tactics were also and especially employed by those cultures which found themselves to be marginalised within a wider polity. The later nineteenth century saw the efflorescence of these tendencies in nationalist politics, historiography, literature, music and art; if it is customary, therefore, to consider the period 1850–1900 as the heyday of European nationalism, then the preceding hundred years might well be regarded as its infancy.

Before examining the evidence from other countries, however, it is important to be clear on three major points. First, it is evident that the search for national roots and the arguments over a nation's history are often intimately bound up with ideas concerning national identity yet they are found in cultural circumstances where the concept of nationalism, strictly defined, would have no meaning. With hindsight, in other words, we can see such investigations as motivated by similar cultural concerns as nationalism, but, as has been argued, it is anachronistic to talk of nationalism before the last decades of the eighteenth century while the political framework for true nationalism requires a fully developed capitalist economy. When examining material prior to the nineteenth century we should talk only of national sentiment and even a term like 'proto-nationalist' would be misleading if it implied a relationship to nationalism proper.[1] In what follows, therefore, 'nationalism' and its cognates should be taken as loose, even impressionistic terms, to signify a sense of national identity and the celebration of origins.

Second, even when appropriately used nationalism is an unwieldy and often an over-reductive concept; for nationalism is the servant of many masters and, dependant on circumstances and ideological persuasion, it can be marshalled for repressive as well as emancipatory ends. The nationalism associated with imperial expansion may share the same beliefs in manifest destiny and cultural aptitudes as the nationalism organised to resist imperial domination. Nationalism, in other words, is effective both as an imperial device to orchestrate national unity and as a more localised politics of resistance to that very imperialism. Examples of both of these nationalisms will be found throughout this study.

Third, while cultural genealogies may eventually support the emergence of nationalist sentiment they are not usually sufficient in themselves to mobilise a full-blown nationalism which is, of course, a product of very many complex changes in culture and society. They are, however, often used within a nationalist framework as the most obvious rallying points around which such an ideology can be orchestrated and implemented. Thus, in this chapter I do not mean to imply that the search for origins *is* nationalism, but instead wish to indicate that it can and should be historically contextualised within the wider matrix of nationalist feeling.

As an example of national identity and resistance we might first consider the case of the Dutch celebration of origins in the late sixteenth and early seventeenth centuries, when the United Provinces of the Netherlands turned to their originating history as Batavians to endorse separation from the Hapsburgs and the devolution of political power among the individual provinces. Perhaps the two best known products of this patriotic enthusiasm are Grotius' youthful treatise, *De Antiquitate Reipublicae Batavicae* (1610) and Rembrandt's late painting, commissioned for the town hall of Amsterdam, *The Conspiracy of Julius Civilis* (1661). The history of Batavia presented in these and like works is not recondite antiquarianism but a partisan response to victory over imperial oppression and they should be seen as explicit exercises in political propaganda, using Batavian resistance to Rome as a precedent for the United Provinces' independence from Spain.

Further north, Sweden and Denmark both marshalled history and antiquarian learning as propaganda aids in their contest for the overlordship of Scandinavia in the early seventeenth century. In Sweden Gustavus II Adolphus and his instructor Johan Bure used antiquarianism to dignify early Swedish history and to combat the Danish history promulgated by Ole Worm under the patronage of the Danish King Christian IV.[2] Between 1637 and 1645 Christian himself was responsible for commissioning the first illustrated history of Denmark, a series of eighty paintings for Kronborg Castle depicting subjects from prehistory to the present day and showing, in Christian's own words, 'the brave and heroic deeds of our forefathers, the old kings of Denmark'. Current ambitions, in other words, could be bolstered and legitimised by appeals to a glorious past reaching back into the remotest epochs of unrecorded time.[3]

A very similar iconographic scheme was devised for Holyroodhouse, Edinburgh, for James VII of Scotland (James II of England) in the 1680s. The Dutch artist Jacob de Wet was commissioned to paint the likenesses of 110 Scottish monarchs from the mythical Fergus I via Caractacus (Plate 4) to Charles II. Drawing on the antiquarian writings of Hector Boece, de Wet's gallery of kings constructed a royal lineage for James which demonstrated his inheritance and legitimacy.[4] Here too antiquarian argument may have influenced de Wet's commission for the 1680s

4 Jacob de Wet, *King Caractacus*, 1684–6, oil on canvas, 214 x 137 cm. Holyroodhouse, Edinburgh. The Royal Collection © Her Majesty Queen Elizabeth II.

witnessed a dispute between Irish and Scottish scholars over the early histories of their countries, with each side attempting to arrogate to itself the glories of the archaic past in constructing their national genealogies.[5]

To return to Scandinavia, pride in their ancient origins can be evidenced in the eighteenth century, too, when research into saga literature and a growing interest in antiquarian study helped to construct a vivid and heroic past. In 1752 Paul-Henri Mallet was commissioned by Frederick V, King of Denmark, to write a history of that country in French. Although Mallet never completed the project, the two resultant volumes on the ancient history of Scandinavia (published in 1755 and 1756) were designed to re-orientate European history around a northern axis. Both in French and in its English translation of 1770 Mallet's *Northern Antiquities*

5 Nicolai Abildgaard, *Europe in the Primaeval Period* (modello), *c.* 1784–90, oil on canvas, 29.5 x 29.5 cm. Statens Museum for Kunst, Copenhagen.

proved instrumental in stimulating pre-Romantic and Romantic investigations into the primal origins of northern European culture.[6] Danish pride in their archaic history is also evident in the second half of the eighteenth century when two attested prehistoric sites in Zealand, one at Ledreborg, and the other at Jaegerspris (the Julianehøj), were developed, in 1756–7 and 1776 respectively, as national monuments to the glorious past. Fake tumuli and cromlechs were also erected at Moesgaard (Jutland) and Fredensborg (Zealand) as garden motifs in this period. Both the Danish and Swedish academies of art started setting competition themes from early Scandinavian history and mythology in the second half of the century and in 1778 Nicolai Abildgaard was commissioned to produce a series of paintings for Christiansborg, the royal palace in Copenhagen, showing the history of the royal line of Denmark reaching back to prehistoric times. Unfortunately these decorations were lost in the 1794 fire which destroyed the palace but Abildgaard's design for *Europe in the Primaeval Period* survives, showing a naked Amazon figure seated next to a dead bear in an uncultivated landscape dominated by a dysse or cromlech (Plate 5). In the light of this attested interest in the remote past it comes as no surprise to note that when the sculptor Johan T. Sergel was asked to devise a monument for King Gustavus III of Sweden (assassinated in 1792), one of his designs was for a prehistoric tumulus with standing stones.[7] The identification of Scandinavian peoples with their barbarian past was still potent in the middle of the nineteenth century. When the young archaeologist J.J.A. Worsaae wrote his short survey of Denmark's early history for King Christian VIII, *The Principal Antiquities of Denmark* (1843), his advocacy of prehistoric sites was

29

informed by more than scholarly interests. The book was published at a time of mounting political tension with Schleswig-Holstein and in these circumstances Worsaae included a patriotic appeal to the Danish people using almost Churchillian rhetoric.

> It is in this way that the relics of prehistory strengthen our links with the Fatherland. We enter, through them, into a more lively empathy with hills and valleys, fields and pastures; for it is through the burial-mounds that lie humped up on their surfaces and through the prehistoric artifacts which have lain safely, down through the centuries, in their recesses, that the land can constantly remind us of the fact that our fathers, a free, independent people, have dwelt from time immemorial in this country; more, they command us to look to our heritage, to resist foreign domination over a soil that shields our fathers' bones and in which our most sacred and venerable memories are rooted.[8]

In France interest in Gaulish origins begins to quicken in the 1780s. Both the Parc d'Ermenonville (c.1782) and the Parc de Betz (1785) contained Druid altars as garden ornaments, perhaps inspired by the appearance of Druidic structures in British gardens in the 1760s and 1770s.[9] These were, however, isolated instances and it is significant that the Comte d'Angiviller, the Directeur General des Bâtiments, had completely overlooked the Gaulish past when recommending subjects for history painters in his reorganisation of the French Academy from the mid 1770s.[10] Notwithstanding this 'invisibility', the Gauls were sporadically mobilised during the revolutionary climacteric to underwrite current political aspirations. When the French government in 1788 attempted to stop the *parlements*' obstruction of the royal will a number of pamphlets appeared defending the *parlements* as inheritors of the political institutions described by Tacitus.[11] In January 1789 the Abbé Sieyès' pamphlet, *Qu'est-ce que le Tiers État?*, arrogated the ancient past of the Gauls and Gallo-Romans to the people and identified the aristocracy with the late-coming Franks.

> Why should the Third Estate not relegate to the forests of Franconia all those families which persist in the foolhardy practice of being descended from the race of conquerors and of having succeeded to the rights of conquest? The Nation, thus purged, would, I believe, be able to console itself by the thought that it was constituted of the descendants of the Gauls and Romans only.[12]

Similarly, the revolutionary and proto-feminist Théroigne de Méricourt appealed to the ancient past to shame her women contemporaries into political action. On 6 March 1792 a petition from the Société fraternelle de Minimes, with 300 signatures, was read out to the Legislative Assembly seeking permission for women to receive military training and to defend the revolution alongside their menfolk. De Méricourt went to the Société on 25 March and delivered a speech supporting and radicalising their position with a thorough-going appeal to sexual equality, justified by archaic precedent:

> Fellow Frenchwomen! I would urge you yet again: let us raise ourselves to the height of our destinies; let us break our chains; at last the time is ripe for Women to emerge from their shameful nullity, where the ignorance, pride and injustice

6 François Rude, *The Departure of the Volunteers of 1792 (The Marseillaise)*, 1833–6. Arc de Triomphe de l'Etoile, Paris.

of men had kept them enslaved for so long a time; let us return to those times when our Mothers, the Gauls and the proud Germans, debated in the public Assemblies, fought side by side with their husbands and repulsed the enemies of Liberty.[13]

The best known survivor of this sort of republican patriotism is François Rude's *Departure of the Volunteers, 1792* (1833–6) on the Arc de Triomphe in Paris which contains the figure of a Gaulish warrior set amidst a group containing Roman or Gallo-Roman defenders of liberty (Plate 6). The association of the Gauls with republican sentiment was not, of course, inevitable and the establishment of the Celtic Academy (1805–13) as an official body in Napoleonic France is a case in point. Part antiquarian, part propagandic, the researches of the Academy were designed to investigate the relics of ancient Celtic culture and to demonstrate the historical pedigree and ethnic coherence of French civilisation, reaching back to the period before the Roman invasion.[14] Similarly, Vercingetorix and other leaders were celebrated later in the century as national patriotic heroes rather than defenders of a particular polity. Vercingetorix, Brennus, Velleda and various renditions of Gauls appear with some frequency in the exhibitions of the 1850s, 1860s and 1870s and Velleda, the Druidess heroine of Chateaubriand's novel *Les Martyrs* (1809) was included as one of the twelve statues glorifying the female sex commissioned by the French government in 1844 for the Luxembourg Gardens. Alphonse de Neuville's engravings of Gaulish chieftains for Francois Guizot's *L'Histoire de*

7   Aimé Millet, *Vercingetorix*, 1863–5. Alise Ste Reine.

France (1870), published just before the Franco-Prussian war, exemplify this transition to nationalist pride in origins. Vercingetorix himself had only recently achieved heroic stature with the publication in 1828 of Amédée Thierry's *Histoire des Gaulois*, where Caesar's mightiest Gaulish opponent is given a good hundred pages of exposure. Henri Martin's *Histoire de France* (1833–6) developed the cult of Vercingetorix further, helping to fix the image of this supreme Celtic warrior. 'His height, his good looks, his strength and his skill in arms, the warlike spirit which shone in his eyes, all produced in him that mixture of admiration and fear which was the ideal of the Gaul.'[15]

Martin's own proselytising on behalf of his hero included a five act heroic drama, *Vercingétorix*, published in 1865. More notable, perhaps, is Aimé Millet's colossal bronze statue of Vercingetorix erected on the site of Gaulish Alesia (Alise Sainte Reine), the spot where Julius Caesar finally overcame Gaulish resistance in 52 BC (Plate 7). This immense figure is the largest of the five sculptures of Vercingetorix commissioned by Napoleon III in the late 1850s and 1860s as part of an extensive exercise in state patronage seeking to portray the Second Empire as heir to the glories of French history.[16] Millet gave the emperor the choice of Vercingetorix 'in action, sword raised' or 'in repose, leaning on a shield and thinking', the pose eventually selected. On the base of the statue is inscribed part of the speech given to Vercingetorix in Caesar's *Conquest of Gaul*, a text which might have been written in justification for Napoleon III's own policies of political unity and foreign expansion. 'The whole of Gaul will be united, and when we are all of one mind the whole world cannot stand against us.' Millet's colossal figure was erected on 27 August 1865, pulled into position by six horses and Morvan oxen before being raised on to the immense pedestal designed by Viollet-le-Duc.[17] Megalomania was certainly in the air when considering Vercingetorix. Antoine Préault, whose own *Cavalier Gaulois* (1849–53) stands on the Pont d'Iena in Paris, was eager to work on a titanic scale that would have eclipsed Millet's achievement entirely. He had already attempted colossal projects, such as a 30 foot plaster figure of Charlemagne (1836), and would later explore ideas for a Joan of Arc and a Lamartine (1874) on gigantic columns. According to the art critic Thoré-Burger, Préault reacted to Millet's statue by declaring,

If the Emperor had commissioned me to make Vercingetorix I would have said 'Sire, I'm leaving for Auvergne. Give me a mountain peak. I'll choose that volcanic *puy* dominating the heart of France and transform it into an Acropolis of Gaulish civilization. I'd have a spiral road, wide enough for an army or crowds of people, wind from the base to the summit. At intervals would be placed, like the guardians of a sanctuary, statues of Gaulish warriors ten metres high. On the top of the mountain, a pedestal composed of the arms, tools and symbolic objects of our ancestors' lives, flanked by four allegorical statues: the Druid, Brennus, The Bard and Velleda or inspiration, poetry, strength and philosophy ten metres high. And above the pedestal would be the equestrian statue of Vercingetorix, a figure twenty metres high on a horse of the same scale, the arms extended calling to arms. The whole in brass, bronze, iron, granite dulled and rusty, the image of the past.'[18]

8 Angelica Kauffmann, *Hermann and Thusnelda* (modello), 1786, oil on canvas, 44.8 x 61.9 cm. Tiroler Landesmuseum Ferdinandeum, Innsbruck.

French attitudes to Vercingetorix should be compared to the contemporary German celebration of Hermann or Arminius, the Teutonic leader who crushed the Roman legions in the Teutoburger Wald in AD 9. The German translation of Macpherson's *Ossian* in 1764 kindled an interest in archaic German history and references to the prehistoric, heroic past of the German people can be found in the writings of Herder and his contemporaries, a *Sturm und Drang* enthusiasm precisely equivalent to British celebration of their primitive ancestors in the same period. Hermann was celebrated in three heroic verse dramas by Klopstock, the so-called 'Bardiet' trilogy of *Hermanns Schlacht* (1769), *Hermann und die Fürsten* (1784) and *Hermanns Tod* (1787) and in a picture painted for Joseph II, the Emperor of Austria, by Angelica Kauffmann in 1786 (Plate 8).[19] Kauffmann shows Hermann returning to his grateful people after the defeat of the Roman legions under Quintilius Varus; captured booty is carried in on the left, Hermann and his wife Thusnelda are in the centre and a bard or Druid gives thanks on the right. The whole scene is studded with gestures and poses borrowed from antique and Renaissance art, while Hermann himself is shown in a pose derived from the noblest warrior of all, the Apollo Belvedere.

In the German war of liberation against the French in the early 1800s (the Freiheitskrieg) Hermann was valorised as a patriotic defender and his example was frequently invoked, inspiring among others Kleist's drama *Hermannsschlacht* (1809) and paintings by his fellow Dresdener, Caspar David Friedrich, such as *Old Heroes' Tomb* (1812) and *The Grave of Arminius* (1813–14) (Plate 9). The modest sarcophagus, installed in a rocky cleft at the base of a cliff, allows Friedrich to present Hermann as though fused with the land he had defended. Stimulated by

9   Caspar David Friedrich, *The Grave of Arminius, c.* 1813–14, oil on canvas, 45 x 70 cm. Kunsthalle, Bremen.

the same patriotic motives, Karl Friedrich Schinkel produced a visionary design for a huge sculptural monument to the great German leader in 1814–15 (Plate 10). It is hard to tell how seriously Schinkel intended this project, whose ambition and scale seem to insist on comparisons with Leonardo's Sforza Monument of 1489. Like Leonardo's designs, the triumphalism of a mounted rider rearing over his

10 Karl Friedrich Schinkel, *Design for a Monument to Hermann of the Cherusci,* 1814–15, black chalk and water-colour, heightened with white on blue paper, 60.9 x 89.9 cm. Nationalgalerie, Staatliche Museen zu Berlin.

12 (*facing page*) Caspar David Friedrich, *Dolmen in the Snow*, c. 1816, oil on canvas, 61.5 x 80 cm. Staatliche Kunstsammlungen Dresden, Gemäldgalerie Neue Meister.

11 Ernst von Bandel *Arminius*, 1875. Detmold.

prostrated foe would have presented enormous technical difficulties, especially on such a gigantic scale, and the monument survives only as an inspired exercise in patriotic celebration.[20] In 1819, and presumably unaware of Schinkel's design, the sculptor Ernst von Bandel began his own project to commemorate Hermann on a colossal scale. Von Bandel persevered over many decades and his gigantic statue of Hermann, eighty-five feet tall, was eventually erected in 1875 near Detmold, amidst the forest in which the Romans were defeated (Plate 11). By the time of its unveiling, however, von Bandel's sculpture was inflected not so much by patriotic thanksgiving for victory over an aggressor but by a militant nationalism, inspired by German unification and the recent victory over the French army at Sedan.[21]

Von Bandel's *Hermann*, whose grandeur of conception and sheer size were reported in illustrated art journals in the 1840s, may have influenced Millet's approach to Vercingetorix (both statues, after all, celebrate military heroes on a colossal scale), but no such explicit prompt need be sought, for the second half of the nineteenth century saw the outbreak of triumphalist ancestor worship across Europe; and even if such giganticism found no echo in Britain, Thornycroft's *Boadicea* on Westminster Bridge (Plate 96) is a typically flamboyant example of this sort of patriotic celebration of warrior ancestors.

Alongside these explicitly patriotic treatments of German history should be placed a more poetic response to the archaic past of Germany, more meditative than celebratory and closer in feeling to Worsaae's empathetic approach to Danish antiquities, quoted earlier. Caspar David Friedrich's paintings of dolmens (Plate 12) were based on studies made on the island of Rügen, off the Pomeranian coast, but his mystical approach to landscape transforms these prehistoric survivors into emblematic tokens of mortality. An aura of ponderous melancholy hangs around

36

these mute relics of the dead, often presented, as here, within the shelter of an oak grove, symbolic of pagan ritual. As with Worsaae's sentiments of the 1840s it seems legitimate to infer that Friedrich's approach is not only a meditation on the passing of time and the erasure of human achievement but also a profound reflection on the deeper continuities that bind a people together.

Finally, in Belgium, celebration of their Celtic ancestors gathered pace around the middle of the nineteenth century. When, in 1849, the government decided to revive the ancient procession of the Ommegang by subsidising each province to construct allegorical cars for procession on the occasion of the national *faites*, the province of Luxembourg offered a glimpse of Belgium's prehistoric past.

> A mass of mimic rock covered with moss was erected, at the base of which the gigantic trunk and limbs of an ancient oak were placed. A wild boar was mounted in front; in crevices of the rock appeared a fox and a wolf, and on its summit a stag, with a cross between the antlers, recalling the miraculous vision of St. Hubert . . . This immense car was drawn by a number of the small Luxembourg ponies, and escorted by groups of persons in the attire of the ancient *Tréviriens*. The whole grouping had a wild and primitive appearance . . .[22]

A more lasting reminder of Belgium's origins, possibly inspired by the examples of Millet and von Bandel, was Jules Bertin's statue of Ambiorix, chief of the Eburones who defeated the Romans in 54 BC, which was erected on a dolmen-like plinth at Tongeren (Tongres) in 1867 (Plate 13). Belgium's recent independence as a sovereign state, following the revolt of 1830, perhaps more than usually required figures like Ambiorix and ancient Tréviriens as symbols of national unity, especially when its cultural patrimony was so diverse.

13 Jules Bertin, *Ambiorix*, 1867. Tongeren.

Such appeals to the archaic past indicate how effective a symbol, because innocuous, the barbarian ancestor could be, redolent of a past so remote as to be either immune from class, religious or party interests or so ambiguous as to allow many different interests to seek confirmation from one and the same source. Like Belgium, very few modern nations can trace a lineal descent from one aboriginal race and their selection and celebration of founding heroes reveals a great deal about contemporary aspirations and ideologies. This rapid survey of the mobilisation of the archaic past in northern Europe should help us understand the similarities and idiosyncracies in the uses made of that past in Britain, for in Britain too, or perhaps especially in Britain, the question of ancestors informed a good deal of debate in this period.

Within the geographical boundaries of what we refer to today as the British Isles the distinction between nation and political state was a matter of some importance in the eighteenth and nineteenth centuries. The political reality of Britain was being forged in the eighteenth century, establishing English political and economic hegemony, but the constitutional relationship of the English centre to the Welsh, Scottish or Irish peripheries was itself in the process of being created. English domination of Wales was already relatively firmly established in political terms, the Act of Union with Scotland in 1707 formalised politically a relationship that had hitherto lacked explicit constitutional force, while English political control in Ireland was waxing and waning throughout this period. Such political realities could not, however, be disentangled from other frames of reference, from differing

38

religious observances, from localised economic networks and legal arrangements, and from other distinctive cultural traditions.[23] These historically specific differences cannot, of course, simply be reduced to or explained by ethnic inheritance but the relationship between the English centre and a broadly Celtic periphery provided (and perhaps still provides) a bedrock difference sufficient enough for some to contest English hegemony and for others to recommend colonial measures in enforcing it, not so much on the basis of a historically complex elaboration of difference but on the basis of an ethnically privileged nationalism. In this context the construction of a patriotic genealogy for Britain was a much more formidable undertaking. The recurrent demands within the Celtic periphery for some degree of autonomy and the political soultions adopted to deal with them indicate that the United Kingdom as a political entity had separatist tensions within it which no amount of transnational sleight of hand could disguise. French schoolchildren might have accepted 'our ancestors, the Gauls' as an obvious reminder of their national identity and their cultural inheritance, but in Great Britain no such simple rallying point existed for the orchestration of national sentiment.

No educated citizen of the United Kingdom was unaware of the dual origin of British culture in ancestral Celtic and Germanic peoples. Those inhabitants who lived in England, parts of Wales and Lowland Scotland spoke English and the majority of the inhabitants of England were customarily believed to be descended in large part from Saxon and other Germanic or Scandinavian invaders. In contrast, many of the inhabitants of Highland Scotland, Ireland and extensive tracts of Wales spoke Gaelic and were presumed to be descended from the aboriginal Celts. If the political reality of the state was not in question, even though granted reluctantly by some, appeals to a national community certainly were. The sheer self-confidence of eighteenth- and nineteenth-century advocates of British national integration (especially in contradistinction to the ethnic and regional rivalries of foreign states) has tended to eclipse the continuing debate between nationalism, defined in cultural and linguistic terms, and political unity in this period.

This study begins in the 1750s and it is in the second half of the eighteenth century that recent scholarship has detected the beginnings of English nationalism.[24] Its effects would eventually result in that overweening sense of history and of destiny so characteristic of the high Victorian period: the belief in the triumph of the Anglo Saxon race as a military, economic, political and cultural power whose enlightened leadership of the world was progressive, inevitable and infinitely sustainable. Yet, while hindsight may show the first stirrings of this vigorous ideology in the middle of the eighteenth century it is important to bear in mind the other strands in a tangled skein. For while Anglo-Saxonism was indeed to become the major constituent in English nationalism, its pre-eminence would not have been so obvious to many participants in the search for British ancestry during the eighteenth and nineteenth centuries; a cogent set of arguments was deployed to celebrate the Celtic past as at least equal to the achievements of the Saxon. The steady eclipse of this 'rival' history can be observed creeping onward as the period progresses, but its eventual subjection to the master historiographic discourse of Anglo-Saxonism in England, and its marginal survival as a strand within Celtic nationalism in the peripheral countries of the United Kingdom, should not blind us to its importance in a time of great intellectual fluidity. For what faced the historians, antiquarians and artists in the latter part of the eighteenth century was nothing short of the need for Britain to achieve historical self-consciousness as a nation, as a people. This is not, of course, to deny the existence of historians and historical writing prior to the 1700s using the past to validate matters of religious or constitutional importance but I would contend that it is only after the 1750s that historical research impinges on such a wide spectrum of ideological concerns.

Generally speaking, then, when it comes to examining the historiography and the art of eighteenth- and nineteenth-century Britain, the literary and artistic recruitment of its aboriginal founders, such as it was, was a more complex phenomenon than its continental equivalents whose celebration of primaeval forebears was relatively striaghtforward, the originators of a genealogical descent which led to the present.[25] In Britain the double Celtic and Saxon settlement made for a more difficult choice and the tension between these two historiographical emphases can be seen to have affected the historical persona and the representation of the Ancient Briton in the arts of painting, engraving and sculpture. Within England, celebration of the Britons tended to be orchestrated such that it worked at a high level of national generalisation with little more involved than a hazy appeal to patriotism. However, within the context of the Celtic periphery a more focused use of the past can be detected.

In Wales, for example, writers could celebrate a line of resistance running from Caractacus to Owain Glyndŵr and other specifically Welsh freedom fighters. The Welsh believed themselves to constitute as a people the remnants of the original Celtic inhabitants of Britain, pushed back into their mountain fastness by Saxon settlers. The reality of this ancestral lineage, as opposed to its semi-mythical status in Welsh mediaeval literature, had been demonstrated by Pezron and Lhuyd in the first decade of the eighteenth century who had revealed the continuity of Welsh linguistic culture from remotest antiquity, where an ancestral Celtic people had once played a significant part on the European stage. These links were underlined in the names used by the London Welsh for two of their societies: The Honourable and Loyal Society of Antient Britons, established in 1715, and the Honourable Society of Cymmrodorion (meaning 'earliest natives' or 'aboriginal people'), established in 1751. The incorporation of Wales into England by Acts of Parliament in 1536 and 1543 was, in other words, merely a political reality; in cultural terms the Welsh people might look to another tradition.[26]

In the context of such antiquity and tradition the history of Celtic Britain could be honoured not just for its own sake, as an historical episode superseded by Saxon England, but for its survival in Wales, for its separateness from the Saxon world. Thus Evan Evans (Ieuan Fardd), in a poem of 1772 entitled *The Love of Our Country* provides a lengthy celebration of the defenders of Welsh culture, beginning with the Druids and Caractacus and proceeding along an uninterrupted line of princes and heroes such as Hywel the Good and Owain Glyndŵr. Even in the nineteenth century, Theophilus Jones's *History of Brecknockshire* (1805) contains a number of references to 'the Saxon conquerors' and the 'vile jargon' of the English language; and, although Jones looks forward to the common interest of England and Wales and the end of traditional prejudices, he can still write of how 'the treachery of the Saxons, whom the aboriginal Britons introduced into the island as friends and allies, and their cruelty in exterminating in cold blood the nobility of the antient inhabitants . . . still rankles in the bosom of the indigenous sons of freedom. . . .'[27] Benjamin Heath Malkin in *South Wales* (1804) observed the tenacity of the Welsh tradition of resistance to English rule: 'The cherished remembrance of what they once were, so long after having ceased to exist as an independent nation, is a not less remarkable feature of the modern Welsh.'[28] A good example of such 'cherished remembrance' is *The Triads of the Isles of Britain*, whose legitimacy regarding the origins of the Welsh people was still maintained by some eighteenth-century Welsh historians. In England the reliability of such literary sources in historiographical terms had been successfully challenged in the sixteenth century, when Polydore Vergil had demolished Geoffrey of Monmouth's *History of the Kings of Britain*. In Wales these accounts still lingered as, for example, in Theophilus Evans' *Drych y Prif Oesoedd (The Mirror of the First Ages)* (1716) which traced the Welsh people back to Noah's grandson Gomer.

This Welsh enthusiasm for fabulous origins was notorious enough to occasion sly comment from the Picturesque tourist Richard Warner. Writing of Molmutius Dunvallo, an early British monarch associated with Malmesbury Abbey by Geoffrey of Monmouth, Warner reminds his English readers that 'the tales of Geoffrey are not now considered as high authority on this side of the Severn'.[29] Warner's dig at Welsh credulity overlooks the fact that Welsh antiquarian writing in the eighteenth century, whether unduly reverential of the past or more rigorously researched, developed a specific inflection of British history and helped to foster a sense of separateness from England. Sometimes we can catch a glimpse of a network of writers, ensuring the continuation of a line of argument about cultural identity which asserts its distinctive claims throughout the eighteenth century and well into the modern era. Thus Theophilus Evans, the writer of *Drych y Prif Oesoedd* was the grandfather of Theophilus Jones, author of the *History of Brecknockshire*, referred to above and Benjamin Heath Malkin, author of *South Wales*, was a friend of Iolo Morganwg, one of the key figures promoting Welsh traditions in this period. Aided and abetted by Iolo, William Owen Pughe's *Myvyrian Archaiology of Wales* (1801-7) and *Cambrian Biography* (1803) propelled these traditions into the nineteenth century.

Like other members of the Gwyneddigion Society, established in London in 1770, Pughe was a radical (a supporter of Horne Tooke and his colleagues in the 1794 treason trials) and the *Myvyrian Archaiology* was criticised by Welsh conservatives as a cover for 'publishing democratic stuff under the fictitious title of the works of the Ancient Bards'. There was some justice in this, given the Gwynnedigion Society's politics in its early years. It recruited from a lower social stratum than the Cymmrodorion Society and its founder Owen Jones (Owain Myfyr) declared in 1789 that 'Liberty in Church and State is the aim of this Society'. The recently re-established Eisteddfod was viewed by Owen Jones and William Owen Pughe as an opportunity to promote political radicalism and from September 1789 the Gwyneddigion Society promoted eisteddfodau in its own name, with Jones controlling the choice of subject for bardic competition ('Liberty' in 1790).[30] The Caradogion Society, the debating branch of the Gwyneddigion, was established in 1790 and, as Helen Ramage has pointed out, its debates (in English) 'can hardly have been other than political' for it was raided by the constables and had its books and papers confiscated.[31] Pughe's celebration of a Welsh tradition should be seen, therefore, as part of his political radicalism, a means of restoring identity and pride to the Welsh people. In this context, the 'celebrated men among the Ancient Britons' of the *Cambrian Biography* are honoured as Celtic leaders whose renown is couched in explicitly British (i.e. Welsh) terms, rather than in the context of a universal patriotism. Arthur is a 'hero and consummate warrior' who 'often led the Britons to battle against the Saxons' and is grouped in the Triads with Cynvelyn (Cunobelinus) and Caradog (Caractacus) as one of 'the three gallant sovereigns of the Isle of Britain'. Other early British heroes in the *Cambrian Biography* are Boadicia (sic), Cadwaladyr (last of the British kings), Caswallon (Cassivellaunus), Gwrtheyrn (Vortigern) and Owain Vinddu. All of these historical and semi or wholly mythical figures are woven into a tapestry of significance whose pattern can best be understood as a celebration of a Welsh pantheon, a pantheon that includes the mythical founding figures of Britain: Hu Gadarn, 'the patriarch of the Cymry', and the fifth century BC lawgivers, Prydain and his son Dynval Moelmud.[32]

In Scotland, ancient Caledonian culture was pressed into this sort of service less frequently than in Wales. At first sight this is somewhat surprising, considering how recent was the Act of Union and how tenaciously Jacobite support was maintained throughout the eighteenth century, especially in the rebellions of 1715 and 1745. A number of reasons may be advanced to explain the Scots' relative lack of interest in patriotic resistance by Caledonians. In the first place, the very fact that Scotland had been separate from England for so long provided an authentic history of separate development and resistance that needed no aboriginal heroes to flesh it out. Secondly, whereas the Welsh tradition asserted the cultural continuity of the Welsh people from remotest antiquity to the present, in Scotland the descendants of the Caledonians were presumed to have survived intact, if at all, in the Highlands and Islands.[33] (William Robertson, for example, claimed in 1755 that in the Highlands and Islands of Scotland 'society still appears in its rudest and most imperfect form'.)[34] Even so, the relationship of the Caledonians to the present inhabitants of the region was a contested issue. In 1729 Thomas Innes had attempted to refute the idea that modern Highlanders were descended from the Caledonians, but their ancient descent was re-established by David Malcolm in 1738 in his *Dissertations on the Celtic Languages* and confirmed in the 1770s by James Macpherson's *Introduction to the History of Great Britain and Ireland* (1771). Macpherson's *Ossian* saga of the 1760s likewise promoted the idea of continuity between aboriginal Celtic peoples and the inhabitants of the Highlands. As a result, by the close of the eighteenth century most educated Scots accepted the idea that the Highlanders were descended, at least in part, from the Caledonians who had confronted the Romans. But this whole question of Highland origins should be contextualised within Scotland as a whole, for 'enlightened' centres such as Edinburgh tended to be dominated by Scots who prided themselves on their break with the feudal and clannish past represented by Gaelic Scotland. As has been frequently pointed out, the Scottish enlightenment, centred on Edinburgh, Glasgow and Aberdeen, can be seen as a wholesale attempt by the intelligentsia to 'improve' Scots culture, language and religion by enthusiastic adoption of the Act of Union and by repudiating the backwardness of the clannish, Jacobite and parochial world of the great Highland chiefs. Sir John Clerk of Penicuik may be instanced as an example of the way in which the Caledonian past might occasion ambiguous reactions; while praising the martial vigour and resistance to Rome of his forefathers, he nevertheless concluded, in words surely conditioned by his opinion of the Act of Union itself, that 'it is a reproach to a nation to have resisted the humanity which Rome laboured to introduce'.[35] From the viewpoint of grandees like Sir John, steeped in classical learning, well travelled and intellectually sophisticated, the benefits of union with an advanced culture, whether Roman in the first to third centuries AD or English in the eighteenth century, overrode patriotic enthusiasm for local traditions. Nevertheless, there was a keen sense of patriotic pride among Scottish antiquarians, none more so, perhaps, than Lord Buchan who erected a Temple of Caledonian Fame at Dryburgh and insisted that antiquarian study of the earliest Scottish history was a patriotic pursuit. His discussion of the spot where the Caledonian leader, Galgacus, faced the Romans under Agricola encapsulates this attitude: 'I shall be apt to throw off my shoes, and say the ground on which I stand is consecrated to the fervour of our patriotism . . . I shall exclaim, My ancestors were defeated, but not subdued.'[36]

As we shall see, one of the deciding factors in the reception of Macpherson's Ossianic writings in the 1760s was the patriotic celebration of a Scottish literature and a Scottish past separate from that of England. Indeed, Macpherson's canny provision of a literary bridge between the attested Caledonian past and the beginnings of genuine Scottish history brought Scots patriots into a position close to that of the Welsh, where an unbroken lineage might be followed from the remotest past to the culture of the clan and to contemporary peasant customs.[37]

As regards Ireland, we have already noted in Chapter Two the patriotic feelings mobilised in the mid eighteenth century by the Catholic Committee and Charles O'Conor, the urgency of antiquarian research in the period of Grattan's Parliament and the publication of a number of investigations into ancient Irish literature, music and history in the late eighteenth century. Yet in common with Scotland and Wales there seems to have been little attempt to translate antiquarian enthusiasm into patriotic icons, whether painted or sculpted, of primaeval ancestors.[38] In part this reflects the Celtic peripheries' only partial success in articulating a sense of historical difference; in part it is due to the lack of effective private or institutional patronage outside London which might have supported localised historical schools of painting and sculpture. When ancient Irish history was tackled, it was Celtic Christianity which dominated the artistic imagination, especially in the nineteenth century. The glories of early Christian Ireland provided a better documented and a more secure period to honour than the more doubtful world of Milesian heroes, for Irish history suffered from the absence of classical reports, out of which might be fabricated patriotic examples. It is true that Irish mediaeval literature and the oral tradition provided a good spread of colourful heroes like Finn and Cuchulain who were every bit as valorous as Boadicea, Caractacus and Galgacus, but their feats of arms, courage and endurance took place in a darker world, well away from the full glare of historical record. Moreover, unlike their mainland equivalents, their typical campaigns were internecine and local as opposed to any national defence of liberty against foreign aggression. James Gandon's late eighteenth-century decorations for the Four Courts in Dublin included the figure of Ollamh Fodhla, who gave the ancient laws to the Irish, but this is a rare instance of mythography[39] and it is not possible to detect any significant consideration of the ancient Irish in art until the 1840s, when Thomas Davis wrote articles in *The Nation* including the most remote periods of Irish history as suitable subjects for a nationalist art and a handful of historical paintings treating such themes were shown at the Royal Hibernian Academy exhibitions.[40]

Nevertheless, within the United Kingdom the supremacy of England meant that the elaboration of a British national identity articulated English concerns in the main. In a period of nascent nationalism the stakes to play for were high indeed. Which ancestors would best secure 'historically' the legitimacy of present claims regarding Britain's place in European and global affairs? Notwithstanding the problems of historiography that bedevilled the whole enterprise of investigation into archaic Britain, the crucial question remained: did the Celt or the Saxon hold up the most flattering mirror to the British people? As Horace Walpole wrote to William Mason, author of *Caractacus*, ruminating on the loss of Britain's American colonies, 'Our empire is falling to pieces; we are relapsing to a little island. In that state, men are apt to imagine how great their ancestors have been . . . the few, that are studious, look into the memorials of past time; nations, like private persons, seek lustre from their progenitors.'[41] Walpole could not foresee the extraordinary growth of the British Empire in the nineteenth century, but his perception remains as acute for an expanding as a contracting state.

Works of art helped in this process of self-definition if only because their iconic simplicity could crystallise concepts otherwise amorphously present in historical and antiquarian scholarship. From about the middle of the eighteenth century an iconographical tradition of British history developed which, arguably, helped to cement the idea of British history in the popular imagination. The establishment of The Society for the Encouragement of Arts, Manufactures and Commerce can be seen as a crucial instigator of this development, through its awarding, from 1760, of premiums for paintings of British history.[42] Yet, what strikes any analyst of the pictorial approach to ancient British history in this period is the repetition of the same subjects. The era that ends with the rise and decline of Roman Britain is represented by a narrow group of subjects with little variation from one dominant pattern of selection. Naturally, such a narrow interpretation of the historical record can be explained partially by the paucity of available subjects from this period; nevertheless, even having made allowances for scant historical evidence, the list of potential subjects is wider than those that were usually depicted. The four key topics typically selected were Caesar's landing in Britain, Boadicea, Caractacus, and the coming of Christianity. These would be repeated time and time again from the 1750s, when this series was inaugurated by Francis Hayman and Nicholas Blakey, while patriotic heroes such as Galgacus, Cassivellaunus, and Cunobelinus, or images of Ancient Britons prior to Roman contact were rarely chosen.[43] The reasons for the discrimination between these two categories of material are elusive. The written histories of this period follow their classical antecedents when narrating the history of the Romans in Britain and there is certainly no priority given to those subjects later illustrated by artists. The most that can reasonably be said is that once Hayman and Blakey had established the selection in the 1750s their work took on a canonical authority which removed the need for extensive reworking. Certainly, the pattern of subjects used in the competitions for the decoration of the Houses of Parliament in the 1840s shows little deviation from that of some ninety years earlier. Of the twenty designs exhibited in 1844 dealing specifically with ancient British subjects seven were of the Roman invasion of Britain, five were of Boadicea and five were of Caractacus.[44] The same repetitive choices can be seen in the illustrated histories of this period. The subjects chosen for Robert Bowyer's edition of Hume's *History of England* (1793-1806) recur without significant variation in George Craik and Charles Macfarlane's *Pictorial History of England* (1837-41).

Is it not likely that this narrow selection represents something akin to the iconic presentation of a heroic myth, with all the drama and force that simplification provides? A brave and dauntless people fight for their liberty against a cruel and merciless invader, helped in their attempts by two of the most inspired patriot leaders ever to take arms. Subdued by the Romans, their resistance is not truly overcome until they surrender spiritually and with commendable docility to the teachings of Christ. There is comfort and confirmation in such a tale, a thousand miles away from the detailed classical accounts of barbarian degradation and the longstanding tradition of pejorative anti-Celtic rhetoric we shall examine in Chapter Six. In the rarified world of abstract patriotism Caractacus and Boadicea join Arthur and Alfred not as Celtic chieftains but as patriot heroes, staunch defenders of these islands against the evils that might beset it from outside. This is not a strategy unique to Britain; Walpole's comments about seeking lustre from progenitors would apply equally well to any of the ancestral genealogies celebrated in northern Europe in this period. History and art join forces in a mythopoeic endeavour whose success can be measured by its efficacy in terms of national belief, its ability to create and sustain that patriotic enthusiasm which overrides the very real fractions, differences and contestations of everyday political and cultural life.

Chapter Four

THE BARDS OF BRITAIN

If Celtic heroes were truly to help the peoples of Britain come to some understanding and celebration of their remotest past a measure of agreement on the worth of their culture was necessary. The Ancient Briton of recorded history was, however, a contested reality throughout the eighteenth century. There was some consensus concerning the evidence of the classical accounts and what they revealed about the status and achievement of the Celtic peoples, but this consensus was fragile and the texts themselves were vulnerable to distortion in the service of zealous commentators arguing for or against the civilisation of the Britons. These complex and constantly shifting arguments were, of course, influential in determining the ways in which the general public may have visualised their remotest progenitors, even if that influence manifested itself in little more than a vague awareness of prehistoric Britain, distilled from skimming general histories or reading guide books to local antiquities. But if the Ancient Briton of scholarly debate was a shadowy figure, based on confused and contradictory evidence, his or her counterpart in heroic myth was for many in the later eighteenth century a better defined and more appealing individual. Notwithstanding the occasional flights of rhetoric put into the mouths of Celtic leaders by Caesar, Tacitus or Cassius Dio, the Britons of the classical texts were for the most part two dimensional creatures, shorn of the philosophy, the emotional identity, even the personality which might explain their patriotic and militant opposition to invasion. But that which the Roman annals lacked might be supplied by imaginative literature, with the voice of the bard providing the thoughts and feelings, the heroism and the pathos missing from the prejudiced accounts of the Britons' conquerors.

For Celtic advocates the bardic tradition was one of the most important cultural forms in ancient British society. Not only had it preserved the authentic ancestral voices of the past, but it also demonstrated the creative genius and literary sophistication of the bards themselves. Bardic literature, along with the closely related field of Druidic learning, indicated the high level of intellectual attainment possessed by ancestral Britons in an heroic age. Hugh Blair's *Critical Dissertation on the Poems of Ossian* (1763), a work of fervent enthusiasm, drew on this tradition to buttress claims for the historical likelihood of Ossian and the nobility of the sentiments recorded in his poems.

Wherever the Celtae or Gauls are mentioned by ancient writers, we seldom fail to hear of their Druids and their Bards; the institution of which two orders was the capital distinction of their manners and policy. The druids were their philosophers and priests; the bards their poets and recorders of heroic actions; and both these orders of men seem to have subsisted among them, as chief members of the state, from time immemorial. We must not therefore imagine the Celtae to have been altogether a gross and rude nation. They possessed from very remote ages a formed system of discipline and manners, which appears to have had a deep and lasting influence . . . there flourished among them the study of the most laudable arts, introduced by the bards, whose office it was to sing in heroic verse the gallant actions of heroic men; and by the druids, who lived together in colleges, or societies, after the Pythagorean manner, and, philosophizing upon the highest subjects, asserted the immortality of the human soul.[1]

For Blair and like-minded enthusiasts, then, Celtic society was quintessentially bound up with those bards and Druids whose cultural achievement added lustre to the remotest antiquity of Britain. Through the agency of the oral tradition, fragments of that achievement were able to survive centuries of obscure existence in Gaelic-speaking areas to be finally recorded and refurbished in the 1760s with the publication of Macpherson's *Ossian* and other works of literary exhumation.

There is, therefore, a very real sense in which the Celtic bard as promoted in the later eighteenth century is the key to the Celtic revival at all levels. The fame of the bard was the inspiration for examination of the bardic tradition, to find there a native equivalent to the archaic poetry of Homer and the Bible. The Celtic literature enjoyed by eighteenth-century readers ranged from renderings of authentic texts to emulations of a presumed bardic tradition, but within this burgeoning literature the discovery of a new poetic voice, a Celtic sensitivity to language and its expressive potential, was paramount. Once identified with a significant literature, Celtic culture took on the same mantle of heroic simplicity that seemed to typify the world of the *Iliad* and the patriarchs. This was far more engaging than the dry and dusty research of antiquarians, for bardic literature revealed above all a relationship to nature and the ultimate mysteries which seemed to be spontaneous and unmediated. As the poet Anna Seward expressed it in 1762, fresh from her first exposure to Ossian,

> Stranger, as was the author of these sombre dramas, to the sciences and arts, even to agriculture itself, and therefore excluded from the immense resources which they yield to the poet; yet, by the force of native genius, the grandly simple objects, which an uncultivated, and almost desert country could produce, are found sufficient for the sublimest purposes of illustration, description, and imagery.[2]

The literary endeavours of the late 1750s and 1760s should thus be seen as effecting a huge change in popular perceptions of archaic British society. By producing a vision of the past sympathetic to the interests and sensibilities of their readers, Gray, Macpherson and others freed Celtic Britain from the exclusive concern of scholarship and encouraged the growth of an imaginative graft on the prosaic stock of antiquarian learning. Thus, however extensive antiquarian interest in Celtic society and culture may have been before the mid eighteenth century, it is nonetheless true that the publication in 1757 of Thomas Gray's ode *The Bard* was one of the most important stimuli to a more widespread public understanding of archaic Britain, and a begetter of that interest in all things Celtic now known as the Celtic revival. Gray's antiquarian knowledge, his contacts with other writers and his learned proselytising for Celtic culture, together with the public success of *The Bard*, would, in their turn, stimulate writers and artists to respond with investigations of their own.[3] Similarly, Macpherson's publication of *Ossian* in the 1760s accelerated this rage for Celtic literature and spawned numerous literary and artistic progeny, though now on a European scale, especially in Germany and France.[4]

The scale of this shift in aesthetic and cultural interest has been well characterised by Edward D. Snyder whose book *The Celtic Revival in English Literature* (1923) is still the authority in the field. In examining several hundred eighteenth-century literary folios written before 1760, Snyder found less than a dozen references to Druidism or literary evidence of a more general interest in Celtic culture. The transformation of this situation during and after the 1760s, when Gray, Mason, Macpherson and Evans had all published texts celebrating the Celtic achievement, is nothing short of a revolution in literary taste. For Snyder, 'the Celtic Revival was something definite; it was a real movement among English men of letters who were united by a common desire to infuse into English poetry the mythology, the history, and the literary treasures of the ancient Celts.'[5] William Blake's attitude to the ancient British past may be taken as an extreme example of this imaginative recuperation. His approach to archaic British history is reliant on the bardic tradition, as opposed to antiquarian or historical research. The truth of Celtic literature was, for Blake, a surer guide to the past than the measured historiography of his age. As late as 1826 he declared that he was 'an admirer of Ossian equally with any other Poet whatever' and that he believed with both Macpherson and Chatterton 'that what they say is Ancient Is so'.[6] In his comments on his picture *The Ancient Britons*, published in the *Descriptive Catalogue* of his 1809 exhibition, the poetic approach to history is presented as a manifesto for the creative imagination, which alone is capable of eliciting the truths of the past hidden from the clumsy, unsympathetic investigations of historians like Hume, Gibbon and Rapin.

> . . . believing with Milton the ancient British History, Mr. B. has done as all the ancients did, and as all the moderns who are worthy of fame, given the historical fact in its poetical vigour so as it always happens, and not in that dull way that some Historians pretend, who, being weakly organized themselves, cannot see either miracle or prodigy; all is to them a dull round of probabilities and possibilities; but the history of all times and places is nothing else but improbabilities and impossibilities; what we should say is impossible if we did not see it always before our eyes.[7]

In this chapter we shall be concerned with aspects of the Celtic revival and its imaginative responses to Celtic culture, looking particularly at the figure of the bard, the values the bards were presumed to hold and the world they were imagined to inhabit. As with any discussion of this phenomenon, our starting point must by Thomas Gray's ode, *The Bard*. Gray's poem is based on a historically suspect account of Edward I's policy after his conquest of Wales in 1282, when he is supposed to have condemned the bards to be hanged because their seditious recitations might inspire opposition to English rule. The story itself is first mentioned in an early seventeenth-century history of the Gwedir family by Sir John Wynn and had become part of the fabric of Welsh history by the time Thomas Carte chose to include it in the second volume of his *History of England* (1750).[8] Gray read Carte's version in 1755 and began work on the theme, but it was the harp recital given in Cambridge by blind John Parry, harpist to the Prince of Wales, which seems to have inspired him to finish the poem.

> There is no faith in Man, no, not in a Welch-man, and yet Mr. Parry has been here, and scratch'd out such ravishing blind Harmony, such tunes of a thousand years old with names enough to choak you, as have set all the learned body a'dancing, and inspired them with due reverence for Odikle [i.e. *The Bard*], whenever it shall appear.[9]

The poem's early reception was uneasy, largely because Gray was using allusions too recondite for the public to understand, even if Gray considered these to be 'a few common facts to be found in any six-penny History of England by way of question & answer for the use of children'. As Charles Hinnant has noted, Gray's interpretation of the massacre was at odds with his contemporaries' opinion of Edward I and of the Welsh he defeated and some of their criticism may have been prompted by this as much as Gray's 'mediaeval' historiography,[10] but the reading public was gradually won over and the poem is now commonly regarded as the key text inaugurating the Celtic revival in eighteenth-century English literature. Like Macpherson's *Ossian*, Gray's *Bard* asserts the primacy of the creative and imaginative life capable of elevating the culture and history of a vanquished people into a realm of eternal remembrance. Literature endures when dynasties have crumbled, even those which sought to eradicate it.

This was, of course, a comforting message for poets, worried about their lack of patronage and social standing in Georgian England. The bard's central position in Celtic society, whether archaic or mediaeval, offered a vision of a quite different state of affairs: Gray's bard, Ossian and the bards of the Ancient Britons all demonstrated the necessity and power of poetry in a more heroic age, in stark contradistinction to its shameful neglect in a polite and civilised era. A good example of this sort of historical comparison is provided by William Boscawen's *Ode for the Anniversary Meeting of the Subscribers to the Literary Fund* (21 April 1795) which contrasts the glorious past of poetry to contemporary indifference and offers a panegyric of the Celtic bard to stand alongside tributes to the poets of classical antiquity.

> Say, Britain, when, in days of yore,
> Thy sons 'gainst Rome's oppressive band
> Stood dauntless on thy sea-girt shore,
> Stern guardians of their native land;
> And, on the deep-wedg'd ranks of war,
> Impetuous whirl'd the scythed car;
> What pow'r their gen'rous valour fir'd?
> The Bard, the patriot Bard, inspir'd!
> From oak-crown'd glades,
> From mystic shades,

Where late he chaunted meek Religion's strain,
Avenger of his country's wrongs,
With harp, attun'd to martial songs,
He rush'd indignant to th'embattled plain!
Nor less his voice, midst factious rage,
Could Discord, baleful fiend, assuage;
The warrior's maddening steel arrest,
And soothe to peace his savage breast!
Taught by his lore in social bands to join,
All lov'd the gentle Bard, all bless'd the song divine.[11]

In Gray's poem the last surviving bard in Wales stands high above the river Conway and the victorious English army, cursing Edward I and prophesying the destruction of the king and his family line. The pungent imagery used to describe the bard and his surroundings still has its impact despite generations of over-exposure in anthologies and school text-books.

On a rock, whose haughty brow
Frowns o'er old Conway's foaming flood,
Robed in the sable garb of woe,
With haggard eyes the Poet stood.
(Loose his beard and hoary hair
Streamed, like a meteor, to the troubled air);
And, with a master's hand and prophet's fire,
Struck the deep sorrows of his lyre.
'Hark, how each giant-oak and desert cave
Sighs to the torrent's awful voice beneath!
O'er thee, oh king! their hundred arms they wave,
Revenge on thee in hoarser murmurs breathe . . .'[12]

This intensely dramatic encounter is not only the justification for the rest of the poem's declamatory style but also constitutes its most immediate and easily comprehensible writing, quite different in kind to the allusive rhetoric used by the bard himself, which gave early readers so much apparent trouble. The translation of such a dramatic mise-en-scène into pictorial imagery proved relatively easy to accomplish; indeed, the precision of Gray's description in this stanza tends to circumscribe all the artistic attempts to illustrate it. The reasons for this lie, no doubt, in the fact that Gray himself was starting from pictorial sources in composing this scene; his image of the bard was informed by two paintings: the head of God the Father in Raphael's *Vision of Ezekiel* and, more precisely, the figure of Moses in Parmigianino's *Moses breaking the Tablets*.[13] The strength of Gray's visual approach was not lost on his contemporaries and Horace Walpole's letter of September 1755 to the illustrator Richard Bentley provides a vivid example of the artistic potential and inspiration of the ode.

Gray has lately been here. He has begun an ode, which if he finishes equally, will, I think, inspirit all your drawing again. It is founded on an old tradition of Edward I putting to death the Welsh bards. Nothing but you, or Salvator Rosa, and Nicolo Poussin, can paint up the expressive horror and dignity of it. Don't

50

14   Richard Bentley, *The Bard*, 1757, pen and ink, 13.3 x 16.4 cm. The Lewis Walpole Library, Yale University.

think I mean to flatter you; all I would say is, that now the two latter are dead, you must of necessity be Gray's painter . . .[14]

Walpole commissioned Bentley to illustrate the poem and, from the surviving drawings, a good idea can be obtained of how the finished design would have appeared in the proposed Strawberry Hill edition of the poem had Walpole continued with it. He must have been dissatisfied, however, for he printed the poem without illustrations. The most developed drawing (Plate 14), finished at Strawberry Hill in early 1757, grapples with the declamatory style of the bard's oratory, his meteor-streaming hair, loose robes and harp, but Bentley positions him on too insignificant a rock to fully engage with Gray's more sublime imagery. The landscape enumerates Gray's descriptions but only as a tame assembly of stage scenery, whose diminutive effects have little imaginative power either individually or collectively. Bentley's individual studies for this draft, however, and his 1766 tailpiece of the bard's suicide for James Dodsley's expanded fifth edition of Gray's poems (Plates 15 and 16) are altogether more successful, providing a more robust handling of the narrative, closer in feeling to the work of succeeding artists.[15]

Gray himself seems to have favoured Paul Sandby's *Bard*, now alas lost, exhibited in 1761 at the Society of Artists. In a letter to Thomas Wharton of October 1760, he speaks with enthusiasm of the scheme: 'he (& Mason together) have cook'd up a great picture of M: Snowdon, in Wch the Bard & Edward the first make their appearance; and this is to be his EXHIBITION-PICTURE for next year, but (till then)

15   Richard Bentley, *The Bard*, 1757, grey wash with brown
pen and ink, 38 x 46.9 cm. The Lewis Walpole Library, Yale
University.

16   J.S. Muller and Charles Grignion after Richard Bentley, *The
Bard*, tailpiece for James Dodsley, *Designs by Mr. R. Bentley for
Six Poems by Mr. T. Gray*, 5th edition, 1766. The Lewis Walpole
Library, Print Collection, Yale University.

it is a sort of secret.'[16] Mason later wrote to Lord Nuneham in ecstatic celebration of Sandby's achievement, demonstrating in his encomium how Gray's own verse had set the pictorial agenda. 'My Lord! Sandby has made such a picture! such a bard! such a headlong flood! such a Snowdon! such giant oaks! such desert caves! If it is not the best picture that has been painted this century . . .'[17]

The sublime potential of the situation, indicated in Mason's description, was to be increasingly taken up by artists, with greater and greater prominence given to the natural surroundings, to the point where the bard's speech becomes of necessity a rhetorical soliloquy rather than a meaningful attempt to address Edward I hundreds of feet away. Thomas Jones's *Bard* (1774) (Plate 17) is a particularly vivid example of this tendency, concentrating on the bard and his sublimely primitive domain as opposed to his haranguing of Edward I and his army. Jones had visited Stonehenge in 1769 and had speculated then whether its grandeur would be diminished when placed in a different location, 'amidst high rocks, lofty mountains and hanging Woods';[18] five years on, his *Bard* was, in this respect at least, a pictorial experiment to test his assessment, using a variety of megalithic features to constitute a Druidic sanctuary. But Jones was also using this mixture of prehistoric antiquity with Welsh topography to increase the sublimity of Gray's imagery. The discovery of Snowdonia as a tourist region capable of offering experiences akin to those of the Alps was slowly developing in the 1770s and Jones has taken full advantage of the sublime aesthetic to position his bard in a truly elemental wilderness. As Walpole's letter to Bentley indicates, the sublime landscape was particularly associated with Salvator Rosa and the overall disposition of Jones's composition seems to owe a debt to Salvator Rosa's *Augures*, which he might well have known from the engraving by Joseph Goupy of *c.* 1740 (Plate 18).

Jones's picture is also significant for its symbolic articulation of the continuities between Welsh mediaeval culture and prehistoric Celtic society. The bard himself and the distant army of Edward I follow the iconography suggested by Gray's poem but the middle ground indicates a much wider historical frame; the megalithic structure silhouetted against the flank of Mount Snowdon emphasises the belief common in some antiquarian circles, and especially in Wales, that the mediaeval bards still retained some vestiges of the rituals and beliefs associated with the bards and Druids of classical texts. The setting sun casts a last glow on the western slopes of Snowdon, throwing the Druidic monument into shadow as Welsh culture gives way to the darkness spreading from England in the east.

The identification of Wales as the home of the Ancient Britons and the celebration of a people with a continuous history older than that of the English found ready embodiment in the figure of the bard, hurling defiance at the English armies bent on the suppression of cultural traditions many millenia in the making. Similarly, the blasted trees in the foreground might be seen as allusions to death and the destruction of bardic culture. Here we touch again on the specifically Welsh dimension of this celebration of cultural continuity. In Chapter Eight we will examine Julius Caesar Ibbetson's telescoping of chronological time, with reference to bards and Druids, where the physical propinquity of native people and historic sites effaces diachronic distance. This essentially emblematic presentation establishes visually a connection which might otherwise have been left unarticulated. We can see it again, more starkly, in one of the frontispieces to the patriots' journal

17 Thomas Jones, *The Bard*, 1774, oil on canvas, 115.6 x 167.6 cm., The National Museum of Wales, Cardiff.

18 Joseph Goupy after Salvator Rosa, *Augures*, *c.* 1740, etching. The British Museum, London.

19 William Bromley after Richard Corbould, *Britannia directing the Attention of History to the Distant View, Emblematical of Wales*, hand-coloured engraving, frontispiece to *The Cambrian Register*, London, 1796. The British Library, London.

of the 1790s, *The Cambrian Register* (Plate 19), which displays the past and present of Wales not as a palimpsest, where the present effaces the past, but as a continuum where the past is available as a source of inspiration in the present. Perhaps the most pungent demonstration of these assumptions can be discerned in Iolo Morganwg's enactment of a Gorsedd on Primrose Hill on 22 September 1792, of which more will be said in Chapter Nine. Iolo's fabrication of tradition was unequivocally asserted as a genuine continuation of archaic ritual; as he explicitly stated, 'The Bardic Institution of the Ancient Britains, which is the same as the Druidic, has been from the earliest times, through all ages, to the present day, retained by the Welch . . . [and] is now exactly the same that it was two thousand years ago.'[19]

Antiquarian scholarship was investigating not only the classical accounts of Celtic society, where Druids and bards are described in some detail but also, especially in Wales, examining the Dark Age and mediaeval legacy of Celtic culture. John Parry, whose harp recital had inspired Gray, had himself published *Antient British Music* in 1742 on the subject of the Welsh bardic tradition. Parry was a friend of the Morris brothers of Anglesey, the prime movers in the Celtic revival in Wales and the establishment of the Cymmrodorion in London and, like them, believed in the great antiquity of Welsh music and suspected that the twenty-four bardic measures of music went back to the Druids. This theory was to prove very influential in the later eighteenth century and, following Parry, a number of publications appeared whose aim was to recuperate Welsh tradition: Evan Evans's *Some Specimens of the Poetry of the Antient Welsh Bards* (1764), Rice Jones's *Gorchestion Beirdd Cymru (Exploits of the Welsh Bards)* (1773),

facing page

21 Richard Corbould, *The Bard*, 1807, oil on canvas, 80 x 67.3 cm. Collection unknown.

22 John Martin, *The Bard*, 1817, oil on canvas, 213.4 x 155 cm. Laing Art Gallery, Newcastle upon Tyne, England.

20 Charles Hall and Samuel Middiman after Philippe Jacques de Loutherbourg, *The Bard*, engraving, frontispiece to Edward Jones *Musical and Poetical Relicks of the Welsh Bards*, London, 1784. Yale Center for British Art, Paul Mellon Collection.

Edward Jones's *Musical and Poetical Relicks of the Welsh Bards* (1784) and *Bardic Museum* (1802), and Iolo Morganwg and William Owen's *Myvyrian Archaiology of Wales* (1801–7). In fact the true Welsh bardic tradition had declined during the Tudor period and by the late seventeenth century had all but died out. Even the Welsh triple harp had changed, its three rows of strings owing more to the Italian baroque harp than its mediaeval original. Yet from these dying embers it proved possible to rekindle aspects of Welsh culture. Early eighteenth-century Welsh printing presses helped foster the language and transmitted the culture to ordinary readers and *The Cambrian Register* had as one of its aims the recording of the fast vanishing oral culture of Wales.[20]

We can see these ideas brought together in De Loutherbourg's *Bard*, engraved as the frontispiece to Edward Jones's *Musical and Poetical Relicks of the Welsh Bards* (Plate 20). It is a highly appropriate image for Jones's text and faithfully follows Gray's visualisation of the bard, giving him a heroic, muscular frame in exactly that tradition of biblical illustration which had inspired Gray in the first place. As the frontispiece to a book whose contents celebrated and re-established the bardic tradition which Edward I had attempted to utterly eradicate, the bard is, as it were, vindicated in his prophecy by the text which follows his appearance. The bardic legacy lives on while Edward's dynastic ambitions were thwarted absolutely.

Richard Corbould in 1807 (Plate 21) and John Martin in 1817 (Plate 22) exhibited pictures of the Bard at the Royal Academy, close enough in general composi-

56

tion to suggest that Martin's version was inspired by Courbould's earlier painting. Corbould had already produced an illustration of the bard for an edition of Gray's poems published in 1796, but his oil painting shows a much more robust handling of the theme, steeped now in sublime landscape as opposed to the mannered surroundings he provided originally.[21] Martin's picture pushes the imagery still further; by turning the bard around he is able, even on this diminutive scale to articulate the rage and vehemence of his oratory, while the giant oaks seem to writhe in agony below the emphatic despoliation of Snowdon by Edward's obtrusive and oppressive castle. These images of the bard demonstrate the extent to which the natural sublime has merged with Gray's historical setting. The bard is now a creature of these mountains, the genius loci of that wild, untamed landscape which stands in opposition to the urban, lowland culture bent on subduing it. As an exercise in romantic primitivism such pictures of the bard have no peers, fusing in one histrionic image the ideas of natural man, poetic genius and untamed nature. Poetic and political liberty are shown to be the intimates of a rugged terrain and wild weather, far away from the soft, enervating and corrupt culture of polite society.

This relationship between the playing out of the drama and its sublime theatre worked both ways. The tendency to encompass aesthetic reactions with historical associations informed a wealth of approaches to the past in this period and William Godwin, for instance, quoting from Gray's *Bard*, was keenly aware of the extent to which Edward I's massacre of the Welsh bards had become a constituent of any tourist's response to the landscape of Snowdonia.

facing page

24 John Downman *The Bard*, c. 1800, black chalk and stump on paper, 36.5 x 20.4 cm. The British Museum, London.

25 Maria Cosway after Richard Cosway, *The Bard*, 1800, soft ground etching. The British Museum, London.

23 Benjamin West, *The Bard*, 1778, oil on wood, 29.2 x 22.9 cm. Tate Gallery, London.

'Old Conway's foaming flood,' with the lofty castle beyond, has acquired a sacredness from the supposed massacre of the Bards in that place. If these scenes were not really transacted, and the passions of the real persons excited there, at least a beautiful association has been produced, by the bare selection of the spot made by the author of the romance, for the imaginary exercise of such feelings.[22]

The elevation of the sublime landscape as a sounding board for the bard's verses is part of a tendency in the work of this period to strip away the context of Gray's narrative and instead to concentrate chiefly on the bard. His solitary presence suffices to mobilise the sentiments marshalled in the poem, and in some images we can observe artists zooming in as it were on the bard himself, as Benjamin West did in his painting of 1778 (Plate 23), rather than attempting to depict the whole encounter in anything other than the most perfunctory detail. Because of this close-up presentation the bard's address to Edward is secondary to the oratorical performance itself; in the (near-) absence of the English armies the bard exists in a sublimely isolated realm, the epitome of poetic inspiration, transcending any genuine mediaeval reality, Welsh landscape or historical encounter.

Two images, produced in the first decade of the nineteenth century, concentrate on the isolated figure of the bard in just this way. The first, a drawing by John Downman (c.1800) (Plate 24) shows the bard at the edge of a precipitous drop with Edward I's army far below, airy spirits in the storm-wracked clouds and an eagle looking up from a rather awkwardly cramped position at the bottom left

of the composition. The drawing is squared up, as if for transfer to a finished design, but the resulting picture (if executed) would appear to have been lost. Downman exhibited an Ossianic subject at the Royal Academy in 1802 and it is plausible to see both designs as part of a broader interest in the heroic past at this period.

Contemporary with Downman's design is Richard Cosway's *Bard*, etched by his wife Maria and published by Ackermann in 1800 as part of a set of 'fancy' subjects (Plate 25). The picture is noteworthy if for no other reason than the ludicrously literal interpretation of the 'lyre' Gray uses to refer to the bard's harp. Cosway's lyre has at least the merit of being more portable than the cumbersome Welsh harps usually given to the bard, as for instance the unwieldy specimen shown in Downman's drawing, but it is woefully and, at this late date, surprisingly out of sympathy with the rather effective figure of the bard himself. It is hard to imagine Cosway being ignorant of the 'correct' form of the bardic harp, given the wealth of illustrations of the bard available to him, and it is worth considering that his lyre was meant to bring the bard closer to some transcendental realm, some Parnassus where cultural specificity was effaced. If so, the attempt surely fails and the resulting image strains credulity. In terms of Celtic culture it is as if the antiquarian exactitude of the later eighteenth century had never been; yet on the other hand the image is too prosaic to be redeemed by visionary excess, where exactitude might legitimately make way for an exploration of the essence of Gray's vision.

For excess and creative exploitation of Gray's poem we must look to William

26 William Blake, *The Bard weaving Edward's Fate*, 1797–8, watercolour and black ink, 41.9 x 32.4 cm (in John Flaxman's copy of 'The Bard. A Pindaric Ode', *The Poems of Thomas Gray*, London 1790). Yale Center for British Art, Paul Mellon Collection.

Blake. Blake had first been drawn to the theme early in his career, exhibiting a now lost watercolour version at the Royal Academy in 1785, and it is surely reasonable to suggest that he continued to feel sympathy for such a cynosure of his own craft.[23] He next paid extensive attention to Gray's poem in 1797–8, including fourteen designs for *The Bard* as part of the set of 116 watercolour illustrations to Gray's poems he produced for John Flaxman (Plate 26); these extraordinary images show an enthusiastic attention to every aspect of the text, using the suggestions within Gray's poetic imagery as a springboard for Blake's own imagination. Their accompaniment of the poem is exact, yet in the liberties taken with the imagery Blake's designs offer a meditation or free improvisation on *The Bard* rather than a straightforward illustration of it. His final version of the subject was his tempera painting, shown in 1809 as part of his one man exhibition (Plate 27). This picture is an exemplary instance of the tendency to present the bard as a heroic icon rather than a historical figure, for Blake's own intentions have survived in the *Descriptive Catalogue* which he published to accompany the exhibition. In it he declared his belief that painting could match the boldness of Gray's poetic conception.

. . . shall Painting be confined to the sordid drudgery of fac-simile representations of merely mortal and perishing substances, and not be as poetry and music

60

27 William Blake, *The Bard, from Gray*, *c.* 1809, tempera and mixed media on canvas, 60 x 44.1 cm. Tate Gallery, London.

are, elevated into its own sphere of invention and visionary conception? No, it shall not be so! Painting, as well as poetry and music, exists and exults in immortal thoughts.[24]

So, in this image Edward and his Queen Elenor, with Mortimer and Gloucester behind them, are shown cowering at the foot of the rock on which the bard stands, with the corpse of a murdered bard floating in the waters of the river Conway and the spirits of three more corporeally represented in the air above. The picture is much darkened and so difficult to read, but even in its present state much of the impact of Blake's design comes through. The use of a poetic interpretation of the subject allows him to combine elements from Gray's narrative and compress the linear unfolding of the whole poem into a powerful cipher, showing the protagonists of the massacre together with the weaving of the prophecy. The extreme dislocations of place and distortions of scale seen in the 1797–8 Flaxman set are not present here, but their influence is felt in the reduction of Gray's text to an artistic configuration which restates rather than merely illustrates its theme.

If Gray's *Bard* was the embodiment of Celtic defiance in the face of English attack, the poem also recognised the eclipse of Celtic culture. It was, in other words, as much a threnody as a call to arms. This mournful recognition of the passing of a way of life is the hallmark of James Macpherson's *Ossian* too. The tales Ossian relates are the supreme example of the Celtic golden age, with valiant heroes, noble deeds and fine emotions, but Ossian is old, his father, Fingal, and his son, Oscar, are dead and with Ossian's coming demise the whole era will be at an end. The pathos of this coming extinction gives an added poignancy to all the tales Ossian narrates; the songs he sings are of a world that will soon be lost forever. It was this lost world, miraculously preserved in the chants of its inspired bard, which burst upon an astonished public in the 1760s. Macpherson's *The Works of Ossian* (1765) was the culmination of a sequence of published 'translations' of poems belonging to an ancient Caledonian epic which Macpherson claimed to have transcribed from traditional Gaelic manuscripts and oral sources, surviving in the Scottish Highlands and Islands. *Fragments of Ancient Poetry, Collected in the Highlands of Scotland and Translated from the Galic or Erse Language* was published in Edinburgh in June 1760. The almost immediate success of this book on both sides of the border prompted enthusiasts to subscribe for Macpherson to travel twice into the Highlands and Islands that year to collect more Gaelic poetry. In 1761 Macpherson moved to London and in December published *Fingal, an Ancient Epic Poem, in Six Books* followed by *Temora, An Ancient Epic Poem, in Eight Books* in 1763. The debate concerning what exactly he invented and what he translated continues to this day and Howard Gaskill has notably rehabilitated Macpherson from the critical obloquy which has so besmirched his name.[25] For Gaskill, the probable truth is that *Fingal* in particular is a composite reworking of genuine Scots Gaelic ballads, a judgement shared by Dr Johnson in his *Journey to the Western Islands of Scotland*: 'He has doubtless inserted names that circulate in popular stories, and may have translated some wandering ballads, if any can be found; and the names and some of the images being recollected, make an inaccurate auditor imagine, by the help of Caledonian bigotry, that he had formerly heard the whole.'[26]

Fingal, King of Morven, his son Ossian, the third-century bard, Ossian's son Oscar and Oscar's lover Malvina, together with a soon to be familiar cast of heroes, warriors and princes, people these romances set in a strange heroic world of Homeric integrity and valour. Fourteen further poems, invented by John Smith and published as *Galic Antiquities* were added to the canon in 1780. The almost immediate debate over the authenticity of Macpherson's translations helped, if anything, to fuel the popular enthusiasm for Ossian. Gray, whose scholarship in Celtic and Scandinavian literature and culture was thorough, had been sent unpublished material by Macpherson but was suspicious of the authenticity of the fragments. As he wrote to Thomas Wharton in June 1760,

> but what plagues me is, I can not come at any certainty on that head. I was so struck, so *extasie* with their infinite beauty, that I writ into Scotland to make a thousand enquiries. the letters I have in return are ill-wrote, ill-reason'd, unsatisfactory, calculated (one would imagine) to deceive one, & yet not cunning enough to do it cleverly. in short, the whole external evidence would make one believe these fragments (for so he calls them, tho' nothing can be more entire) counterfeit: but the internal is so strong on the other side, that I am resolved to believe them genuine, spite of the Devil & the Kirk. it is impossible to convince me, that they were invented by the same Man, that writes me these letters. on

the other hand it is almost as hard to suppose, if they are original, that he should be able to translate them so admirably. what can one do?[27]

Writing to William Mason a month later Gray was still sceptical: 'I continue to think them genuine, tho' my reasons for believing the contrary are rather stronger than ever: but I will have them antique, for I never knew a Scotchman of my own time, that could read, much less write, poetry; and such poetry too!'[28]

Others were less hesitant; William Stukeley, whose own antiquarian publications of the 1740s had developed increasingly extravagant theories of Druid worship at Avebury and Stonehenge, was completely satisfied with Macpherson's work and in his *A Letter from Dr. Stukeley to Mr. Macpherson, On his Publication of Fingal and Temora* (1763) wrote at some length on Ossian's vindication of the hypotheses Stukeley had advanced in his own work on the Ancient Britons. So too, Macpherson's *Dissertation* prefixed to *Fingal* emphasised the historical value of the oral tradition, and *Temora* repeated this claim for the historicity of its narrative. Macpherson's most passionate advocate was the Scots clergyman Hugh Blair who wrote the preface to the *Fragments* and a lengthy defence of Ossian in *A Critical Dissertation on the Poems of Ossian, the Son of Fingal* from which I have already quoted.[29] The *Critical Dissertation* tended to be included in all the English editions of *Ossian* as an antiquarian introduction to the texts. Blair's reasoning is emphatic and makes early use of the Four Stages theory of human progress, then being developed in Scottish intellectual circles.[30]

> The compositions of Ossian are so strongly marked with characters of antiquity, that although there were no external proof to support that antiquity, hardly any reader of judgement and taste could hesitate in referring them to a very remote aera. There are four great stages through which men successively pass in the progress of society. The first and earliest is the life of hunters; pasturage succeeds to this, as the ideas of property begin to take root; next, agriculture; and lastly, commerce. Throughout Ossian's poems, we plainly find ourselves in the first of these periods of society; during which, hunting was the chief employment of men, and the principal method of their procuring subsistence.[31]

In a sense, though, Hugh Blair's learned defence of *Ossian* was beside the point when considering popular enthusiasm for the texts. Of course the genuineness of the poems needed to be debated, and vast amounts of ink were expended in the process, but the attraction of *Ossian* continued even after a torrent of scholarly proofs and disproofs, claims and counterclaims had thrown the whole issue into hopeless confusion.[32] Beyond the scruples of the antiquarians and the literati there lay a deeper and essentially non-historical response to *Ossian* which is summed up by William Shenstone, writing to a Scottish friend in 1761. 'The public has seen all that Art can do; they want the more striking efforts of wild, original, enthusiastic Genius. It seems to exclaim aloud with the chorus in ''Julius Caesar'': ''Oh rather than be slaves to these deep learned men, Give us our wildness and woods, our huts and caves again.'' '[33] The wraith-like heroes, stalking the gloomy landscape of Macpherson's sagas have a phantasmagoric attraction; their unfinished portraits require completion and the reader's imaginative effort is required to bring Ossian's world into tangible life. If we read sympathetically we make these characters and this landscape our own and it is this sympathetic investment which helps to explain the phenomenal impact of *Fingal* and its related works. John Greenway has pointed out in a persuasive reading of the whole affair, that *Ossian* functions as a modern myth, expressing values held to be significant in the late eighteenth century and it was Macpherson's achievement in orchestrating those values that accounts for *Ossian*'s success. Macpherson's skill lay in his ability to give his readers the impression that they were witnessing an almost unmediated encounter with the authentic past and, most importantly, the thoughts, emotions and sensibility of that past, particularly with regard to the creative process of the primitive mind and its 'spontaneous' reaction to nature. Macpherson managed to create the illusion that the reader was experiencing directly the 'raw nature and noble passion' of his ancestors just before that era passed into historical oblivion.[34]

Furthermore, as has recently been suggested, in Scotland a defence of the authenticity of *Ossian* against English suspicion might become almost a patriotic cause. The Act of Union and the failure of the Jacobite risings had dissolved one aspect of Scottish culture; Macpherson's *Ossian* promised the celebration of another Scotland, differentiated from England not by politics but by history and tradition. As Richard Sher has noted, for the Scots intelligentsia the 1760s were marked by two severe difficulties in their relations with England: the failure of the Westminster parliament to extend Pitt's militia bill to Scotland, and the London literary establishment's refusal to recognise the worth of contemporary Scottish dramatists. The main players in encouraging Macpherson to produce his Ossianic work were keenly aware of these difficulties and had founded the so-called Poker Club to agitate for a Scots militia. Ossian's world of military heroics, related in an epic rivalling or surpassing Homer's provided retribution for a nation unfairly slighted in literary, political and military terms.[35] Given this background it is not surprising that partisans of *Ossian* could be vehement in their defence of the poems. When the Celtic scholar William Shaw published his sceptical examination of the texts, *An Enquiry into the Authenticity of the Poems ascribed to Ossian* (1781), he was 'accused of not being a good Scot, of being a traitor to the National Cause, and perhaps even being a spy on the English payroll.'[36] At least one of Shaw's readers, however, used his perfidy to good effect; when James Barry painted his monumental cycle of paintings, *The Culture and Progress of Human Knowledge* (1777–84) for the Society of Arts he included the figure of Ossian among the 125 portraits of men of genius populating Elysium, and, following Shaw's thesis, portrayed him as an *Irish* bard.[37]

The debate concerning the genuineness of Ossian was finally brought to a head in 1805 with two publications: the *Report* of the Committee set up by the Highland Society of Edinburgh to investigate the nature and authenticity of the poems and Malcolm Laing's edition of *The Poems of Ossian*, which undertook a critical examination of the material. Laing was a historian; he had completed volume six of his fellow Scot Robert Henry's *History of Great Britain* (1793) and written his own *History of Scotland* (1800), containing a *Dissertation on Ossian* which had searchingly exposed the fraud. He was also a correspondent of Pinkerton's, whose own *History of Scotland* (1788) had attacked Ossian and his supporters with his customary anti-Celtic vigour. Laing's conclusion was devastating.

When we return to the Poems of Ossian, I should insult the reader's understanding were I to expatiate on the gross contradictions between the generous heroes, the chaste and lovesick maids, clad in complete steel; feasting from sparkling shells, in the halls of mossy towers, traversing the northern ocean in large ships, yet subsisting solely on venison; and those naked, sanguinary barbarians, armed with a small shield, a dart, a dagger; almost destitute of iron, which they prized like gold; residing promiscuously in wattled booths, and possessed of no navigation but currachs, which crossed the Irish channel . . . during a few days only at the summer solstice.[38]

The very historicity which had seemed to guarantee the poems' authenticity at a time of Celtic enthusiasm and widespread primitivist belief now, as that enthusiasm and belief waned, proved their greatest weakness. Textual and philological questions, the accuracy of Macpherson's transcriptions, his knowledge of Gaelic, the possibility of such a long-standing oral tradition, were all points of attack on which Macpherson was pressed hard; but the idea that he had fabricated a bogus culture was easier to comprehend, to debate and ultimately to ridicule. Macpherson's confection of heroic chivalry and nobility of sentiment could not be sustained without an excessive suspension of disbelief. And even when disbelief was suspended in the 1760s and 1770s, there is still a sense of defensive apologetics in the discussion, despite the texts being trusted; Hugo Arnot's *History of Edinburgh* (1779) bears witness to the difficulties Ossian provoked.

To reject the authority of the poems of Ossian, we apprehend impossible; yet, to admit such dignified sentiments, such purity of manners, as have not prevailed generally among the most polished nations, to subsist in the earliest and most illiterate stages of society, contradicts every principle which an observation of its progress has enabled us to form.[39]

Nevertheless, even after the 1805 assaults on Ossian, works like George Chalmers' *Caledonia* could still use Ossian as a source of historical evidence when championing the identity and status of the earliest Caledonian peoples, in contrast to the historical disdain or vehement opposition of historians like Robertson, Laing and Pinkerton.[40] One response to the sceptics was to embark on a circular argument respecting cultural traits. Enthusiasts might discern 'Ossianic' sentiments and manners in the peoples of the Highlands and Islands and argue that these Gaelic speakers were in lineal descent from Ossian's world thereby demonstrating the possibility of refinement in their Gaelic ancestors too. Macpherson's claim to have discovered a Gaelic literary tradition with links to the era of the third century AD encouraged the belief that clan culture was, in essence, a survivor from a heroic Dark Age itself descended from the aboriginal Caledonians described by Tacitus. In his *Essay on the Authenticity of the Poems of Ossian* (1807) Patrick Graham used a Montesquieu-like functional model to explain those cultural survivals in Gaelic Scotland.

We know, that the mode of living, the domestic accommodations, and even the external scenery, which daily strikes the eye, have a powerful influence in forming the character, and in giving a tone to the ideas of a people. Even in the Highlanders of the present day, whose characters have not undergone a change

28 James Parker after James Barralet, *Fainasollis Borbar and Fingal*, 1783, stipple engraving. Yale Center for British Art, Paul Mellon Collection.

29 James Parker after James Barralet, *The Fall of Agandecca*, 1783, stipple engraving. Yale Center for British Art, Paul Mellon Collection.

by the contact of foreign manners, we may still trace the mode of thinking and of acting, which distinguishes the personages of Ossian. Accustomed to traverse vast tracts of country, which have never been subjected to the hand of art; contemplating, every day, the most diversified scenery; surrounded everywhere by wild and magnificent objects; by mountains, and lakes, and forests, the mind of the Highlander is expanded, and partakes, in some measure, of the rude sublimity of the objects with which he is conversant.[41]

In fact, it was precisely the rude sublimity of Ossian which proved so successful. Unlike Gray, Macpherson chose to recount events separate from any historical tradition and to place them in a world clearly lacking a specific topography. As is well known, there are no detailed indications of place in Ossian, merely evocations of mood and atmosphere: mist, gloom, cloud-wracked mountains, and roaring torrents. The protagonists, similarly, are rarely described in other than the most generalised terms, quite bereft of any detailed description of clothing, war gear or other accoutrements which might help to provide specific, individuating markers. As Hugh Blair put it, '. . . amidst the rude scenes of nature and of society, such as Ossian describes; amidst rocks, and torrents, and whirlwinds, and battles, dwells the sublime; and naturally associates itself with that grave and solemn spirit which distinguishes the author of Fingal.'[42] This very lack of specific description in the Ossianic texts allowed artists treating the material to invent images of these Celtic heroes and their environment with scarcely any factual restraint. 'Ossianic' indeed became a generalised term to describe effects of landscape and of weather, so amorphous was its reference.

Two Ossianic paintings by James Barralet, exhibited in 1778 at the Free Society and known to us in Parker's engravings of 1783, exemplify the licence occasioned by Macpherson's renderings of a Scottish heroic age. Both are taken from *Fingal*, the first is of *Fainasollis, Borbar and Fingal* (Plate 28) the second is *The Fall of Agandecca* (Plate 29). Given that the action is presumed to take place in the third century AD, with the Romans in the wings, the vaguely classical uniforms worn by Barralet's warriors might conceivably be justified by the text – after all, Samuel Wale's title-page illustration of the first edition of *Fingal* (1761) had pictured Ossian as a theatrically attired classical-looking bard in a heroic landscape (Plate 30) – but the mediaeval castle in Barralet's *Agandecca* can hardly be justified and the provision of kilts and tam-o'-shanters in *Fainasollis* gives the impression of a fancy dress occasion. Nevertheless, despite this farrago of costumes melding the vernacular and the antique, it is just conceivable that Barralet was attempting to underline the connection between contemporary Highlanders and their remote ancestors of the heroic period. Certainly others were prepared to detect a heroic affinity in Highland dress; William Gilpin, for example, who toured the Highlands in 1776, saw an immediate link between Highland dress and the antique.

But to see the plaid in perfection, you must see the highland gentleman on horseback. Such a figure carries you into Roman times; and presents you with the idea of Marcus Aurelius. If the bonnet were laid aside (for the elegance of which but little can be said) the drapery is very nearly Roman.[43]

30   Isaac Taylor after Samuel Wale, titlepage of James Macpherson, *Fingal; an Ancient Epic Poem in Six Books*, London, 1762, engraving. The Lewis Walpole Library, Yale University.

31 (*below*)   Alexander Runciman, *The Death of Oscar c.* 1770-2, pencil, pen and wash, 35.4 x 49.5 cm. National Gallery of Scotland, Edinburgh.

Of all the Ossianic subjects produced in this period, the most notable was Alexander Runciman's treatment of the saga in his ceiling decorations for Penicuik House, Midlothian, in 1771–2 (Plate 31). Here, in the interior of a large and recently completed Palladian mansion belonging to Sir James Clerk, Runciman painted not the life of Achilles he had originally proposed but a cycle of Ossianic pictures painted on a huge scale in emulation of the Renaissance frescoes he had recently studied during his five years in Italy, chiefly at Sir James's expense. The ceiling was destroyed in a fire of 1899, and is known to us today chiefly from the sketches which still survive.[44] Runciman worked in the spirit of Macpherson and used non-specific costume and indistinct surroundings to position the story in an imaginative realm, alluding to an archaic past yet outside of history. His *Death of Oscar* conveys the full impact of this approach, with histrionic gestures and exaggerated emotion heightening the pathos of the scene. Oscar's pose seems to have been modelled on a combination of Michelangelo's *Adam* in the Sistine Chapel and the classical statue of the *Dying Gaul*, the very image of the nobility of a warrior's death.[45]

The misfortune of losing Runciman's designs at Penicuik is doubled by the knowledge that his ablest contemporary, John Hamilton Mortimer, never produced an Ossianic subject despite being approached by Macpherson in person to illustrate his works, if a story circulating at the height of the forgery debate can be believed. Writing to Malcolm Laing in September 1799, to congratulate him on his *Dissertation on Ossian* John Pinkerton mentioned the incident.

> You saw, I suppose, in one of our Magazines, a year or two ago, a story authenticated with the name. The person was present when M'Pherson brought to Mortimer the painter, an Ossian for him to draw designs. It was full of corrections and alterations written on the margin, and showed that M'Pherson had no prototype but his own fancy.[46]

The same story, considerably enlarged, can be found in Richard Fenton's *A Tour in Quest of Genealogy* (1811), quoting a relation of his Welsh friend, Jones, and suggesting that the incident, if true, should be dated to the winter of 1761 when Macpherson had just moved to London and was preparing *Fingal* for the press.

> This gentleman happened to be on a visit to Mr. Mortimer, when Mr. Macpherson called to consult him about a set of designs for his Ossian, which he was now about to serve up whole, having already treated the public with a taste of it, and for that purpose had brought his manuscript with him. He described it as a bulky quarto volume, with 'a small rivulet of text running through a large meadow of margin.'[47]

The vigour of Mortimer's line and the pungency of his creations would have produced an Ossian far removed from the rococo winsomeness of most illustrators and we can get some idea of what his treatment might have been by looking at a work of his follower, Charles Reuben Ryley, who exhibited six subjects from Ossian at the Royal Academy between 1783 and 1789. *Oscar bringing back Annir's Daughter* (1786) (Plate 32) is very Mortimer-like with its banditti type warriors and heroic ambience, though it reveals a tender sensibility and sense of

32   Charles Reuben Ryley, *Oscar bringing back Annir's Daughter*, 1785, oil on canvas, 31.4 x 41.2 cm. Tate Gallery, London.

pathos somewhat distant from Mortimer's mordant expression and darker emotional range.

The indiscriminate visualisation of this heroic age can be demonstrated by examining the fate of a particular 'Ossianic' visage. In Runciman's *Death of Oscar*, the figure of Fingal on the left of the composition, clutching his face with his hair streaming out to the side, is one of the artist's happiest inventions. It is possible that Runciman had Gray's *Bard* in mind here,

> (Loose his beard and hoary hair
> Streamed, like a meteor, to the troubled air)

whose predicament as the last of his kind found an echo in Fingal's own dynastic situation, now that his grandson was dying. Fingal's visage was borrowed in its turn by James Barry for his evocation of paternal grief in an equally shadowy era on the margins of history, *King Lear weeping over the Body of Cordelia* of 1774. From Barry it reached J.H. Mortimer for his etching of *Lear* published in 1776, and then William Blake for his watercolour of *Lear grasping his Sword* (c.1780).

Barry's treatment of Lear indicates the extent to which the archaic past in the proto-Romantic imagination might combine antiquarian understanding of British antiquity with the embroidered representations of the literary imagination. That Barry had an interest in the subject is borne out by his repeated reworking of it. The 1774 oil painting was engraved in aquatint in 1776 (Plate 33), in etching c.1790 and the figure of Lear alone in lithography c.1803.[48] More significant, perhaps, is the greatly enlarged and ambitious picture of this subject produced for

70

Boydell's Shakespeare Gallery in 1786–8 (Plate 34). Here the background contains 'improved' megalithic architecture of a sort which Inigo Jones might have recognised as primaeval Doric and which provides a context of archaic civilisation appropriate to the story.[49] This coupling of the heroic past with the megalithic remains of prehistory can also be found in at least one attempt at an Ossianic subject. Elizabeth Harvey, in her *Malvina lamenting the Death of Oscar*, exhibited at the Paris Salon in 1806 (Plate 35), positions Malvina in front of a large

35 Elizabeth Harvey, *Malvina mourning the Death of Oscar: her Companions trying to console Her. Scene from Ossian*, exhibited 1806, oil on canvas, 86 x 72 cm. Musée des Arts Décoratifs, Paris.

trilithon with Fingal's Cave in the distance,[50] but this conjoining of the heroic with the prehistoric was as rare for Ossian as it was for Lear, both of whose natural habitat was the misty, storm-wracked and indeterminate world conjured up by sublime rhetoric.

The one artist who might be said to have worked naturally in the gap between history and literature was William Blake. Blake's interest in the origins and earliest history of Britain resulted in the production of a number of works, some of which are relatively straightforward interpretations of mythical or historical events while others are as abstruse and dense in meaning as anything he produced. In 1793 he planned a series of twenty-two subjects for *The History of England, a small book of Engravings*, of which the first eight are concerned with the mythical and Celtic past of England:

1. Giants ancient inhabitants of England
2. The Landing of Brutus
3. Corineus throws Gogmagog the Giant into the Sea
4. King Lear
5. The Ancient Britons according to Caesar [The frontispiece *del.*]
6. The Druids
7. The Landing of Julius Caesar
8. Boadicea inspiring the Britons against the Romans
   The Britons' distress & depopulation
   Women fleeing from War
   Women in a Siege

These topics had evidently interested him for some time; watercolours of *The Landing of Brutus in England, Lear and Cordelia in Prison* and *The Landing of Julius Caesar* (all *c.*1779) are extant and David Bindman has suggested that *A Breach in a City, the Morning after a Battle* (*c.*1790–5), a version of a lost watercolour exhibited at the Royal Academy in 1784, could be related to the cluster of subjects listed under number 8 in Blake's list.[51] References to Boadicea, Bladud, Arthur and Merlin can be found in his mature writings, but it is especially in *Jerusalem* (1804–20) that Blake concentrates on the archaic history of Britain and on Druidical religion (see Chapter Five). In addition there are pencil drawings, among the so-called visionary heads, of *Cassibelane* (Cassivellaunus), *Caractacus* and *Boadicea* (all *c*.1819–25) and a lost tempera painting, *The Ancient Britons*, was exhibited as part of his one man exhibition in 1809, with the following accompanying text:

> In the last Battle of King Arthur, only Three Britons escaped; these were the Strongest Man, the Beautifullest Man, and the Ugliest Man; these three marched through the field unsubdued, as Gods, and the Sun of Britain sat, but shall arise again with tenfold splendor when Arthur shall awake from sleep, and resume his dominion over earth and ocean.[52]

Paraphrasing Blake's own description, the painting showed these three Britons overwhelming their Roman enemies, while below them dead and dying Britons and Romans strew the field of battle, the last of the bards falls dying among them, singing to his harp and in the distance, among the mountains, are seen Druid Temples 'similar to Stone Henge', behind which sets a bloody sun. Blake's interpretation of the subject was, as we might expect, more than historical and included the story of King Arthur with a further symbolic twist of Blake's own. The three Britons are three of the four parts (the fourth being 'like the Son of God') of an originally united man who 'was self-divided, and his real humanity slain on the stems of generation',[53] this being the major theme of Blake's contemporary poem *Jerusalem*. The Strong Man represents the human sublime and is portrayed as a receptacle of wisdom, the Beautiful Man represents the human pathetic (the male and female principles) and is portrayed as imbued with intellectual beauty and the Ugly Man represents human reason and is portrayed as bestial and intellectually incapable.

According to Robert Southey, Blake's *Descriptive Catalogue* entry for *The Ancient Britons* 'begins with a translation from the Welsh, supplied to him no doubt by that good simple-hearted, Welsh-headed man, William Owen, whose memory is the great storehouse of all Cymric tradition and lore of every kind.'[54] Blake's source for the three last Britons does indeed seem to have been the Welsh Triads, which he probably encountered in the *Myvyrian Archaiology of Wales* (1801–7) edited by his friend William Owen Pughe. The interplay between the two men has been graphically and probably too easily characterised by Southey as mutual madness: 'Poor Owen found everything which he wished to find in the Bardic system, and there he found Blake's notions, and thus Blake and his wife were persuaded that his dreams were old patriarchal truths, long forgotten, and now re-revealed.'[55]

As we have seen, the association of the Welsh with the Ancient Britons and the bards with the survival of Druidical learning from archaic times was not necessarily unreasonable, particularly in the context of the radical circles in which Blake moved in the 1790s. What complicates Blake's use of the Triads in this instance is that Edward Williams (Iolo Morganwg) had adulterated a genuine literary tradition.

Iolo had compiled, or rather invented, a number of triads as an appendix published with a collection of his own poems in 1794 and then contributed an entirely bogus *Third Series of Triads* to the *Myvyrian Archaiology of Wales*.[56] Blake's source was, therefore, corrupt, adding a further intermediate presence to an already creatively interpreted scenario.

Henry Crabb Robinson was one of the few to visit Blake's exhibition and in his *Reminiscences of Blake* describes the show: 'There were about 30 oil paintings, the colouring excessively dark & high, the veins black & the colour of the primitive men very like that of the red Indians. In his estimation they wd. probably be the primitive men.'[57] Blake seems to have been particularly proud of this colouring, comparing it to the 'sickly daubs' of Titian, Rubens and Correggio, whose men were like leather and whose women were like chalk. Bewailing the fact that today's copier of nature cannot find 'a civilized man, who has been accustomed to go naked' he looked to the frecoes of Michelangelo and Raphael to represent 'The flush of health in flesh exposed to the open air, nourished by the spirits of forests and floods in that ancient happy period . . . in Mr. B.'s Britons the blood is seen to circulate in their limbs; he defies competition in colouring.'[58]

Seymour Kirkup, who also visited the show, considered the picture to be Blake's finest work, noting its 'fury and splendour of energy . . . contrasted with the serene ardour of simply beautiful courage; the violent life of the design, and the fierce distance of fluctuating battle'.[59] That the picture has disappeared is an immense disappointment. Kirkup estimated its size as 14 feet by 10, making it far and away the most ambitious painting Blake ever attempted and the attention paid to its aesthetic principles and spiritual philosophy in the *Descriptive Catalogue* indicates that Blake presented it as something of a summation of his artistic and metaphysical beliefs. Kirkup made a copy, done from memory, in about 1870 which he gave to Swinburne, but that too is lost; the original seems to have vanished without trace after the failure of the 1809 exhibition.[60]

As with Blake's interpretation of *The Bard*, his vision of ancient Britain might stand as the epitome of the imaginative and creative approaches to that era undertaken by artists and writers. History is activated by suggestion, supposition and empathetic projection to produce a fabulous account of Celtic Britain, its people and its culture, the whole picture bodied forth in the rhetoric of partisan enthusiasm as a panegyric on a lost domain. *The Ancient Britons*, in its fervent propaganda for Celtic Britain, signals the high water mark of that sensibility first inaugurated by Gray and Macpherson sixty years before. Blake himself should have the last word.

The Britons (say historians) were naked civilized men, learned, studious, abstruse in thought and contemplation; naked, simple, plain in their acts and manners; wiser than after-ages . . . this Picture . . . supposes that in the reign of that British Prince, who lived in the fifth century, there were remains of those naked Heroes in the Welch mountains; they are there now, Gray saw them in the person of his Bard on Snowdon; there they dwell in naked simplicity; happy is he who can see and converse with them above the shadows of generation and death.[61]

Chapter Five
THE DRUIDS

Although the figure of the bard was instrumental in establishing and maintaining the eighteenth-century Celtic revival, his importance was not unique for, as we have seen, the bardic community was intimately linked with that of the Druids. These latter, for antiquarians and the general public alike, were self-evidently the most memorable and significant members of ancient British society and their philosophy and religious practices were a source of seemingly endless fascination. Indeed, their combination of benevolent and malevolent qualities, coupled with a relatively full classical report ensured that these primitive British priests became the chief representatives of their culture as a whole in the popular and antiquarian imaginations. Even today their conceptual hold has hardly weakened and the general public is easy enough with the idea of Druids at Stonehenge, or in sword and sorcery literature and the like. If we compare this picture with the current archaeological thinking from which it deviates it is evident that the late twentieth-century imagination still receives its picture of the Druids through the mediating screen of romantic interpretation rather than the enquiries of historians and archaeologists. Whilst investigating second hand book shops for various tomes relevant to this project it was not unusual to find serious studies such as Stuart Piggott's *The Druids* (1968) and A.L. Owen's *The Famous Druids* (1962) shelved under 'occult' rather than 'archaeology' or similarly sober classifications. Was this a bookseller's attempt to subvert the Druidic lunatic fringe by infiltrating works that debunked the romantic image, or was it an ironic indication that, where Druids are concerned, archaeology is subordinate to a more whimsical approach?

In the extant classical literature references to the Druids appear in a number of texts scattered over some six centuries, from about 200 BC to AD 400. Modern English translations of this material have been usefully brought together and discussed in Kendrick's *The Druids: A Study in Keltic Prehistory* (1927) and Stuart Piggott in his own later study, *The Druids*, has provided an admirably lucid guide to a complex historical, literary and philosophical story which makes it superfluous to go over the same ground in exhaustive detail here. For our purposes, looking at the use made of these sources in the eighteenth century in particular, it is sufficient to note that two traditions of writing about the Druids came down from classical antiquity, characterised by Piggott as the Posidonian and the Alexandrian. The Posidonian accounts are named in respect of Book 23 of the *Histories* of the Greek author Posidonius, written towards the close of the second century BC. Although Posidonius was domiciled in Apamea, Syria, he had travelled in Gaul and much of what he has to say was probably derived from first hand sources. Posidonius' influence on later writers was enormous; his historiography followed in the footsteps of his great predecessor, the Greek historian Polybius, and his knowledge ranged over a huge domain, including philosophy, ethnology and science. Even at the close of the first century AD his influence was apparent: Tacitus' ethnological material in the *Germania* (AD 98), for example, is indebted to Posidonius' studies. The *Histories* themselves are lost and are only known to us today from their quotation by other writers, such as Diodorus Siculus in his *Historical Library* (*c.*36 BC), Strabo in his *Geography* (*c.*7 BC) and Caesar in his *Gallic Wars* (*c.*52 BC), though Caesar also had his personal experience of the Celts on campaign to guide him. This tradition of writing is even-handed in its description of Celtic culture, detailing the philosophy and rituals of the Druids whether benign or murderous. In this vein further details of Celtic customs can be found in Pomponius Mela's geography, *De Chorographia* (*c.* AD 43), Lucan's *Pharsalia* (*c.* AD 65), the elder Pliny's *Natural History* (*c.* AD 77), Tacitus' *Annals* (*c.* AD 117), Ammianus Marcellinus' *History* (*c.* AD 391) and other classical accounts.

The later Alexandrian tradition is, in contrast, essentially a second order writing, derived only from previous authors as opposed to personal experience, and it elaborates a much more respectful image of the Druids, especially in relation to their 'Pythagorean' philosophy and knowledge of the workings of nature. From the first to the third centuries AD writers like Dio Chrysostom, Clement of Alexandria, St Cyril, Origen and Diogenes Laertius are the chief representatives of this tendency. By this period the Druids themselves were probably a spent force in Celtic society, now mainly under Roman occupation. The Druids in Gaul had been suppressed under Tiberius and Claudius because the Romans abhorred their sacrificial practices and probably also recognised that the Druids' teachings represented a potentially subversive rallying point. The Roman attack on Anglesey in AD 61, prompted by similar concerns, may have fatally weakened their position in British society. For Alexandrians, then, the opportunity for direct encounters with Druids or those who knew of them was remote and the work of enthusiastic elaboration supplied the lack.

Some of these sources were studied in the Middle Ages, others, like Tacitus, were ignored or forgotten until unearthed in monastic libraries in the Renaissance, but most of this material was published in editions of varying accuracy between the 1470s and the 1550s, with translations into English and other modern European languages often following. New editions and new translations appeared in the seventeenth, eighteenth and nineteenth centuries, allowing scholars to peruse without too much difficulty the full range of the Greek and Roman reports.[1] The Druids described in these classical accounts furnished the historians and antiquarians of the eighteenth and nineteenth centuries with the materials from which to fashion their interpretations. These 'Druids as wished for' have been extensively discussed by Thomas Kendrick, A.L. Owen and, most recently, Stuart Piggott; suffice it to say that for Celtic enthusiasts a selective and partial reading of the classical sources laid the groundwork for the erection of increasingly ornate speculation concerning the Druids and their doctrines.

In the climate of Celtic enthusiasm which developed after the 1760s such antiquarian speculation helped to construct an image of the Druid as a primaeval seer, versed in the mysteries of nature, worshipping in oak groves and/or in megalithic temples. The historian and witness of his community, the Druid guarded the people's memory, handing down ancestral wisdom from generation to generation. As a supreme patriot he might animate his people to defend their liberty in time of war, despite his own pacifism. Druidic religion involved the collection of mistletoe and the making of sacrificial offerings, sometimes animal and sometimes human. These last, which involved ritual killing, were used as auguries, with the victims' death throes interpreted for what they portended. Such, in crude outline, constituted the standard image of the Druid. When tourists visited megalithic sites they carried some of this speculation with them, peopling the stones with a farrago of historical and imaginative detail. In his *Observations on Cumberland and Westmoreland* (1786), William Gilpin describes the Castlerigg stone circle, near Keswick, and talks of megalithic architecture in general as

> strong proof of the savage nature of the religion of these heathen priests. Within these magical circles we may conceive any incantations to have been performed; and any rites of superstition to have been celebrated. It is history, as well as poetry, when Ossian mentions the *circles of stones*, where our ancestors, in their nocturnal orgies, invoked the spirits which rode upon the winds – the awful forms of their deceased forefathers; through which, he sublimely tells us, *the stars dimly twinkled*.[2]

It is in this imaginative guise above all that the image of the Druid is disseminated in a variety of contexts in the later eighteenth and early nineteenth centuries. In literary and historical texts, in paintings, sculptures and engravings, on armorial bearings, commemorative medals and trade tokens the familiar bearded figure presides as priest and instructor, the fount of learning and the penetrator of nature's sublimest mysteries.[3] One of the most pungent of these images is an extremely rare early lithograph by Raphael Lamar West first published in 1803 in André's *Specimens of Polyautography* (Plate 36). The visionary intensity of West's Druid manages to suggest both the Druids' association with nature and the numinous quality of their autochthonous knowledge. This image, in its compression and visual impact may be viewed as the presiding spirit of this chapter.

Antiquarian interest in the Druids can be detected from at least the late sixteenth century. Camden's *Britannia*, from its first edition in 1586, contained information and speculation on the Druids which helped to bring them into public reckoning and stimulated further enquiries. The first part of Michael Drayton's poem *Poly-Olbion* (1612), for example, makes reference to the Druids as philosophical bards and this description was elaborated in the notes to the poem provided by the antiquary John Selden. The Druids must have become part of the public's stock of historical information for writers to include them in literary productions of this period. Act III of John Fletcher's play *Bonduca* (probably first performed in 1613–14) opens with a scene set in 'A Temple of the Druids', where Druids assist Bonduca, her daughter and the British commanders Caratach and Nennius to offer a sacrifice to the Celtic gods Tiranes and Andate, accompanied by music and song. Kendrick is of the opinion that this text above all others established the Druids in the popular imagination[4]. From the 1580s to the 1620s, then, the Druids were becoming recognised as the ancient priests of England and in that guise they

36 Raphael Lamar West, *Bearded Man with an Oak Garland*, 1802, pen and brush lithograph. The British Museum, London.

are to be found in a number of seventeenth-century works of literature and antiquarianism.

Visually, too, the image of the Druid was beginning to take shape. Inigo Jones included a Druid in his staging of Lodowick Carlell's masque *The Passionate Lovers* (Plate 38), representing him as bare legged, long haired and bearded, clothed in a shaggy tunic, wearing an oak garland and carrying a phial and a dagger.[5] It is possible that this interpretation was loosely derived from reading John

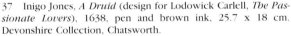

37   Inigo Jones, *A Druid* (design for Lodowick Carlell, *The Passionate Lovers*), 1638, pen and brown ink, 25.7 x 18 cm. Devonshire Collection, Chatsworth.

38   W. Dolle, *A Druid*, engraving, in Aylett Sammes, *Britannia Antiqua Illustrata*, London, 1676. The British Library, London.

Selden's *Jani Anglorum Facies Altera* (1610) who based his account, in turn, on Conrad Celtes' description of six statues believed to represent Druids which had been found at the base of the Fichtel Berg in Germany. Jones's costume was, of course, designed for an ephemeral occasion but Aylett Sammes's engraving of a Druid, sticking demonstrably closer to Selden's description, which appeared in his *Britannia Antiqua Illustrata* (1676) (Plate 38) was widely disseminated; Sammes's visualisation was copied by Henry Rowlands and William Stukeley in the eighteenth century and still dominated the iconography of the Druid in the early years of the nineteenth century. Sammes's Druid carries a staff, a leather bag and a book, is bare legged, long bearded and dressed in a cowled costume. The whole image is reminiscent of contemporary images of hermits for example the figure of Mutius, engraved in Jan and Raphael Sadeler's *Solitudo, sive vitae patrum eremicolarum* (1594), the first of four series of engravings based on drawings of hermits by Marten de Vos (Plate 39).[6] Given the association of the Druid with religion, learning and withdrawal from everyday life the use of a pre-existing iconographic schema representing exactly those qualities is perhaps to be expected.

By the early eighteenth century the Druidic tradition had begun to solidify. In his 'Templa Druidum', the opening section of an unpublished manuscript known as

MVTIVS excellens virtute, reliquit eremum
Sæpius, ad fratres corripuitq̃, gradum .

Languida debilium fanauit corpora: vita
Orbatos facra contumulauit humo.

Sadeler excud:

Monumenta Britannica (1665–93), John Aubrey was the first to claim that Stonehenge and Avebury were probably associated with the Druids. Extracts from Aubrey's writings were included in Edmund Gibson's 1695 edition of Camden's *Britannia*, which gave them a wide airing, and the whole manuscript was later read by William Stukeley in 1717 prompting his own investigations into Druidism published in the 1740s.[7] Further impetus to Druidic study was provided in 1723 when Henry Rowlands, vicar of Llanidan, published *Mona Antiqua Restaurata*, to prove that Anglesey was the heartland of the Druidic order in Britain, supplying an extensive account of Druidic rites on Anglesey and the archaeological remains on the island associated with them. Rowlands's re-engraving of the Druid from Sammes's *Britannia Antiqua Illustrata* was instrumental in ensuring the survival of this iconic type (Plate 40).

In literature, too, the Druids' presence was securely established. They appear in 'Britain', part IV of James Thomson's *Liberty, A Poem* published in 1736, whose political theme opposes the cynicism of Walpole's government and the dereliction of England under George II. The poem as a whole is concerned with the reawakening of public virtue and social harmony which, for Thomson, are the true marks of freedom and political stability and can be traced in the long progress 'from Celtic Night to present Grandeur'. Thomson's Druids are teachers and patriots whose doctrine of metempsychosis emboldens the Britons to resist Roman invasion.

> BOLD were those BRITONS, who, the careless Sons
> Of Nature, roam'd the Forest-Bounds, at once,

39 (*facing page*) Jan and Raphael Sadeler after Marten de Vos, *Mutius*, engraving, from *Solitudo, sive vitae patrum eremicolarum*, 1594. The British Library, London.

40 'Dna A M' *The Chief Druid from a Statue* in Henry Rowlands, *Mona Antiqua Restaurata*, Dublin, 1723. The British Library, London.

Their verdant City, high-embowering Fane,
And the gay Circle of their woodland Wars:
For by the *Druid* taught, that Death but shifts
The vital Scene, they that prime Fear despis'd;
And, prone to rush on Steel, disdain'd to spare
An ill-sav'd Life that must again return.
Erect from *Nature's* Hand, by *tyrant Force*,
And still more *tyrant Custom*, unsubdu'd,
Man knows no Master save creating HEAVEN,
Or such as Choice and common Good ordain.
This general Sense, with which the Nations I
Promiscuous fire, in BRITONS burn'd intense,
Of future Times prophetic. Witness, *Rome*,
Who saw'st thy *Caesar*, from the naked Land,
Whose only Fort was *British* Hearts, repell'd,
To seek *Pharsalian* Wreaths. Witness, the Toil,
The Blood of Ages, bootless to secure,
Beneath an *Empire's* Yoke, a stubborn *Isle*,
Disputed hard, and never quite subdu'd.[8]

Thomson's later *Castle of Indolence* (1748) includes a Druid-bard who has the task of rousing from indolence those souls who will respond and who achieves this with talk of spiritual progress and enlightenment as humankind advances from age to age. Again, Thomson stresses the idea of the Druid as sage, teacher and moral example, whose belief in metempsychosis makes him an appropriate conduit for the idea of spiritual progress advancing generation by generation.

This may sound like the typical effusions of a poet embroidering scant historical material, but the idea of the Druid as a source of wisdom was widespread in the period. As we have seen, the Alexandrian tradition of writing on the Druids existed as a store of suggestive remarks on their learning and this material was used from early on to bolster the status of the Druids. In the sixteenth century Hector Boece in his *Chronicles of Scotland* (1526) made them exponents of early humanism and John Leland described them as philosophers who had founded Cambridge and were willing converts to Christianity.[9] By the time John Milton wrote *Areopagitica* (1644), his pamphlet in defence of freedom of the press, he was voicing a fairly orthodox view in declaring

> . . . the studies of Learning in her deepest sciences have been so ancient and so eminent among us, that writers of good antiquity and ablest judgement have been persuaded that even the school of Pythagoras and the Persian wisdom took beginning from the old philosophy of this island.[10]

As the eighteenth century grew to its maturity, marked by the enthusiastic espousal of Celtic culture, celebration of the Druids reached new heights. Two examples from the 1740s are indicative of this burgeoning interest, as promulgated in the writings of extreme advocates of the Alexandrian tradition.

William Stukeley in the preface to *Stonehenge, a Temple Restor'd to the British Druids* (1740) declares,

> . . . I shall shew likewise, that our predecessors, the Druids of *Britain*, tho' left in the extremest west to the improvement of their own thoughts, yet advanc'd their inquiries, under all disadvantages, to such heights, as should make our moderns asham'd to wink in the sunshine of learning and religion.[11]

Stukeley's contemporary, the architect John Wood the elder, investigated Stonehenge and Avebury in 1739, and published the results as *Choir Gaure vulgarly called Stonehenge, Described, Restored and Explained* (1747). The preliminary results of this research, however, were directed towards the city whose remodelling is Wood's abiding testament. In the preface to his book *An Essay towards a description of Bath* (1742) Wood declared his intention

> to prove the City of Bath to have been the Metropolitan Seat of the British Druids; whose University having been Founded by King *Bladud*, the Building [i.e. the stone circles at Stanton Drew] still so far exists within eight Miles of our Hot Fountains as to prove the Work to have been a stupendous Figure of the Pythagorean System of the Planetary World.[12]

Bladud, the legendary founder of Bath is shown to Wood's satisfaction to have travelled to Greece in 506 BC where he taught Pythagoras and was known as Abaris, the northern sage recorded in classical texts. And not only did Wood construct an archaic history for Bath, his own town planning may have been informed by Druidic assumptions. It was Stuart Piggott who first noticed the intriguing possibility that the King's Circus, designed in 1725 and erected 1754–66, was perhaps inspired by Inigo Jones's plan of Stonehenge, so that Wood's rebuilding of Bath may be read, at least on one level, as the physical articulation of his theories concerning the city's Druidical glory in Bladud's era.[13]

By the close of the century, enthusiasm for the Druids' learning was an accepted position in numerous publications. Robert Henry, for example, in his *History of Great Britain* (1771)[14] celebrated the Druids' mechanical and scientific learning while Edward Davies in his *Celtic Researches* (1804) aimed to show how the 'philosophy of Greece originated in the Celtae'. Davies' panegyric on Druidic learning is unabashedly partisan.

> Their studies embraced those elevated objects which had engaged the attention of the world in its primitive age – The nature of the Deity – of the human Soul – of the future State – of the heavenly bodies – of the terrestrial globe, and of its various productions. Their conceptions were great and sublime, their speculations comprehensive in their sphere, pervading most of the arts and sciences which had interested the earliest periods. Perhaps there was no order of men amongst the heathens, who preserved the history and the opinions of mankind, in its early state, with more simplicity, and with more integrity.[15]

Reading passages such as this it is evident that we are at the climax of enthusiasm for the Druids, coinciding with the fervour of the Celtic revival that begins in the 1760s. Apart from his Ossianic writing, James Macpherson's *Introduction to the Ancient History of Great Britain and Ireland* (1771) had championed the Celtic peoples as the ultimate noble savages, well-versed in natural philosophy, valiant, free of malice, kind, considerate, but a terror to their enemies in all of which activities the Druids might be seen as crucial instructors. In the same year Dr John Smith of Salisbury published a full account of the Druids' interest in astronomy in a volume whose lengthy title renders further description superfluous: *Choir Gaur; The Grand Orrery of the Ancient Druids, Commonly called Stonehenge, on Salisbury Plain, Astronomically explained, and Mathematically proved to be a Temple erected in the earliest Ages, for observing the Motions of the Heavenly Bodies.* John Smith of Edinburgh's *Galic Antiquities* (1780) eulogised the Celts as a highly civilised people, among whom the Druids practised the perfection of knowledge, which they would in turn pass on to the Greeks. The nobility of behaviour and sentiment so evident in *Ossian* could thus be ascribed to the Druids' teaching.

> What wonder, then, if every noble and amiable virtue flourished, under the patronage of this venerable order, to the degree that we find it represented in the poems of Ossian? Or what wonder if poetry arrived at such perfection, in a country where there was not only, from age to age, a standing order of poets [the Bards], but such men as these [the Druids] to be its teachers, encouragers, and rewarders?[16]

Perhaps the longest poetic treatment of Druidism was John Ogilvie's *Fane of the Druids* (1787), a fifty-page celebration of 'the ritual ceremonies and observancies of this celebrated order of men'. Based on a comprehensive, yet highly selective understanding of the classical authors, the poem adopts an attitude of respect and admiration for the Druids' learning and civilisation. 'The Argument' for the poem provides a succinct summary of its contents.

> Introduction. Manners, habitations, etc., etc., of the first inhabitants of North Britain. Face of the country. Mansion of the Druid, and account of his person, dress, and character. Assembly of the Druidical order. Speech of the Arch-Druid. Building, and consecration of the Fane. Signal of approbation from heaven. Ceremony of lopping the mistletoe. Sacrifice. General feast. Office of the chief Druid in the Fane. Office of the Bardi, and subjects of their songs. Sublime ideas of the Deity. Oblation of the Warriour. Office of the Euvates, and of the sacred Virgins. Ceremony, time, and manner of gathering the Mistletoe, and honours paid to him who brought it. Wonderful fable of the serpent's egg. Druidical tenets and principles. Astronomical discoveries. Doctrine of the Metempsichosis, and application of it to promote the practice of virtue. Of the mundane dissolution, and renovation. Moral lessons. Effect on character and practice. Manner of receiving young warriors after conquest. Peace and general felicity. Comparison of their manners with those of modern times. Conclusion.[17]

Ogilvie's success with this poem was sufficient for him to publish a further thirty-eight pages as *The Fane of the Druids. A Poem. Book the Second* in 1789. Evidently, his idealised portrait suited the public mood, grown used by this date to antiquarian proselytising for the Druids, their patriotism and their respect for nature's mysteries. As a testament to the high regard in which Druids were held in this period, it is surely significant that those few Druids appearing in fashionable masquerades begin to do so in the 1770s[18] and that the Grand Lodge of the Order of Druids, a friendly society which survives to this day, was first established in 1781.[19] Promoted by antiquarian enthusiasm, these late eighteenth-century Druids offered a vision of wisdom and insights into cosmic harmony not altogether unlike our discovery, two hundred years later, of ecological sensitivity and intuitive wisdom in the peoples of the Amazon rainforest.

Amidst this celebration of the Druids as philosophers another strand can be discerned, linking their religion to that of the patriarchs. Stukeley in *Stonehenge: A Temple Restor'd to the British Druids* said that the Druids came to Britain during the lifetime of Abraham or very shortly afterwards and brought the patriarchal religion with them. For Stukeley, the only crucial distinction between their religion and Christianity was that the Druids believed in a Messiah who is to come, whereas Christians believe in one who has come already.

> And tho' the memoirs of our Druids are extremely short, yet we can very evidently discover from them, that the Druids were of *Abraham's* religion intirely, at least in the earliest times, and worshipp'd the supreme Being in the same manner as he did, and probably according to his example, or the example of his and their common ancestors.[20]

He further explained that both this book and its companion, the forthcoming *Abury, A Temple of the English Druids* (1743) should be considered as sections of a larger future work to be called *Patriarchal Christianity, or a Chronological History of the Origin and Progress of true Religion and Idolatry*. Stukeley's motives in proclaiming this were partisan. As both an Anglican clergyman and an antiquarian he felt the need to defend his church from the assaults of Deism, especially as promoted by John Toland, the Irish free-thinker, whose *Christianity not Mysterious* (1696) claimed that God gave mankind from the first some rules to live by, so making the precepts of revealed religion superfluous. Toland had also written on the Druids, probably drawn to them as a result of his interest in metempsychosis. This had developed in Holland, where Toland had gone in 1692–3 to study for the Presbyterian ministry but where he became especially influenced by the Hermetic philosopher and alchemist F.M. Van Helmont who placed a particular emphasis on metempsychosis. The second letter in Toland's *Letters to Serena* (1704) attempted to establish the origin of this belief with the Pythagoreans and Egyptian priests and his two books on the Druids, *A Critical History of the Celtic Religion and Learning* (1702) and *A History of the Druids* (1726) can be seen as an extension of the same interest.[21] Toland added cairns, standing stones and cromlechs to Aubrey's ideas about megaliths as Druidical sites and he also promoted the religious observances of the Druids but he was sarcastic about their 'supposed learning' and their deception of the people. 'To arrive at perfection in Sophistry requires a long habit, as well as in juggling, in which last they were very expert: but to be masters of both, and withal to learn the art of managing the mob, which is vulgarly called *leading the people by the nose*, demands abundant study and exercise.'[22] This sort of criticism was a cover for Toland's more general attack on Christianity from a Deist point of view, seeing the priesthood as a pernicious barrier between the individual and natural religion. Stukeley's patriarchal views are to be considered, therefore, as an attempt to contest Toland's account. By proposing that the Druids believed in the revelation of religious doctrine and the Trinity and that the Anglican church preserved their teaching, Stukeley attempted to show that even seemingly dissimilar religious systems were in fact united in revelation and he therefore tended to load Druidism with an even greater freight of doctrinal significance than usual. As Owen memorably put it, 'Stukeley sometimes writes as though he were a man who speaks and accompanies his remarks with gestures which have no apparent relevance to his subject, but who is being annoyed by a small fly.'[23] It is doubtful whether Stukeley's readers could follow the labyrinthine path of his doctrinal thinking, with the probable result that his advocacy of patriarchal revelation and the Druids was understood simply as antiquarian research rather than a contribution to contemporary religious dispute.

Irrelevant or not, the links between Druidism and patriarchal religion became well established in later eighteenth-century writing on Celtic Britain. William Cooke, vicar of Enford, Wiltshire, published *An Enquiry into the Patriarchal and Druidical Religion, Temples, etc.* in 1754, promoting a confident re-statement and development of Stukeley's ideas.

> For the Patriarchal Religion was not confined to the Patriarchs and their Descendants, tho' it was preserved pure through them, while most of the Nations fell into great Corruptions; nor to the land of *Canaan* in which they chiefly resided. Great Parts of *Asia, Africa*, the continent of *Europe* and the *British Isles* were no strangers to the same Doctrine, and abound with Monuments of the same Worship.[24]

Given Stukeley's attempts to combat Deism there is a certain irony in reviewing the growth of these ideas, for when orthodox religion was itself increasingly affected by the challenge of deistic thinking there is a sense of ecumenical rapprochement in some of this material, such that the Druids might be accepted without great demur by liberal-minded Christians not, as Stukeley intended, as representatives of patriarchal religion but as a benign pagan priesthood who shared intuitively the fundamental tenets of Christianity. *The Monthly Review's* warm appreciation of William Owen Pughe's *The Heroic Elegies and Other Pieces of Llywarc Hen* (1792) is a case in point: 'Mr. Owen gives a most pleasing picture of the religion of the Druids, which, he says, is no more inimical to Christianity than the patriarchal theism of Noah and of Abraham. He attributes it to a severe and inflexible morality. Its doctrine of the transmigration of souls has been held by many christians . . .'[25]

This less sharply focused image of the Druids reaches its apogee at the turn of the century. In his poem, *A Descriptive Account of the Old Serpentine Temple of the Druids at Avebury* (1801), the vicar of Avebury, Charles Lucas compared the Druids' social prestige with contemporary indifference to the Anglican clergy. Just as Thomson had presented archaic Britain as a lost golden age for learning and patriotism compared to the corruption of the 1730s, so Lucas looks back longingly to a time when the priesthood was at the intellectual and moral centre of British life. Manifestly, this vision of the Druids was reliant not only on an Alexandrian interpretation of their training and doctrines but also on the patriarchal connections established by Stukeley and others. Given a more hostile, Posidonian-derived interpretation Lucas' effusions would appear merely ludicrous.

> Methinks I see the venerable Arch-druid
> Proceeding to the Fane, Thousands attend
> His solemn footsteps, or uncover'd crowd
> Along the spacious Way, and prostrate bow,
> As slow along he passes; See! he ascends
> The higher Cove, with awful silence
> The multitude attentive stand without
> The Dike; within, his Brethren their allotted
> Places take: – Each Word proceeding from his lips
> The greedy Crowd devour; on him alone
> All eyes are fix'd, all ears arrested wait,
> His Word the only Truth, his Wishes Law.[26]

John Martin's aquatint for John Britton's *Topographical Sketches of North Wiltshire* (1826) (Plate 41) shows a similar sort of scene; here a funeral procession enters the 'Ancient Temple at Avebury, Wiltshire, as presumed to have been originally'. All is decorous and ordered, the vast crowds move forward with the solemn pageantry appropriate for religious ceremonial. It takes little more than a moment's contemplation to note that the success of this image lies in its complete avoidance of any descriptive detail. The figures are on such a minute scale that the rites which accompany this funeral cannot be specified; all we are left with is a vague sense of religiosity conveyed by the disciplined patterns of the celebrants. The same benign image of Druidic worship is found in a slightly earlier plate representing Stonehenge from Meyrick and Smith's *Costume of the Original*

41 Robert Havell after John Martin, from a sketch by John Britton, *Ancient Temple at Avebury Wiltshire, as presumed to have been originally*, 1824, aquatint, in John Britton, *Topographical Sketches of North Wiltshire*, London, 1826. Exeter Central Library.

42 Robert Havell after Charles Hamilton Smith, *Grand Conventional Festival of the Britons*, hand-coloured aquatint, plate 11 of Samuel Rush Meyrick and Charles Hamilton Smith, *The Costume of the Original Inhabitants of the British Islands*, London, 1815. Yale Center for British Art, Paul Mellon Collection.

Inhabitants of the British Islands, entitled 'Grand Conventional Festival of the Britons' (Plate 42). The accompanying letterpress is long and detailed, drawing chiefly on old Welsh literature such as Taliesin, Aneurin, the *Goddodin* and similar material, and examines the ceremonies associated with the Helio-arkite cult at Stonehenge on the morning after May-eve. The inner trilithons are covered with hangings depicting the story of the dragon king, while Druids, with bards in attendance wait to sacrifice the sacred cattle. As with Martin's image, all is calm and ordered here; it is a vision of a highly structured and hierarchical society, with religion almost literally presented as its controlling centre. Both of these images are, of course, merely fantastic flights of imagination when compared to the little we do know of Druidism and Piggott in particular has exposed the romantics' Druid for the fabrication it is. But is it not also conceivable that these celebrations of Druidism, with their wistful yearning for respect and authority, should be seen as expressive symptoms of the unease occasioned by the political unrest that marked the 1810s and early 1820s?

We have been looking at favourable interpretations of Druidic customs, based on optimistic use of the Alexandrian tradition, but such uncritical enthusiasm did not pass unchallenged and it is necessary to backtrack a little here and look at more disparaging accounts. Toland's sceptical views on Druidic mystification were not unique in the eighteenth century and a number of writers would not countenance Druidic enthusiasm. The Druids of Burke's *Enquiry*, for example, ruled by fear and guarded the secrecy of their rituals to maintain the people in thrall to them.[27] The Irish antiquary Edward Ledwich went further and attempted a wholesale assault on Druidism in the pages of *Archaeologia* itself in his *Dissertation on the Religion of the Druids* of 1785.

> On no subject has fancy roamed with more licentious indulgence than on that of the Druids and their institutions. Though sunk in the grosses ignorance and barbarism, their admirers have found them in the dark recesses of forests, secluded from mankind and almost from day, cultivating the abstrusest sciences and penetrating the sublimest mysteries of nature: anticipating the discoveries of Pythagoras, Epicurus, Archimedes, and Newton: and all this without the aid of letters or of experiments: without those progressive steps in civilization which polish and refine the mind, and naturally lead it to the study of abstracted knowledge.[28]

Ledwich then offers a dispassionate examination of the Greek and Roman sources; given the tendency of some of the classical evidence to picture a society of utter barbarism and cruelty, he attacks in particular the idea of the Druid-philosopher, criticising the ill-founded conjectures of Rowlands, Macpherson and other enthusiasts.

> Had they reflected on what occasions the philosopher's presence was necessary, they certainly could never think them such as became an enlightened and polished man. He was not called from his retirement to communicate discoveries advantageous to society, the result of his applications to natural philosophy or politics: it was not to open new sources of trade and manufactures, or new improvements in legislation: no, it was to behold one of his own species

stretched on his back, his breast dissected with the stroke of a sword, while the Vates stand around, and with curious eyes view the convulsions of the members, the streaming of the vital fluid, and from the spectacle deduce cruel presages. These Vates were the same as the Roman Haruspices, the lowest of the sacerdotal order, and so odious their employment that they were scarcely admissible to the rank of senators.[29]

Ledwich was mobilising the more critical Posidonian material to make his case and there is no doubt that it seemed better founded than talk of Pythagorean learning and patriarchal worship. Yet, even though the abominations of the Druids may have offended the Romans and might equally offend the morals of modern Europe, there is a sense in which the antiquarian and literary cataloguing of their foul rites chimed perfectly with that love of the macabre so evident in Gothick novels, grave poetry and the rest of that literary tendency associated with the second half of the eighteenth century. There is, in other words, an element of *Grand Guignol* in even the most disapproving texts. A representative literary example of this more negative view can be found in Robert Holmes' otherwise undistinguished poem *Alfred* (1778), whose description of the Druids is unremittingly bloodthirsty.

> No more th'impenetrable groves among,
> With sacred spoils, and idol-trophies hung,
> From altars foul dark wreaths of smoke
> Imbosom the religious Oak;
> When rous'd by Mona's bloody-mantled Priest.
> Impatient Homicide, his Druid-crew
> With eyes of madness watch the midnight spell,
> And drown with deaf'ning yell
> The scream of Captives stretch'd in furnace blue.[30]

William Wordsworth's Salisbury Plain poems likewise use the Druids at Stonehenge as a device to compare the wanderer's isolation and misery with the brutality of primaeval existence. Wordsworth's unpublished draft *A Night on Salisbury Plain* (1793–4), based on his own experience of Stonehenge in 1793, revels in necromantic gore and the supernatural.

> For oft at dead of night, when dreadful fire
> Reveals that powerful circle's reddening stones,
> 'Mid priests and spectres grim and idols dire,
> Far heard the great flame utters human moans,
> Then all is hushed: again the desert groans,
> A dismal light its farthest bounds illumines,
> While warrior spectres of gigantic bones,
> Forth-issuing from a thousand rifted tombs,
> Wheel on their fiery steeds amid the infernal glooms.[31]

As the identity of the Druid, mystagogue or murderer, was in contention, so Wordsworth's thoughts rehearsed the alternatives and this first draft also contains one stanza dedicated to the Druids' astronomical knowledge; but the variants which succeed it are chiefly notable for their presentation of the Druids as cruel overseers of a horrific rite, notably the wicker-man in which sacrificial victims were burnt alive. In *The Growth of a Poet's Mind*, completed in 1805 and first published in 1850 as *The Prelude*, Wordsworth again returned, and this time at some length, to the Druids and their monuments on Salisbury Plain. The verses are interesting not only for their articulation of a variety of opinions concerning the Britons and the Druids, but also for their emphasis on reverie and the temporal and spatial dislocation of the monuments engendered by it. For Wordsworth the vestiges of the past well up out of the darkness or are situated in a featureless solitude which encourages the poet's imagination to range through time and space. This mode of presentation is analogous to the iconic compression used by some landscape artists in this period when depicting Stonehenge, as we shall see in Chapter Eight.

There on the pastoral Downs without a track
To guide me, or along the bare white roads
Lengthening in solitude their dreary line,
While through those vestiges of ancient times
I ranged, and by the solitude overcome,
I had a reverie and saw the past,
Saw multitudes of men, and here and there,
A single Briton in his wolf-skin vest
With shield and stone-axe, stride across the Wold;
The voice of spears was heard, the rattling spear
Shaken by arms of mighty bone, in strength
Long moulder'd of barbaric majesty.
I called upon the darkness; and it took,
A midnight darkness seem'd to come and take
All objects from my sight; and lo! again
The desart visible by dismal flames!
It is the sacrificial Altar, fed
With living men, how deep the groans, the voice
Of those in the gigantic wicker thralls
Throughout the region far and near, pervades
The monumental hillocks; and the pomp
Is for both worlds, the living and the dead.
At other moments, for through that wide waste
Three summer days I roam'd, when 'twas my chance
To have before me on the dreary Plain
Lines, circles, mounts, a mystery of shapes
Such as in many quarters yet survive,
With intricate profusion figuring o'er
The untill'd ground, the work, as some divine,
Of infant science, imitative forms
By which the Druids covertly expressed
Their knowledge of the heavens, and imaged forth
The constellations, I was gently charmed,
Albeit with an antiquarian's dream,

I saw the bearded Teachers, with white wands
Uplifted, pointing to the starry sky
Alternately, and Plain below, while breath
Of music seem'd to guide them, and the Waste
Was chear'd with stillness and a pleasant sound.[32]

Wordsworth's reference to 'an antiquarian's dream' suggests that his image of the Druid was more sardonic, and that the antiquarians' investigation of Druidic learning was at best a pleasant fiction which disguised the fact that the world of the Britons in general was harsh and comfortless, well removed from any idea of primitive philosophers. As he worked on his poem, the eighteenth-century's celebration of the Druids' civilisation and learning, typified by Henry's *History of Great Britain*, was slowly giving way to a less enthusiastic view. Henry himself was sceptical about reports of Druidic science and natural philosophy, given the acknowledged limitations of knowledge in the ancient world,[33] and John Lingard's *History of England* (1819), confirms and extends this approach. Despite his reasonably sympathetic exposition of Druidic learning, Lingard calls the doctrine of metempsychosis 'an absurd fiction';[34] he does not associate the Druids with Stonehenge and Avebury at all, because the classical authorities do not either[35] and he has a sharp retort for those who would interpret classical reports of groves and outside worship as indications of the Druids' sophisticated rapport with the spiritual realm: 'Some fanciful writers have pretended that they rejected the use of temples through a sublime notion of the divine immensity: though the absence of such structures may, with more probability, be referred to their want of architectural skill'.[36] In this climate of opinion it would have been hard for Wordsworth to accede uncritically to enthusiasm for Druidic learning and it is significant that the stanza dealing with the Druids' astronomical knowledge in *A Night on Salisbury Plain* was dropped in that poem's eventual published appearance as *Guilt and Sorrow* (1842), so emphasising the Druids' association solely with human sacrifice and the terror of the stones.

The other major poet of the period to devote attention to the Druids was, of course, William Blake and passages like the following can be read, at one level as sharing both Wordsworth's repulsion and his rhetorical exploration of blood sacrifice.

The Serpent Temples thro' the Earth, from the wide Plain of Salisbury,
Resound with cries of Victims, shouts & songs & dying groans
And flames of dusky fire . . .[37]

But for Blake, Druidism was more than simply a barbarous episode in the archaic history of Britain. We have already examined aspects of his interest in ancient Britain, with relation to the figure of the bard, and in his lost painting *The Ancient Britons* some notice was taken of Blake's tendency to rearrange the early history of Britain for his own spiritual and philosophical purposes. Blake's representation of Druidism provides a further example of the ways in which archaic history could be manipulated for particular religious, political or cosmological ends. His writings and associated images are a complex mixture of history and conjecture, melding certain aspects of the antiquarian tradition with his own cosmology.[38] From Stukeley or those influenced by him, for example Edward Davies and William

Owen Pughe, he seems to have derived the idea of Druidism as a patriarchal religion of great antiquity, whose origins predated Abraham himself. For Blake, these early Druids, guided by divine vision, preached a type of religion later revealed as the gospel of Jesus. Druidism in its original form thus exemplified the spiritual age, untarnished by the logo-centric and material era which followed it. But in his writings Blake concentrated on the degenerated Druidism which succeeded this original religion; Druidism now becomes a symbol of religious oppression as genuine spirituality rooted in the individual capitulates to an empty, systematic theology with moral authority given into the hands of the priesthood.

In holding such opinions Blake was not necessarily alone. Henry had followed Stukeley and others in asserting that the Druids got their religion from Noah's grandson, Gomer, but added to his measured account of their knowledge and philosophical status the further recognition that many of their practices were extremely cruel. By seeing this latter aspect of Druidism as the token of a religion in decline Henry was able to balance both the Alexandrian and the Posidonian traditions, with one following the other. As he noted, what the Romans witnessed was not Druidism in its primal glory: 'at the period when this history begins [the coming of the Romans], the religion of the ancient Britons had degenerated into an absurd, wicked, and cruel superstition'.[39] In addition, Henry threw out hints that these latter-day Druids operated like a corrupt and over-numerous priesthood, living a monastic life, collecting tithes and being supported in their privileged lifestyle by the people. Similarly, Edward King, in his *Munimenta Antiqua* (1799), made an emphatic distinction between pure patriarchal Druidism and its lapsed state, as it had been witnessed by the Romans.

> Surely, there can hardly be a more painful reflection; or one that tends more to cause an honest mind to shudder with indignation; – than that by the perverseness and blindness of the human heart, such grand associations of ideas should ever have been perverted to impious, and to idolatrous purposes; instead of being directed to the worship and honour of HIM, who created the whole expanse from [Stonehenge] surveyed . . . It is an happy circumstance, that we do not, at this distance of time, with precision, understand *what* the abominations here practised, in the latter most corrupted ages of Druidism were; though the first original designation, in conformity with Patriarchal usages, is manifest enough.[40]

For Blake, this corrupt Druidism stands for any institutional control of spirituality but symbolises in particular contemporary Deism, whose advocates had admitted the mechanistic Newtonian universe as a true picture of the creation and so radically restricted God's role in daily life. (This, of course, is an almost exact reversal of Toland's position, where the Druids' decline into sophistry stands for the corruption of Deism into organised Christianity). Druidism in its degenerate form, with its human sacrifices and occult ceremonial, epitomises the blindness, venality and cruelty of an entirely false religion. This argument is consistent with Blake's attack on organised religion throughout his writings. In *The Marriage of Heaven and Hell* (1790) he had expressed his belief that the Priesthood had systematised what had originally been a poetic understanding of the world until 'men forgot that All deities reside in the human breast'.[41]

92

Druids occur in various of Blake's projects from about 1793 but these theories were worked out chiefly in work he began about 1804, especially his prophetic books, *Milton*, produced between 1804 and 1808 and, in a much more developed form, *Jerusalem*, on which he was occupied from about 1804 to 1820.[42] The message contained in *Jerusalem* has proved difficult to elucidate fully, but its central pre-occupation concerns Albion, the eternal man, and his emanation Jerusalem, or spiritual freedom. The narrative recounts the degeneration of Albion from a free and spiritual existence to religious, philosophical and political slavery, 'the Ancient World of Urizen in the Satanic Void'. In Plate 27 of the book Blake sets out the argument at length.

Jerusalem the Emanation of the Giant Albion! Can it be? Is it a truth that the Learned have explored? Was Britain the Primitive Seat of the Patriarchal Religion? If it is true, my title-page is also True, that Jerusalem was & is the Emanation of the Giant Albion. . . . 'All things Begin & End in Albion's Ancient Druid Rocky Shore.' Your Ancestors derived their origin from Abraham, Heber, Shem and Noah, who were Druids, as the Druid Temples (which are the Patriarchal Pillars & Oak Groves) over the whole Earth witness to this day.

You have a tradition, that Man anciently contain'd in his mighty limbs All things in Heaven & Earth: this you received from the Druids. 'But now the Starry heavens are fled from the mighty limbs of Albion.' Albion was the Parent of the Druids, & in his Chaotic State of Sleep, Satan & Adam & the whole World was Created by the Elohim.[43]

The two lines quoted by Blake are derived from his own work, *Milton*. In Book One of that poem a diminutive rider is dwarfed by a giant trilithon and logan stone set against a night sky (Plate 43) to accompany the following lines:

Thence stony Druid Temples overspread the Island white,
And thence from Jerusalem's ruins, from her walls of salvation
And praise: thro the whole Earth were rear'd from Ireland
To Mexico & Peru west, & east to China & Japan: till Babel
The spectre of Albion frown'd over the Nations in glory & war.
All things begin & end in Albion's ancient Druid rocky shore
But now the Starry Heavens are fled from the mighty limbs of Albion.[44]

These Druid temples symbolise the rule of restrictive reason and Blake interspersed an entire megalithic landscape in a later copy of *Milton*, dated *c*.1814–15, to illustrate his characterisation of Satan as 'Newton's Pantocrator weaving the woof of Locke' with spirituality 'Mocking Druidical mathematical Proportion of length, Breadth, Highth.'[45] The same philosophy is outlined in *Jerusalem*; in Plate 70 (Plate 44) where a giant trilithon, framing an eclipse of the sun, accompanies verses which detail the spread of mechanistic reason emanating from

. . . Three Forms, named Bacon & Newton & Locke,
In the Oak Groves of Albion which overspread all the Earth.[46]

In both poems the human spirit, symbolised by Jerusalem, is destroyed and virtue becomes instead the product of law ruled by reason, such that human sacrifice,

43 William Blake, *Milton a Poem in 2 books*, c. 1807–9, plate 4, relief-etching and white-line engraving with water-colour and grey wash, 15.2 x 9.5 cm. The British Museum, London.

44 William Blake, *Jerusalem The Emanation of The Giant Albion*, c. 1804–20, plate 70, relief-etching and white-line engraving, 21.9 x 15.9 cm. The British Museum, London.

which is Satan's work, can be sanctioned in the name of morality. Blake's account of Stonehenge is emphatic in his detestation of Enlightenment reason.

> In awful pomp & gold, in all the precious unhewn stones of Eden
> They build a stupendous Building on the Plain of Salisbury, with chains
> Of rocks round London Stone, of reasonings, of unhewn Demonstrations
> In labyrinthine arches (Mighty Urizen the Architect) thro which
> The Heavens might revolve & Eternity be bound in their chain.
> Labour unparallel'd! a wondrous rocky World of cruel destiny,
> Rocks piled on rocks reaching the stars, stretching from pole to pole.
> The Building is natural religion & its Altars Natural Morality,
> A building of eternal death, whose proportions are eternal despair.
> Here Vala stood turning the iron Spindle of destruction
> From heaven to earth, howling, invisible; but not invisible,
> Her Two Covering Cherubs, afterwards named Voltaire & Rousseau,
> Two frowning Rocks on each side of the Cove & Stone of Torture,
> Frozen Sons of the feminine Tabernacle of Bacon, Newton & Locke;
> For Luvah is France, the Victim of the Spectres of Albion.[47]

45 William Blake, *Jerusalem The Emanation of The Giant Albion*, c. 1804–20, plate 69, relief-etching and white-line engraving, 21 x 14.9 cm. The British Museum, London.

46 William Blake, *Jerusalem The Emanation of The Giant Albion*, c. 1804–20, plate 25, relief-etching and white-line engraving, 21.9 x 16.1 cm, The British Museum, London.

The Druids appear as repressive forces throughout *Jerusalem* and their temples are illustrated on a number of occasions. Plate 69 of *Jerusalem* (Plate 45), for example, shows a human sacrifice by the daughters of natural religion, the issue of Albion's rational mind, their Druidic temple in the background, while Plate 25 (Plate 46) shows a disembowelled figure on the Druids' stone altar. This is presumably Albion himself, personified as a painted Briton with cosmic symbols on his body. The symbols are derived from a tradition established as early as the late sixteenth-century drawings of John White who portrayed Ancient Britons with elaborate tattooing (Plate 63), but when Blake says that 'The Sun fled from the Briton's forehead, the Moon from his mighty loins'[48] he is indicating that man has fallen away from the true patriarchal religion. And, following David Erdman's interpretation in *Blake: Prophet against Empire*, we can say that Albion's loss is also secular, a loss of liberty occasioned by England's political and military responses to the wars with revolutionary and Napoleonic France.[49] The Druidic temples in *Jerusalem* are thus emblematic of moral and political tyranny whose destruction will only come about when Albion awakes and draws together his disintegrated self. In the final plate of Jerusalem (Plate 47) we are offered such a

47 William Blake, *Jerusalem The Emanation of The Giant Albion*, c. 1804–20, plate 100, relief-etching and white-line engraving, 14.7 x 22.3 cm. The British Museum, London.

vision, after the annihilation of 'the Druid Spectre', showing the emanations of Jerusalem: Los, the Spirit of Poetry, carrying the sun, his wife Enitharmon, Spirit of Inspiration and Spiritual Beauty, tending the heavens and Urthona, Spirit of Productive Labour, in the centre, all three 'Awaking into [Albion's] Bosom in the Life of Immortality'. The serpent-like form of megalithic architecture behind them, presumably restored to its original spiritual purposes, is derived from Stukeley's famous plan of Avebury and its surroundings, but only in Blake's hands could such a radical transfiguration of antiquarian speculation have been achieved.

As we have seen, in emphasising the cruelty and repression of Druidism Blake participated in an increasingly widespread poetic and historical attitude. The best visual equivalent of this approach can be found in a mezzotint engraved by William Geller in 1832 (Plate 48). Geller is known today as a minor follower of John Martin, working in the north of England, and this print is almost a caricature of Martin at his most apocalyptic. Extreme contrasts of light and shade, violent weather and hordes of agitated figures combine to produce an image reeking with superstition, blood sacrifice and idolatry and thus a thousand miles away from Pythagorean learning and patriarchal Christianity. The disciplined ranks of worshippers, solemnly participating in elevated ritual, as seen in the engravings after Martin and Hamilton Smith discussed above, are replaced here by a savage tumult, whipped on by Druid instigation to an emotional climax within the brooding, bloody circles of Stonehenge.[50]

One aspect of Geller's print that should be noted is its pretensions towards fine art, for hitherto in this discussion, with the signal exception of Blake, Druidic visual imagery has been derived from antiquarian texts in the main. William Gilpin,

48 William Overend Geller, *The Druid's Sacrifice*, 1832, mezzotint and etching. Salisbury and South Wiltshire Museum.

writing in 1786, was puzzled that Druidic subjects had received such little attention from artists.

> As singular a part as the Druids make in the ancient history, not only of Britain, but of other countries, I know not, that I ever saw any of their transactions introduced as the subject of a capital picture. That they can furnish a fund of excellent imagery for poetry we know: and I see not why the scenes of [Mason's] Caractacus might not be as well suited to picturesque, as dramatic representation . . . I know few of the less animated kind [of pictorial subject], which would admit more picturesque embellishment, than a Druid-sacrifice. The peculiar character, and savage features of these barbarous priests – their white, flowing vestments – the branch of misleto, which they hold – the circular stones (if they could be brought into composition) – the spreading oak – the altar beneath it – and the milk-white steer – might all together form a good picture.[51]

There was, in fact, an extant fledgling tradition of Druidical images in precisely this vein, but the fact that Gilpin was ignorant of it suggests that its appeal was extremely limited. Nevertheless, as early as the 1750s serious artists had essayed Druidical subject matter. Francis Hayman produced *The Druids; or, the Conver-*

49 Simon François Ravenet after Francis Hayman, *The Druids; or, the Conversion of the Britons to Christianity*, 1752, engraving. Yale Center for British Art, Paul Mellon Collection.

sion of the Britons to Christianity in 1752 as Plate 3 for John and Paul Knapton and Robert Dodsley's projected history of Great Britain in fifty prints (Plate 49). It is the earliest image of Druids in a fine art context in England but the overall project was abandoned after the production of only six prints when the proprietors went bankrupt and a limited print-run explains why Hayman's work failed to have the influence it might otherwise have enjoyed.[52] The lengthy letterpress accompanying the print is concerned with the nature of Druidism, its ceremonies and its teaching and the (mythical) mission of Aristobulus, ordained bishop by St Paul, who was meant to have converted many of the Britons in AD 56 before suffering martyrdom. Hayman's picture shows Aristobulus coming upon the Druids in the midst of their most sacred ceremony, cutting the mistletoe with a golden sickle, or 'golden Pruning-knife' as the text has it. Cairns with sacrificial fires smoke in the background and two white bulls are readied for sacrifice on the right; the chief Druid ascends the oak in search of mistletoe while others prepare to catch it in a white woollen sheet below. All of this is a literal rendering of Pliny's account of Druidic ceremonies in his *Natural History*.[53] Meanwhile, the force of Aristobulus' preaching has already converted a group of Britons who willingly turn to the superior religion.

Just over a decade later another significant attempt was made to exploit this sort of subject. John Hamilton Mortimer's *St Paul preaching to the Ancient Britons* (Plate 50) (exhibited at the Free Society in 1764) won the 100 guineas top prize from the Society of Arts for the best historical painting and was noted at the time as an auspicious start to the revival of history painting in England. It was eventually bought in 1770 by Dr Benjamin Bates of Little Missenden, Buckinghamshire, a member of Sir Francis Dashwood's Hell Fire Club and a consistent patron of the artist. Bates apparently got the painting cheap from Mortimer who was using it for a game of fives when his patron visited his studio. He later donated the picture to High Wycombe church and Mortimer himself was buried near this early example

50 John Hamilton Mortimer, *St Paul preaching to the Ancient Britons*, 1764, oil on canvas, 350 x 366 cm. Guildhall, High Wycombe.

51 Joseph Haynes after John Hamilton Mortimer, *St Paul preaching to the Britons*, etching, 1780. Yale Center for British Art, Paul Mellon Collection.

of his powers. In 1777 Mortimer exhibited a finished drawing on the same theme at the Society of Artists which survives (reversed) in Joseph Haynes's etching of 1780 (Plate 51).[54] Even after making allowances for the different media and Mortimer's growing maturity as an artist, the contrasts between the two images are extreme. The 1764 painting, clearly indebted to seventeenth-century Bolognese artists such as Guercino, is generalised to the point where its subject matter is indistinct; the figures on the right of the composition who are presumably the Druids referred to in an alternative title are almost lost in the deep, and possibly symbolic, chiaroscuro, but even in the full glare of day there would be little to differentiate them as Druids, nor do the lay Britons exhibit any markers of their Celtic originals. The 1777 composition is, on the other hand, informed by a much more searching historical iconography; the man immediately behind the altar on the left is clad in skins and the woman in what we might call barbarian déshabillé, while the group of Druids on the extreme left of the composition have a monumental, dignified presence. This is very much an image of ancient British civilisation, benighted certainly but not savage or degenerate. It is also worthwhile speculating that Mortimer had been advised and inspired by his friend and occasional collaborator Thomas Jones, whose *Bard* (Plate 17) was exhibited in 1774 and had shown a more studied attitude to the Celtic past. Jones could have discussed his own picture and Mortimer's *St Paul preaching to the Ancient Britons* with Mortimer when both artists were working for Bates at Little Missenden in January 1775 and the 1777 drawing would therefore represent a response to Jones's criticisms. In addition, Mortimer seems to have borrowed some details from Grignion's engraving of Hayman's *Conversion of the Britons to Christianity* (first exhibited in 1761 at the Society of Artists) insofar as his original sketch for the 1777 drawing includes on the left a smoking cairn very similar to those shown on the left of Hayman's picture. Like Hayman's picture this is an entirely fictitious subject and, like his, it can be seen as an Anglican propaganda piece, linking the early British church with the apostolic tradition rather than the Vatican succession. Paul de Rapin-Thoyras's *History of England*, whose first volume was translated in 1725, had included this story, while admitting its mythical status and it is even conceivable that Mortimer derived it from his own copy of Speed's *History of Great Britaine* of 1611.[55]

We see these Druids again, or at least variants of them, in Mortimer's *Sacrificial Scene* (Plate 52), a drawing of the 1770s, where an assembly of oak-wreathed priests are involved in an unexplained moment of high drama in front of a sacrificial altar.[56] If this is a Druidical scene it is tempting to suggest that Mortimer was perhaps illustrating Henry Brooke's drama *Cymbeline* (1778). Brooke's play is an adaptation of Shakespeare's and concerns the love of Leonatus for Imogen, the daughter and sole heir of Cymbeline, King of the Britons. Their unsanctioned marriage produces a catastrophe; Imogen is disinherited and Cloten, her stepbrother, made heir while Leonatus is banished. Having been tricked into believing Imogen was unfaithful Leonatus, back in Britain, orders her killed and by the beginning of Act 5 has nothing to live for, despite saving Cymbeline's kingdom from his Queen's treachery. One hundred Roman captives, 'with fillets and fresh garlands, duly bound' are to be sacrificed to the goddess Andate. A 2,000 year old oracle proclaims that when a voluntary victim gives his life for others all human

52   John Hamilton Mortimer, *Sacrificial Scene* (also known as *Allegory of the Arts*), 1770s, pen and black/brown ink on paper, 24.5 x 36 cm. The Cleveland Museum of Art.

sacrifice shall cease and Mortimer seems to depict the moment when Leonatus rushes forward,

> Hold-Stop your horrid rites! Refrain your hands,
> Ye bloody servants of a barbarous godhead –
> Behold I give those valiant Romans freedom!
> Come, bring your fire and steel, your racks and engines –
> On me, alone, be emptied all your stores,
> All your artillery of death – I claim,
> And scorn your utmost efforts.[57]

The mixture of horror and heroism, artfully contrived by Brooke to maximise public reaction, is well caught by Mortimer whose drawing revels in a frantic emotional urgency whilst flirting with the violence it depicts.

Without qualification, the most public Druidical painting of the late eighteenth century was Vincenzo Waldré's *St Patrick lighting the Paschal Fire on the Hill of Slane*, part of the painted ceiling in St Patrick's Hall, in Dublin Castle (Plate 53). The Knightly Order of St Patrick was established in this hall on 17 March 1783 and the Irish viceroy, Lord Temple, afterwards first Marquis of Buckingham was installed as its first Grand Master. Waldré was employed at Stowe, Buckingham's seat, as architect, artist and designer in the 1780s and Buckingham commissioned him to undertake the decoration of St Patrick's Hall sometime around 1787. The overall scheme divides the ceiling into three compartments with large oil paintings on

53   Vincent Waldré, *St Patrick lighting the Paschal Fire on the Hill of Slane*, *c.* 1787–1801, oil on canvas, 325 x 683 cm. St Patrick's Hall, Dublin Castle, Dublin.

canvas set into each one. In the central and largest panel George III is accompanied by personifications of Liberty and Justice, on either side and approximately half the size are renditions of the two key founding incidents in recorded, as opposed to fabulous, Irish history: *King Henry meeting the Irish leaders* and *St Patrick lighting the Paschal Fire on the Hill of Slane*. The latter picture depicts the incident when Patrick, newly arrived in pagan Ireland lights the Paschal Fire in defiance of the Druids, positioned on the margins amidst a landscape thick with standing stones. Waldré exhibited the two smaller pictures in Dublin in 1801 and 1802 but it is unclear when the ceiling as a whole was completed.[58] The overall scheme, however, has a clear message: the benevolent impact of advanced religion and civilisation on the Irish people and, as such, it is precisely the kind of programme we might expect a viceroy to recommend.

Furthermore, although the incidents depicted are taken from Irish history their spiritual and secular content provides an overall iconography of church and state supporting the legitimacy of George's rule over Ireland. The 1780s and 1790s were of critical importance in Ireland's political development. Grattan's Parliament (1782–1800) was no longer subordinate to the English privy council in matters of legislation even if the administration was in the hands of an English-appointed lord-lieutenant. This delicate arrangement assuaged the grievances of Protestant patriots and some Catholics just enough to dampen public enthusiasm for a more radical political solution. Conciliation and mutual benefits for England and Ireland were of signal importance in a revolutionary climacteric, with Wolfe Tone's United Irishmen inspired by events in America and France to agitate for an Irish republic entirely independent of England. Waldré's ceiling should be seen as a product of these years, promoting a vision of progress and political accord.

A generation earlier, James Barry had also essayed a conversion scene, *The Baptism of the King of Cashel by St Patrick*, which he exhibited in 1763 at the Dublin Society for the Encouragement of Arts, Manufactures and Commerce. As

54 James Barry, *The Baptism of the King of Cashel by St Patrick*, c. 1799–1801, oil on paper laid down on canvas, 63.5 x 64.8 cm. Dublin Castle, Dublin.

William Pressly has noted,[59] its purchase by three MPs for the Irish House of Commons may be seen as part of the 'nationalist' pride that would come to the fore with Grattan's Parliament. In 1780, in recognition of his support for a more independent Ireland Barry himself was made a member of the Order of St Patrick, a Dublin patriots' club (not to be confused with the Knightly Order of St Patrick and associated with Waldré's painting of St Patrick). Barry's painting, recently rediscovered, disappeared in the burning of the Irish House of Commons on 27 February 1792, and Barry composed an oil sketch of the same subject between 1799 and 1801 (Plate 54). Barry probably took the story from Keating's *General*

55 Jacob Thompson, *The Druids cutting Mistletoe – a view of Long Meg and her Daughters (a Druidical Circle near Salkeld, Cumberland) in the Distance*, 1832, oil on canvas, 100.3 x 124.5 cm. Private collection.

History of Ireland (1723), a work he took notes from at a later date, and chose the moment when Patrick accidentally pierces King Oengus' foot with his staff. In the background a cromlech and trilithons hint at the Druidical superstitions overcome by Christianity, while the Doric temple in the foreground echoes the idea of primaeval simplicity in architecture found in the trilithons of Barry's *King Lear* (1786–8) (Plate 34) and to the same purpose, the demonstration of primitive civilisation in Celtic antiquity. The heroism and moral rectitude of the antique world is arrogated to the Celts.[60]

Although the contest between Christianity and Druidism remained by far the most popular exploration of Celtic religion, occasional scenes of Druidic rites, teaching and ceremony were exhibited in this period, as for example Jacob Thompson's *The Druids cutting Mistletoe* (Plate 55). Thompson's picture, exhibited at the Royal Academy in 1832, shows the same Pliny-derived scene of mistletoe harvest as had Hayman but includes, as an added bonus, the Cumbrian stone circle known as Long Meg and her Daughters in the background. The unattributed illustration in Charles Knight's contemporary *Old England* (Plate 56) takes this more positive view of Druidism to a pitch of banality, with the arch Druid holding court as though engaged in some outside conversazione with academic colleagues of a natural history faculty. Yet again this points up the contradictory positions adopted on Druidism. In contrast to Geller's almost contemporary engraving we are presented here with two benign images of some lost arcadia, without the

56 ?Stephen Sly after Thomas Scandrett, *Group of Arch-Druids and Druids* in Charles Knight (ed) *Old England: A Pictorial Museum of Regal, Ecclesiastical, Municipal, Baronial, and Popular Antiquities*, London, 1845.

57 (*below*) T.H. Maguire after Edmurd Thomas Parris *Joseph of Arimathea Converting the Britons*, 1847, lithograph. The Victoria and Albert Museum, London.

slightest suggestion of bloodthirsty rites and dark superstition. If this is a pagan world it is pagan in the way Greece was pagan, as opposed to the idolatry and fetishism of a more benighted culture. Idealised interpretations like these were rare, however, and conversion scenes still dominated the depiction of the Druids, especially in the nineteenth century.

In the Houses of Parliament fresco competition of 1843 E.T. Parris submitted *Joseph of Arimathea converting the Britons* (Plate 57) and won a £100 premium

58 Charles George Lewis after John Rogers Herbert, *The First Preaching of Christianity in Britain* (1842), 1847, engraving.

for his pains, but he was attacked in the *Illustrated London News* for painting a myth and for doing it feebly.[61] Parris had made his reputation as an illustrator and diorama painter but those critics who insinuated that his professional practice was inadequate preparation for history painting were presumably ignorant of his earlier attempts at the genre, for example his small *Landing of Julius Caesar at Dover*, exhibited at the British Institution in 1825. In *Joseph of Arimathea* Parris adopts a similar composition to Mortimer's *St Paul*, with Joseph standing in front of an oak, surrounded by Britons and Druids, some of whom are suspicious while others already submit to his teaching. But in the place of Mortimer's depiction of inspired eloquence and its dignified reception we have here a more insipid performance, presumably intended to indicate that Joseph's meekness and saintly demeanour were inspiration enough. The same rather bloodless representation of conversion to Christianity is found in J.R. Herbert's contemporary oil painting, *The First Preaching of Christianity in Britain* (Plate 58), where an anonymous missionary preacher wins an easy victory over a compliant group of Britons gathered outside Stonehenge. The token Druid among them doffs his oak garland as the Christian message breaks in upon his pagan cosmology.[62]

In all of these representations the triumph of Christianity is accomplished with scant resistance and the lesson to be derived from that seems clear. As early as the Tudor period antiquarian scholars had promoted the idea that the Druids had converted easily to the teachings of Christ, so helping to establish the longevity of the Church in Britain and buttress claims for its separation from Rome.[63] Later, as we have seen, eighteenth-century belief in the Druids' connections with patriarchal religion allowed their paganism, as recorded in the classical texts, to be re-examined as a more appealing doctrine closer to Christian precepts. In all of this there was comfort for a modern Christian nation to learn that from its infancy it had been predisposed to Christianity and had readily converted when confronted with the real thing. In the nineteenth century especially, with missionary endeavour overseas a growing phenomenon, these conversion scenes would presumably have elicited favourable responses. Seen from another angle, of course, the mur-

59 William Holman Hunt, *A Converted British Family sheltering a Christian Priest from the Persecution of the Druids*, 1850, oil on canvas, 111 x 141 cm. The Ashmolean Museum, Oxford.

derous Druids with their hecatombs and necromantic law were anything but compliant, but only one artist seems to have been bold enough to tackle the violence of the contest between Druid and Christian head on.

William Holman Hunt's *A Converted British Family sheltering a Christian Priest from the Persecution of the Druids* (Plate 59) is probably the best known painting taking Druidism, even incidentally, as its subject. In the foreground an exhausted missionary is tended by converted Britons while outside their primitive hut his less fortunate colleague is hunted down at the command of an imperious Druid. The proximity of the megalithic temple, amidst whose stones the Druid asserts his power, hints at an attempt at conversion whose failure will result in death or even ritual sacrifice. Hunt's scene is set in the first century AD, so linking the conversion of the Britons to apostolic rather than Roman Catholic endeavour, independent of papal control. As we have seen, Francis Hayman had drawn on a similar tradition one hundred years earlier in his *Conversion of the Britons to Christianity*, but here the comparison ends, for Hunt's religious purposes, in a climate of religious controversy, must be seen as determining his choice of subject as a critique of the Church of England rather than a defence of it. As Lindsay Errington has demonstrated,[64] Hunt's aesthetic was essentially allied to that of the Tractarians, paying close attention to the realities of the material world but investing material features with spiritual, symbolic qualities discernible to the religious observer. In a long description of the picture to its purchaser, Thomas Combe, Hunt demonstrated how symbolic the picture was: the corn and the grapes, conventional symbols of the eucharist indicate the civilising influence brought about by Christian teaching, the net symbolises the net of religion, catching souls, as well as these converts' independence of the Druidical prohibition against catching fish which were sacred. Similarly, the bramble on which the missionary has snagged his clothes is symbolic of the crown of thorns. Slumped on his seat, the missionary himself is posed like the dead Christ in a conventional *pietà*. This, then, is not merely the retelling of a pseudo-historical narrative but an ideologically motivated assertion of primitive Christianity, close to the original teachings of Christ, here identified as the origin of religious worship in the British Isles from which modern Protestant worship had strayed.

For most Victorians, however, the most ready access to Druidic ceremony would have been in the opera house. Vincenzo Bellini's opera *Norma* (1831) focused attention on the Druids quite decisively and its popularity in England must have helped keep the subject at the forefront of public awareness. The origins of the opera are relatively well established. Bellini was already a great admirer of *Ossian* in Cesarotti's translation and either Bellini or his librettist Felice Romani had read Alexandre Soumet's play *Norma* (a verse tragedy in five acts, first performed in early 1831 at the Théâtre Royale de l'Odéon, Paris), although the increased emphasis on the Druids and their rituals is very much Romani's emphasis. Romani's credentials for the libretto were excellent. In 1820 he had written a libretto, *La Sacerdotessa d'Irminsul*, with a heroine called Romilda whose character owes a considerable debt to Velleda, the tragic Druidess heroine of Chateaubriand's novel *Les Martyrs*.[65] *Norma* takes place in pre-Christian Gaul at an unspecified date in the first century BC and recounts the tragic history of a Druidess who breaks her holy vows for love of a Roman proconsul, Pollione, and sacrifices herself on a burning funeral pyre after confessing her crime to her people. Given the association of Druids with patriotism and liberty in Britain, it is interesting to note the suggestion that Bellini may have written his opera in the cause of Young Italy, highlighting revolt against foreign oppression in *Norma* just as numerous Italian risings were taking place against the Austrians in the 1820s and 1830s and being brutally suppressed. Milan, after all, was still under Austrian rule and the censor objected to the opera's opening chorus because its references to Caesar and the enemy eagles might be subversive of the house of Hapsburg. His suspicions were vindicated in 1847 when the Milanese audience, prompted by the 'Guerra' chorus in Act II, erupted into a spontaneous and violent demonstration against the Austrian regime.[66]

Norma was first performed at La Scala on 26 December 1831, with Giuditta Pasta singing the title role and came to London for its first performance in June 1833 at His Majesty's Theatre (The King's Theatre), with Pasta still playing the part of Norma. The opera was performed again, in English, in the 1837 season, at the Drury Lane Theatre, under the management of Burn, who was interested enough in Celtic subjects to put on a (disastrous) revival of John Fletcher's *Bonduca* that winter.[67] In London, the opera was presented again in English translation in 1841–42, with Adelaide Kemble making her sensational operatic debut as Norma, in

60   Abraham John Mason after Edward Corbould, *Scene from Bellini's Norma*, c. 1842, wood engraving.

German translation in 1842 and again in English in 1843. From 1847 to 1861 *Norma* was staged every year at Covent Garden with London's favourite prima donna, Giulia Grisi, dominating the interpretation of the part, having graduated from her supporting role as Adalgisa in the La Scala production of 1833.[68] Alessandro Sanquirico, the sceneographer at La Scala, seems to have designed a predominantly classical set for *Norma* but when the opera was performed in London a more primitive setting was devised. Edward Corbould's drawings of the 1840s for *Norma* (Plate 60) show him using the full panoply of the by now standard Druidic imagery in the British artistic tradition.

Norma's historical setting concerns the confrontation between the Gauls and Romans and the Druids' key role in mobilising patriotic resistance to foreign invasion. In Britain, too, the idea of the Druid as patriot was well established. Looked at positively, the Druids' status in Celtic society, their training in certain arcane mysteries committed to memory, their inspiration of resistance to Rome and Rome's retaliatory policy of extermination all pointed to an image of the Druid as a philosopher-patriot whose wisdom and knowledge of tradition held Celtic society together until it was deliberately destroyed by the Roman invaders. For some, like Pughe and Davies, the tenets of Druidism implied a pacifist stance, indeed Davies blamed the suppression of Britain on the Druids' abhorrence of violence,[69] but most commentators were happy to see the Druids promoting opposition to Rome in a spirit of militant patriotism. As George Chalmers expressed it in 1807,

Whatever may have been the speculative tenets of Druidism, the Druids taught the duties of moral virtue, and enforced the precepts of natural religion. They inculcated a strong desire of liberty, with an ardent love of their country, which strikingly appeared, in the struggle for both, which was made against the Roman legions, by the Gauls, by the Britons, and, above all, by the Caledonians.[70]

It so happens that in all of the classical accounts the best known instance of Druidic opposition to Rome was that recorded in Book XIV of Tacitus' *Annals* which relates the events of AD 61. In that year Paulinus Suetonius, the governor of Britain, attacked Anglesey (Mona), 'which had become a refuge for fugitives', slaughtered the Druids and cut down their sacred groves. Unlike earlier Roman accounts, which did not indicate that the Druids participated in battle, this famous passage placed them in the midst of the struggle.

> The enemy lined the shore: a dense host of armed men, interspersed with women clothed in black, like the Furies, with their hair hanging down, and holding torches in their hands. Round these were the Druids uttering dire curses, and stretching out their hands towards heaven. These strange sights terrified our soldiers.[71]

The association of Anglesey with Druidism was thus assured and Rowlands's *Mona Antiqua Restaurata* was particularly influential in buttressing this claim throughout most of the eighteenth and nineteenth centuries. We can see the results in, for example, W. Sotheby's *Poems, consisting of a tour through part of north and south Wales* (1790) which includes a long sequence on the Roman destruction of Druidism on Mona, a poetic meditation inspired by the megalithic remains on the island.

> Visions of old flash wild on fancy's eye:
> Mid armed ranks to desperation wrought
> The bards invoking vengeance from above
> Lift their clasp'd hands to heaven, and thunder forth
> Deep execrations on the foe . . .
> . . . Lo, th'avenging eagle sails
> Along the lurid air, and fires the groves
> Of *Mona*, while expiring on their shrines,
> The Druids to th'infernal gods devote
> The foe, and die triumphant.[72]

Robert Smirke's design for an early nineteenth century edition of Hume's *History of England* (Plate 61) is a visual rendition of this same key moment. The Romans advance into the gloomy recesses of the Druid sanctuary with firebrands but are momentarily checked by the appearance of the white-bearded Druid who appears to be calling down imprecations while two of his companions are brutally dispatched. One of these appears to be a bard, for his right arm still clasps a harp. A mossy oak, a trilithon, and a sacrificial altar complete the picture.

The poignancy of British defeat on Anglesey and its identification with later bardic suppression was ripe for romantic treatment. The same sentimental impulse that entranced a whole generation with songs of dying Indians and the lamenta-

61 Thomas Milton after Robert Smirke, *The Massacre of the Druids*, engraving, in David Hume, *History of England*, London, 1810.

tions of the last of various races helped to weave a literary shroud for the aborigines of Britain, whether dying bards or slaughtered Druids. Walter Scott's son-in-law, J.G. Lockhart, invokes this tradition in all its pathos at the end of *Valerius; a Roman Story* (1821), one of the very few novels of this period to touch on Celtic Britain.[73] The story concerns the adventures of Valerius, the son of a centurion who had fought against Galgacus under Agricola and married a Briton. Despite this promising background, most of the action is set in Rome and the references to Celtic and Roman Britain are few, but they are significant for all that. In Rome Valerius sees British gladiators, their body tattoos vivid enough to suggest recent capture, he also meets a veteran of Agricola's campaign in Caledonia, who had been captured and forcibly tattooed by the British. Finally, as the novel draws to a close, his Celtic servant accompanies their departure from Rome with 'an old British boat-song' sung by Silurian boatmen in commemoration of an old chief's escape to Anglesey after his village was burned and his kindred slain.

The night is dark above the water,
The hills are all behind us far;
We cannot see the hill of slaughter,
Where in their tents the steel-clad Romans are.

Row gently through the gentle sea –
Row gently, for my wound is deep –
Soon, soon in safety shall ye be –
And I, too, brothers, – for I fain would sleep . . .[74]

111

These undistinguished verses are vaguely reminiscent of Ossianic diction, while the setting and subject matter recall both the death of Arthur and the Young Pretender's flight to Skye, but this hackneyed rhetoric is itself conditioned by the reader's knowledge that Mona did not remain a safe haven, that the Britons had been finally hunted down even there. In the context of the novel this old British boat-song was already a faint and feeble reminder of a world that had passed away for ever, and with its passing the Druids disappeared from history.

Chapter Six

ANCESTORS AND OTHERS: THE ORIGINS OF ENGLAND

It is well known that the nineteenth century witnessed the emergence in England of a strong Anglo-Saxon bias to its history, powerful enough to construct an image of English nationality and British destiny in almost exclusively Anglo-Saxon terms. The recognition of the dominance of England within the United Kingdom and the celebration of the English way of life as a superior form of civilisation was not necessarily an exclusive preoccupation of the English, nor was it universally believed by English people. Nevertheless, as a generalisation it needs little qualification; the Victorians fashioned themselves as Anglo-Saxons first and foremost.[1] Such an emphatic racial identity offered a reductive reading of English civilisation based on the ethnic attributes of Celt or Saxon and ignored the finely nuanced texture of cultural development over thousands of years. It also did violence, of course, to the realities of mixed descent in England as well as confirming a hierarchical distinction between the Celtic and Saxon peoples of the United Kingdom. Yet, as an expedient in securing an intelligible national history this vindication of Saxon England at the expense of the Celts had much to recommend it. The Celts, after all, seen from a negative viewpoint, had been defeated by the Romans and then overwhelmed by the Saxons. Their original Druidic religion was pagan, repressive and bloodthirsty and even after conversion their strand of Christianity was to be abandoned at the Synod of Whitby. The Saxons, on the other hand, could be celebrated as a successful military power with a vigorous democratic tradition who had become the zealous promulgators of orthodox Christianity. In elevating Saxon origins and repressing this other Celtic descent Victorian histories of England were doing more than 'solving' a historiographical problem; they were enunciating a myth of race and destiny that sustained a host of contemporary ambitions. As we shall see, this emphasis on Anglo-Saxon origins could result in its more extreme formulations in out and out racist judgements on the worth of the Celtic peoples of Britain. We need to ask, therefore, why a negative view of archaic British culture arose and why this should have been sufficient to cause the Celtic origins of Britain to be repressed or at least played down by many nineteenth-century writers.[2] What, in other words, propels an Anglo-Saxon bias such that Celtic British culture is seen to be effaced rather than supplemented by the Saxon incursions of the fifth century AD?

As always, changes in historiography are themselves affected by and constitutive of much wider ideological concerns. When considering pejorative comments about Celtic brutishness in nineteenth-century texts it is important to remember that the prevailing thought on 'savage' cultures in the eighteenth century had been sanguine about the prospect of their development to what Europeans regarded as civilisation. The theory of social progress had been successfully promulgated throughout Europe and the savage origins of a people were, to that extent, expected and unproblematic. In France, Turgot's *Tableau philosophique des progrès successifs de l'esprit humain* (1750) and Condorcet's *Esquisse d'un tableau historique des progrès de l'esprit humain* (1795) both divided the history of human progress into epochs marked by social, technological and intellectual differences.[3] Simultaneously, Scottish intellectuals set out to analyse the determining factors such as geography, climate and social relations that might explain the diversity of human cultures. Lord Monboddo's *Of the Origin and Progress of Language* (1773-92), for example, used a model of progressive staged developments to assert the barbarous origins of all nations, 'even the most polished and civilized'.[4] Similarly, Adam Ferguson's *An Essay on the History of Civil Society* employed the comparative example of Native Americans to underline the progress of European society.

> The Romans might have found an image of their own ancestors, in the representations they have given of ours; and if ever an Arab clan shall become a civilized nation, or any American tribe escape the poison which is administered by our traders of Europe, it may be from the relations of the present times, and in the descriptions which are now given by travellers, that such a people, in after ages, may best collect the accounts of their origin. It is in their present condition that we are to behold, as in a mirror, the features of our own progenitors; and from thence we are to draw our conclusions with respect to the influence of situations, in which we have reason to believe that our fathers were placed. What should distinguish a German or a Briton, in the habits of his mind or his body, in his manners or apprehensions, from an American, who, like him, with his bow and his dart, is left to traverse the forest; and in a like severe or variable climate, is obliged to subsist by the chase? If, in advanced years, we would form a just notion of our progress from the cradle, we must have recourse to the nursery; and from the example of those who are still in the period of life we mean to describe, take our representations of past manners, that cannot, in any other way, be recalled.[5]

What united all these authors was, broadly, an adherence to the so-called Four Stages theory of human progress which saw all human cultures as developing from hunting and gathering to the pastoral state, thence to agriculture and finally to commercial civilisation. Prior to the 1750s theories of cultural change had, of course, been advanced based variously on metaphorical transitions from youth to old age, vigour to degeneracy and the like, but only the Four Stages theory stressed the mode of subsistence as the key differentiating factor and thereby articulated a fully progressive development at odds with any nostalgia for a lost golden age.[6] As a developed position the theory probably originated with Adam Smith's jurisprudence lectures given at Glasgow University in 1752–3 and it grew in sophistication and reach over the next thirty years with the successive publication of Lord Kames's *Essays on the Principles of Morality and Natural Religion* (second revised edition, 1758), Adam Ferguson's *Essay on the History of Civil Society*

(1766), John Millar's *Origin of Ranks* (1771) and Adam Smith's own *Wealth of Nations* (1776).

Yet, notwithstanding the popularity of such theories in the late eighteenth and early nineteenth centuries, it is clear that as the nineteenth century developed descent from the savage Celtic peoples described by Caesar and Tacitus was increasingly regarded as an inauspicious beginning to British history. Thomas Nicholas wrote *The Pedigree of the English People* (1868) specifically to combat the view prevalent in Victorian popular histories of an exclusive Saxon descent for the English people. Nicholas, as a Welsh antiquary and one of the prime movers in the establishment of the University College of Wales at Aberystwith in 1867 had a real interest in contesting any notions of Anglo-Saxon triumphalism, arguing instead for the mixed origins of the English and attempting to defend the Celts from prejudices based on faulty history and a distaste for the race as a whole.

> We therefore conclude that in the Ancient Britons are found a people greatly removed from barbarism, and that for hundreds of years before Caesar's arrival they had been marked by the same characteristics. To represent them as our popular and unenquiring historical writers have usually done is to belie history, travesty facts, and do a manifest and gratuitous injustice to a brave people.[7]

In asserting that 'the aborigines were by no means the low type of barbarians which ill-informed writers have too commonly represented them to be'[8] Nicholas was doing something that would have been unnecessary for eighteenth-century believers in social progress. The origin of nations in barbarism was taken for granted, such that worries over whether one's ancestors were 'low' or not was beside the point. By the mid nineteenth century, however, the question of descent had become of much greater significance. We must ask, therefore, why Nicholas felt impelled to argue for an 'improved' Celtic character, why were theories of social progress no longer adequate to accommodate the 'savagery' of British origins and why mid-Victorian Britain had such a pejorative view of Celtic culture. For it is manifest that Nicholas was attempting to confront an ideology whose import was that the aboriginal Britons were a backward and inferior race.

In fact, the ultimate origins of this anti-Celtic prejudice lay deep in the past and were steeped in issues of race and national identity from the beginning. English incursions into Ireland, Wales and Scotland from the mediaeval period onward had revealed the existence of a cultural difference whose dimensions gave the lie to any notion of a truly united people. Sixteenth- and seventeenth-century reports on the Celtic peoples of Britain created a stereotypical image of a primitive, poverty-stricken and potentially unruly society whose culture existed at a profound distance from that of their English neighbours and would-be compatriots. The satirical representations of the Welsh, Scots and Irish in the plays and, later, novels of the seventeenth and eighteenth centuries underlined the idea of their backwardness in terms of civic progress and the refinements of modern living. For example, as Keith Thomas has observed, by the sixteenth century it had become customary for the English to boast that they kept their domestic stock at a distance, unlike the despicable Irish, Welsh and Scots, many of whom slept under the same roof as their cattle.[9] Likewise, a traveller to England in 1672 noted that it was considered an affront to call any man a Welshman.[10]

Thus, despite growing communication and trade and even after the various Acts of Union the peoples of Wales, Scotland and Ireland were recognised and distinguished as separate from the English.[11] As we might expect, political union could not efface cultural separation; indeed, cultural difference (real or imagined) might be used to justify English policy, particularly in the case of Ireland. A typical example is provided by Richard Cox's *Hibernia Anglicana* (1689).

> Feuds continued with the greatest Pride, most hellish Ambitions and cruellest Desires of Revenge, and followed with the most horrible Injustices, Oppressions, Extortions, Rapines, Desolations, Perfidious Treasons, Rebellions, Conspiracies, Treacheries and Murders, for almost two thousand Years . . . That we never read of any other People in the World so implacable, so furiously, so eternally set upon the Destruction of one another . . . the Irish have as much Reason to thank God and the English for a more Civil and Regular Government exercised over them.[12]

From the late sixteenth century, histories and accounts of Ireland had appeared in which the Irish were frequently depicted in just this way, a barbarous and backward people whose violent and unruly nature was epitomised by their conduct at times of military and political strife. We can catch the measure of the strength of these pejorative depictions in Geoffrey Keating's preface to *The General History of Ireland* (1634, translated into English 1723) where he attempts to remedy the distortions of English historians, likening them to beetles who fly over flowers to settle on dung.

> Never was any Nation under Heaven so traduced by Malice and Ignorance as the ancient Irish . . . I . . . resolv'd to vindicate so brave a People from such scandalous Abuses . . . It grieved me to see a Nation hunted down by Ignorance and Malice, and recorded as the Scum and Refuse of Mankind, when upon a strict Inquiry they have made as good a Figure, and have signalled themselves in as commendable a manner to Posterity as any People in *Europe*.[13]

While the treatment meted out to the Irish was more extreme than that given to the Scots and Welsh, it is nevertheless true that these peoples too were often subjected to invidious comparisons, harsh judgements and deliberate distortions of their culture and traditions by English writers. As Edward Snyder has pointed out, the roots of English anti-Celtic sentiment reach all the way back to Giraldus Cambrensis' descriptions of Ireland and Wales in the 1180s and 1190s in his *Topographia Hibernia* and *Itinerarium Cambriae*. These, together with other mediaeval writings, such as Walter Map's *Cambriae Epitome* (1170s) and *De Nugis Curialium* (1181–92) and Ranulf Higden's *Polychronicon* (1342), were variously taken up and augmented in Holinshed's *Chronicles* in 1577 and, most importantly of all, in Camden's *Britannia* in 1586, via which route they were transmitted to the readers of the seventeenth and eighteenth centuries. Similarly, the stage Irishman or Welshman, the epitome of stupidity and brutishness, is familiar from sixteenth-century drama and still firmly established in eighteenth-century theatre.[14] As Snyder observes, by the beginning of the eighteenth century anti-Celtic satire had become something of an English literary tradition, and this tradition grew stronger by the decade. Writers such as Walpole, Wilkes and Johnson are seen by Snyder as typical rather than unusually prejudiced in their comments on Celtic peoples and Celtic culture. John Torbuck's popular *A Collection of Welsh Travels and Memoirs of Wales* (1738) included William Richards' *The Briton Described* which may rank as the most salacious anti-Celtic satire of the century but its eminence in the field of prejudice is one of degree not kind.[15] In reviewing the phenomenon as a whole, especially in the minor poetry of the literary magazines, Snyder can only conclude: 'Throughout the magazines we find traces of an anti-Celtic prejudice so strong that we begin to wonder how any Celtic revival at all was possible.'[16]

The existence of potential or actual political dissent in these regions, especially Ireland and Scotland, provided an additional impetus for an often hostile or, at best, condescending view of contemporary Celtic culture and this characteristic judgement continued into the eighteenth century. Horace Walpole, for example, could write thus of the Scots in 1780. 'But what a nation is Scotland; in every reign engendering traitors to the state and false and pernicious to the kings that favour it the most! National prejudices, I know, are very vulgar; but, if there are national characteristics, can one but dislike the soils and climates that concur to produce them?'[17] Scotland had rebelled against Charles I in 1638, against the Commonwealth in 1650 and was marked by Jacobite insurrection throughout the eighteenth century, most dangerously in 1715 and 1745. Although the London Welsh tended to be ostentatiously loyal at their meetings, sporting the Prince of Wales' ostrich plumes to signify Welsh allegiance, this very ostentation perhaps signifies a recognition that Wales was not reliably loyal. Thomas Carte described Wales in his *History of England* as 'a country in which ambition, love of change, violence and sedition, had long reigned'.[18] Parts of Wales evinced Jacobite leanings in the eighteenth century and showed signs of Jacobin sympathies in the 1790s and there was renewed tension in the 1830s and 1840s, most prominently with the Merthyr Rising of 1831 and the so-called Rebecca Riots (1839–43).[19] Ireland had by far the most volatile history, with a lengthy chronicle of forced occupation, civil disturbance and insurrection throughout the sixteenth, seventeenth and eighteenth centuries. The espousal of Jacobinism by the United Irishmen and the rebellion of 1798 were followed in the nineteenth century by nationalist revival in the 1840s and the rise of Fenianism in the 1860s. Such political dissent with its attendant violence could be employed as the 'proof' of Celtic failure to accept the finer tenets of civilisation. This was particularly true for Ireland, where the political struggle was not only a constant feature of the period with which this study is concerned but also punctuated by violent atrocities. Contemporary Irish 'brutality' could thus support a judgement on the Celtic peoples as a whole, contemporary and aboriginal, and such a judgement tended towards the conclusion that the Celts had been and in some quarters still were prone to some of the worst excesses of savagery. Thus 'disloyal' political aspirations leading to insurrectionary violence and the poverty born of economic deprivation could be regarded not as the effect of an imperfect political and economic union with England, but as the natural condition of the Celtic race. One of the earliest sustained examples of this sort of thinking occurs in John Pinkerton's attack on the Celts in his *A Dissertation on the Origin and Progress of the Scythians or Goths* of 1787:

. . . what their own mythology was we know not, but it in all probability resembled that of the Hottentots, or others of the rudest savages, as the Celts anciently were, and are little better at present, being incapable of any progress in society . . . here in Britain, [we] know the Celts to be mere radical savages, not yet advanced even to a state of barbarism; and if any foreigner doubts this, he has only to step into the Celtic part of Wales, Ireland, or Scotland, and look at them, for they are just as they were, incapable of industry or civilisation, even after half their blood is Gothic, and remain, as marked by the ancients, fond of lyes, and enemies of truth.[20]

Pinkerton's splenetic tone throughout the *Dissertation* was widely criticised, even by less than partisan individuals such as Walpole, and defenders of Celtic culture were quick to point out the mixed Celtic and Saxon inheritance in British culture.[21] Nevertheless, the viciousness of Pinkerton's attack, the intemperate quality of his language and his reliance on swingeing generalisations can all be seen as informed by the anti-Celtic tradition of the previous century as well as looking forward to some of the more excessive flights of rhetoric associated with mid nineteenth-century Saxonism. The epitome of the latter tendency is Robert Knox's *The Races of Men* (1850), whose anti-Celtic prejudice is cut from the same hyperbolic cloth as Pinkerton's. For Knox the Celtic character can be summed up as 'Furious fanaticism; a love of war and disorder, a hatred for order and patient industry; no accumulative habits; restless, treacherous, uncertain: look at Ireland.'[22] The Celtic race, as evidenced by the people of Scotland, Ireland and Wales, should be banished from Great Britain 'by fair means, if possible; still they must leave. England's safety requires it. I speak not of the justice of the cause; nations must ever act as Machiavelli advised: look to yourself.'[23]

Such attacks, some of the fiercest anti-Celtic assaults in the English language, articulate a move away from the doctrine of social progress as Adam Ferguson and others had understood it. As we have seen, the standard eighteenth-century view of 'primitive' peoples was that they were in their social and cultural childhood compared to the maturity of European civilisation; Ferguson himself, we should recall, was a Gaelic-speaking Highlander and so was perhaps the most prone of all the Edinburgh savants to a favourable view of 'backward' cultures; but his views were not untypical. Even Hume, whose criticism of Ferguson's *Essay* was severe, believed in the possibility of progress. The following description of the ancient Irish in his *History of England*, while disapproving, records an accident of history and geography which 'civility', 'education' and 'laws' could ameliorate.

The Irish from the beginning of time had been buried in the most profound barbarism and ignorance; and as they were never conquered or even invaded by the Romans, from whom all the western world derived its civility, they continued still in the most rude state of society, and were distinguished by those vices alone to which human nature, not tamed by education, or restrained by laws, is for ever subject.[24]

Samuel Johnson's views of the Highlands and Western Isles of Scotland, albeit more complex and discriminating, still allowed him to make similar observations on Scottish Gaelic culture.

118

Yet men thus ingenious and inquisitive were content to live in total ignorance of the trades by which human wants are supplied, and to supply them by the grossest means. Till the Union made them acquainted with English manners, the culture of their lands was unskilful, and their domestick life unformed; their tables were coarse as the feasts of Esquimeaux, and their houses filthy as the cottages of Hottentots.[25]

For writers like Hume or Johnson, then, the issue of race was unimportant as regards cultural aptitudes. The ignorance and brutishness of the Celtic peoples, lamentable though it might be, could be transformed by the beneficial influence of that enlightened culture located in London and Edinburgh. There was nothing intrinsic to the Celts that doomed them to an 'inevitable' character or condition. Racial theory, insofar as it existed at all in the eighteenth century, was concerned with difference rather than hierarchy. Johann Frederick Blumenbach, for example, argued for one species of man with five divisions – Caucasian, Mongloian, American, Ethiopian and Malay – in his extremely influential *De Generis Humani Varietate Natura Liber* (1775) but explicitly denied the inferiority of any one race. When the word 'race' was used it was understood as little more than descent or lineage.[26] The fact that the Irish or Scots (or for that matter the peoples of America or Africa) were living in cultural conditions seemingly inferior to the English was a recognition of unrealised potential, the infancy of a more developed social, technological, moral and intellectual world.

Nowhere is this concept so succinctly expressed than in Robert Henry's *History of Great Britain*; his innovative methodological division of each book into thematic chapters allowed ample room for the discussion of learning.

Nations, as well as particular persons, have their infancy, in which they are not only small and weak, but also rude and ignorant. Even those nations which have arrived at the highest pitch of power and greatness, and have been most renowned for wisdom, learning, and politeness, when they are traced to their infant state, are found to have been equally weak and ignorant . . . We need not, therefore, be surprised to find, nor ashamed to own, that there was a time, when the inhabitants of this island were divided into a great many petty states or tribes, each of them consisting of a small number of rude unlettered savages.[27]

Henry was born and raised in Scotland and benefited from the Scottish intellectual tradition discussed above. His elaboration of the Four Stages theory of human development provided a historiographic rationale for the investigation of barbarous cultures. Thomas Peardon has suggested that Henry's immediate precedent was Goguet's *Origin of Laws, Arts, and Sciences, and their Progress among the most ancient Nations* (English translation published in Edinburgh in 1761) but Henry's sustained application of such thinking to British history was novel. Despite initial wariness on behalf of the publishers (Henry had to publish the earlier volumes of his *History* at his own expense) and some severe criticism, especially from the jealous Gilbert Stuart who attempted to orchestrate a campaign of criticism against the book, the *History* proved popular on both sides of the border.[28] Nowhere in Henry's work does he suggest that the culture he is describing is immutable; indeed, the very division of his account into eight separate categories for each period (civil and military history, ecclesiastical history, constitutional history, government and law, learning, the arts, commerce, manners and customs) implies that explanations for material included in one category may be sought elsewhere in the cultural matrix, rather than by appeals to unchanging racial qualities.

However, from about the last quarter of the eighteenth century race begins to be defined as an immutable given, a fact of biology as opposed to descent. On this new view, analysis of the shortcomings of primitive society, as regards learning, industry, justice, the arts, religious disposition and so on, provided information about specific cultural tendencies whose underlying framework could only be partially altered. Hence, the presumed backwardness of certain peoples was not simply an accident of time or geography but an inevitable consequence of their (biological) race. This alteration in thinking resulted in some particularly important racial distinctions being drawn in England between the Celts and the Saxons, for now the apparently more primitive nature of Celtic culture could be ascribed to blood rather than economic or cultural factors. We have already witnessed an early example of this new attitude in Pinkerton's *Dissertation on the Origin and Progress of the Scythians or Goths*, whose anti-Celtic argument can be summed up in his own pithy judgement '[The Celts] have been savages since the world began, and will be for ever savages while a separate people; that is, while themselves, and of unmixt blood.'[29]

In brief, the question of race should be seen initially as part of the late eighteenth-century's fascination with origins and only later as a systematic contribution to the hierarchical classification of mankind. There is, therefore, a wholesale change of context in which the writings of Pinkerton and Knox were received. Similarly, the wide variety of positions adopted on the question of race between the 1780s and the 1880s precludes any possibility of summarising the debate in terms of one or two overbearing racial theories. What we can say, however, is that the sheer volume of historical, ethnological and other writings devoted in whole or in part to the question of race indicates the extent to which it had become of importance in nineteenth-century British culture. The flowering of ethnology in the 1820s and 1830s provided a seemingly objective basis for discrimination between peoples and the new science was responsible for giving a racist flavour to that Anglo-Saxonism which had flourished since the Tudor period primarily as a celebration of liberty and martial valour. In Britain, James Cowles Prichard's *Researches into the Physical History of Man* (1813), an immediate best seller, opposed the idea of the inherent inferiority of any race and defended the idea of one human species (monogenesis) but Prichard's subsequent development of the concept of 'permanent varieties' in human races came as close to the separate species view of the polygenesis camp as made no difference. Prichard's pre-eminence in the field was maintained as the *Researches*, amended in the two subsequent editions of 1826 and 1836, grew and developed into three separate treatises, but his most significant contribution to Victorian anthropology was the publication of a new work, *The Natural History of Man* (1843), which is particularly noteworthy for its emphasis on the shape of the skull as an indicator of human development, distinguishing the cranium, chin and forehead as key features. His favourable comments on the Germanic tribes' superior moral energy, civilisation, understanding and intellectual qualities helped establish the ground work for the more developed racist ethnology of the 1840s and 1850s.[30] Prichard was no simple minded Teutonic polemicist, in fact, as a fine linguist who knew Celtic and had published *The Eastern Origin of the Celtic Nations* in 1831, his promotion of German virtues was relatively dispassionate, but his conclusions about German superiority indicate the direction of anthropological thinking in mid Victorian England.

As Prichard's reliance on skull formation attests, the emergence of physiognomy as a scientific discipline had developed the idea of human differentiation at the biological level.[31] Blumenbach had used skulls as the basis for his classifications and Johann Caspar Lavater's contemporaneous *Essays on Physiognomy*, originally published 1774–8, revealed the extent to which the human head might be studied and examined on a comparative basis. Lavater's work was widely published in Europe and remained popular throughout the nineteenth century; while his conclusions did not support the racist interpretations that later theories would display, his work nevertheless laid down the basis for succeeding investigations. The calibration of human types on the basis of skull measurements had also been promoted by Pieter Camper, whose use of the 'facial angle' as a measurement of human potential would prove extremely influential, despite the reservations held about it by Blumenbach and physiognomists like Charles Bell and even Prichard himself. Camper's *Works* were published in English in 1794, three years after his death. The emergence of phrenology, with its stress on the relationship between skull formation and intelligence, cultural aptitudes and the like can be regarded as a less scrupulous and increasingly dubious development of these ideas. Phrenology was definitively established by the writings of Frans Joseph Gall and Johann Caspar Spurzheim in the early 1800s. Gall's *Functions of the Brain* (1825) appeared in English translation in 1835, but British writers had already begun to popularise his and Spurzheim's ideas in the 1810s. The most famous phrenologist in Britain was the Scot George Combe, who had attended Spurzheim's lectures in Edinburgh in 1815 and had been deeply influenced by the new science. His own research, especially his book *On the Constitution of Man* (1835) purported to demonstrate that within the 'superior' Caucasian division of mankind, the Teutonic branch was uppermost, with the Celts struggling far behind Teutonic potential and achievement.[32]

The impact of these new investigations was such that by the 1840s the centrality of race to any discussion of human culture was not in doubt and the triumph of Anglo-Saxon culture could be sought in biological rather than cultural explanations. The rise of Victorian racial theory was to replace Pinkerton's barely controlled outbursts with the cooler and more deadly prose of pseudo-scientific discourse, whose dispassionate and measured style might advance the anti-Celtic case in an entirely reasonable manner. At first this was achieved not so much by denigrating the Celt but as a by-product of exalting the Saxon, such that the Anglo-Saxon's seeming industrial, military and imperial pre-eminence in the nineteenth century was explained in terms of qualities of character and behaviour whose combination was unique to the race. Furthermore, the royal family's links with Germany helped to promote the idea of Saxon power in two dominant European countries, a contemporary union of peoples sharing a common archaic homeland. The English, as the presumed lineal descendants of Saxon forefathers, were destined to greatness because of their racial inheritance leaving their Celtic compatriots far behind. The following comment from the 1840s is typical of this sort of comparison.

> The English people are naturally industrious – they prefer a life of honest labour to one of idleness. They are a persevering as well as an energetic race, who for the most part comprehend their own interests perfectly and sedulously pursue them. Now of all the Celtic tribes, famous for their indolence and fickleness as the Celts everywhere are, the Irish are admitted to be the most idle and the most fickle.[33]

This kind of simple-minded racial Saxonism, together with the racist excesses of the short-lived *Anglo-Saxon Magazine* (1849–50) and the Teutonic enthusiasms of authors such as Knox and Thomas Carlyle were continually challenged in works of history and ethnology; but even if the more facile Celtic-Saxon racial contrasts were successfully contested there remained a residue of this thinking in almost all areas of public life. Charles Pearson's *The Early and Middle Ages of England* (1861) indicates only too well the way in which ethnological speculations had colonised historical writing by mid century.

> The British physique, if we may judge from the better specimens of the human remains found in barrows, was that of a weak and impulsive, but not an unintelligent race. The average capacity of the skull is smaller than that of Saxon and Roman crania, but its form is less irregular; and, indeed is often exquisitely symmetrical. The predominance of the middle or emotional compartment, and a certain deficiency in the back part, indicating weak will, are its chief features: the frontal development is commonly good, though not equal to the Greek type. Modern theory would view with suspicion the prehensile thumb, equalling in length the forefinger of the hand, as if something of a lower nature had not yet been worked out in the growth of the race . . . To complete the imperfect details of this picture of early life, we may reproduce in fancy the British chief, with his 'glib' of matted chestnut hair and his moustache, with his broad chest and long arms, and high cheek bones of his race . . .[34]

Between them, the combination of traditional anti-Celtic satire, disparaging accounts of the Celtic periphery and its culture and the rise of racial theory constructed an image of the Celtic peoples whose inferiority to their Saxon equivalent was immediately apparent. Part of the antipathy shown to the Celts may have been fuelled by prejudiced reactions to the large movements of Celtic casual labourers into industrial areas of nineteenth-century England and Lowland Scotland. Here, for example, is Thomas Carlyle, writing in 1839.

> Crowds of miserable Irish darken all our towns. The wild Milesian features, looking false ingenuity, restlessness, unreason, misery and mockery, salute you on all highways and byways . . . he is the sorest evil this country has to strive with. In his rags and laughing savagery, he is there to undertake all work that can be done by mere strength of hand and back; for wages that will purchase him potatoes. He needs only salt for condiment; he lodges to his mind in any

62   George Cruikshank, *Murder of George Crawford and his Grandaughter*, etching, from W.H. Maxwell, *History of the Irish Rebellion in 1798*, London, 1845.

pighutch or doghutch, roosts in outhouses; and wears a suit of tatters . . . The Saxon man if he cannot work on these terms, finds no work. He too may be ignorant; but he has not sunk from decent manhood to squalid apehood: he cannot continue there. American forests lie untilled across the ocean; the uncivilised Irishman, not by his strength but by the opposite of strength, drives out the Saxon, takes possession in his room. There abides he, in his squalor and unreason, in his falsity and drunken violence, as the ready-made nucleus of degredation and disorder.[35]

Northern Welsh and Irish migrant labour worked in Lancashire, Highlanders worked on Clydeside and Irish navvies followed the railway building campaigns like an army of occupation. Like all prejudices, rumour and hearsay created an image of the dangerous, unlawful Celtic labourer that did not stand up to even cursory examination, but between 1800 and 1860 Irish immigrants, in particular, were repeatedly distinguished as a social minority with specific problems. We can detect an echo of this, interestingly enough, in Frederic Stephens's *Memoir of George Cruikshank*. In 1824 Maxwell's *History of the Irish Rebellion in 1798* was published, illustrated with engraving by Cruikshank (Plate 62). Cruikshank's visual denigration of the Irish rebels of 1798 as bestial, ape-like louts still occasions comment and criticism today[36] and Stephens, in attempting to justify Cruikshank's approach, makes explicit reference to Irish immigrant labour.

123

The representatives of such horrible countenances as he gives the Irish are hardly to be found even amongst the reapers one sees at work during the English harvest, which is saying a great deal.*

* Readers not yet past middle life may remember to have encountered such semi-savages at the times in view here, and known them for ruffians of the vilest sort, the terror of the countryside, the curse of police-courts, and infamous for their conduct, violence and drunkenness.[37]

Such an unfavourable verdict was compounded by debates over Celtic and Saxon liberty in primaeval times, an issue which returns us to the heart of this study. On this argument, the cultural inheritance of Celt or Saxon included attitudes towards democracy and the rule of law. The myth of Anglo-Saxon freedoms and their origin in the political institutions of the Germanic peoples can be traced back to the sixteenth century when the work of antiquarian scholars such as John Leland, John Bale and John Foxe was promoted, by Archbishop Matthew Parker and others, as a means of recovering the history of the Saxon church. Parker's motive was to demonstrate that Henry VIII's break with the papacy might be legitimised historically as a return to a purer and more ancient form of worship and these researches stimulated the development of Anglo-Saxon studies in Tudor England; but during the Stuart period this antiquarian learning was recruited for quite other constitutional purposes – as a justification for parliamentary opposition to an over-powerful monarchy. The origins of English common law and of Parliament itself were presumed to lie far back in the historical record. Taking their cue from Richard Verstegen's *Restitution of Decayed Intelligence* (1605), supporters of Germanic origins, such as Nathaniel Bacon, argued for the preservation of Teutonic freedoms with their concomitant severe restrictions on the royal prerogative.[38] Bacon's *An Historicall Discourse of the Uniformity of the Government of England* (1647) proved to be very influential, running to six editions by 1760, and may be regarded as one of the key texts linking English historical freedoms with Saxon descent.

Compared to the Victorians' stress on the Saxon origins of liberty, it is notable, however, that equivalent arguments for Celtic freedom were sometimes included alongside these seventeenth-century celebrations of Saxon culture. Sir Edward Coke had argued thus in Parliament in the 1610s, locating the origins of that institution in the British 'conventus' as well as the Saxon witenagemot.[39] Other political or constitutional features recorded in the classical texts and applicable to both Celts and Saxons, such as the provisional nature of kingship vested in the 'dux bellorum', the elected leader in time of war, were used to substantiate a liberal view of Celtic power relations. As Algernon Sydney noted in his *Discourses Concerning Government* (1698)

[Caesar] describes the Britons to have been a fierce people, zealous for liberty, and . . . obstinately valiant in the defense of it . . . He calls them a free people, inasmuch as they were not like the Gauls, governed by laws made by great men, but by the people . . . The Saxons, from whom we chiefly derive our original and manners, were no less lovers of liberty . . . But we know of no time in which the Britons had not their great council to determine their most important affairs: and the Saxons in their own country had their councils . . .[40]

The popular histories of eighteenth-century England continued this tradition; Whig in tone, they championed the slow and steady growth of democratic institutions which might restore the British people to liberties lost at the time of the Norman Conquest. Both Paul Rapin de Thoyras's *History of England* (1724-6; translated 1732) and Thomas Carte's *A General History of England* (1747) make reference to the idea of the dux bellorum and the concept of Celtic British liberty appears in Sir William Blackstone's *Commentaries on the Laws of England* (1765-9).[41] The elaboration of ancient British liberty in the late eighteenth century, coeval with the Celtic literary revival, can be most easily detected in the works of two clergymen historians keen to advance research into the earliest British history. John Whitaker, in his *History of Manchester* (1771-5), was a resolute champion of the Ancient Britons' individual liberties and parliamentary democracy, celebrating the heights their civilisation had reached before the Romans arrived; in like manner, Henry's *History of Great Britain* contains one of the fuller eighteenth-century discussions of Celtic liberty, confidently asserting the limited authority of British kings, the Celtic origins of English common law, the Britons' love of liberty and their abhorrence of slavery.[42] This tradition of Celtic liberty, although built on flimsy historical foundations, was thus still a valid constituent of British historiography in the last quarter of the eighteenth century. Agitation for parliamentary reform inspired T.H.B. Oldfield to publish his *History of the Original Constitution of Parliaments, from the time of the Britons to the present day* (1797) in which he firmly asserted the Britons' use of a representative assembly, as well as later Saxon developments of democracy.[43] As we shall see in the next chapter, the identification of the Britons with the cause of freedom was prevalent in the creative literature of this period as well, with a flood of poems in celebration of the Britons' defence of liberty.

Yet, within a generation the more vigorous claims of Saxon freedoms had eclipsed this interpretation of Celtic Britain, such that by the mid nineteenth century the Saxon foundation of England had become the dominant historiographic model. The origins of constitutional freedoms and the origins of the English people were both to be identified with the Teutonic tribes who had invaded this country in the fifth century. As Luke Owen Pike observed in 1866

> There are probably few educated Englishmen living who have not in their infancy been taught that the English nation is a nation of almost pure Teutonic blood, that its political constitution, its social custom, its internal prosperity, the success of its arms, and the number of its colonies have all followed necessarily upon the arrival, in three vessels, of certain German warriors under the command of Hengist and Horsa . . . when Germany is in distress, we are invariably reminded that Germans are our kinsmen.[44]

This more resolute Anglo-Saxon interpretation of British history, marked by an uncritical enthusiasm for all things Saxon can be detected from the last quarter of the eighteenth century. Bishop Percy's preface to his translation of Mallet's *Northern Antiquities* succinctly encompasses the distinction which was to be drawn increasingly between the Saxon and Celtic peoples.

> The Celtic nations do not appear to have had that equal plan of liberty, which was the peculiar honour of all the Gothic tribes, and which they carried with them, and planted wherever they formed settlements: On the contrary, in Gaul,

all the freedom and power chiefly centred among the Druids and the chief men, whom Caesar called *Equites*, or Knights: But the inferior people were little better than in a state of slavery; whereas even the meanest German was independent and free.[45]

Bishop Percy's preface to Mallet outlines a position taken further in publications such as that of the radical Obadiah Hulme, who embellished his *Historical Essay on the English Constitution* (1771) with panegyrics to the free-born Saxon such as the following: 'I am of opinion, that if ever God Almighty did concern himself about forming a government, for mankind to live happily under, it was that which was established in England, by our Saxon forefathers.'[46] Sharon Turner's *History of the Anglo-Saxons* seemed to provide, in its attention to hitherto unpublished sources, the justification for such claims. Turner was a personal friend of William Owen Pughe and had defended the earliest Welsh poetry against charges of forgery in his *Vindication of the Genuineness of the Antient British Poems* (1803); he was, therefore, no enemy of the Celts, and took Pinkerton to task for his abusive treatment of them,[47] but his careful examination of Saxon institutions provided the kind of historical authentication that defenders of Celtic liberty could not hope to supply. Turner's *History* proved immensely popular, running to seven editions by the 1850s, and after its publication no serious historian would essay a Celtic origin for the English constitution and English liberties.

> Our language, our government, and our laws, display our Gothic ancestors in every part: they live, not merely in our annals and traditions, but in our civil institutions and perpetual discourse. The parent tree is indeed greatly amplified, by branches engrafted on it from other regions, and by the new shoots, which the accidents of time, and the improvements of society have produced; but it discovers yet its Saxon origin, and retains its Saxon properties, though more than thirteen centuries have rolled over, with all their tempests and vicissitudes.[48]

Turner's identification of constitutional liberties with the Saxons was a strong element within his treatment of the period and helped to bolster public interest in his research, but that very Saxon achievement of liberty eclipsed any Celtic pretension to democracy. Turner's friend Robert Southey, for example, could assert provocatively in his *Colloquies on Society* (1824) that the material conditions of life for the labouring classes had deteriorated in terms of health, diet and housing from that of the Britons; nevertheless this Rousseau-like position was tempered by his significant insistence that the aboriginal Celtic peoples enjoyed no liberty whatsoever and lived in a state of slavery.[49]

The idea of Celtic liberty thus disappeared without trace and by mid century the slavery endured by the Celtic peoples had become something of an historical commonplace. Thomas Wright's *The Celt, the Roman and the Saxon* (1852) is typical in declaring 'The mass of the Celtic population, as we learn from Caesar, were serfs, without civil influence or even civil rights; the mere slaves of their superior orders.'[50] The Celts as patriotic defenders of liberty had figured in literature and in historical writing throughout the first three quarters of the eighteenth century and had been widely celebrated as dauntless free-born patriots in the

1770s, 1780s and 1790s, but the more searching historiography typified by Turner's *History of the Anglo-Saxons* was to undermine the whole tradition. We have already noted the growth and development of a set of ideas whose combination was to construct in the nineteenth century an ideology of Saxon racial superiority over the Celtic peoples. Now, with the historiographic triumph of Saxon liberties the place of the Ancient Britons in English history had effectively become marginal.

The results of this are plain to see. By the middle of the nineteenth century the displacement of Celtic culture from its original position as a foundation of British history had developed to the point where the more extreme advocates of Saxonism could talk of England as an uniquely Saxon country, pure in its blood, with little or no taint of a degraded and inferior Celtic culture. A number of authors attempted to challenge such views, among them Richard Tuthill Massy in his *Analytical Ethnology: the mixed tribes in Great Britain and Ireland examined* (1855) and Thomas Nicholas in his *Pedigree of the English People* (1868). Popular writers, using mass circulation journals, could also push the debate along; Thomas Huxley in 'The Forefathers and Forerunners of the English People' (1870) and Grant Allen in 'Are We Englishmen?' (1880) reinforced Massy and Nicholas' insistence on mixed descent and attacked those contemporary racial theories, backed up by physiognomy, facial angles, phrenology and negrescence, which sought to demonstrate the innate superiority of the Anglo-Saxon racial type.[51] Looking back on thirty years of argument and invective Allen wearily concluded.

> The fact is, Keltic blood has so long been regarded as in some way obviously inferior to Teutonic, that most of us are ashamed to acknowledge it, even if we suspect its presence. The idle, superstitious Kelt has been so often contrasted with the clear-headed, energetic, pushing Anglo-Saxon, that everybody has hastened to enroll himself under the victorious Anglo-Saxon banner.[52]

In such a climate of opinion, it is evident that the perception of the Celtic peoples of prehistory could not be dispassionate or objective. The people who were presumed to have built Stonehenge, who had faced the Romans and followed Druidic teachings would be admitted into English history not as progenitors but as an inferior race whose origins and achievements were as nothing compared to the lustre of Saxon civilisation. Irish, Welsh and Scottish histories might contest such a vision, just as some ethnologists dissented from it in their work, but English history and anthropology, dominated by Saxon enthusiasm, constituted the master narrative of the age. In any case, to oppose such entrenched views was to work with the same parameters, to accept the idea of racial and cultural hierarchies and raise the Celts' position within them, rather than attempting to dismantle the whole ideological apparatus which supported those hierarchies.

The real break with the views examined here was to come with the growing development of a better informed anthropology and archaeology, whose examination of prehistoric culture was materialist in focus and empiricist in methodology. Growing tensions in the late nineteenth century with an imperially aggressive Germany would, in addition, cool some of the ardour hitherto expressed for the Saxon race, just as the *entente cordiale* with France might demonstrate how Celtic peoples should together safeguard civilisation from disruption. The shortcomings of Victorian thought on race and culture should not, however, encourage feelings of superiority from us today. No investigation of cultural origins can be isolated from questions of genealogy, perceptions of racial differentiation and other ideological assumptions and we are, of course, kidding ourselves if we believe that late twentieth century scholarship is not riven with ideological biases every bit as severe as those which orchestrated perceptions of the Celtic and Saxon peoples in the eighteenth and nineteenth centuries.

Chapter Seven

THE IMAGE OF THE BRITON

The Ancient Briton of the pictorial imagination has a surprisingly long ancestry and as early as the 1570s Lucas de Heere and Jacques le Moyne had produced illustrations of how aboriginal Britons might have appeared. De Heere's designs remained in manuscript, but Le Moyne's drawings were collected and augmented by John White, the Governor of Virginia and a talented draughtsman in his own right, and were engraved as a supplement to Theodor de Bry's publication of Thomas Harriot's *Briefe and true report of the new found land of Virginia* (1590) so that comparisons could be made between the Ancient Britons and the Native Americans of Virginia, whose way of life constituted the text (Plate 63).[1] These designs were quickly taken up by John Speed and used in his *History of Great Britaine* (1611) (Plate 64). As iconic types de Bry's and Speed's images proved effective and retained their hold for a considerable time. Thomas Jefferys turned to them as the best available illustrative source for the Britons in his *A Collection of the Dresses of Different Nations, Ancient and Modern* and so perpetuated their appeal into the late eighteenth and early nineteenth centuries (Plate 3). With scant archaeological evidence available to contest or supplement the classical accounts it is evident that once an adequate visualisation of their several descriptions had been achieved it would be difficult to improve or displace it. The plates published by de Bry effectively provided this visual construct, exhibiting all the features so prominent in the classical reports. Ancient Britons were naked or clothed in skins, they wore their hair long and the men were clean-shaven except for the upper lip, their skin was tattooed or painted with strange designs, their weapons included swords, spears, shields and chariots. Such was the iconic power of de Bry's stereotypes that attempts to add to the canon were only partially successful. Sammes's *Britannia Antiqua Illustrata*, for example, offered a fresh interpretation of the subject, adding the black robed and swarthy Silurian to the standard presentation of Ancient Britons but no subsequent artist took up this figure.

As Britain's economic sphere of influence expanded more information about tribal communities became widely available to the general public through the publication of travel accounts. The comfort a reader might draw from comparing their advanced and historically rich culture with the primitive existence of these savages was inevitably qualified by the realisation that British society must have looked as unsophisticated, barbarous and inferior to Roman eyes as native cultures looked to contemporary Europeans. John Aubrey recognised this explicitly in 1659:

64 (*facing page*) Anon, *The Portraitures and Paintings of the Ancient Britaines* wood block print, in John Speed, *The History of Great Britaine under the Conquests of the Romans, Saxons, Danes and Normans*, London, (1611), 1627 edition.

63 Theodor de Bry after John White, *The Truue Picture of One Picte*, engraving, from Thomas Harriot, *A Briefe and True Report of the New Found Land of Virginia*, Frankfurt, 1590. The British Library, London.

Let us imagine then what kind of countrie this was in the time of the Ancient Britons. By the nature of the soil, which is a sour woodsere land, very natural for the production of oakes especially, one may conclude that this North Division was shady dismal wood: and the inhabitants almost as savage as the Beasts whose skins were their only rayment . . . They knew the use of Iron. They were 2 or 3 degrees I suppose less salvage than the Americans.[2]

From the earliest encounters with native peoples, but especially in the eighteenth century, one strand of European thinking would compare civilised culture unfavourably with those who could live without the comforts of modern life. The primitivist belief that a simpler and less sophisticated life was in some (or all) respects a more desirable life found its justification and origin in highly coloured accounts of Native American and South Seas communities. 'Hard' primitivism, concentrated on life in harsh climates, stripped of the debilitating luxury of more civilised cultures, and fostered admiration for the stoic virtues of, for example, the hardier tribes of North America. 'Soft' primitivism, concentrated on life in ideal climates, such as Tahiti, where man was freed from toil, disease and danger, and engendered dreams of lost golden ages and paradise on earth.[3] As we shall see, both patterns of primitive life, but especially that celebrated by 'hard' primitivism, could be applied to the presumed way of life that obtained in primaeval Britain. Admiration for a difficult and dangerous existence exalted the strength, purity and discipline of peoples exposed to the ravages of nature and it is chiefly in this guise that the British noble savage was set to make an appearance alongside the exotic inhabitants of remote lands. By the early nineteenth century the hardihood of the

Ancient Britons, especially the Caledonians, was a well understood concept. John Lingard wrote of these latter in his *History of England*.

> They went almost naked: and sheltered themselves from the weather under the cover of the woods, or in the caverns of the mountains. Their situation had hardened both their minds and bodies. If it had made them patient of fatigue and privation, it had also taught them to be rapacious, bloody and revengeful. When Severus invaded their country, the Roman legions were appalled at the strength, the activity, the hardihood, and ferocity of these northern Britons.[4]

In one sense, these Britons were the personification of the elemental man, unencumbered by the trappings of civilisation, free to live a life of basic needs and quick gratification. And in this minimal existence they found a ready support in their iconic construction, where illustrators showed them alone, haughty and unfathomable, striking poses on an essentially empty stage. All of these presentations, of course, were specifically designed for book illustration and it would be surprising were any artist much before the 1750s to have thought of the subject in any other context than that of historical or antiquarian illustration. Yet, precisely because Ancient Britons were to be found in these surroundings, their visual presentation tended towards the iconic rather than the discursive. These were racial or national types, generic specimens standing for their tribal culture, and little explanatory context was provided to soften their stark isolation amidst the whiteness of the page. Even in the early nineteenth century, when print technology and public taste allowed for a more generous mise en page, the absence of detailed archaeological knowledge restricted the context that could be provided.

65   Robert Havell after Charles Hamilton Smith, *An Arch Druid in His Judicial Habit*, hand-coloured aquatint, plate 10 of Samuel Rush Meyrick and Charles Hamilton Smith, *The Costume of the Original Inhabitants of the British Islands*, London, 1815. Yale Center for British Art, Paul Mellon Collection.

66   Robert Havell after Charles Hamilton Smith, *British Fishing and Husbandry*, hand-coloured aquatint, plate 5 of Samuel Rush Meyrick and Charles Hamilton Smith, *The Costume of the Original Inhabitants of the British Islands*, London, 1815. Yale Center for British Art, Paul Mellon Collection.

The delight in vestments, utensils, architecture and other surroundings evident in the romantic depiction of mediaeval life finds no echo here. Such a visual presentation tended to reinforce, perhaps, the association of the Ancient Briton with a harsh and comfortless existence, living a life of spartan rigour and integrity in a world barely touched by human intervention. It is a vision of heroic fortitude.

Samuel Rush Meyrick and Charles Hamilton Smith's *The Costume of the Original Inhabitants of the British Islands* may be taken as one of the earliest illustrated books to provide a fuller context for the Britons. These two authors in particular attempted to place the depiction of the Briton on a firmer footing, dispensing with the de Bry stereotypes and paying attention to archaeological discovery in presenting their illustrations; but they also reveal a wish to revivify the past through the agency of sympathetic antiquarianism, to make those dry bones live. As Stephen Bann has shown,[5] it is this melding of history and imaginative projection that marks romantic historiography and in this the contributions of visual artists are of signal importance. As we saw in Chapter Two, Meyrick and Smith attempted to supply believable surroundings for their figures, including war gear, clothing and built structures where appropriate. I argued then that these illustrations were to a great extent illusory, presenting speculative hypotheses with the iconic clarity of documentary truth, as though these images were as securely grounded in material evidence as was mediaeval research. Yet, with regard to the rhetoric of that presentation the way in which these Britons are represented, their muscular bodies, the poses they strike, their rudimentary or non-existent clothing, their accompanying weaponry, their indominitable gaze and dignified self-possession, a good case can be made for a primitivist interpretation as well. Certainly, when depicting the Ancient British warrior the images follow the prevalent hard primitivist tendency, placing native Britons in stern and barren surroundings as a general rule (Plate 2).

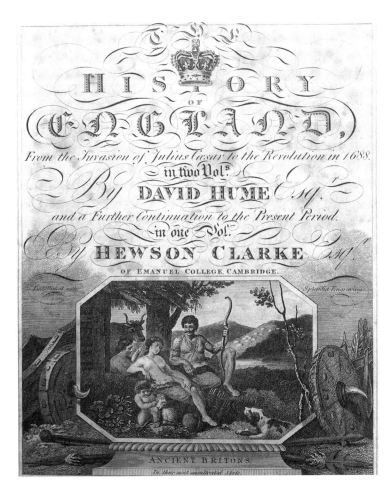

67 Charles Warren after Henry Corbould, *Ancient Britons in their most Uncultivated State*, engraving, titlepage of David Hume *History of England*, continued by Hewson Clarke, London, 1813.

The two major exceptions to this are both concerned with non-military matters. The image of the Arch Druid (Plate 65), dressed and accoutred in a medley of prehistoric gear, is an attempt to deal with the material culture of prehistory as far as it was understood in the 1810s. Decked out in his finery the Druid has as tangible a presence as any mediaeval abbot ready to celebrate the mass. The second instance is the plate entitled 'British Fishing and Husbandry' (Plate 66), where, instead of the usual clichéd images of warriors or Druids, a completely different sentiment informs an image of almost arcadian gentleness. A similar tendency can be seen in Henry Corbould's contemporary title-page vignette for Hewson Clark's edition of Hume's *History of England* (Plate 67). Here 'Ancient Britons in their most uncultivated state' are shown relaxing amidst a landscape of bucolic bliss. Only the framing implements of war (themselves borrowed from the trophy plate by de Loutherbourg (Plate 128) to be discussed in Chapter Ten) hint at a harsher reality. These few instances of 'soft primitivism', depicting British savages at their ease amidst the bounty of nature, are noteworthy because they are so untypical in their offer of an alternative visualisation of Ancient Britain. It is tempting to speculate that the coincidence of these publications with the end-game of the Napoleonic Wars is not entirely accidental and that the martial supremacy of the patriotic Briton now yields a little to the blessings of peace and prosperity.

Understandably, however, Britons in their uncultivated state were not the stuff

of which good pictures are made; no matter how well wrought, the antiquarian illustrators' depictions of Britons as generic specimens held little attraction for artists whose training and vocational imperatives insisted on the nobility of a dignified subject. For the archaic past to come alive it needed to become part of history, where recorded deeds might provide education and instruction, both philosophical and moral, and artists whose ambition aimed higher than antiquarian illustration need look no further than Caesar's account of his invasions of Britain. Nicholas Blakey treated the theme in 1751 as part of John and Paul Knapton and

facing page

68 (*top*) Simon François Ravenet after Nicholas Blakey, *The Landing of Julius Caesar*, 1751, engraving. Yale Center for British Art, Paul Mellon Collection.

69 (*below*) Anker Smith after Edward Burney, *The Landing of Julius Caesar*, 1793, engraving, in Robert Bowyer's edition of David Hume's *History of England*, London, 1806.

70 Robert Smirke, *The Landing of Julius Casar*, engraving, in David Hume, *The History of England*, London, 1824.

Robert Dodsley's projected series of fifty historical prints 'Representing the most memorable Actions and Events, from the landing of JULIUS CAESAR to the Revolution' (Plate 68). Blakey shows the struggle at close quarters. Roman missiles fly rather unconvincingly above the battleground and the foreground melée reveals a desperate struggle in progress. Only the background figure of Caesar himself and his calm ranks of disciplined legionnaries hint at the eventual outcome of the engagement. Blakey deliberately chooses to show the two sides as evenly matched, just at the moment when an ensign of the 10th legion emboldens his comrades by carrying the standard into the British lines. The accompanying letterpress underlines Blakey's depiction in describing the Britons' 'brave and obstinate resistance'.[6]

Thereafter, this moment was frequently chosen in illustrations of British history, as for example Burney's and Smirke's plates for two early nineteenth-century editions of Hume's *History* (Plates 69 and 70), but neither improve on Blakey's design, revealing instead a poor knowledge of anatomy and a feeble sense of composition. As a theme, however, this moment never lost its popularity and the competition for the decoration of the new Houses of Parliament encouraged a number of artists to attempt it. Edward Armitage was awarded a £300 premium, the top prize, for his design which restates Blakey's conception on an altogether more heroic scale (Plate 71). What is interesting about all these images is that the depiction of the Roman invasion is usually viewed from the British perspective, on the shore or in the water, rather than from the Roman one on the boats. The spectator's sympathies are thereby elicited to side with the defenders of barbarism rather than the emissaries of a civilised power. Within the context of patriotic nationalism this sentiment had received a widespread airing throughout the eight-

71   William Linnell after Edward Armitage, *The Landing of Julius Caesar*, 1847, lithograph. The Victoria and Albert Museum, London.

eenth century, the Britons being widely regarded as 'Freedom's plain sons', in William Shenstone's phrase.[7] As Edward Snyder has remarked,

> . . . most of the Celtic-English poetry appealed to the love of liberty. In an age when the agitation against slavery was first assuming importance and the great struggle for freedom was reaching its climax in France and America, it is not strange that people should have glorified the Celts, whose struggles to retain their freedom in spite of the inroads of more powerful nations have been uninterrupted. In fact, the Celtic-English poetry of the age (except for Macpherson's) is chiefly marked by reference to the love of liberty.[8]

As early as 1730, in William Hay's poem *Mount Caburn*, Britain's current military prowess had been compared to the resistance to Rome offered by the Ancient Britons. Hay's purpose is to praise the feats of the Georgian navy as a counter to invasion and conquest.

> Had ancient BRITONS thus been skilled in Fight,
> They had restrained the ROMAN Eagle's Flight;
> Ambitious CAESAR ne'er had reach'd this Shore,
> And Shewn his Troops a World unknown before . . .
> Far to the East, but almost in my view,
> There is the Place where first those Eagles flew:
> Where naked BRITONS did his Power oppose,
> And shew'd arm'd Legions no inglorious Foes:
> Then mighty CAESAR might relate at ROME,
> He came, he saw, but could not overcome;

136

For Liberty long resolute they stood,
And were the last the ROMAN Arms subdu'd.[9]

William Collins' *Ode to Liberty* (1746) is less specific about a contemporary military guarantor of freedom but, like Hay, Collins assumes that liberty, 'ador'd by Britain', is coeval with the Celtic prehistory of these islands even if the blessings of liberty seem to be intangible in the mid eighteenth cenutry.

Then too, 'tis said, an hoary Pile,
'Midst the green Navel of our Isle,
Thy Shrine in some religious Wood,
O Soul-enforcing Goddess stood!
There oft the painted Native's Feet,
Were wont thy Form Celestial meet:
Tho' now with hopeless Toil we trace
Time's backward Rolls to find its place;
Whether the fiery-tressed *Dane*,
Or *Roman*'s self o'erturned the Fane,
Or in what Heav'n-left Age it fell,
'Twere hard for modern Song to tell.[10]

Two verse dramas of the 1750s, Richard Glover's *Boadicea* (1753)[11] and William Mason's *Caractacus* (1759), are indicative of the easiness with which Celtic Britain was popularly associated with the defence of liberty against Roman aggression. Both showed Celtic peoples battling the Romans, inspired by that sort of dauntless patriotic zeal which is guaranteed to move any audience's feelings. Despite their eventual defeat and the loss of their liberty, these British warriors are ennobled as children of freedom, cherishing quite naturally and intuitively a concept of liberty which was in seemingly short supply in later eras. In Mason's play Caractacus' daughter, Evelina, condenses these assumptions in one pithy encomium on her father.

My father, rapt in high heroic zeal,
His ev'ry thought big with his country's freedom[12]

The almost constant state of warfare in the second half of the eighteenth century provides the context for such poetic appeals to a time-honoured British love of liberty. From the Seven Years War (1759–63) to the American Revolutionary War (1775–83), the French Revolutionary War (1793–1802) and the Napoleonic Wars (1803–15) Britain was engaged in a long sequence of military struggles, with France as the perennial opponent. James Thomson's and Thomas Arne's 'Rule Britannia' from David Mallet's masque *Alfred* (1740), first performed at Cliveden, the country seat of the Prince of Wales, at the height of the war with Spain, is the precursor and still popular survivor of a mass of similar celebratory effusions from this period. Ancient British heroes were pressed into service to support the war effort as exemplary ancestors of the contemporary British warrior, risking not real death and disability but poetic mangling at the hands of patriotic enthusiasts. *A Poetical Sketch of Caractacus' History* by Sneyd Davis was included in Thomas Pennant's *Tours in Wales* (1778–81) and is a good example of this sort of writing.

Davis makes an explicit connection between the British fight against Rome and contemporary warfare with France.

> O for more sparks of thy heroic fire!
> If aught regarding this dull orb of earth,
> Boils not thy rage, and thy great spirit chafes,
> To see the rivals of all-conquering Rome,
> Thy hardy Britons, foil'd by tinsel France?
>
> Assist, inspire our host! But chiefly thou,
> The champion, guardian-genius of this isle,
> Hover around our tents; thy airy lance
> Direct, and spread thy visionary shield!
> Call, rouse thy countrymen! To arms, To arms.[13]

The Reverend Edward Davies's *Aphtharte, or the Genius of Britain* (1784) is one of the lengthiest of these tributes to Celtic resistance, listing Nennius, Cassibelan, Caradog, Arviragus, Boadicea, Vortimer, Ambrotius, Uter and Arthur as the earliest of 'Great Albion's chieftans and her patriot kings'; in their turn to give way to Saxon heroes.

> See the Majestic Band!- what numbers more
> (Brave sons of freedom) generous Albion bore!
> With hardy limbs she built her martial race,
> And hearts to tear the mountains off their base.
> In vain, my Cambrians! to repel the foe
> All have ye done, that Virtue's self could do.
> Give now the friendly hand, since Heav'n ordains
> Odin's brave sons to share your happy plains:
> From your join'd blood a hardy race will rise,
> And Kings, whose names shall shine above the skies.[14]

Such a sanguine interpretation of the Saxon incursion into Britain was, perhaps, acceptable in a poem celebrating a lineage of British heroes, but it was more usual to explore the drama of the encounter between the two peoples. Abraham Portal's *Vortimer, or the True Patriot* (1796) deals with the beginnings of the Saxon invasion of Britain, casting these newcomers as essentially predatory. The tragedy of Celtic defeat is witnessed by a Roman, Ambrosius, one of whose dramatic functions is to comment on the British character. As he tells us, he has

> Observ'd the native genius of the Britons.
> Rich in unpolish'd worth, disdaining art,
> Freely they love and hate: honest and brave;
> Their unsuspecting nature often wrought on,
> To serve the purpose of smiling villainy. –
> Thro' death devoted to a patriot Prince.
> But is their darling liberty endanger'd,
> They rage and foam, and the weak web of law
> Indignant burst.[15]

Later in the play he remarks to Hengist and Horsa

> To peace averse, you may too late confess,
> That Britons arm'd in freedom's holy cause,
> Like the white cliffs that bound their native isle,
> Smile at the raging storm, and lift their heads
> Bold, and superior.[16]

Following the outbreak of war with France in 1793, a spate of literature celebrated the freedom-loving Ancient Britons. William Tasker's *Arviragus, A Tragedy* (1796) is prone to patriotic sentiments that were by now thoroughly clichéd. Caesar's conquest of Britain is described by Arviragus, son of Caractacus, using rhetoric derived ultimately from the speech of Vercingetorix in Caesar's *Gallic War*.

> He, whose brave legions never knew repulse,
> Who reign'd triumphant o'er the vanquished globe,
> First learnt to tremble at the British arms,
> And fled with tarnish'd laurels back to Gaul.
> Nor could the nation's conqueror subdue
> Our free-born fathers: 'till he sow'd dissension
> Among the chiefs, conquering by art not arms.
> For know, that Britain, world within itself,
> While her brave sons shall mutually accord,
> May hurl defiance to the world at large.[17]

All of these passages, and the numerous others from which these are but a small selection, share a perception of the Celtic peoples as lovers of liberty and dauntless defenders of their freedom. It seems fair to say that in general terms the patriotic invocation of Celtic martial valour served the purpose, in the later eighteenth century, of securing the historical identification of Britain with liberty, asserting the 'natural' defence of freedom in these islands. We have noted in Chapter Three, however, that different readings of this history might be prompted in Scotland and especially in Wales; yet, despite these regionally nuanced uses of the archaic past, it is important to stress that outside of a specifically Celtic context the patriotism of the British resistance to Rome could be mapped on to almost any co-ordinates. Caractacus, for example, was used for English political purposes on at least two occasions. Sanderson Miller built Radway Castle (1747–50) to mark the spot where Charles I raised his standard before the battle of Edgehill. It includes an octagonal tower with niches in one of which was to be placed the figure of Caractacus in chains.[18] To equate the royalist cause with Caractacus was to arrogate to Charles I the qualities of supreme patriotism usually vested in the Celtic warrior leader. Twenty-five years later at a Whig meeting in Shropshire to protest against the war with America, a reading took place of 'Some Additional Lines to Caractacus' (a reference to Mason's verse drama, though not by him, despite his well-known Whig politics), recommending conciliation and greater liberty for the colonists.[19] It is, perhaps, a token of just how ill-defined a symbol of British liberty Caractacus was that his person could be used for such distinctly antithetical political purposes. But the fate of national heroes is often just this, to add a spurious credibility or historical lustre to any expedient invocation of patriotism. We need also to remind

ourselves of what was discussed in Chapter Six, that as soon as this Celtic liberty was investigated more scrupulously, in terms of its legal, judicial and political dimensions, it was difficult to substantiate it in any meaningful way. At the very moment when Celtic defenders of liberty were being celebrated in art and literature, their lack of liberty and primitive justice were being exposed in historical and antiquarian debate. The more searching demands, particularly of nineteenth century historians, would elevate Saxon freedoms over Celtic autocracy and in this context the nobility and heroism of Caractacus and Boadicea could become compromised, their shining examples might look a little tarnished.[20] For many such commentators Celtic patriotism was not enough.

Thus far we have been examining images of Celtic resistance to Rome and the appeals to patriotism implied by them; but not all representations of Romans and Ancient Britons were antagonistic. The benefits of Roman civilisation, notwithstanding their eclipse after 410 AD, were a legitimate part of the historical record. It seems fair to postulate that the growing imperial domain of Britain would excite some interest in the spectacle of an 'advanced' culture instructing a subject people and indeed most of these images date from the middle of the nineteenth century. Prior to this period very few attempts were made to portray the beneficial effects of Roman culture on the Ancient Britons. Hamilton's crude illustration of Julius Agricola in Edward Barnard's *History* (1790) (Plate 72) is one of the very few eighteenth-century examples of such illustrations. Its explanatory letterpress has a

curious mixture of admiration and detestation for the Roman occupation of Britain.

> Julius Agricola a Roman Governor in Britain under the Emperor Domitian introducing the Roman Arts & Sciences into ENGLAND, the Inhabitants of which are astonished and soon become fond of the Arts and manners of their cruel Invaders.

In the nineteenth century there is less of this type of equivication. In 1831 Henry Perronet Briggs exhibited at the Royal Academy a picture whose theme concentrated on the idea of benighted savages being freed from the fetters of ignorance and superstition by enlightened knowledge (Plate 73). The picture had been commissioned by the Hull Mechanics Institute and was entitled *The Progress of Civilization. The ancient Britons instructed by the Romans in the mechanical arts.* The commission is interesting insofar as it seems to be one of the earliest visual examples where Celtic Britons and the nineteenth-century artisan are mapped on to one another, a theme we shall return to later. The Mechanics' Institute guidebook made the point of Briggs' picture absolutely clear. '. . . A Roman unfolding to some Britons an architectural elevation, while a scowling Druid is overlooking them, with a sinister expression of countenance well contrasting with the open confiding expression of the half-kneeling Britons.'[21] The few other examples of such subjects treated in the nineteenth century likewise tend

74   Edward Henry Corbould, *The Britons deploring the Departure of the Last Roman Legion*, 1843, watercolour, 91.5 x 137 cm. Private collection.

towards the beneficial results of Roman rule. The open, confiding expression of recently civilised Britons is, in pictorial terms, emblematic of a belief in the cultural benefits of domination by a more advanced power. As with the contemporary British empire, the introduction of civilisation might effect an intellectual and spiritual change in subject peoples; certainly the beneficiaries of imperial rule seen in Edward Henry Corbould's *The Britons deploring the Departure of the last Roman Legion* (Plate 74) have a dignity and pathos at odds with the martial vigour and heroic patriotism of their savage forebears. Corbould's picture and John Everett Millais' *Romans leaving Britain* (Plate 75) are possibly the most developed pictorial statements of the Victorian ideal of imperial harmony, especially at the personal level.[22] Millais' picture, in its mawkish effacement of imperialism by personal relationships, calls to mind Rudyard Kipling's much later treatment of the theme, where Roman garrison troops mouth the sentiments of British soldiers on imperial service, most notably in *The Roman Centurion's Song*:

> Legate, I come to you in tears – My cohort ordered home!
> I've served in Britain forty years. What should I do in Rome?
> Here is my heart, my soul, my mind – the only life I know
> I cannot leave it all behind, command me not to go[23]

But what of the immediate impact of Roman rule? William Bell Scott's *Building a Roman Wall* (1855–60) (Plate 76), painted for Wallington Hall, the Trevelyan

142

75 John Everett Millais, *The Romans Leaving Britain*, 1853, pen, ink and sepia drawing. Present whereabouts unknown. Reproduced from John Guille Millais, *The Life and Letters of Sir John Everett Millais*, London, 1899.

76 William Bell Scott, *Building a Roman Wall*, 1855–60, oil on canvas, 185.4 x 185.4 cm. Wallington Hall, Northumberland.

77 Stephen Sly After William Bell Scott, *The Free Northern Britons surprising the Roman Wall between the Tyne and the Solway*, wood engraving, *Illustrated London News*, 12 August, 1843.

family home near Newcastle, shows subdued Britons put to use as labourers under the control of Roman officers. In the background the Britons' unruly compatriots threaten this work of civilisation, as they had in Scott's earlier *Romans and Caledonians* (Plate 77), exhibited in 1843 in the Houses of Parliament fresco competition. British experience of native unrest and the problems of imperial control were particularly vivid in this period, with events of the 1840s and 1850s in Afghanistan and India still an unhappy memory and it is likely that images of the Roman occupation of Britain gained a topical currency from such an obvious point of comparison.[24] J.C. Bruce's book, *The Roman Wall* (1851), in dealing with the remains of the most spectacular vestige of Roman occupation in these islands neatly encapsulates the kind of imperial comparisons that were commonplace in mid-Victorian Britain.

> Another empire has sprung into being, of which Rome dreamt not . . . Her empire is threefold that of Rome in the hour of its prime. But power is not her brightest diadem. The holiness of the domestic circle irradiates her literature, and all the arts of peace flourish under her sway. Her people bless her. We may . . . learn . . . on the one hand to emulate the virtues that adorned [Rome's] prosperity, and on the other to shun the vices that were punished by her downfall. The sceptre which Rome relinquished, we have taken up. Great is our Honour – great our Responsibility.[25]

The sentiments of this passage are echoed in the art displayed at Wallington Hall. Scott's *Building a Roman Wall* hangs as part of a sequence of pictures of local

78 Thomas Woolner, *Prayer*, 1867, Wallington Hall, Northumberland.

79 Thomas Woolner, *Prayer*, 1867, Wallington Hall, Northumberland.

history whose final image celebrates the industrial revolution in Victorian England. Before them stands the scupltural group by Thomas Woolner known variously as *Civilization* or *Prayer* (Plate 78).[26] Woolner's sculpture has on its pedestal relief carvings of barbarism and pagan worship as a counterpoint to the mother and child carved in the round as though the child was literally elevated by Christian civilisation above the brutishness of primal society. On the pedestal Woolner shows the human spirit trapped in barbarism: a mother feeds her child (raw?) meat on the end of a dagger and prays that he may become a successful warrior; the results of this unredeemed upbringing are shown by a warrior mowing down his enemies in a scythe-wheeled chariot and Druids sacrificing their victims in wicker cages (Plate 79). This is a far cry from the *Death of Boadicea*, Woolner had exhibited at

80   Ford Madox Brown, *Building a Roman Fort at Mancenion*, 1879–80, 318 x 146 cm. Gambier-Parry spirit fresco. Manchester Town Hall.

Westminster Hall in 1844 as a competition piece for the new Houses of Parliament. In that context, celebrating patriotic heroism, Woolner's attitude to Ancient British life was much less pessimistic and he depicted 'the dying queen, mastered by the anguish of the hour, [lying] like a royal martyr in the arms that sustain her'.[27] In contrast, at Wallington that enthusiasm for material and spiritual progress evident in Bruce's text finds an explicit echo in a celebration of Britain's historical development from pagan barbarity to Christian prosperity. Manifestly, however, the barbarian Britons of this history are a different class of people to the staunch defenders of British liberty discussed earlier in this chapter and it is interesting to note the extent to which artists like Scott were now prepared to portray subdued Britons not as idealised patriots but as navvies, with coarse features and sun-burnt limbs. We see them again in Ford Madox Brown's *Building a Roman Fort at Mancenion* (Plate 80), the first in a series of historical pictures for Manchester Town Hall. As at Wallington, the Roman invaders' superior intelligence and civilisation is in some contrast to the Celtic labourers toiling at their behest. Their faces are a neat demonstration of the impact of pseudo-sciences such as phrenology on Victorian attitudes to Celtic peoples. As Mary Cowling has brilliantly demonstrated,[28] phrenology had a decisive impact on artists as well as the general public who 'read' their images according to its principles. George Combe's *Phrenology applied to Painting and Sculpture* (1855) was a best-selling and highly influential work, much discussed in artistic circles, and Cowling details many other serious and popular contributions to the field. Two concepts embedded in much mainstream phrenology have a particular bearing on the Celtic natives labouring in Scott and Brown's pictures: the general idea that the lower classes of civilised nations correspond physiognomically to savages (a development of Haeckel's recapitulation theory, ontogeny repeating phylogeny); and the specific identification of the lower classes in Victorian Britain with the dark complexion and temperament of the aboriginal Celt.[29] This is made patently clear if we examine the Celts in Scott's picture, particularly the reclining figure in the left foreground and

146

compare their physiognomies with their Roman overseers. It is evident that in this case physiognomic differences do not merely draw attention to different races but to a definite hierarchy of race, with the orthognathous Roman features contrasted with the prognathous jaw, large mouth, snub nose and receding forehead of the Celt. For a middle-class English viewer, reassured that his or her physiognomy was orthognathous and quite distinct from the working-class visage, Scott's labourers were properly and precisely delineated as anthropologically subordinate to those who controlled them in the Roman era, just as they were to those who controlled them now.[30]

We might compare such images with two passages from Macaulay. In his *History of England* (1848) Macaulay offers a resolutely negative view of archaic British culture.

> Nothing in the early existence of Britain indicated the greatness which she was destined to attain. Her inhabitants, when first they became known to the Tyrian mariners, were little superior to the natives of the Sandwich Islands. She was subjugated by the Roman arms; but she received only a faint tincture of Roman arts and letters. Of the western provinces which obeyed the Caesars she was the last that was conquered, and the first that was flung away. No magnificent remains of Latian porches and aqueducts are to be found in Britain. No writer of British birth is reckoned among the masters of Latian poetry and eloquence.[31]

Fifteen years earlier, on 10 July 1833, Macaulay had contributed to the East India Company debate in Parliament, as Secretary to the Board of Control. In the peroration to his speech he looked forward to

> the proudest day in English history. To have found a great people sunk in the lowest depths of slavery and superstition, to have so ruled them as to have made them desirous and capable of all the priveleges of citizens, would indeed be a title to glory all our own . . . there are triumphs which are followed by no reverse. There is an empire exempt from all natural causes of decay. Those triumphs are the pacific triumphs of reason over barbarism; that empire is the imperishable empire of our arts and our morals, our literature and our laws.[32]

These perceptions of Britain's past degradation and present civilisation take further the ideas of national progress instanced in the passage quoted above from Bruce's *Roman Wall*. Macaulay's insistence on the worthlessness of primitive British society articulates a more sombre view of British history, where the culture of ancient Britain offers not an unproblematic beginning to the story of national progress but instead stands as a highly inauspicious and ultimately false start to that society now triumphing in the nineteenth century. Such sentiments are very close to the informing philosophy of the central corridor programme of frescoes for the new Houses of Parliament. When the parliamentary commissioners decided to decorate the national seat of government the relationship between history and contemporary aspirations was not in doubt and Macaulay's election to the commission in 1844 suggests that his view of British history was a critical determinant of that relationship. Defined in 1847, the iconography of the corridor shows explicitly the uses to which British history was to be put: 'Six subjects have been selected: in three Britain appears sunk in ignorance, heathen superstition and slavery; in the other three she appears instructing the savage, abolishing barbarous rites, and liberating the slave.'[33] These six subjects were respectively the Phoenicians in Cornwall, a Druidical sacrifice, Anglo-Saxon captives on sale in Rome, Cook in Tahiti, English authorities stopping a Suttee sacrifice and the emancipation of black slaves. Evidently, the context of these images is both imperial and progressive. English authority is exercised on races or cultures whose contemporary condition is assimilated to prehistoric and Dark Age Britain. In both cases we are to be shown peoples in need of redemption by a superior intellectual or moral authority, with England's current civilised culture an example of the benefits that accrue once this redemption has been achieved. Part of this thinking was well established by the mid nineteenth century. As we have seen, since at least the late sixteenth century Ancient Britons had been compared to Native Americans in particular on the assumption that 'as they are, so were we'. The imperial context of Victorian expansion overseas added a new dimension to this clichéd assumption, concentrating equally on the interaction between native peoples and 'superior civilisations'. Robert Vaughan, for example, in his *Revolutions in English History* (1859) used the contemporary parallel to elicit sympathy for Britons subjected to imperial Roman ambition:

> Some rough experience then came on the rude communities of this island. For civilized men do not often estimate the suffering of the not civilized according to a law of humanity. It is deemed enough to estimate it according to a law of caste. The blood of the rude flows – their hearts are broken – but what of that? Is such blood human – do such hearts really feel?[34]

Understandably, the subjugation of Celtic Britain was an awkward episode in the national history of a state currently pursuing expansionist foreign policy and the pictorial treatment of the subject is caught up in the problem. Are Caractacus and Boadicea national heroes or ignorant savages resisiting civilisation? Even within the Houses of Parliament this question receives two answers. The central corridor programme suggests that Celtic Britain was a place of ignorance and superstition requiring civilisation, yet painters such as Armitage, Watts and Selous exhibiting in the 1843 competition and sculptors like Woolner in the 1844 exhibition depicted Celtic leaders as heroic patriots and presented British resistance to Roman invasion as a noble defence of national freedom. Indeed, Boadicea was intended as a subject in Maclise's fresco programme for the Royal Gallery. But which of these competing interpretations would best explain the meaning of the Romans in Britain? For if, as seems likely, such images were inflected with connotations of contemporary imperialism their impact on the British audience is problematic. Were these ancestors of whom Britons should be proud or embarrassing reminders of the barbarous, even savage origins of British civilisation? Similarly, what sympathy could the Britons elicit if their cultural inferiority and resistance to Roman rule was being mapped on to the cultural difference and resistance to British imperialism of contemporary subject peoples? In short, did the Victorian viewer project him or herself into the Roman or the Celtic character? Plainly such confusion over the treatment of Celtic Britain is not just a question of historical truth, but a muddled response to the problematics of writing a British history at all.

It should, I hope, be apparent to the reader that the arguments concerning the

Celtic peoples, both historical and contemporary, which were outlined in Chapter Six provided an important context for the way in which images of those peoples were received and understood. With the transient exception of the eighteenth-century's celebration of the Celts as patriots and defenders of liberty, it is clear that the standard image of Celtic culture was not overly positive and, as the nineteenth century developed, the rise of racial theory encouraged a condescending or hostile attitude. A good example of the prevalence of racial thinking applied to British history can be found in W. Cosmo Monkhouse's discussion of John Henry Foley's sculpture of *Caractacus* (Plate 81), now in the Mansion House, London. The figure is widely regarded as Foley's masterpiece, marking something of a high point in mid Victorian sculpture, and its inclusion as one of six sculptures commissioned by the City of London to celebrate characters in British literature testifies to its contemporary significance.[35] Monkhouse concurred with the aesthetic evaluation of Foley's work but his account reaches a pitch of exquisite embarrassment when considering Caractacus' race and culture. He begins by quoting Hume's account of the Claudian invasion in AD 43, where the Roman assault is compared to European subjugation of Africans and Native Americans, but plainly wishes to demur from this comparison:

> . . . we may be pardoned for thinking, or finding it difficult not to think, that there were some distinctions, not unimportant between an ancient Briton and a being even as noble as a North American Indian. Although the ancient inhabitants of these islands painted themselves with woad, and we cannot help admitting that they were barbarous, we wince at such an epithet as 'savage' being applied to them. In a word, however uncultivated and wild they may have been, we feel that they were not degraded, and that they possessed the essence of that noble character and the capacity for improvement which only needed time and cultivation to develop them into such an altogether admirable race as ourselves. We have, however, fortunately, an alternative consideration which will enable us to view with comparative complacency any revelations discreditable to the ancient Britons, and that is, that, thanks to the Romans, Picts, Danes, Saxons, and others, we have probably little or none of their blood in our veins.[36]

What we have here, neatly conjoined in one piece of criticism, is evidence of an intellectual or ideological tussle between two points of view. Monkhouse begins, or so it seems, with a judgement on Celtic Britain owing a fair deal to eighteenth-century notions of social progress, with talk of 'essences' and 'capacity for improvement', but his conclusion runs counter to this position by postulating his readership's racial separation from 'the ancient inhabitants of these islands'. This more severe view, which is deemed a 'fortunate' alternative, and the 'comparative complacency' it is presumed to encourage are telling indices of just how problematic any association with the Celtic peoples might be.

Monkhouse goes on to make a further significant point that the success of Foley's *Caractacus* lies in his surpassing the particularities of Celtic culture to become 'a splendid specimen of humanity' and an icon of heroic patriotism. Evidently, part of his reasoning here is a recapitulation of standard academic theory concerning the avoidance of meretricious detail in the search for ideal qualities of form and spirit; but given the context of Monkhouse's earlier remarks there is a

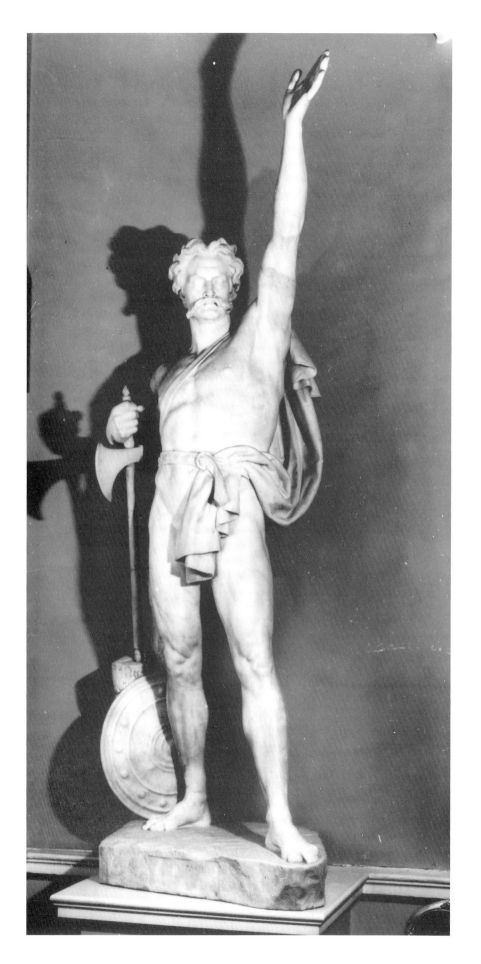

further connotation of the suppression of those very racial qualities that had provoked the passage quoted above. As Monkhouse stresses, the figure of Caractacus should be one 'in which barbarity should be overcome by inward fire and outward beauty'. By insisting on a more abstract depiction of the Celtic leader Monkhouse offers a strategy which might remove the figure from the context of history to position it within an almost purely symbolic world. The iconic presentation of aboriginal Britons, the usual preserve of antiquarian illustration, is here recommended not to produce an image of a generic type but its contrary, a bloodless Briton stripped of any specific markers of race and culture. Thus, despite Monkhouse's claim that Foley has depicted 'a Celt . . . of the finest type',[37] Caractacus as national hero should ideally transcend the particular Celtic historical and cultural context that some viewers evidently found so worrying.

It is arguable, indeed, that this requirement of transcendence is the mark of mythopoeia and that the creation of an effective national history relies, paradoxically, on the avoidance of historical detail. Art, insofar as its imagery can only admit so much discursive potential, is thus perfectly placed to construct the icons a national history requires. The conjunction between fine art and popular history is illuminating, for both modes of presentation simplify their subject to achieve clarity of exposition. Both rely on cliché, mythography and decontextualisation to make their point irrespective of any loses in accuracy of description. *1066 and All That* and its Victorian predecessor, Gilbert Abbott A'Beckett's *The Comic History of England* (1847), are brilliant burlesque reminders of where such presentation ends, but their thumb-nail treatments of the 'key' moments in British history are only finitely removed from the distillation and inevitable over-simplification of the standard pictorial approaches to British history. When the Knaptons and Dodsley advertised their intention in 1750 to publish their fifty prints after Blakey and Hayman representing British history, they were aware of the difficulties of such an enterprise: '. . . in the Choice of Subjects, Care will be taken that they be First; Important, or Interesting: Secondly Striking, or such as will make a good Picture; Thirdly, So different from each other as to afford an agreeable Variety.'[38] In a further advertisement they elaborated on the tensions between history and its visual presentation.

> There are some important Events and remarkable Periods of History, which will not afford any subject for the Painter: As on the Other Hand some Actions and Occurrences, that would make very agreeable Pictures, are not of Importance enough in the History to merit a Place in such a Series of Prints. Some subjects must likewise be avoided, because of their Similitude in Painting to others . . . However, in so large a Tract of Time, there is no doubt but that the History of England will afford the Painter a sufficient Number of Subjects, various in their Nature, striking in their Circumstances, and important to the History.[39]

Similarly, Robert Bowyer was evidently aware of the potential for a pictorial national history. The second dedication of his 1806 edition of Hume's *History of England* is addressed 'to the Legislature of Great Britain' and describes the pictures of his Historic Gallery (from which the engraved plates in the *History* were taken) as assisting in 'enforcing the important lessons of English History' and capable of forming 'a School of Historic Painting; or to answer any other national purpose that may to the Wisdom of Parliament seem fit'.[40] In the 1795 *Elucidation* of his project Bowyer described the aim of his illustrations as being 'to rouse the passions, to fire the mind with emotion of heroic deeds, or to inspire it with detestation of criminal actions'.[41] These honest appreciations of the issues involved in illustrating British history indicate at once how engravings might aid and abet that tendency in popular history to construct its narrative as a series of sensational events concerning great names.

Furthermore, we must ask ourselves how history was envisaged, mediated thus in copper plate engravings. For once illustrations stand in place of the narrative they are presumed to support, it is as though an editorial redaction has taken place, stripping the narrative of whatever complexity it might possess. Thus, while some elements in these prospectuses chimed with the 'philosophical' reflections of enlightenment historiography, the sheer iconic punch of visual images and their tendency to schematise complex events into a unified vision meant that only the most basic reflection could, in truth, be activated by pictures. The iconic simplicity of a depicted event – its facticity – militates against that kind of reflection engendered by the analysis of history. The selections made for engraving in the 1750s and the 1790s by the Knaptons, Dodsley and Bowyer were predicated, to some extent, on assumptions about the audience to be addressed and the ideology to be promoted. The rationale of the Knaptons and Dodsley asserts the need to balance the claims of aesthetics and historiography; Bowyer bases his selection on the potential to provide ethical or civic instruction. Both, however, are agreed that it is possible and desirable to offer a visual quintessence of a complex historical narrative, yet the embellishment of history with illustrative material such as this can only be a distraction, a simplistic interpolation into a complex narrative rather than a quintessence of it, and closer to mythography than historiography.

Obviously the measured consideration of the complexity of historical events could not be rendered in images whose whole function was that of seizing moments of physical crisis, moral dilemma or dramatic incident for the inspiration of their spectators. And whereas readers of British history from the Norman conquest onwards might situate these images within a richly detailed narrative, readers of pre-Conquest history had less and less alternative to such visualisations as the materials for narrative history grew more scant. The earlier the period under consideration, the greater the power of its iconic visualisation, where images selected from aesthetic or patriotic motives had little check from a narrative alternative which might temper their drama with a more nuanced understanding, rendered in exhaustive prose.

We can consider the decoration of the Houses of Parliament as an epitome of the difficulties involved in presenting an appropriate national history in visual terms. Although Victorian assumptions about race, progress and society, to name but three, were distinctive, they nevertheless shared with their Georgian predecessors the desire to use history for example and instruction. Any selection from history, any ordering of events or characters as 'representative' or 'crucial' must be founded on assumptions about the function of such a selection. Like the Knaptons and Bowyer, the Commissioners wished to fuse the concerns of aesthetics with those of a patriotic historiography and it is perhaps a measure of the difficulty of achieving this 'fusion' that when the competition for the redecoration was announced in 1843 the choice of specific historical subjects was left virtually open. We have already encountered the results of this freedom in the mutually antagonistic accounts of archaic British society that resulted. This antagonism can be explained, as I have argued, by the ambiguous interpretations of Celtic Britain in play throughout this period. Nevertheless, whether these interpretations were positive or negative they were highly reductivist visions of ancient Britain choosing either to exalt or to excoriate the Celtic peoples of these islands. To have attempted a more judicious representation, mingling Celtic patriotism with ignorance, valour with cruelty, simplicity with superstition would not have produced effective, purposeful images and it is perhaps reasonable to suggest that Monkhouse's reaction to Foley's sculpture of Caractacus was entirely justified. Only a mythopoeic presentation of patriot heroes such as Boadicea and Caractacus could guarantee an unequivocal response.

Caractacus was frequently depicted in the eighteenth and nineteenth centuries and was quickly reduced to a set of iconic co-ordinates whose displacement from history we have already noted in Foley's sculpture. Like Boadicea, his figure attracted early dramatic interest and, as the supremely chivalric Caratach, his character dominates the action of John Fletcher's *Bonduca* (1613–14), a play which remained well known throughout the seventeenth and eighteenth centuries and was adapted for performance in 1695, 1696, 1778 and 1837. As a pair, however, Caractacus and Boadicea articulate different ideas of the British leader; Boadicea's inspiration lies in her sense of personal and patriotic outrage and the exhortatory fervour of her oratory, while Caractacus is aligned with an innate nobility of spirit capable of sustaining him even in defeat. Caractacus in chains before Claudius predominates over all other interpretations of his history.

Although the relevant modello is lost, it is possible that Sir James Thornhill's designs for eight pictures representing '8 heroic Virtues taken from several stories of the Antients, Greeks, & Latins & Britons' may have included Caractacus in chains. The series was painted for Benjamin Styles at Moor Park, Hertfordshire, in 1725–7 but was destroyed when the decorations were replaced in 1732.[42] With Thornhill's picture gone, and its precise subject unknown, it is appropriate to see Caractacus' iconographic tradition beginning in earnest at mid century. Francis Hayman's *The Noble Behaviour of Caractacus, Before the Emperor Claudius* of 1751 (Plate 82), produced as part of the Knaptons and Dodsley's series of historical engravings, appears to have inaugurated this tradition, while its attendant letterpress articulates the features of the story that were to remain dominant in subsequent visual elucidations of the theme. Caractacus, 'this illustrious Prisoner, who had so bravely resisted the Power of the *Romans* for upwards of nine Years', is brought before the Emperor and Empress. Hayman shows the moment after his speech to Claudius

> so sensible and affecting, yet with an Air and Manner so noble, and so much superior to his present Fortunes, that the Emperor, struck with the Greatness of his Mind and the Gallantry of his Behaviour, immediately order's his Chains to be taken off, and restor'd his whole Family to Liberty.[43]

Hayman is genuinely inventive in his personification of the British chief, finely built, proud and disdainful in his stance and depicted with a flowing moustache as

82   Charles Grignion after Francis Hayman, *The Noble Behaviour of Caractacus, before the Emperor Claudius*, 1751, engraving. Yale Center for British Art, Paul Mellon Collection.

specified in Caesar's account of Celtic appearance. Behind him servants lug war booty into the hall, a collection of idols presumably meant to represent Celtic deities. (Booty it certainly is, being Hayman's reworking of an illustration of British gods he had filched from Sammes's *Britannia Antiqua Illustrata*.[44])

In 1792 Fuseli attempted the same encounter, this time with Caractacus in mid speech (Plate 83). Coincidentally, George Richards published his *Songs of the Aboriginal Bards of Britain* in the same year, one of whose 'songs' is *The Captivity of Caractacus*, and it is possible that this was the spur to Fuseli's imagination. Fuseli's closer focus and a concentration of light on the Briton make a more unified, and more melodramatic composition but the debt to Hayman is clear. Interest in Caractacus had revived thanks to William Mason's extremely popular *Caractacus, a dramatic Poem*, published in 1759 and republished in seventeen different editions between 1759 and 1811. As a stage play Caractacus was performed in London and the provinces in 1776, 1777 and 1778.[45] William Hamilton chose to depict the climax of Mason's drama in his *Caractacus, King of the Silures deliver'd up to Ostorius the Roman General by Cartismandua, Queen of the Brigantes* (Plate 84) but such scenes were never as popular as those depicting Caractacus' nobility in the presence of Claudius at Rome. Hamilton's subject, in a symbolic context, might be seen as an equivalent betrayal to Samson's

83   A. Birrell after Henry Fuseli, *Caractacus at the Tribunal of Claudius at Rome*, 1792, engraving. Yale Center for British Art, Paul Mellon Collection.

84   William Bartolozzi after William Hamilton, *Caractacus King of the Silures deliver'd up to Ostorius the Roman General by Cartismandua, Queen of the Brigantes*, 1788, engraving. The British Museum, London.

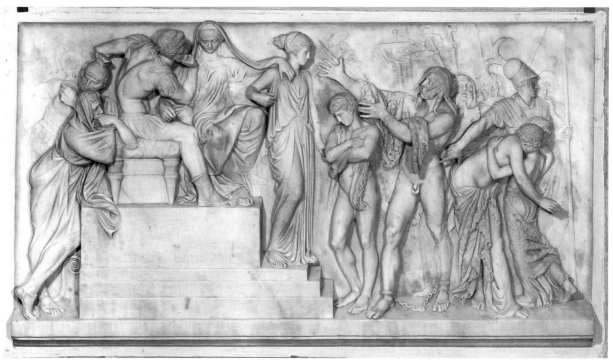

85 Thomas Banks, *Caractacus pleading before Claudius*, 1777, 91 x 192 cm. Stowe School.

by Delilah and certainly the poignancy of the moment was ripe for visual interpretation; but Caractacus at Rome was an altogether more positive image of the aboriginal Briton, whose iconographic predecessors included Paul before Felix and, ultimately, Christ before Pilate.[46] If Walpole was right to claim that a time of political crisis might cause Britons 'to seek lustre from their progenitors' then this surely was the incident of greatest refulgence.

Thomas Banks' *Caractacus before Claudius* (Plate 85), now at Stowe, was commissioned in Rome by George Grenville, the future Marquis of Buckingham and exhibited at the Royal Academy in 1780. As Flaxman noted of it, Banks depicted the same moment as had Hayman and Fuseli:

> the subject is historical, but the characters are heroic, and a dramatical gradation of passion is expressed in a few figures; from the patriot's undaunted attitude, you perceive he is saying, 'nor wouldst thou have disdained to receive me with articles of peace, because I am descended of noble progenitors, and I have ruled over many warlike nations' while the Emperor listens with attentive respect.[47]

Banks's version lacks a little of the dramatic fire of Fuseli's, but his debt to antique art is more marked, as was Mason's verse drama of course, with a consequent generalisation of detail and only an abbreviated reference to a specific historic encounter. Although academically correct, Banks' classicising treatment of Caractacus encourages a presentation in which he is depicted as somehow transcending his historical culture; the moustache, semi-nudity and coarse animal skin clothing mark him out as a Celtic leader but the smooth modelling and nobility of pose speak the refined language of decorum. Banks' *Caractacus* helps throw some

156

86 John Linnell after George Frederick Watts, *Caractacus led in triumph through Rome*, 1847, lithograph. The Victoria and Albert Museum, London.

light on Monkhouse's later recommendations for Foley which share this concern for nobility of expression and sentiment; for instead of Banks' etherealised emblem of patriotism the Victorian sculptor had presented his Caractacus as a Celt of flesh and blood. Even the musculature of the two is different; where Foley has rendered unclassical proportions, Banks has kept his figure within the accepted constraints of bodily perfection.

Once established as a subject, Caractacus remained relatively popular as a vehicle for artists. Engravings in illustrated histories appear frequently from the 1770s onwards and a number of painters exhibited work on the theme at the Royal Academy and British Institution. Perhaps predictably the debating club of the London Welsh, the Caradogion Society (active *c.*1790–8) had a picture of Caractacus before Claudius hanging in its meeting room.[48] As we might also expect, the 1843 and 1844 fresco competitions for the new Houses of Parliament inspired a number of painters to try their hand at a Caractacus theme. Of these only George Frederick Watts' design is known to us (Plate 86). Like his friend Armitage, whose *Caesar's First Invasion of Britain* won the top award, Watts was the winner of one of the three £300 prizes. By choosing an episode earlier in the narrative than the convocation with the emperor Watts departed from the established mode of representation and, as we shall see in a moment, upset some reviewers as a result. Nevertheless, Watts attempts here to represent Caractacus' undaunted nobility of spirit amidst the splendours of the enemy capital. An anec-

157

dote relates that Watts derived the pose of Caractacus' head from sketching the head of a lion in London's zoological gardens, 'thrown back for an instant as if at bay'.[49] This would seem to take the idea of noble savagery to ludicrous extremes, but the British chieftan's leonine hauteur was striking enough to encourage a similar comparison from a contemporary reviewer: 'the grand old man, firm as a riven rock, and in his barbaric pride, as grim and as unconquerable as a mastiff, strides through the crowded streets with more the air of victor than of vanquished.'[50] Yet, compared to Caractacus' oratorical victory over Claudius, Watts's depiction of his appearance as a captive occasioned some criticism in the pages of the *Athenaeum*, whose reviewer commented,

> A British captive led in triumph to 'make a Roman holiday'! – Would the Delaroches or the Delacroix's adorn their Palais de Justice with Napoleon dying under the eyes of English sentinels! . . . There was a moment in the history of the Ancient Briton which an artist had done well to select: we mean the chief's appearance before Claudius, when the captive by his inborn greatness, towered alike superior to his adversary and to his own fate. Here he is but a chained savage, led in humiliating procession by his victors.[51]

This criticism is significant, for it articulates yet again that dilemma concerning the representation of Celtic Britons as savages or as patriots. It seems clear that Boadicea and Caractacus needed to be established at some distance from their savagery if they were to function as patriotic examples and that this was a particularly acute problem in the nineteenth century when a pejorative view of Celtic culture was in the ascendant. The heroic view of Caractacus, established from as early as the mid eighteenth century, managed to withstand the intellectual assaults on the Celtic peoples of Britain mounted from the 1780s onwards and particularly in the Victorian period, but it did so by constructing an image of the British leader which suppressed his historical and cultural reality. Watts's cartoon threatened to return Caractacus to that reality, to mark him with the signs of barbarity that a patriotic tradition had so sedulously covered over. We have already examined Monkhouse's encounter with this difficulty in discussing a much more idealised representation, Foley's Mansion House sculpture of Caractacus. If Foley could be criticised for retaining those vestigial markers of the Celt in his figure it is easier to understand the concerns of the *Athenaeum*'s reviewer. What both critics seem to have wanted was a heroic figure, safely removed from specific details of race and culture.

Even writers who dissented from Anglo-Saxon triumphalism tended to construct such a panegyric for Caractacus as to place him alongside Arthur or Alfred in a mythopoeic realm rather than emphasising his Celtic inheritance. An example is provided by a contemporary of Monkhouse's, Thomas Nicholas, whose *Pedigree of the English People* attempts to offer an alternative to the rampant Saxonism of the period. His description of Caractacus epitomises the patriotic appeal located within the British chieftain's character and helps explain how Caractacus, as the supreme patriot, might encourage a sympathetic identification that transcended the 'problem' of Celtic barbarism.

> This piussant prince, after the noblest efforts on record for the defence and honour of his country, was destined to defeat at the hands of Ostorius, and to

87 'Dna A M', *Boadicea Q of ye Iceni: ex Dione* in Henry Rowlands *Mona Antiqua Restaurata*, Dublin, 1723. The British Library, London.

betrayal at the hands of Queen Cartismandua . . . But his defeat was not an easy or sudden thing. For nine whole years had this heroic man kept the field against the power of Rome, fighting many battles and inflicting terrible losses on the imperial army. When led a captive to Rome, his arrival created one of the most exciting and impressive spectacles history has depicted . . . What Briton can read the speech put into his mouth by Tacitus without emotion?[52]

As a subject for historians Boadicea has as long a lineage as Caractacus, appearing first in the sixteenth century after Boccaccio's discovery of Tacitus in the library of Monte Cassino. She appears in Holinshed's *Chronicle* (1578) and in texts such as Petruccio Ubaldini's *Lives of the Noble Ladies of the Kingdom of England and Scotland* (1591); and as a vehicle for imaginative interpretation she received full length dramatic treatment in John Fletcher's *Bonduca* (1613–14, first published in 1647), Sir Robert Howard's *Bonduca* (1669), Charles Hopkins's *Boadicea* (1697) and Richard Glover's *Boadicea* (1753).[53] Cowper's ode *Boadicea* (1782), a product of the Celtic enthusiasm of the late eighteenth century remained popular well into the middle of the next century, to be contested in its turn by Tennyson's ambitious version of 1859. Her historical stature and potential for epic mythography is witnessed by her inclusion as one of the six subjects for paintings suggested by the committee set up by the Society for the Encouragement of Arts in 1758–9 to award premiums for History and Landscape painting.[54] In the late seventeenth century Aylett Sammes, like Holinshed and Speed before him, had her portrayed as a steadfast queen,[55] and this depiction was in turn used by Henry Rowlands in 1723 when illustrating *Mona Antiqua Restaurata* (Plate 87). This

88 Charles Grignion after Francis Hayman, *Boadicea in her Chariot*, engraving, frontispiece to volume 1 of Tobias Smollett, *Complete History of England*, London, 1757. The British Library, London.

89 Thornton after ? Francis Robert West, *Portraits and Dresses of the most Remarkable Personages and Sovereigns in England proir to the Norman Conquest*. Plate I in Edward Barnard *History of England*, London, 1790. The British Library, London.

90 John Tomlinson after Thomas Stothard, *The City of London burnt by the Troops of Boadicea Queen of the Icena*, 1803, engraving.

91 William Sharp after John Opie, *Boadicea*, 1795, engraving, in Robert Bowyer's edition of David Hume *History of England*, London, 1806. The British Library, London.

regal and imposing figure owes more, of course, to contemporary dress than to a close reading of classical texts and it was not until later in the eighteenth century that a more antiquarian depiction of Boadicea began to emerge. Francis Hayman provided an illustration of *Boadicea in her Chariot* for the frontispiece to Smollett's *Complete History of England* (Plate 88), showing her bare-breasted, with a chain necklace and carrying a spear, a wicker shield and the hare used as an augury before the onset of her campaign, according to Cassius Dio. A wolf laps from the river in the foreground, while behind her some rather ghostly Druids sanctify her rebellion with appropriate ceremonial. Perhaps Hayman's Boadicea was rather too rough and ready for polite taste, for a generation later she had left this barbarian world for something much less historically specific. At the close of the eighteenth century, Boadicea was represented in three illustrations which depict much more general and regal qualities than Hayman had employed, as though his example could not be followed. West's figure of Boadicea for Barnard's *History of England* (Plate 89) is still a relatively primitive individual, borrowing her spear and cross garters from Rowlands but she is dressed in a more nondescript style with an animal skin and 'primitive' necklace and belt as markers of her barbarian origins and lacks Hayman's attention to classical accounts. Thomas Stothard, on the other hand, devised an image of *The City of London burnt by the Troops of Boadicea Queen of the Icena* (sic) for George Raymond's *History of England* (Plate 90) showing her as a neo-classical heroine and John Opie portrayed her in similar guise exhorting her followers for Bowyer's edition of Hume's *History of England* (Plate 91). In all of these examples Boadicea has been depicted as some archaic but classicised heroine, whose features, demeanour and accoutrements propel her out of history into the transcendent world of tragedy.

Such hesitant revisions of the fanciful Boadicea were overtaken by Meyrick and Smith's *The Costume of the Original Inhabitants of the British Islands* (Plate 92). Here, as with all their figures, the image of Boadicea is an attempt to give an accurate visualisation of the Queen of the Iceni based on antiquarian learning. Roman accounts and Roman artefacts depicting Celtic peoples have been used to produce an illustration of an historical personage, rather than an empty symbol. Yet notwithstanding this attempt at historically accurate representation, most nineteenth-century artists were to choose more fanciful interpretations of Boadicea just as their predecessors had failed to follow Hayman's more literal interpretation of the British queen. If sober antiquarianism diminished Boadicea to the point where her historical existence threatened to eclipse her almost mythic force, it is hardly surprising that creative artists would choose to ignore Meyrick and Smith's revisionism. Stothard's second image of *Boadicea* of 1812 (Plate 93), for example, in its combination of declamatory drama with an almost credible interpretation of British tribesmen readying for war, provided a dramatic and heroising image that Meyrick and Smith's costume book was unable to supply. It is, after all, the drama of Boadicea and not her culture that gives the story its appeal. As with Cleopatra, we do not really want to know about the niceties of contemporary dress and the organisation of her society; instead we hold on to the unfolding of the drama, the poignancy of her rhetoric and that powerful, primal mixture of sex and death.

Boadicea's tragedy and her historical significance inspired numerous artists,

including W.H. Brooke in the 1825 edition of Hume's *History of England*, H.C. Selous and E.M. Ward, both exhibitors in the 1843 Houses of Parliament cartoon competition, and Maclise in the Royal Gallery of the Houses of Parliament. E.H. Corbould even translated the imagery into male terms for his frontispiece to James Taylor's *Pictorial History of Scotland* (1852), representing *Galgacus addressing his army* (Plate 94). Here the iconography of a war leader inspiring a massed crowd of warriors is maintained, with the Caledonian leader Galgacus standing where Boadicea would normally be positioned. Of all of these images Selous's (Plate 95) shows the extent to which Boadicea's character had been reinterpreted by the 1840s. The dignity and disciplined anger of the earlier illustrations gives way here to a frenzied harangue whose histrionics are echoed in the writhing, plunging figures of her people. It is tempting to believe that Tennyson had seen Selous' image and was inspired by it when drafting his own experimental poem *Boadicea* in 1859.

> Far in the East Boadicea, standing loftily charioted,
> Mad and maddening all that heard her in her fierce volubility,
> Girt by half the tribes of Britain, near the colony Camulodune,
> Yell'd and shriek'd between her daughters o'er a wild confederacy.
> 'Lo the colony, there they rioted in the city of Cunobeline!
> There they drank in cups of emerald, there at tables of ebony lay,
> Rolling on their purple couches in their tender effeminacy.
> There they dwelt and there they rioted; there – there – there – they dwell no
> more.
> Burst the gates, and burn the palaces, break the works of the statuary,
> Take the hoary Roman head and shatter it, hold it abominable,
> Cut the Roman boy to pieces in his lust and voluptuousness,
> Lash the maiden into swooning, me they lash'd and humiliated,

> Chop the breasts from off the mother, dash the brains of the little one out,
> Up my Britons, on my chariot, on my chargers, trample them under us.'[56]

The apotheosis of Boadicea is, without doubt, Thomas Thornycroft's colossal sculpture of *Boadicea and her Daughters* (Plate 96) which now stands at the end of Westminster Bridge in London. Thornycroft began the project in 1856 and was encouraged from the start by Prince Albert. In the light of Meyrick and Smith's failure to inspire British artists with a more resolute approach to antiquarian exactitude in treating this theme, it is interesting to note that Thornycroft debated

96   Thomas Thornycroft, *Boadicea*, 1871. Westminster Bridge, London.

the relative merits of realism and inspiration with the Prince consort. 'The comparative advantages of realistic treatment were contrasted against the artistic and poetic views: and his decision was decidedly to the latter. He would make the chariot regal: "You must make," said the Prince, "the throne upon wheels." '[57] Here surely is the stimulus for these representations. The attraction of Boadicea is that she is patriot, woman and mother seeking to avenge political, sexual and familial wrongs. Her struggle against the Romans, her defeat and eventual suicide while originating in history occupy a mythic and elemental space. Like Foley's *Caractacus*, exhibited in the same year Thornycroft began his project, the poetic interpretation eclipses the historical figure. William Cowper's poem *Boadicea* had anticipated the Victorians' linking of her story with national pride and imperial success and when Thornycroft's sculpture was finally erected in 1902 it bore a quotation from that poem on its podium.

> Regions Caesar never knew
> Thy posterity shall sway.

The idea of future decline awaiting those who had once defeated Britons allowed a historical calamity to be contextualised within present success. The stain of disgraceful rout and subjugation is bleached out by the triumph of contemporary imperial domination. Thus, in the same way as the nobility and heroism of Boadicea or Caractacus transcended the savage degradation of their tribal community, so their proleptic indication of future imperial glory transcended their historical defeat.

164

Chapter Eight
THE MEGALITHIC LANDSCAPE

Stone circles, dolmens, menhirs and other visible relics of British antiquity had excited antiquarian speculation for some while before the period with which this study is concerned. As unusual features in the landscape they could not escape attention and the folklore associated with many monuments attests to a long standing vernacular curiosity in them as magical sites.[1] How far back this superstitious interest goes is difficult to judge, but their appeal to widespread scholarly attention is essentially a phenomenon of the seventeenth-century and afterwards. The chief exception to this rule is, naturally enough, Stonehenge, the most striking monument of them all, which was being written about as early as the mid twelfth century and was first illustrated in two fourteenth-century manuscripts. As Christopher Chippindale has so ably demonstrated,[2] Stonehenge has the longest recorded history of public response of any prehistoric monument. From its position close to a public highway it was almost impossible to ignore and this, together with its structural daring, was enough to ensure that from its early mediaeval recognition to its popular standing today it has become the pre-eminent megalithic site in Europe. Even now, for the general public at any rate if not for the archaeologist, Stonehenge is both an enigmatic symbol and the key physical demonstration of what prehistory left behind.

Although the earliest written records concern Stonehenge alone, by the time of Leland and Camden in the second half of the sixteenth century one or two other sites were entering literate awareness as antiquarian endeavour began to sketch in the primaeval map of Britain. This process accelerated in the seventeenth century and afterwards as these pioneering studies were supplemented by a steadily increasing volume of antiquarian research over the whole of the British Isles. By the second half of the eighteenth century a high proportion of prehistoric sites had been examined by antiquarians and recorded in their texts as the earliest remaining visible antiquities, the only surviving physical traces of the Ancient Britons and the beginnings of British history. Yet, despite this antiquarian interest and even after the growth and development of landscape painting in Britain in the eighteenth century it was uncommon for an artist to approach these sites as suitable subjects for landscape painting. Depictions providing accuracy of the sort that archaeologists might find useful today certainly had value for the antiquarian, either as a subject to be engraved or as a finished picture for a cabinet of curiosities, but such productions were essentially illustrative topography and well outside the concerns of the ambitious artist competing for reputation in the London art world. Practically all depictions of prehistoric features produced prior to the late eighteenth century came into being to satisfy these somewhat mundane demands and were of purely topographical and antiquarian interest. Prehistoric monuments would not become subjects for serious landscape painters until the close of the eighteenth century when the taste in landscape painting for classicising subjects or portraits of country houses and their estates was no longer dominant and a new aesthetic celebrating the sublime was firmly established. And even in these altered circumstances it is significant, as Louis Hawes has noted, that prehistoric landscape paintings are predominantly watercolours;[3] in the period 1750–1850 only a handful of images were produced in oils, the characteristic vehicle for the most serious pictorial statements.

There is, nevertheless, a fundamental change of emphasis in the depiction of prehistoric remains in the latter part of the eighteenth century, with topographical accuracy shouldered aside in a bid to capture the character of the monuments. In looking at these different approaches to prehistoric remains we shall be witnessing, essentially, the rival claims of two sorts of truth regarding the appearance and meaning of the monuments, the prosaic and the imaginative. In the eighteenth and early nineteenth centuries antiquarianism itself embraced both fanciful imaginings and disciplined inquiry, but the growth of a more rigorous archaeology in the mid nineteenth century would effectively split antiquarianism into two. Archaeology needed to discriminate between hard 'scientific' truth and imaginative projection and may be said to have developed the antiquarian tradition of empirical research to achieve this. What was left of antiquarianism would eventually become identified only with unsystematic and speculative thought and with a propensity for romantic identification with the past. Needless to say, such an absolute distinction between archaeology and antiquarianism was more apparent than real, but it does serve to point out the steadily widening gap in methods, training, institutions, readership and objects of study between the two approaches. Seen in this light, the sober renditions of topographical artists may be regarded as allied to that antiquarian impulse which developed into archaeology, while the more creative approaches of imaginative artists seem closer to those archaeologically suspect elements within antiquarianism tending towards sympathetic projection and speculation. The relationship of images to prehistoric monuments is thus complicated by the fact that one generation's enthusiasm is another's excess and work which might be suitable for the generous antiquarian mind seems frivolous when judged by the stricter canons of archaeology.

David Loggan's engraving of Stonehenge (Plate 97) exemplifies the early antiquarian approach; he provides a detailed and informative double image of the monument whose physical appearance is located within the context of an explanatory letterpress designed to provide a digest of opinions concerning the origin and purpose of the structure. The presentation of the site is unemphatic and matter of fact, with an even light illuminating Stonehenge to give a clear picture of its physical peculiarities. In functional terms, topographical renditions of prehistoric remains may be said to attempt a neutral depiction of their subject, often to the point where illustrative demands override most artistic concerns. The provision of information is the salient feature of such images and remains the criterion by which a successful rendition should be judged. Necessarily, any departure from

97   After David Loggan, *The Prospects of Stonehenge from the West and from the North*, last quarter of the seventeenth century, engraving. Wiltshire Archaeological and Natural History Society Museum, Devizes.

visual accuracy will compromise the purpose of the image and the topographical treatment of prehistoric monuments is often sober to the point of tedium, notwithstanding the technical abilities of the artists involved. Even Stukeley, hardly an opponent of speculative antiquarian enquiry nor its depiction in his later work of the 1740s, could produce quite straightforward illustrations of prehistoric remains early in his antiquarian career, as for instance the view of Stanton Drew published in his *Itinerarium Curiosum* (Plate 98).

This tradition of representation would remain strong throughout the eighteenth

98   William Stukeley, *A View at Stanton Drew*, engraving, from *Itinerarium Curiosum: Centuria II*, 1776. Wiltshire Archaeological and Natural History Society Museum, Devizes.

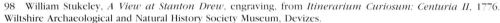

and nineteenth centuries and needs to be distinguished from the more imaginative projections of artists whose work is the chief focus of this chapter. To make such a distinction is not always easy. James Malton's *Stonehenge* (Plate 99) is an accomplished production, carefully articulated in terms of composition and cleverly focused through lighting and the disposition of the staffage. He employs the increasingly standard depiction of the monument against a darkening sky and provides the viewer with a memorable and compact image. Certainly, as regards topography, this image is a considerable improvement, in accuracy and in presentation, on that kind of banal record exemplified in much of the work of an earlier generation. But if we compare Malton's picture with one of the 1840s by William Turner of Oxford (Plate 100), it is evident that the topographical tradition has been infected by another set of values whose import is to dramatise the relics of prehistory. A sober and unemphatic presentation is in the process of giving way to the demands of aesthetics, emotion and association. The development of the latter aesthetic may be said to typify the more ambitious depictions of prehistoric monuments. Its origins lie with the development of the Sublime as an aesthetic category from the late 1750s with the earliest pictorial demonstrations of this approach to prehistoric subjects appearing in the third quarter of the century, as for example Thomas Hearne's 1779 watercolour of Stonehenge. Hearne's image of the monument was published in William Byrne's *Antiquities of Great Britain* (1786) and gained some influence thanks to the popularity of Byrne's volume (Plate 101). Indeed, Hearne's presentation of a closely focused view of Stonehenge under a threatening sky might almost be said to have launched the dramatic interpretation of prehistoric monuments exploited by later artists.[4] It was their achievement to shift the megaliths out of the prosaic world of topographical illustration and into the realm of imaginative suggestion.

It would be fair to say that we still visualise the monuments in these romantic terms, as a quick perusal of the covers of popular guides to prehistoric Britain will make clear. Colour photography may have heightened the available effects but the building blocks of the system are all there: the strong tonal contrast of the monument against its background, the low vantage point to increase the majesty of the image, the lowering or crepuscular sky, and the overall atmosphere of enigmatic power. We, however, are at the end point of this long tradition and take it for granted that megalithic structures may be illustrated prosaically or dramatically, depending on context. Further, we do not find it remarkable that serious twentieth-century artists as well as photographers should wish to investigate the megaliths as subject matter or inspiration.[5] We need to remember that the familiar presence of these monuments, our customary habits of visualising them, the iconic character they possess for us on site or in illustration is the result of a shift in romantic aesthetics when a long standing recalcitrance was overcome, when what had been rebarbative and uncouth suddenly found a means of presentation, and took on a transfigured identity.

That Stonehenge and similar monuments could become possible artistic subjects at all is due in no small part to the growth of domestic tourism, supplementing the Grand Tour abroad as a means of education and recreation. Travel within the United Kingdom was, of course, far less costly and time consuming than its continental equivalent and was enjoyed by a great many more people as a result.

99 James Malton, *Stonehenge*, 1800, watercolour, 55.9 x 80 cm. The Victoria and Albert Museum, London.

100 William Turner of Oxford, *Stonehenge, Stormy Day*, 1846, watercolour and touches of bodycolour with some scraping out on cartridge paper, 45.7 x 67.8 cm. The Ashmolean Museum, Oxford.

101 William Byrne and Thomas Medland after Thomas Hearne, *Stonehenge*, 1786, engraving, in William Byrne, *Antiquities of Great Britain*, London, 1786. Wiltshire Archaeological and Natural History Society Museum, Devizes.

The so-called 'Discovery of Britain' was dramatically accelerated by the almost continual state of war between Britain and France from 1793 until 1815, which conflict severely restricted the possibility of foreign travel for many tourists. A spate of popular handbooks and tourist guides poured from the presses, alerting tourists to the delights of Wales, the Wye Valley, Scotland, the Lake District, the West Country and other areas of natural beauty.[6] Prehistoric remains began to be included within this literature as sites of interest alongside other relics of the past. Their presence in otherwise rural surroundings helped add cultural and historical associations to some landscapes otherwise empty of interest. In this guise they functioned as local equivalents to the ruins of the classical world, an elegiac reminder of the collapse and decay of human endeavour, though without the added poignancy, of course, of having descended into utter destruction from the heights of civilisation.[7] Prehistoric remains could hardly stimulate sensations of loss and regret for what had passed into oblivion as was the case with the relics of Greece and Rome, but their antiquity and mystery might occasion more general reflections on the course of human history. A good example of this is Southey's *Inscription for a tablet at Silbury Hill* (1796), where the standard topoi of funerary verse are deployed to animate this most enigmatic of prehistoric monuments.

This mound in some remote and dateless day
Rear'd o'er a Chieftan of the Age of Hills
May here detain thee, Traveller! from thy road
Not idly lingering. In his narrow house
Some warrior sleeps below, whose gallant deeds
Haply at many a solemn festival
The Scauld hath sung; but perished is the song
Of praise, as o'er these bleak and barren downs
The wind that passes and is heard no more.
Go, Traveller, and remember when the pomp
Of Earthly Glory fades, that one good deed,
Unseen, unheard, unnoted by mankind
Lives in the Eternal register of Heaven.[8]

Southey's verse is typical of a growing tendency to employ association and sentiment as poetic equivalents for antiquarian enquiry. It is indicative perhaps of the extent to which antiquarianism was becoming a more rigorous pursuit that such romantic tendencies, still active in poetry and paintings of prehistoric monuments, tend to drop out of antiquarian writing as the nineteenth century develops. William Lisle Bowles, poet, antiquarian and Wiltshire clergyman, was one of the last antiquarian enthusiasts, described as having 'a fancy . . . for repairing to Stonehenge on the fourth of June, attired in the glories of Druidical attire, or his conception of it'.[9] On publishing his *Parochial History of Bremhill* in 1828 he was taken to task by George Crabbe, his contemporary, colleague and near neighbour, in a heavily ironical criticism.

You feel and in places raise feelings in your reader. But this accords not with topography. He who writes concerning monuments of all or any kind, if I may judge by the little I read of them, should have no more of feeling than the things themselves. Cold, stern judges of dead and decayed materials for investigation.[10]

Crabbe's harsh views on topography indicate the growing gap between serious antiquarian scholarship and the sympathetic involvement with the past that had been part of an earlier tradition. As the nineteenth century progressed it became more and more difficult to keep both accuracy and sympathy simultaneously in play. Antiquarianism was metamorphosing into a variety of 'scientific' disciplines and, in the process, shaking off the rhetorical and speculative nature of its eighteenth-century practice. It was this 'softer', more imaginative antiquarianism that was kept alive in the tourist guides and in the paintings of prehistoric monuments.

In the first volume of his *Munimenta Antiqua* the antiquarian Edward King provides a detailed example of this imaginative antiquarianism, where a susceptible mind confronted with Stonehenge opens itself up to the full associative impact of antiquarian speculation.

I chanced, the first time I visited this structure, to approach it by moonlight; being later on my journey in the evening, than I intended. This, however, was a circumstance; advantageous to the appearance: insomuch, that although my mind was previously filled with determined aversion, and a degree of horror, on reflecting upon the abominations of which this spot must have been the scene; and to which it gave occasion, in the later periods of Druidism; yet it was impossible not to be struck, in the still of the evening, whilst the moon's pale light illumined all, with reverential awe, at the solemn appearance produced by the different shades of this immense group of astonishing masses of rock; artificially placed, impending over head with threatening aspect; bewildering the mind with the almost inextricable confusion of their relative situations with respect to each other; and, from their rudeness, as well as from their prodigious bulk, conveying at one glance, all the ideas of stupendous greatness, that could well be assembled together: whilst, at the same time, the vast expanse of landscape from this summit of an hill, added an idea of boundless magnificence, similar to that produced by a view of the wide extended ocean.[11]

In complete contrast, William Clarke's *Antiquarian Itinerary*, published in seven volumes from 1815 to 1818, provides a good example of early nineteenth-century antiquarian description in transition between the enthusiastic evocations of writers like King and the sterner standards of nascent archaeology. In his description of the standing stones known as the Pyramids, or Devil's Arrows, near Boroughbridge, Yorkshire, Clarke's text is a hybrid, echoing still with eighteenth-century speculation, but written in a quite unemphatic and disinterested style.

A little westward of the bridge stand these stupendous monuments of antiquity: their latter name they probably obtained during the dark ages of superstition: they are three large stones, of a pyramid form, fluted towards the top, and stand nearly in a line from North to South . . . The country people have a tradition, that Severus, dying at York, left the empire to his two sons, Carracalla and Geta, which was acceptable to the empress, and approved by the soldiers; but not by the two brothers. A reconciliation being brought about, by the mediation of the empress and a sister, in memory whereof four Obelisks were erected: but three

171

now are only remaining, one being taken down last century. Several are of opinion that they were erected long before the arrival of the Romans in Britain, and that here was, in British times, the great Temple of the Druids, where was held the midsummer meeting of all the country round, to celebrate the quarterly sacrifice, accompanied with sports, games, races, and all kinds of exercises, with universal festivity: This was like the Olympian Games: and that these obelisks were as the matae of the races, the remembrance of which is transmitted in the present great fair held at Boroughbridge, on Saint Barnabas' day.[12]

It is evident that the reader of this passage is assumed to be after some sort of explanation that would make a visit to the Devil's Arrows worthwhile. Rather than inviting him or her to marvel at the mystery of these stones, Clarke attempts instead to guide speculation into a more familiar context of history and classical learning. As a result the reader has been offered several inducements to visit the Devil's Arrows. While their present name can be scoffed at as a superstitious error, their conjectural history allows mention to be made of a Roman origin which is in turn displaced by a more remote British/Druidic explanation, itself elaborated with references to classical culture. Finally, the Devil's Arrows are linked to the present in terms of the survival of local vernacular festivities. The fanciful nature of these explanations is to some extent beside the point; their interest for the twentieth-century reader is in their positioning of the Devil's Arrows within a coherent context that a nineteenth-century reader could comprehend. What both texts share, notwithstanding differences in scholarship, approach and rhetoric, is precisely their ability to construct the image of prehistory for their readers. Changes in attitude within antiquarianism thus leave their impress on a larger audience whose interest in archaic Britain would have been less committed but whose curiosity had been aroused. By these means megalithic sites became objects of discussion to a wide public, newly awakened to the potential historical interest of their own country's remote past. It is scarcely an exaggeration to claim that monuments like the Devil's Arrows became publicly visible through the agency of speculative antiquarian rhetoric.

Public interest does not, however, produce significant art on its own. If prehistoric sites were to become subjects for painters, as opposed to illustrations in antiquarian or topographical literature, they needed to be amenable to artistic treatment, to be quite simply paintable. It was not enough that they held intrinsic interest as historical relics; unsupported by an explanatory letterpress, subjects for landscape painting needed to work on the spectator immediately and had to find their place within the dominant aesthetic taste in landscape painting. This is not to claim that historical associations were forgotten when approaching such subjects (indeed, as we shall see, that association remains a powerful constitutive part of the meaning of landscape paintings containing prehistoric remains), but it is to emphasise that prehistoric sites, without any redeeming pictorial qualities, would not constitute a serious subject for an ambitious landscape painter. Topography was always prone to dismissive criticism from academicians and connoisseurs who valued art precisely insofar as it had the power to avoid the particular, and was able to inform the mind with grander and more general truths in place of mundane reality. 'Tame delineation of a given spot' or 'mapwork' were the sneering epithets chosen by Fuseli to describe topography, whose limitations he compared with the nobler art of landscape painters like Claude.[13] Relics of British prehistory were particularly prone to the tame renditions of topography, for, as many commentators had noted, they possessed little pictorial appeal or natural beauty. Such unpromising raw material, seen in conventional terms, was below the dignity of landscape painting.

The old prejudice against the remains of Britain's barbarous past was an important part of this difficulty. As with the writing of history, the questions that needed answering were first whether these monuments held any further interest beyond their appeal to antiquarian scholarship, and second whether they could find their place within the more general concerns of the age. Was there, in short, a frame of mind that provided a rationale for their inclusion? As we have seen, Augustan thinking concluded that there was not. Samuel Johnson's tart dismissal of a prehistoric site visited in the course of his Scottish tour is indicative of this prejudice.

> About three miles beyond Inverness, we saw, just by the road, a very complete specimen of what is called a Druid's temple. There was a double circle, one of very large, the other of smaller stones. Dr. Johnson justly observed, that, to go and see one druidical temple is only to see that it is nothing, for there is neither art nor power in it; and seeing one is quite enough.[14]

For landscape painters too it was necessary to find art or power in prehistoric remains before they could become artistic subjects, and the discovery of pictorial appeal in prehistoric sites should be seen as part of a larger shift in aesthetic philosophy, dating from about the middle of the eighteenth century. The reason stone circles, cromlechs and other prehistoric sites became possible subjects for artists aiming to reach a wider public was thus bound up with a new approach to landscape which developed an aesthetic context for these antiquities avoiding the limitations of topography. Johnson's strictures, although shared by others of his generation, were already beginning to look outmoded by the 1780s, indeed the contrary case had been growing for some time. Edmund Burke's *A Philosophical Enquiry into the Origins of Our Ideas of the Sublime and Beautiful* (1757) contains one of the earliest descriptions of Stonehenge to seize on its 'rudeness' as a positive quality, capable of moving the spectator by virtue of the very features which a previous generation would have denigrated as tasteless.

> Another source of greatness is *Difficulty*. When any work seems to have required immense force and labour to effect it, the idea is grand. Stonehenge, neither for disposition nor ornament, has any thing admirable; but those huge rude masses of stone, set on end, and piled each on other, turn the mind on the immense force necessary for such a work. Nay the rudeness of the work increases this cause of grandeur, as it excludes the idea of art, and contrivance; for dexterity produces another sort of effect which is different enough from this.[15]

Burke's identification of the sublime as a legitimate aesthetic category was instrumental in the revaluation of prehistoric monuments, providing them with an aesthetic context every bit as important as the historical context supplied by ingenious antiquarian suggestion. Samuel Pepys, crossing Salisbury Plain by night in 1668 had been upset by the looming presence of Old Sarum which he found 'prodigious so as to fright me'.[16] A hundred years later tourists were learning to cherish that frisson of terror as Sublimity. While the sublime is more usually associated with natural features, its relationship to man-made structures was always important. Although it is sometimes difficult to distinguish between sublime and picturesque approaches to a monument, particularly as the original definitions of these qualities become blurred through repetition and use, it is possible to assert that associations of power, force and endurance are often the key elements in written descriptions and in paintings of Stonehenge and similar prehistoric relics; and these elements are especially characteristic of the sublime.

Other difficulties remained. As Burke had noted, 'Stonehenge, neither for disposition nor ornament, has any thing admirable' yet disposition and ornament may be regarded as key determinants in the composition of pictures. The problem for artists was that these megalithic remains did not lend themselves to an ordered arrangement, their forms did not combine as ready-made pictorial compositions, nor were their constituent parts aesthetically pleasing as individual elements. It is noteworthy, for example, that Picturesque theory was unable to incorporate prehistoric remains within its domain. First promoted by William Gilpin, the celebration of the Picturesque was one of the crucial developments in late eighteenth-century landscape sensibility, occupying the mid-ground between the sublime and the beautiful. As an aesthetic credo it enabled artists to depict topographical sites without lapsing into pure informative notation and may be said to have provided one of the crucial devices for recuperating the mediaeval past. Gilpin's *Observations on the Western Parts of England* provides the key document in our understanding of the Picturesque approach to the prehistoric and repays careful examination.

> Stonehenge, at a distance, appeared only a diminutive object. Standing on so vast an area as Salisbury Plain, it was lost in the immensity around it. As we approached, it gained more respect . . . but when we arrived on the spot, it appeared astonishing beyond conception. A train of wondering ideas immediately crowded into the mind. Who brought these huge masses of rock together? Whence were they brought? For what purpose? By what machines were they drawn? Or by what mechanic powers erected? . . . But it is not the *elegance of the work*, but the *grandeur of the idea*, that strikes us. The walk between the two circles, which is a circumference of three hundred feet, is awfully magnificent: at least it would have been so, if the monument had been entire. To be immured, as it were, by such hideous walls of rock; and to see the landscape and the sky through such strange apertures must have thrown the imagination into a wonderful ferment. The Druid, though savage in his nature, had the sublimest ideas of the object of his worship, whatever it was. He always worshipped under the canopy of the sky, and could not bear the idea of a roof between him and heaven . . . Wonderful, however, as Stonehenge is, and plainly discovering that the mind, which conceived it, was familiar with great ideas, it is totally void, though in a ruinous state, of every idea of picturesque beauty; and I should suppose was still more so in its perfect one. We walked round it, examined it on every side, and endeavoured to take a perspective view of it, but in vain; the stones are so uncouthly placed, that we found it was impossible to form them, from any stand, into a pleasing shape.[17]

Gilpin's account is at its most enthusiastic as it approaches a sublime aesthetic. He can praise 'the grandeur of the idea' and finds Stonehenge 'astonishing beyond conception'; but while its presumed Druid architect 'had the sublimest ideas of the object of his worship', Stonehenge itself is 'void . . . of every idea of picturesque beauty'. Gilpin's definition of 'picturesque beauty' was not in 1798 the loose and impressionistic term it was to become in the hands of others and examination of his grounds for debarring Stonehenge from the Picturesque canon helps to explain why it, and similar structures, were proving problematic for eighteenth-century artists. He had stated in 1792, 'Picturesque composition consists in uniting in one whole a variety of parts; and these parts can only be obtained from rough objects',[18] but an aesthetic designed to celebrate the rough and the irregular stops short at Stonehenge because no composition is possible. The crux of this difficulty has a crucial bearing on artists' approaches to prehistoric monuments, for landscape painting requires a level of pictorial coherence that a topographer might be excused from achieving. Gilpin's aesthetic credo celebrated roughness and ruggedness, but he was also insistent that the forms compose, and in these terms he was correct to exclude Stonehenge from the picturesque.

Uvedale Price, whose *Essay on the Picturesque* (1794) had attempted to refine Gilpin's definitions and usage, went further than Gilpin by seeking the picturesque in qualities of roughness and variety rather than an overall harmony of parts, claiming that picturesque subject matter should not necessarily be defined with reference to painting. His description of a decayed classical temple certainly avoids any mention of 'uniting in one whole' and seems to relish the chaotic abandonment of ruined structures.

> Observe the process by which time, the great author of such changes, converts a beautiful object into a picturesque one. First, by means of weather stains, partial incrustations, mosses, &c. it at the same time takes off from the uniformity of the surface, and of the colour; that is, gives a degree of roughness, and variety of tint. Next, the various accidents of weather loosen the stones themselves; they tumble in irregular masses, upon what was perhaps smooth turf or pavement, or nicely trimmed walks and shrubberies; now mixed and overgrown with wild plants and creepers, that crawl over, and shoot among the fallen ruins.[19]

Price's delight in the triumph of time witnessed in the profusion of decay is, however, as inapplicable to megalithic remains as is Gilpin's need for unity. For, first, it was uncertain whether these monuments *were* decayed. The arguments raging over the true state of ancient British culture gave no clear answer to this question. Were Stonehenge and other megalithic structures once proud ceremonial sites whose restored state would have showed a magnificence now lost through the ravages of time? Or were they the preserved relics of a primitive culture whose architectural or constructional skills were extremely limited? Secondly, from the viewpoint of the contemporary artist these megalithic sites did not display that profusion of decay so lovingly described by Price. Drab irregular blocks of stone lay in various arrangements in upland areas singularly bereft of a rich flora. The starkness of these structures was rarely qualified by the picturesque qualities Price so admired.

102 Henry Thomson, *Distress by Land*, 1811, oil on canvas, 237.5 x 146 cm. Stourhead, Wiltshire.

Faced with these problems of representation, artists whose ambition and ability eschewed the strictly topographic were offered only one viable aesthetic solution. The Sublime became the chief non-topographical approach used in depicting prehistoric antiquities, but the gain in power and drama that such an aesthetic allowed was offset by a tendency towards a similarity of treatment which would end eventually in stock responses, cliché and bombast. A good example of this is provided by Henry Thomson's *Distress by Land* (Plate 102), with Stonehenge presiding over the desperate plight of a mother and her children, cruelly exposed to a savage storm. Sublime approaches to megalithic temples cannot be repeated indefinitely, however, without losing their impact and this perhaps explains why landscape paintings of prehistoric sites are relatively uncommon, unless produced as exercises in topography. Most of the serious, ambitious artists examined in this

176

chapter tackled prehistoric landscape as one relatively short moment in a long creative life, mindful perhaps of the danger involved in over-using a pictorial formula; it is the topographers, whose creative sights were set that much lower and whose treatment of the sites was that much more restrained, who tend to demonstrate a continuing interest in the subject.

The Reverend Richard Warner's description of a visit in 1808 to the Constantine Tolmen in Cornwall captures in literary terms the spirit of the sublime approach and should be compared to Clarke's more measured account of the Devil's Arrows quoted previously.

> Our curiosity had already been excited by a distant view of the famous Druidical Remain in Constantine parish, called by the *initiated* the *Tolmen*, or Hole of Stone, by the unlearned the *Cornish Pebble*, whose huge bulk lifting itself high in air, is seen for miles before it is approached . . . Nothing can be more striking than the appearance of this object. It diffused around it the magic influence ascribed by the poet to these druidical remains;
>
> > . . . 'And aw'd our souls,
> > 'As if the very Genius of the place
> > 'Himself appear'd, and with terrific tread
> > 'Stalk'd through his drear domain.'
>
> Highly appropriate to its tremendous character is the savage spot on which it stands. The first idea that impressed our minds on approaching it, was the *gloomy nature* of that superstition which had selected such a desert for its rites, the focal point of solitude and desolation, where nothing met the eye around but nature in her primaeval rudeness; vast rocks of granite starting out of the ground, of every form, and in every direction; occupying the same places, and maintaining the same positions into which they had been thrown, by the last general convulsion of our planet. But, however extraordinary these individual masses might have appeared to us, had they been seen independently of the Tolmen, our attention was almost entirely occupied, and our wonder entirely absorbed, by this superlative object; which, like Milton's Satan,
>
> > . . . 'Above the rest,
> > 'In shape and gesture proudly eminent,
> > 'Stood like a tower.'[20]

Some forty years later Wilkie Collins would describe another Cornish landscape in very similar terms, so habitual had the sublime interpretation of prehistoric remains become. His evocation of the terrain near the Cheese-Wring and The Hurlers, near Liskeard, is, if anything, more of an invitation to the landscape painter than Warner's, but the same litany of barren landscape, convulsive nature and primaeval man is very much in place.

> We now left the tram-way, and stood again on the moor – on a wild and lonelier part of it than we had yet beheld . . . The whole plain appeared like the site of an ancient city of palaces, overthrown and crumbled into atoms by an earthquake . . . No human beings were discernible anywhere; the majestic loneliness and stillness of the scene were almost oppressive both to eye and

ear . . . Everywhere, the view had an impressively stern, simple, aboriginal look. Here were tracts of solitary country which had sturdily retained their ancient character through centuries of revolution and change; plains pathless and desolate even now, as when Druid processions passed over them by night to the place of the secret sacrifice, and skin-clad warriors of old Britain halted on them in council, or hurried across them to the fight.[21]

In descriptions like these, as district from the more sober, archaeologically influenced topographical guides, the prevailing descriptive mode for prehistoric structures was one of oratorical excess, invoking mystery, sublimity and remoteness in a welter of romantic rhetoric. Poets and poetasters alike seem to have felt duty bound to surround their local antiquities with an atmosphere of doom and superstition. Wordsworth, for example, in his *Guide Through the District of the Lakes*, although aware that the surprise he had experienced when he first saw Long Meg and her Daughters might have led him to over-rate its importance, nevertheless provides his readers with a full-blown exercise in romantic appreciation of the stone circle.

A weight of awe not easy to be borne
Fell suddenly upon my spirit, cast
From the dread bosom of the unknown past,
When first I saw that sisterhood forlorn;
And Her, whose strength and stature seemed to scorn
The power of years – pre-eminent, and placed
Apart, to overlook the circle vast.
Speak, Giant-mother! tell it to the Morn,

While she dispels the cumbrous shades of night;
Let the Moon hear, emerging from a cloud,
When, how, and wherefore, rose on British ground
That wondrous Monument, whose mystic round
Forth shadows, some have deemed, to mortal sight
The inviolable God that tames the proud.[22]

The attraction of this sort of thinking for artists was immediate and profound and resulted in a tendency to exploit the ineffable aspects of such monuments when depicting them. This is not to deny that more prosaic, topographically 'objective' views were also produced, as indeed one can point to less rhapsodic descriptions of antiquities in tourist guides, but it is to acknowledge that the dominating tendency within pictorial representation of British antiquities as subjects for serious painting was one of imaginative projection. The invocation of the Sublime, and similar romantic or quasi-romantic strategies allowed Stonehenge and other monuments to exist not simply as sites in the landscape but as sites within the imagination. The rhetoric that clothes them is a means whereby their mute and baffling presence can be translated out of their topographical situation into a realm of power, mystery and the primaeval.

Furthermore, as a means of finding an artistic subject in 'unpicturesque' prehistoric remains an additional heightening of effect was well nigh essential. Treated sublimely, the stones themselves, instead of providing a dull grey centre to the

103 William Andrews Nesfield, *Circle of Stones at Tormore, Isle of Arran* 1828, watercolour, 25.4 x 30.5 cm. The Victoria and Albert Museum, London.

composition could be activated by light to become the brightest part of the picture, their unpicturesque arrangement could be organised through contrasts of light and shade, while meteorological drama added the necessary vivifying spark to animate the remains. If we compare William Nesfield's *Circle of Stones at Tormore, Isle of Arran* (Plate 103) with J.B. Pyne's *The Druidical Circle, Keswick*

104 James Baker Pyne, *Druidical Circle, near Keswick*, 1848, watercolour, 33.5 x 50.5 cm. Manchester City Art Galleries.

(Plate 104) it is clear that Nesfield's presentation is an over-dramatised but much more effective performance when contrasted with the more sober renditions of these sites required by topography. The need for a dramatic presentation was particularly acute for prehistoric monuments whose size and arrangement lacked the residual nobility of Stonehenge, say, or Callanish. Approached from a distance, most megaliths seemed mean and devoid of pictorial interest; close to, their bland grey surfaces held far less appeal than the crumbling masonry and shattered battlements of later ruins. The surrounding landscape was often featureless and dull. Small wonder, then, that painters might rely on extremes of weather or strongly contrasted effects of light to enliven their pictures.

In similar vein landscape artists would often represent Stonehenge or similar monuments such that they were detached from their surroundings and depicted instead with the power and immediacy of a close-up view. This had the benefit of avoiding the belittling effect of topography, where the attempt to portray the entire site would often require that it be displayed on a relatively diminutive scale. Approaching megalithic structures from a distance was often a disappointing experience; discovered too early and from too far away, their grey humped forms could be fatally trivialised and their sublimity badly compromised in consequence. Coming in close to the megaliths, on the other hand, gave the impression of greater height and a more massive construction and forced their grandeur on the eye. At Stonehenge, the optimum position was standing among the stones, or close to them, with their colossal immediacy providing a dramatic contrast between the monument and the emptiness of Salisbury Plain. (Is not our frustration at the site today, fenced off and forced to view it from a distance as we are, a nostalgic regret for this lost experience?) Thomas Jones, had noted in the summer of 1769 that the isolation of Stonehenge in such a barren spot helped explain its effect, which might be lost in combination with a landscape itself remarkable.

> . . . that Stupendous Monument of remote Antiquity – I can not help thinking, but that it's Situation adds much to it's grandeur and Magnificence, the vast surrounding Void not affording any thing to disturb the Eye, or divert the imagination, or any Scale whereby to judge of it's comparative magnitude but the flocks and Herds – Whereas, were this wonderful Mass situated amidst high rocks, lofty mountains, and hanging Woods – however it might contribute to the richness of the scene in general – would lose much of it's own grandeur as a Single Object – The Experiment is easily tried upon Canvass.[23]

Those travel accounts which allow Stonehenge to emerge out of mist or darkness are making the same point in literary terms: Stonehenge is visualised as surrounded by a blankness, from which it erupts forcefully and entire. Edward Clarke visited the monument in 1791.

> . . . notwithstanding the rebuffs of the rain and the wind, [we] had spirit enough of the antiquarian to venerate and admire this stupendous monument of our forefathers. In the middle of a barren plain, where hardly a tree is visible, or any vestige of human habitation, these gigantic pillars of stone present their aged bosoms to the astonished spectator.[24]

105 Thomas Girtin, *Stonehenge during a Thunderstorm*, 1794, watercolour over pencil with pen, 10.5 x 14.8 cm. The Ashmolean Museum, Oxford.

Carrying a reader across this blankness is relatively easy; Clarke's vocabulary signifies levels and degrees of emptiness and prepares us for the looming presence of the monument amidst this waste, but we are not shown Stonehenge prematurely across this written description of a barren plain. The eye, however, unlike the imagination, cannot be so circumscribed, as spectators we cannot choose but see what lies in front of us, foreground and distance alike, and we need therefore to be offered an immediate encounter with the megaliths, as though the journey to them was effaced, if their maximum impact is not to be lost. We can witness such an approach put into practice quite literally in Richard Fenton's account of a visit to Stonehenge in the autumn of 1807.

> . . . we had not got many miles before our conductor ordered a halt, insisting, for reasons he was certain we should hereafter approve of, that we should contrive to proceed the remainder of the road with the blinds of our chaise up; a motion we most cheerfully complied with. Thus in darkness and durance we travelled rapidly for a few miles, till our captain, with a most majestic tone, issued the word of command, 'Stop, down with the blinds;' when, lo! we found ourselves within the area of the gigantic peristyle of Stonehenge. In every approach to this stupendous pile, particularly that which we took, it is seen for some miles before you reach it, and every eye will discover it too soon; so that on this extended plain at such a distance it appears nothing, and by the time you are at it all astonishment ceases; but when it burst suddenly and all at once on the eye, as it did on ours, not familiarized by a graduated approximation, the effect is wonderful.[25]

Yet this expedient and its equivalent in the melodramatic presentations of some paintings should not in every case be dismissed as mere bombast designed to titivate an otherwise unrewarding spectacle. Thomas Girtin's small watercolour of 1794 (Plate 105) strips away almost all landscape context for the structure, vividly contrasting a close-up view with a violent thunderstorm overhead.[26] The barren foreground and the cursory indication of sheltering sheep amidst the stones propel the image from the topographical realm to the elemental. Stonehenge loses its specific locale through such compression and becomes instead almost a cipher, encoding much more general and essential matters than merely topographical or antiquarian detail. Seen with this immediacy, against a threatening sky, Britain's antiquities are reduced to an almost emblematic presentation of human endeavour withstanding the onslaught of time. For it is above all that quality of stolid endurance that marks the rhetoric and the visual depiction of these monuments. Their remote situation and exposure to the elements become tokens of a titanic struggle between the forces of nature and the vestiges of human culture.

The discomfort experienced by some tourists in visiting these sites is included in their accounts as an earlier devotee might have shown his pilgrim's badge; to truly come to terms with the awesome spectacle of Stonehenge one needed to experience some of the forces arrayed against it, to take upon oneself a sort of penitential sacrifice. The topographical artist and writer John Hassell wrote an extended account of Stonehenge based on his visit there c.1787–8, concentrating particularly on the physical situation of the monument and the ravages of time. All the elements are present to position his reader within an associative framework of barren landscape, inclement weather, age and oblivion. In this context Stonehenge is as much a spur to meditation as it is an object of antiquarian study.

> . . . throughout the whole of the way between Salisbury and Stonehenge, a space of nearly nine miles, I will venture to say I never beheld a more comfortless extension of uncouth, barren, unpicturesque subject in my life. . . . During the storm, a poor old shepherd, whose appearance was almost as antiquated, and rather more defaced by time than the stones themselves, retired to them for shelter from the turbulence of the weather . . . As we left the place, we could not help drawing a comparison between the hoary inhabitant of these downs, and the venerable remains of antiquity by which he stood. While one at the age of seventy-five was bending under the weight of age and infirmity, his fellow natives of the plains, remained nearly in the same state they had done for more than seventeen hundred years; and seemed likely to withstand the ravages of time for a much longer period.[27]

Standing in a landscape removed from everyday experience it is as though the traveller, and the reader, hold their normal life in abeyance whilst investigating this other timescale. The sublime approach to Stonehenge and related monuments thus encourages their presentation as emblems of time, decay and man's insignificance in the cosmic scale. Stonehenge is *the* image of antiquity in the British imagination precisely because its origins are so obscure, and it rivals the ruins of Egypt, Greece and Rome not because of any poignancy we might feel for vanished glories but for the simple fact of enduring century after century. Samuel Bowden's topographical poem *Antiquities and Curiosities in Wiltshire and Somerset* (1733) talked memorably of the impact of Stonehenge on the poet, 'lost in the Circle of devouring Days'.[28] The same point was made quite explicitly in the final plate for Rudolph Ackermann's publication *The English Dance of Death* (Plate 106) where a structure closely modelled on Stonehenge occupies the background, and thus the most remote period, in a landscape littered with Time's victims.[29]

106 Thomas Rowland-son, *Time, Death and Eternity*, nd (engraved for Rudolph Ackermann, *The English Dance of Death*, London, 1816), pen over pencil, 12.4 x 19.3 cm. The Henry E. Huntington Library and Art Gallery.

We encounter this temporal dimension again in the opening stanza of T.S. Salmon's Oxford English Verse prize poem for 1823, *On Stonehenge*.

> Wrapt in the veil of time's unbroken gloom,
> Obscure as death, and silent as the tomb,
> Where cold oblivion holds her dusky reign,
> Frowns the dark pile on Sarum's lonely plain.[30]

Similarly, as Louis Hawes has suggested, the hare running towards us in Constable's great watercolour of Stonehenge (Plate 107) may have been added to contrast the

107   John Constable, *Stonehenge*, 1835, watercolour, 38.7 x 59.1 cm. The Victoria and Albert Museum, London.

fleetingness of everyday life with the vastness of the elemental timescale suggested by the lowering sky which threatens the monument.[31] Constable's own text, accompanying the picture when it was exhibited at the Royal Academy in 1836 certainly hints as much.

> The mysterious monument of Stonehenge, standing remote on a bare and boundless heath, as much unconnected with the events of past ages as it is with the uses of the present, carries you back beyond all historical records into the obscurity of a totally unknown period.

As has frequently been pointed out, Constable's 'bare and boundless heath' seems to echo aspects of Shelley's *Ozymandias*, first published in 1818, whose meditation on the vanity of human aggrandisement and cultural ambition ends with these lines

> . . . Round the decay
> Of that colossal wreck, boundless and bare
> The lone and level sands stretch far away.

The futility of man's temporary achievement when set against the crushing pressure of aeon following aeon makes Constable's *Stonehenge* almost a species of vanitas painting, with the double rainbow perhaps signifying divine grace, a more lasting and worthwhile treasure than the puny efforts of mankind to combat eternity.[32]

Those artists who approached megalithic structures imaginatively rather than topographically offered a context of colossal energies and the passage of time that seems to hint at a growing awareness of the remoteness of prehistory. Although it would be foolish to imply that artists were avid readers of the latest geological and archaeological research, we need to remember that the investigation of time via the agency of the geological record was a matter of general public interest in this period. The slowly dawning realisation that the earth itself was far older than the Biblical record and that man himself had a prehistory of many thousands of years is, as we have already seen, part of a widespread alteration in thinking about prehistory in the late eighteenth and nineteenth centuries.[33] Of course, no artist working before 1850 would have had any inkling of the true age of megalithic architecture, but the repetitive insistence on prehistoric remains somehow fighting it out with the elements from time immemorial offers the spectator a different sense of time, almost outside of history, than the 'correct' chronologies debated by antiquarians and historians. Similarly, but carrying the poetic connotation in the opposite direction, the habitual eighteenth- and early nineteenth-century association of the most archaic epochs of British history with Celtic Britons is carried over into geological nomenclature. In 1835 Sir Roderick Impey Murchison designated the so-called 'grauwacke' palaeozoic strata he had studied in the Wye Valley after the original Celtic inhabitants of that area: '. . . seeing that the region in which the best types of [formation] occurred was really the country of the Silures of the old British King Caractacus, I adopted that name [Silurian].'[34] Murchison's nomenclature, which included a 'Caradoc' subdivision, was followed in 1879 by Charles Lapworth, who designated the stratum between Murchison's 'Silurian' and Sedgwick's 'Cambrian' as 'Ordovician', after another Celtic tribe, the Ordovices of north Wales. The deliberate choice by geologists of a historical rather than a natural name to classify these strata is surely significant. The identification of geological features with Ancient British tribes is, of course, an imaginative conceit but it is a conceit whose appropriateness depends on a habit of mind that was by now deeply ingrained. Although few if any Victorians would have confused geological with historical time many would have understood Murchison and Lapworth's coinages as appropriate precisely because the Ancient Briton and monuments such as Stonehenge were as primordial historically as the strata christened in their honour were geologically.

As Roy Porter has remarked, with reference to the vogue for 'scientific' poetry and landscape painting in the late eighteenth and early nineteenth centuries; 'The rise of this Sublime and Romantic appreciation of scenery is inseparable from that rich form of analysis of the Earth in terms of great antiquity, the majesty of slow and profound process, the investigation of subterranean depths, which is the geological way of seeing.'[35]

The use of the sublime mode for depicting prehistoric antiquities was equally fortuitous in its openness to a cosmic scale of operation, suggesting vast chronologies in the presence of these prehistoric antiquities. Because this suggestion is necessarily imprecise, working through connotation and displacement, the opening up of a wider timescale cannot, as it were, be checked or calibrated and so provokes an infinite recoil into the primordial. Significantly, artists had found a poetic device to signify the remoteness of prehistory in a period when time itself was changing shape and definition, so that the hyperbolic antiquity of the megaliths signalled by the Sublime transcends their recognised historical limits and hints at a vaster time-frame. New geological and archaeological thinking was developing an expanded chronological field within which the dates of British prehistoric remains could become truly primaeval, but the artistic portrayal of these monuments as relics of such a primaeval era had, as it were, almost anticipated this new thinking long before the evidence was available to justify it. Poetic truth had outrun the patient research of scientific method.

Constable's painting, for all its technical brilliance and imaginative approach is nevertheless responding to and continuing something of a traditional formula for the representation of Stonehenge. As we have seen, the invocation of a sublime approach required the venerable stones, fitfully illuminated by strongly contrasted sunlight, to be positioned against a stormy sky. Shepherds or solitary travellers heighten the sense of loneliness and provide a convenient yardstick, as Thomas Jones had noted, with which to judge the scale of the monument, emphasising its isolation on a barren plain, open and exposed to the fury of the elements. In paintings of Stonehenge and similar monuments it is indeed this quality of desolation that is most often emphasised. Turner's *Stonehenge* (Plate 108), exhibited at the Egyptian Hall, Piccadilly, in 1829, is perhaps the apogee of this approach, trembling on the very edge of excess in its portrayal of death and the terrors of nature. Ruskin believed that the lightning indicated God's judgement on the Druidical religion which is an attractive, if fanciful, hypothesis. On that plain of Salisbury, [Turner] had been struck first by its widely-spacious pastoral life; and secondly, by its monuments of the two great religions of England – Druidical and Christian.

108   Robert Wallis after J.M.W. Turner, *Stonehenge* (*c.* 1827), 1829, engraving for *Picturesque Views in England and Wales.*

He was not a man to miss the possible connection of these impressions. He treats the shepherd life as a type of the ecclesiastical; and composes his two drawings so as to illustrate both.

In the drawing of Salisbury, the plain is swept by rapid but not distressful rain. The cathedral occupies the centre of the picture, towering high over the city, of which the houses . . . are scattered about it like a flock of sheep . . . In the foreground stands a shepherd leaning on his staff, watching his flock . . . Turn now to the Stonehenge. That, also, stands in great light; but it is the Gorgon light – the sword of Chrysaor is bared against it. The cloud of judgement hangs above. The rock pillars seem to reel before its slope, pale beneath the lightning. And nearer, in the darkness, the shepherd lies dead, his flock scattered.[36]

Symbolism apart, the association of barrenness and cosmic violence with the site is typical of the sublime approach engendered by the emotional impact of Stonehenge itself. It is almost as if these stark depictions functioned as objective correlatives for the imaginative turmoil provoked by this most ancient and incomprehensible of British monuments.

The sublime rhetoric that made such remains artistically possible was also a rhetoric somehow suitable for their imagined Druidic connection. Ruskin's over-determined reading of Turner's *Stonehenge* is probably too literal but it is likely that storms, barren wilderness and suffering staffage connoted in the most general sense impressions of paganism, dark powers and even damnation. Louis Hawes

186

109   James Giles, *The Weird Wife*, 1831, oil on canvas, 80 x 116.9 cm, Royal Scottish Academy, Edinburgh, Diploma Collection.

quotes a sonnet on Stonehenge by 'C.H.', first published in 1828, which articulates perfectly these associations of Druidical terror.

> Mysterious pile, what necromantic lore
> Evoked thee into light? Moons wax and wane,
> The Roman, and the Saxon, and the Dane
> Have wandered where the Druids long of yore
> Purpled thy circles with unhallowed gore;
> Cities and realms have vanished, while in vain
> On thee descend the thunder and the rain.
> And twice ten hundred winters round thee roar.
> Yet vaunt not, giant wonder![37]

The strong association of Druidism with megalithic sites meant that on occasion the boundary between landscape and history or genre painting might be crossed, as for example in James Giles's *Weird Wife* (Plate 109) where a mysterious figure animates a prehistoric site in a tangible reminiscence of Druidism and the supernatural. Giles's inclusion of this cowled woman is of the same order as Wilkie Collins's ruminations on the aboriginal inhabitants of Cornwall quoted above, as though speculation on the monument had engendered some visionary glimpse of another epoch. There is something here of that sentiment devotees of M.R. James have come to treasure, the suspicion that the secure world of present reality is paper thin and that at particular sites, associated with older and darker beliefs, this fragile membrane is liable to rupture, collapsing the present into the past.

Debate over the origins and purpose of prehistoric antiquities was still active throughout the eighteenth and even the nineteenth centuries with champions of British, Roman and Scandinavian origins all presenting evidence for their suppositions. Increasingly, however, the association of such monuments with a Celtic British past had become the received opinion and the majority of travel writers referred to dolmens, stone circles and menhirs as relics of Druidical religion. As the promoter of a system of judgement which relied heavily on purely pictorial criteria, Gilpin would not admit such adventitious speculations to dominate his aesthetic responses to Stonehenge, yet within the realm of taste, the aesthetic response to prehistoric antiquities, carefully distinguished by Gilpin from his reactions to them as relics of history, was increasingly informed by historical and cultural knowledge. The publication of Archibald Alison's *Essays on the Nature and Principles of Taste* (1790) aimed to demonstrate how our responses to material reality can never be free of knowledge, such that the pleasure or disgust we experience in front of something will always be conditioned by our understanding of it. Alison's doctrine of association helped legitimise again that antiquarian tendency which had existed in literary and pictorial approaches to the monuments for some years. The invocation of Druidical worship, with its attendant horror and fascination, when confronted with prehistoric sites was not, after all, a discovery of the 1790s, and the fusing of aesthetic and associative responses is caught, for example, in John Macpherson's description of stone circles in the Western Isles.

> There is something agreeably romantic in the situations chosen for these temples. The scene is frequently melancholy and wild, the prospect is extensive but not diversified. A fountain and the noise of a distant river were always esteemed as requisite neighbours for those feats of dark and enthusiastic religion.[38]

The last line of this description moves the account from present experience of wild and melancholy landscape to an awareness of the circles' origins, such that both factors contribute to the 'agreeably romantic' sensation. Associationism was certainly a useful corrective to narrowly founded aesthetic theories like Gilpin's and we must assume that landscape paintings containing prehistoric remains produced in this period would have carried an associative charge of Druid worship for most spectators. Gilpin's approach, which had allowed associations to contribute in very much a secondary role, is challenged here by a more cognitive reaction where association assumes a primary importance. In *The Beauties of Wiltshire* (1813), the Wiltshire topographer and antiquarian John Britton based his approach to Stonehenge on just such a cognitive response and was thus able to admit the aesthetic limitations of the site without in any way demeaning or diminishing its impact. In fact, Britton's account could almost have been written as a point by point refutation of Gilpin's picturesque criticisms of Stonehenge.

> At a distance this monument appears only a small, trifling object; for its bulk and character are lost in the vastness of the open space around it. On a nearer approach, and closer examination, it commonly fails to astonish, or even to satisfy the stranger. People generally visit it with exaggerated prepossessions;

110   Julius Caesar Ibbetson, *Costume of the Peasantry in the Island of Anglesea - behind the group, a Druidical Cromlech, Snowdon in the distance*, n.d., pen and watercolour, 21.8 x 28.2 cm. Private collection.

and imagination always exceeds reality. As a mere object of sight, Stonehenge is not calculated to make a strong or extraordinary impression on the mind of the common observer. It must be viewed with the eye of the antiquary or artist; and contemplated by a mind fully stored with historical knowledge to be properly understood and appreciated. To such a person it cannot fail to afford consummate interest and pleasure.[39]

Association could transform particular sites to the point where responses to history and to physical reality were completely interfused. It should be seen, therefore, as the perfect distillation of antiquarian enthusiasm, the apogee of that sympathetic involvement with antiquity, bringing together factual and imaginative approaches to bring the past to life. As such, it is very much an eighteenth-century phenomenon whose survival into the 1830s looked increasingly whimsical when compared with a more rigorous archaeology and whose disappearance, as we have seen, was lamented by Crabbe.

The impact of associationism can be seen as further reinforcement of that tendency to telescope time by bringing together elements of the present and the past as examples of a living continuity within British culture. J.C. Ibbetson provides an exemplary instance of this approach in one of his designs for James Baker's *Picturesque Guide through Wales and the Marches* (1794) (Plate 110). It is

111 John Sell Cotman, *Devil's Den, Wiltshire c. 1802–3*, watercolour on paper, 16.3 x 21.1 cm. The Frances Lehman Loeb Art Center, Vassar College.

entitled *Costume of the peasantry in the island of Anglesea – behind the group, a druidical cromlech, Snowdon in the distance*, which itemisation can be read as a physical enactment of a chain of associations. Contemporary Welsh peasants are positioned in front of the Plas Newydd cromlech as though this relationship was self-explanatory as a demonstration of lineage. Once this link has been made, the association of cromlechs with Druidism brings in its train an invocation of bards whose sacred precinct was Snowdon. Furthermore, as we have seen, the extermination of the Druids on Anglesey by the Romans could be mapped onto the extermination of the bards by Edward I. Ibbetson's design functions like an emblem, triggering associations in the mind of the well-read viewer.

Meanings and associations proliferated around these monuments precisely because their historical co-ordinates were not fixed. Even today the chronology, purpose and construction of megalithic sites is a matter of some dispute. Before the advent of systematic archaeological excavation, radio-carbon dating and the full panoply of techniques now brought to bear on prehistoric culture it was impossible to discriminate with any refinement between rival theories. The transition, therefore, between topographical and imaginative landscapes was easily accomplished if only because the definition of prehistoric culture was so fluid. As we have seen with reference to Stonehenge, the rhetorical utilisation of storm and darkness, whether written or painted, acts to detach the motif from any normal relationship with the world. Whereas topography seeks to position a site within a precise historical and geographical framework, the sublime landscape transcends the normal fixing of place and time such that prehistoric sites are propelled into an imaginative world free of such mundane triangulation. Poetic association, unrecorded time and cosmic drama are the constituents of a realm marked by imprecision, metaphor and suggestion.

We can see this particularly clearly in a group of four watercolours by John Sell

190

112   John Sell Cotman, *The House of the Three Stones, Llanberris, c.* 1803, wash and pencil on white paper, 19.2 x 29.7 cm. University of Michigan Museum of Art.

Cotman, all produced around 1801–4. Cotman's *Devil's Den* (Plate 111) depicts the neolithic cromlech still standing in Clatford Bottom, near Marlborough, and was painted for his Wiltshire patron, John Britton.[40] Its stark and monumental appearance shows the extent to which Cotman was participating in that sublime approach to prehistoric antiquity already evident in the work of Hearne and Girtin. The brooding and atmospheric quality of this watercolour is evident again in Cotman's *House of the Three Stones, Llanberris* (Plate 112). This is a drawing of a natural feature rather than a prehistoric antiquity but Cotman's approach to it seems to emphasise the connotation of Druidic Cyclopean architecture evident in its local name.[41] Certainly his presentation of both sites shares a uniform interest in the massiveness of the rock, the power of the construction and the remoteness and desolation of the surroundings. Both of these watercolours thus emphasise that association of primaeval features with wilderness and desolation found in the written accounts of this period. Two drawings produced at meetings of the Sketching Society show Cotman developing this imaginative approach towards a highly poetic interpretation.[42] The first of these (Plate 113), dated 23 March 1803, takes its subject from Ossian, illustrating the lines

> We bend toward the voice of the King.
> The Moon looks abroad from her cloud:
> The grey-skirted Mist is near – the Dwelling of Ghosts.

Here, the hints of sepulchral gloom and weird rites immanent within the sublime approach to prehistoric monuments are realised in the eerie figures who make their obeisance to a remotely sited tomb marker. Given that Ossianic heroes lived in a pagan world, it is curious that Cotman should have included a cross here. Nevertheless, its looming presence and bulky proportions surely owe something to primitive, menhir-like forms and the primaeval is interfused with it in equal

191

113 John Sell Cotman, *Weird Scene: We bend towards the voice of the King*, 1803, monochrome watercolour, 21.2 x 31.4 cm. The British Museum, London.

114 John Sell Cotman, *Behold yon Oak*, 1804, pencil and grey wash on buff laid paper, 31.2 x 44.7 cm. Norfolk Museums Service (Norwich Castle Museum).

measure. Necessarily, Ossianic subject matter could not be located in real space or time and its imaginative presentation here should remind us of the similarly allusive approach used in depictions of megalithic monuments. As with the lack of hard historical knowledge about genuine examples of prehistoric culture, so the very imprecision of Macperson's descriptions was an invitation to the imagination, for no 'historical' restrictions of accuracy could apply to a period of such remoteness, no one interpretation could be privileged over another.

The second of these Sketching Society drawings is dated 26 January 1804, and takes its subject from the first act of Mason's *Caractacus* (Plate 114).

> Behold yon oak,
> How stern he frowns, and with his broad brown arms
> Chills the pale plain beneath him: mark yon altar,
> The dark stream brawling round its rugged base:
> These cliffs, these yawning caverns, this wide circus,
> Skirted with unhewn stone . . .

In this drawing the imaginative and poetic approach to British antiquity reaches the heights of sublimity. A superbly gnarled and blasted oak dominates the foreground, while behind are grouped the megalithic stones that constitute the Druids' sacred site. The image is of a piece with Cotman's Ossianic subject in its heroising approach, its invocation of the macabre and its sense of pictorial drama. It is the finest example of the way in which an imaginative artist could work with the bombast and rhetoric surrounding megaliths and the subject of Druidism to produce work of dreamlike intensity.

Chapter Nine

GARDEN DESIGN AND THE PREHISTORIC PAST

The eighteenth century saw the rise of the landscape garden as a symbolically ordered environment whose careful design, incorporating the placement of specific motifs, might provoke the interested spectator to instructive contemplation. The 'meaning' of particular gardens was most often made apparent by the inclusion of built structures; their identity and position within a design acted rather like staffage in painting to deliver a message or point a moral. These structures, at first fanciful and somewhat frivolous, were soon deployed in a more rigorous presentation as gardens began to take on a more serious purpose than that of mere recreation. The harbinger of this change was Richard Grenville, Earl Temple, who continued his uncle Lord Cobham's work at Stowe from 1749. The Temple he added to the Grecian Valley was a close imitation of actual Greek examples and can be said to have initiated a more accurate, archaeological approach in the design of similar garden ornaments.[1] Thenceforward many of the more prestigious British gardens would include at least one carefully designed emblem of the past as a spur to meditation and reverie. The cult of the past allowed, indeed promoted contemplation of the relics of antiquity, and their metonymic presence in landscape gardens is of a piece with the growth of archaeology and antiquarianism in this period.

Necessarily, given the overwhelming dominance of classical education and the stature of classical art within contemporary aesthetics, the vast majority of all such structures were intended to evoke the culture of Greece and Rome. Classical architecture, in combination with a cunningly designed mise-en-scène of water, lawn and plantation, provoked a heady combination of nostalgia, exhortation and example for the interested spectator. It hardly needs pointing out that the inclusion of prehistoric remains in landscaped gardens was a response to a quite different set of values; cromlechs and stone circles could not be considered remotely comparable to these classicising schemes, either as specimens of architecture or as tokens of a lost culture. Although megaliths could take their place in histories of architecture and in speculations about the dawn of human culture, prehistoric remains could not provide a lesson in architectural ideals, nor were their forms capable of evoking a vision of Arcadian perfection. Nevertheless, their powers of association were every bit as pungent on a small scale as the porticoes, rotundas and bridges of classical revival and we should make some attempt to understand the development and rationale of the prehistoric garden motif.

Garden designers were not, of course, restricted to classical forms, as is evidenced by the occasional use of Gothic and other motifs in landscaped gardens; the ruinous condition and irregular form of Gothic architecture might be used to add a picturesque note to the scene whilst simultaneously reminding the spectator of the tattered remnants of the British mediaeval past. But it goes without saying that Gothic and especially prehistoric features were relatively impoverished in their references when compared to the wealth of cultural tradition enshrined in classical forms. However, if we accept that many visitors to even the most elaborate classical schemes were tourists who may have responded superficially to their more abstruse meanings, then the comparative poverty of associative meanings conjured up by primitive schemes proves less of a weakness. In every case, Classical, Gothic or Druidic, the overriding function of such antique emblems was to stimulate meditation on the cultures that gave them birth, and at that level a cromlech might provoke reflection as successfully as a Doric peristyle.[2]

Considering the impact of Celtic and Druidic research on the late eighteenth-century mind it was almost inevitable that someone at least should have attempted to use prehistoric remains within a garden setting. It might indeed be argued that the shift in garden design sensibility from a precisely programmed intellectual meaning to a looser encouragement of mood, a shift established by the garden designs of Capability Brown in the 1760s and 1770s, provided the most appropriate moment for the inclusion of Druidical structures in landscaped gardens.

The few known instances of megalithic motifs in garden design are the subject of this chapter, and while their occurrence is sporadic and often marginal they indicate the existence of a little known aesthetic, a minor variant of the taste for the bizarre, to add to the better documented impact of Gothic and Chinese taste on the English garden.[3] They demonstrate, too, that interest in primitive British culture was manifest across the entire spectrum of the arts. As we have noted, familiarity with Celtic Britain was, by the close of the eighteenth century, not simply a matter of historical scholarship, the preserve of antiquarian enthusiasts alone, but a widely disseminated phenomenon which might be discerned in historiographical debate, book illustration, poetry, drama, painting and sculpture as well as in landscape gardening. The patrons of these prehistoric schemes and the public who visited them were thus pursuing a relatively orthodox interest within this larger context of widespread enthusiasm for archaic Britain.

The role of megalithic structures in gardens is complicated by their relationship to a number of ideas. As we have already seen, no one dominant view of the archaic past held sway in this period and in consequence a variety of different readings may have been occasioned by one and the same monument. Most garden motifs were open to ambiguous readings, but prehistoric ensembles in particular gained in interpretative possibilities from the absence of reliable historical knowledge. Druidic temples, grottoes, circles and related structures were empty vessels into which could be poured a variety of different associative meanings, few of them mutually exclusive. Thus, from a purely architectural point of view a Druid's temple might exemplify the most primitive European architecture known, the first stage in the long progress towards civilised living. The more fanciful Druid's hut or Druid's grotto might also play a part in this historicist scheme, employing natural forms and minimally altered materials to demonstrate the infancy of architecture as the simplest structure. The association of Druids with extremely primitive shelters is made explicit in Inigo Jones's account of Stonehenge, where their indifference to architecture is used to prove that they could not have been its builders.

> The *Druid's* led a solitary contemplative life, contenting themselves with such habitations, as either meer necessity invented, to shelter them from contrariety of seasons, without *Art*, without *Order*, without any whatever means tending to perpetuity: or, such as *Nature* alone had prepared for them in dens, and caves of desert and darksome woods; esteeming it, questionlesse, the highest secret of their mystery, rather to command in caves and cottages, than live like Kings, in Palaces, and stately houses.[4]

Something of this attitude is revealed in the Duke of Norfolk's plan to restore the Deepdene to its primaeval state of dense woodland. Extensive planting was carried out from the 1760s to the 1780s, in a bid to transform the coombe near Dorking which forms the garden into a living memorial of a place where he believed ancient rituals had taken place.[5]

Equally, however, primitive architecture associated with the Druids, especially megalithic structures, might be seen from an aesthetic rather than historicist standpoint, since it possessed all the qualities of irregularity and abandonment that made ruins so attractive. William Shenstone's *Unconnected Thoughts on Gardening* (first published in 1764) summed up a common attitude in declaring

> RUINATED structures appear to derive their power of pleasing, from the irregularity of surface, which is VARIETY; and the latitude they afford the imagination, to conceive an enlargement of their dimensions, or to recollect any events or circumstances appertaining to their pristine grandeur, so far as concerns grandeur or solemnity . . .[6]

Thomas Whately went further in his *Observations on Modern Gardening* (first published in 1770), speculating in detail on how similar feelings might be occasioned by sham ruins

> Whatever building we see in decay, we naturally contrast its present to its former state, and delight to ruminate on the comparison. It is true that such effects properly belong to real ruins; but they are produced in a certain degree by those which are fictitious; the impressions are not so strong, but they are exactly similar; and the representation, though it does not present facts to the memory, yet suggests subjects to the imagination: but in order to affect the fancy, the supposed original design should be clear, the use obvious, and the form easy to trace; . . . the mind must not be allowed to hesitate; it must be hurried away from examining into the reality, by the exactness and the force of the resemblance . . .[7]

The simple forms of megalithic remains and the limited number of functional explanations provided for them meant that they could be easily simulated, answering all of Whately's strictures on imitation. As ruins, therefore, megalithic remains would stand as reminders of decay, damaged by centuries of exposure to the elements, rather than as crude structures left as their makers had intended them. Such a reaction would become less tenable as primitivist delight in elemental structures gained ground over the idea of deterioration, but the idea of 'restored' monuments never entirely disappeared and that idea necessarily implied that megalithic structures are damaged relics from the archaic past. As ruins megaliths might evoke the collapse of human endeavour, just as some landscape painters were perhaps suggesting when depicting the real thing, but unlike their originals, whose locations on bare uplands was proving problematic for artists, sham megaliths could enjoy a more picturesque setting within the confines of an established park.

Broadly speaking, we can divide prehistoric garden structures into two main categories. From the 1730s to the 1760s they are essentially a sub-species of the hermitage, a freakish no-style amalgam of coarse materials whose rough working signifies 'primitive'. From the 1770s a new taste develops for genuinely prehistoric-looking cromlechs and stone circles, whose meaning and purpose are derived from a more secure reference in extant remains. Although this bi-partite division is not absolutely clear cut, it provides a useful structure for the exposition which follows in this chapter.

With one or two exceptions the use of prehistoric imagery in early eighteenth-century garden settings was as part of a larger design or ensemble. The visitor would approach the Druidical structure while enjoying a leisurely progress through architectural and other associative reminders of many different periods or cultures. The archaic connotations of a particular motif were thus subsumed within a larger frame of miscellaneous experiences, with sometimes no more serious purpose than the stimulation of those reactions that are expected from today's visitors to Disneyworld. Richard Owen Cambridge caught the flavour of such farragoes in 1754.

> I remember the good time, when the price of a haunch of venison with a country friend was only half an hour's walk upon a hot terrace; a descent to the two square fish-ponds overgrown with a frog spawn; a peep into the hog-stye, or a visit to the pigeon-house. How reasonable was this, when compared with the attention now expected from you to the number of temples, pagodas, pyramids, grotto's, bridges, hermitages, caves, towers, hot-houses &c. &c.[8]

The playful mixing of Gothick, Hindu, Chinese and Classical structures in such gardens is the mark of their style and serves to distinguish them from more serious and programmatic schemes such as the landscape gardens at Rousham and Stowe. The fact that prehistoric features tend to be found in these sportive miscellanies serves at once to indicate the extent to which their appearance there is occasioned by curiosity and novelty rather than by intellectual concerns. Nevertheless, while their inclusion within such schemes may seem frivolous, their presence reminds us that Druids, dolmens and stone circles had become part of the historical furniture of the eighteenth-century mind by about 1740 and that visitors would have been expected to know what it was they were gazing at.

The mid 1730s provide the starting point for the inclusion of primitive structures in garden design and, as with ornamental structures as a whole, a suggestive and imaginative approach to the past dominates the first few decades before a more considered response, based on antiquarianism, offers an alternative to it. Thus, early enthusiasm for the primitive is expressed in playful references to sorcery, arcane knowledge and the legendary past and may be considered as launched with

Summer Hermitage.

Winter Hermitage.

115 Paul Decker, *Winter Heremitage*, engraving, in *Gothic Architecture Decorated*, London, 1746. The British Library, London.

the erection in 1735 of Merlin's Cave in Richmond Park. Designed by William Kent for Queen Caroline, this building has been seen as the *fons et origo* of all the hermit cells and rustic retreats to follow. By linking Merlin with primitive architecture – giving the building a beehive-like thatched roof reminiscent of the ancient British or Druidical houses pictured in antiquarian illustrations of the time – Kent seems to have sanctioned a like blurring of focus in the structures of other designers.[9] This association of primitive structures with the ancient history of Britain can be detected in visitors' reaction to the Hermitage or Ossian's Hall at Dunkeld House in Perthshire. The hermitage itself was completed in 1757, but the fourth Duke of Atholl refurbished it in 1783 with a mirror room, stage devices and paintings of Ossian by George Steuart. Although widely praised by visitors, some tourists complained, with justification, that it was not primitive enough and out of keeping with its wild situation above the falls of the river Braan. Stung by these criticisms, John MacCulloch, author of a guide to Dunkeld, pointed out that a comfortable room was preferable to 'sitting down on a damp stone and under rotten leaves, among rheumatisms and ear-wigs' and that tourists who required a more spartan reminder of Ossian should visit the nearby Ossian's Cave, a dolmen-like structure 'quite comfortless enough to satisfy the warmest ambition on this subject'.[10] The debate over Ossian's Hall indicates how taste was altering with a growing identification between primitive architecture and archaic Britain becoming the norm. This aesthetic coalesced with the existing iconography of primitive dwellings suitable for saints and hermits' meditations. For example, Paul Decker's *Winter Hermitage*, illustrated in his *Gothic Architecture Decorated* (Plate 115), employs the most primitive construction as a marker of its function and so underlines the association of crude structures with noetic isolation. For if contemplation

117 Thomas Wright, *Druid's Cell, or Arbour of the Hermitage Kind*, engraving, plate E of *Universal Architecture Book I, Six Original designs of Arbours*, London, 1755. The Victoria and Albert Museum, London.

116   Thomas Wright, *Grotto of the Bramage Kind*, engraving, plate I of *Universal Architecture Book II, Six original Designs of Grottos*, London, 1758. The Victoria and Albert Museum, London.

implies spatial removal from the social world in the choice of a remote setting, so its temporal flight from the contemporary could be signified in the choice of a primitive, even pre-architectrural building.

Thomas Wright's contribution to garden embellishment went further than Decker's modest primitivism and in his *Universal Architecture* (1755 and 1758) he included an arbour and a grotto with Druidical associations. The grotto, 'of the Bramage Kind, suppos'd to be the Habitation of a Bramin or Druid' (Plate 116) is generalising in its references, as one might expect from the variety of its designated occupants;[11] the arbour (Plate 117), on the other hand, is positioned next to a

menhir and a cromlech and makes its historical association clear. This 'Druid's Cell, or Arbour of the Hermitage Kind, purposely designed for a Study or philosophical Retirement' is itself an exercise in Gothick taste, but Wright's instructions for its location indicate that the context of ideas surrounding such a structure was already quite specific: '. . . the Situation required for it, must be near the Sea, or in the Neighbourhood of Rocks and Mountains, the wildest Face of Nature being the properest Accompanyment, as it partakes in some measure both of the Genus of the Cave and Grotto.'[12] Wright is a shadowy figure of the period. He was an architect and an astronomer about whom only a modest amount of information has survived. He had travelled in Ireland in the 1740s, publishing on his return one of the first surveys of Irish antiquities, *Louthiana – or an Introduction to the Antiquities of Ireland* (1748). He proposed but never published a sequel to this work entitled *Observations on Remains of Antiquity in Ireland*, a companion to a further unpublished study, *Observations on the Most Remarkable Remains of Antiquity Relating to the Druids, Romans and Saxons taken on a Tour through England*. This interest in archaic Britain was bolstered no doubt by the survey of the Stanton Drew stone circles Wright undertook for Lord Sandwich in the 1760s and fragmentary evidence of other aspects of his life bears this out. In his garden designs at Stoke Gifford, where he worked off and on for Lord Botetourt and the Duchess of Beaufort between 1749 and the early 1780s, Wright included a small arbour in a wood named Bladud's Temple, after the legendary son of Cunobelinus who founded Bath; and his own house, Byers Green Lodge, near Bishop Auckland, displayed in the dining room 'depictions of astronomical curiosities, the aurora borealis at Stonehenge, comets and eclipses'.[13]

It seems more than likely that Sir Charles Kemys-Tynte's Druid's Temple in the grounds of Halswell House, Somerset (1756) would have followed Wright and Decker's lead, especially as he subscribed to Wright's *Universal Architecture*. Although this structure has long since disappeared, Sir Charles' diary for 1756 reveals that the Druid's Temple was thatched,[14] and Arthur Young's description of 1772 hints at its overall appearance, set beside a stream in a thickly wooded grove: 'the Druid's temple, built, in a just stile, of bark, etc. the view quite gloomy and confined: the water winds silently along, except a little gushing fall, which hurts not the emotions raised by so sequestered a scene.'[15]

It is probable that Sir Francis Dashwood's Druid's Hut at West Wycombe (1760s) was also of this type.[16] Our regret for its loss can only be matched by our disappointment that he had not built it thirty years earlier when the speculation surrounding him and his Hell Fire Club cronies might have invented some exciting uses for it. At Stourhead, the architect Henry Flitcroft included a Druid's Cell in the building programme for Henry Hoare's garden and again we can see how the design is essentially poetic rather than specific in its references. In a letter of November 1771 Henry Hoare described the construction of the Druid's Cell (or Hermitage) on the zig-zag path leading up from the lake to the Temple of Apollo.

> It is to be lined inside and out with the old Gouty nobbly Oakes, the Bark on, which Mr Groves and my neighbours are so kind to give me; and Mr Chapman a clergyman showed me one yesterday called Judge Wyndham's Seat which I take to be of the year of our Lord one thousand, and I am not quite sure that it is Anti Diluvian. I believe I shall put in to be myself The Hermit.[17]

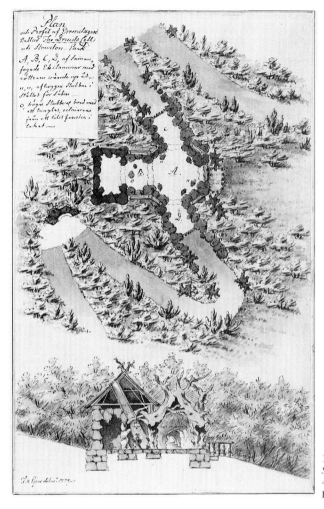

118   Frederik Magnus Piper, *Druid's Cell, Stourhead*, 1779, watercolour and ink, 43.5 x 28 cm, Kungl. Akademien för de Fria Konsterna, Stockholm.

Although the Druid's Cell was dismantled in 1814 we have a good idea of its appearance from the plan and section of it drawn by the Swedish artist F.M. Piper in 1779 (Plate 118). Piper shows Hoare's 'nobbly Oakes' and the rough masonry of the structure set amidst a bosky landscape and only the elegant balustrade, offering a vantage point over the lake towards Stourton, mars the primitive simplicity of the design.

At Hawkstone Hall, Shropshire, a more theatrical presentation of Druid life was on offer. Hawkstone was developed by Sir Richard Hill from 1783, building on the work of his father and grandfather who had begun to refashion the estate from about 1719. The Hawkstone Inn was opened in 1790 to cater for large numbers of tourists coming to view Sir Richard's 'curiosities', such as Neptune's Whim, Amphitrite's Flower-Garden, the Temple of Patience, the Swiss Bridge, the Scene at Otaheite, Reynard's Banqueting House and other delights.[18] Visitors to Grotto Hill were led into the gloomy recesses of its rock-hewn chambers and then entertained by the appearance of the Druid inhabitant, decked in laurels, with coloured light falling on his face. Richard Warner experienced the scene:

201

119   Thomas Sandby, *The Grotto Virginia Water*, c. 1780–90, watercolour over ink and pencil outline, 20.8 x 27.5 cm. Yale Center for British Art, Paul Mellon Collection.

Passing through another dark subterraneous cavern, we suddenly found ourselves at the entrance of a small chapel, where the light of purple hue, or rather 'darkness visible,' will just allow the eye to distinguish an altar, and other appropriate appendages. Whilst contemplating these, a venerable figure, clothed in the stole of a Druid, slowly pacing from a dark recess in the apartment, crossed before us to the altar made his obeisance, and departed; leaving us much surprised at, and almost ashamed of, the very singular impression which our minds could be made to experience, even from childish toys, if presented to them under particular circumstances.[19]

The shifting identification of all these structures is one of their most marked characteristics, with free association of ideas standing in for a definite aesthetic. The equation of archaic with primitive was stretched to allow many substitutions of ideas such that a Hermitage or Grotto might house a philosopher, an ascetic, a Druid or Merlin himself. All of these translations indicate the extent to which 'Druidic' and related concepts were as yet only provisionally defined in conceptual and architectural terms. Thomas Sandby seems to have further confused the issue when designing the Grotto or Robber's Cave (Plate 119) as part of his development of Virginia Water for Henry Frederick, the Duke of Cumberland, sometime in the 1780s. The huge stones from which the cave was formed had been dug up on

202

Bagshot Heath and were 'supposed to have belonged to a Druids' Temple', which feature Sandby retained in his orthostatic arrangement of some of them.[20] Josiah Lane did something similar for Lord Arundel at Wardour Castle in 1792, including monoliths from a nearby megalithic tomb at Tisbury when constructing a grotto. Lane was a grotto specialist and followed his father Joseph in that line of work, building a number of impressive structures in the south of England.[21] In 1794, working for William Beckford at Fonthill, Lane placed 'a rude erection in imitation of a Cromlech' above the Hermit's Cell he had constructed in the slope beside the lake. It is just possible that Lane again used megalithic remains in the grotto he constructed here, if the account of this grotto provided by the Richard Warner is reliable, for Warner describes it as being constructed from large unquarried rocks: 'The structure was formed of *tumblers* found near the spot; and although a little objectionable at first from a formality in its execution, it is now so broken and relieved by planting, as to afford a picturesque object to the eye.'[22]

The second category of Druidical structure, which comes into prominence in the 1770s, can be seen as more specific in its associations than the shadowy world of hermits, Druids and Merlin we have been examining so far. Instead we find the deliberate invocation of specific archaeological features from Britain's archaic past, a conscious emulation of extant remains. A handful of estates (among them Stonor, Temple Druid, Amesbury Abbey, Wilton, Plas Newydd and Strichen House) already possessed genuine prehistoric remains so that the inclusion of ancient British structures within the landscape was already accomplished, but there seems to be little evidence that these survivors were incorporated as garden features as prominently as their artificial cousins would be. In fact, the simulation of megalithic remains seems to be positioned mid-way between the inclusion of genuine prehistoric structures in estates and the construction of Druids' cells, blending a tolerable accuracy of form with a taste for the bizarre.

Three examples of simulated megaliths prefigure their popularity in the late eighteenth century. Near Batheaston stands the structure known as the Three Shire Stones, marking the conjunction of Gloucestershire, Wiltshire and Somerset. Erected in 1736, its structural form echoes that of a cromlech and its builders may have used genuine prehistoric megaliths to construct it.[23] A more ambitious project is recorded in Stukeley's preface to *Abury* (1743), dedicating his account of Avebury to the Earl of Pembroke, where he rather cheekily puffs his own 'fine and costly model of *Stonehenge*, which your lordship introduces in the garden at *Wilton*; where, I may be bold to say, it shines amidst the splendours of *Inigo Jones's* architecture'.[24] This venture is confirmed in a description of Wilton House written in 1759, where we learn that the Earl of Pembroke had indeed commissioned Stukeley to erect in the gardens 'a Stonehenge in Miniature, as 'twas supposed to have been in its first glory'. Pembroke had already used a prehistoric barrow to close a vista at Wilton and the house is, of course, situated very close to Stonehenge; he had had Stukeley survey the monument for him in 1719 but this scheme to reconstruct Stonehenge does not appear to have lasted in situ for any length of time.[25] Lord Glenorchy was more successful at Taymouth Castle in the 1750s, constructing one of the earliest bogus stone circle in the British Isles.[26] Generally, however, it was not until the late 1770s that a taste developed for artificial remains of this type.

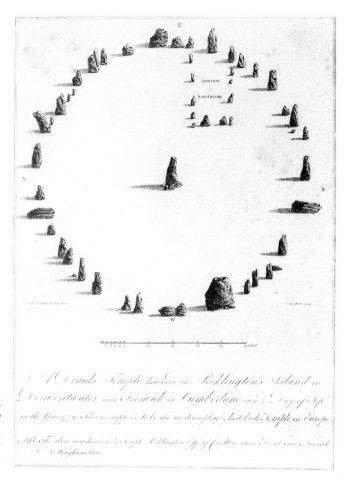

120 John Peltro after Joseph Pocklington, *A Druid's Temple discover'd on Pocklington's Island in Derwentwater*, 1779, engraving. Wiltshire Natural History and Archaeological Society Museum, Devizes.

One of the earliest appears to have been erected by Joseph Pocklington on an island in Derwentwater, developed between 1778 and 1783. Described as The Druid Temple it was a stone circle, 56 feet in diameter, on the island's southern shore (Plate 120). Pocklington described it as 'supposed to be the most compleat and last built Temple in Europe', a statement that may have led many a picturesque tourist astray had not his whole enterprise on the island come in for such vigorous criticism from visitors and residents of Keswick alike.[27] Warner, for example, suggested half-seriously that owners like Pocklington who 'diminshed the stock of public pleasure' by violating natural beauties should be 'the objects of severe taxation': 'Mr. Pocklington's erections on and near the lake of Keswick would, if my suggestion were adopted, make an ample return into the coffers of the Exchequer.'[28] Elizabeth Diggle's response to Pocklington's structure, if typical of the average tourist to the Lake District, suggests a healthy scepticism concerning such follies.

I had walked half over the island without perceiving any signs of one. 'Till I heard my aunt ask . . . if that was the Druid's temple, if his master had found it, in its present state? I looked round & could see nothing but a few round stones set in a circle like boys playing at Marbles. The man answered to the first question 'yes ma'am'; to the second 'n . . . o ma'am, master had these stones put up to look like one that was found near Penrith; but the Lake is always knocking em down', & well it may thought I.[29]

Pocklington's errors seem to have included a woeful lack of understanding and sympathy for his island's location, a failure to produce a tolerable facsimile of a genuine circle and a total absence of dramatic understanding. His taste, so far as we can judge it, appears to have been running completely counter to the dominance of the Sublime and the Picturesque in this period. Properly handled, the introduction of megalithic architecture could enhance an appropriate landscape as we can see from George Cumberland's *An Attempt to Describe Hafod* (1796), a panegyric of the estate in Cardiganshire developed by Thomas Johnes in the mid 1780s.

. . . in front, the wooded valley, with the Ystwyth, in its bottom, opens before us, crowned on the left with sloping, lofty hills; while, in the midst, a smooth mound, half concealed with oaks, rises among the shades, and seems designed by nature as a centre; whence, not too high, nor too low, the whole expanse around, of intermingled beauties, may continually feed the mind: where, if a druid's temple never stood, a druid's temple is unquestionably called for; and I cannot help expressing a hope, that a rude imitation will one day there be placed.[30]

Johnes knew those promoters of the picturesque, Uvedale Price and Richard Payne Knight, his mother's cousin, who made frequent visits to Hafod. Like Sir Richard Hill's Hawkstone Hall, the estate was developed to attract tourists and rapidly acquired a celebrity among visitors and connoisseurs alike.[31] As Malcolm Andrews has pointed out,[32] Hafod was designed by Johnes to offer a predominantly sublime experience and the erection of the Druid Temple amidst this landscape would have echoed the aesthetic of those images of Stonehenge discussed in Chapter Eight. In the winter of 1795 Johnes discussed the Druid Temple with the architect Thomas Harrison and relayed his progress to Cumberland.

. . . I have long thought of the Druidical Temple for your famous Knoll, and this last winter I . . . desired [Harrison] to make his remarks on whatever Druidical Temples he should and give me a Sketch of one. I understand from him that I can have Stones of any size from the Quarries on the Mersey. Upright stones will be all we shall want, for our Flat Slates are to be had very large to cover it. I should imagine ten or twelve very large Upright Blocks would be sufficient.[33]

In the event Johnes does not seem to have actually built the Druid Temple after all but Cumberland's description and Johnes's serious consideration of the plan are telling reminders of how easily megaliths might be included in landscape design at this date. The stone circles at Auldgarth, Dumfries, and Ravensdale Park, Louth, are further examples of this type of folly,[34] as is that at Bierley Hall, Oakenshaw, near Bradford (Plate 121). Here Richard Richardson, the son of the famous Yorkshire doctor and botanist of the same name, developed the gardens between 1725 and

121   Druid's Circle at Bierley Hall, Bradford, *c.* 1740–50?.

1750 by creating four small lakes linked by artificial cascades from the stream flowing through the estate. Grottoes and a Druidical circle (now nearly destroyed) were added to enhance the overall design and may have been intended to evoke a more mystical approach to nature.[35] Richardson, like Johnes at Hafod, was something of a bibliomaniac and connoisseur of the fine arts and his interest in gardening was part of the same taste. That a stone circle could be admitted into the garden design of a virtuoso indicates the extent to which prehistoric antiquities had begun to colonise the imagination and inform the taste of the literati. As at Hafod, the appropriateness of the structure may have been the deciding element and it is possible that Richardson's circle was modelled on or at least inspired by the genuine prehistoric circle at St Ives, Bingley, nearby.[36]

The fashion for prehistoric garden features was sufficiently widespread in the late eighteenth century for William Mason to include one in the sarcastic review of landscape ornament he included in his didactic poem *The English Garden* (1783).

> . . . the common mode,
> Which, mingling structures of far distant times,
> Far distant regions, here, perchance, erects
> A fane to Freedom, where her BRUTUS stands
> In act to strike the tyrant; there a Tent,
> With crescent crown'd, with scymitars adorn'd,
> Meet for some BAJAZET; northward we turn,

206

And lo! a pigmy Pyramid pretends
We tread the realms of PHARAOH; quickly thence
Our southern step presents us heaps of stone
Rang'd in a DRUID circle. Thus from age
To age, from clime to clime incessant borne,
Imagination flounders headlong on,
Till, like fatigu'd VILLARIO, soon we find
We better like a field.[37]

As the author of *Caractacus* Mason was far from an unsympathetic critic, but it is easy to see how a scholarly approach to the past might have been offended by these miscellanies of history. Mason's criticism is not aimed at prehistoric structures as such, but at their inclusion in a farrago of picturesque 'effects'. Some eight lines earlier Mason champions the use of early mediaeval ruins in English gardens as opposed to Roman structures and it is clear from this passage that his criterion of appropriateness is chiefly one of historical relevance.

But Time's rude mace has here all Roman piles
Levell'd so low, that who, on British ground
Attempts the task, builds but a splendid lye
Which mocks historic credence. Hence the cause
Why Saxon piles or Norman here prevail:
Form they a rude, yet 'tis an English whole.[38]

It is apparent from Mason's selective scrutiny that the prehistoric garden structure had become such a victim of whimsy by the 1780s that despite its historical appropriateness and legitimacy as 'a rude, yet . . . English whole' it could not escape the taint of gimcrack superficiality.

Nevertheless, despite this limitation megalithic structures did enjoy a certain vogue, although it was not circles but cromlechs that were of most interest as garden additions. An impressive example was erected at Park Place, near Henley, in 1788 (Plate 122); uniquely, this was no sham monument but the real thing. The cromlech had been unearthed on Jersey in 1785 and was offered to the Governor, General Henry Seymour Conway, as a token of thanks from the people of Jersey for his services to them during the war against France.[39] The stones were re-erected on a hill overlooking the Thames and the whole managed so well that 'the Druids' temple seems to have been born and bred on the spot where it stands' as far as Horace Walpole was concerned. Walpole, who was Conway's cousin and great friend, had visited Park Place that August and wrote a number of letters praising what he found there.

I have been at Park Place, and . . . the Druidic temple vastly more than answers my expectation. Small it is, no doubt, when you are within the enclosure, and but a chapel of ease to Stonehenge; but Mr Conway has placed it with so much judgement, that it has a lofty effect . . . It now stands on the ridge of the high hill without, backed by the horizon, and with a grove on each side at a little distance; and being exalted beyond and above the range of firs that climb up the sides of the hill from the valley, wears all the appearance of an ancient castle, whose towers are only shattered, not destroyed; and devout as I am to old castles, and

122　William Alexander, *The Druid's Temple at Park Place*, n.d., watercolour, 15.2 x 22.6 cm. Maidstone Museums and Art Gallery.

small taste as I have for the ruins of ages absolutely barbarous, it is impossible not to be pleased with so very rare an antiquity so absolutely perfect, and it is difficult to prevent visionary ideas from improving a prospect.[40]

If Park Place was unusual insofar as it made use of a genuine megalithic structure, its effect was indistinguishable from other artificial monuments. In his proposals for John Harford's estate at Blaise, near Bristol, the architect John Nash had included a Druid Temple (Plate 123) to be placed in the gorge. Nash had worked for Johnes at Hafod in 1794 and might conceivably have seen the plans for the proposed Druid Temple there. In any case, as Nigel Temple has pointed out, Nash had been working close to the genuine site of Pentre Ifan in 1793 whilst superintending the construction of Cardigan Priory and Cardigan Gaol and could have received his inspiration direct. Although the work does not appear to have been carried out, George Repton's drawing of the structure underlines the extent to which a concern with archaeological reference has replaced the earlier whimsical taste for Druids' Temples of bark and thatch.[41] There is a further possibility that George Repton gave Nash the idea from his fathers' work at Cobham Hall, for Humphrey Repton may have been responsible for the introduction of a cromlech and standing stones in the grounds there, sometime around 1800, as part of a commission to redesign Lord Darnley's gardens (Plate 124).[42]

Of all the megalithic structures placed in gardens of this period the most

123   George Repton, *Druid Temple*, *c.* 1798–1805, sepia wash, 9.5 x 15.5 cm. The British Architectural Library, RIBA, London.

124   ? Humphrey Repton, Megaliths at Cobham Hall, Kent, *c.* 1800.

125   Druid Temple near Swinton, Yorkshire, *c.* 1800–20.

complex and extensive was that erected in the early 1800s at Swinton Hall, near Masham in Yorkshire by William Danby (Plate 125). The complex includes a grotto and a 100 foot elipse of monoliths and trilithons containing altars and ritual standing stones. Unfortunately, no evidence appears to have survived concerning Danby's Druidic interests, and attempts to interpret the temple as an expression of genuine religious feeling are more ingenious than illuminating.[43] Nevertheless, in building such an elaborate complex Danby, or his designer, showed their awareness of contemporary thinking on Druidic religion; indeed, the elliptical form of the temple may be seen to have been inspired by Stukeley's famous diagram of the serpent temple at Avebury.

Another extensive use of Druidic features can be found in the garden of George Henry Law, Bishop of Bath and Wells, at Banwell in Somerset. Law developed the garden from the mid 1820s and attracted many tourists to its celebrated caves, with their deposits of animal bones belonging to extinct species. On approaching Banwell Cottage the visitor could see 'all its rich embellishments; the Druidical circle and trilithon; broad surfaces of verdant turf; parterres of flowers; clusters of flourishing trees; and tasteful fancy structures, of diversified form and designation.'[44] The fancy structures included Law's Bone House where were displayed some of the choicest specimens from the caves below, while the Bone Cave itself was reached via a trilithon and had inscribed on its outer wall the following lines

Here where once Druids trod in times of yore
And stain'd their altars with a victim's gore
Here now the Christian ransomed from above
Adores a God of mercy and of love.[45]

126   John Buckler, *The Obelisk on Banwell Hill, Somersetshire, as it appeared in 1839, before the present tower was built*, pencil and wash, 18 x 31 cm. Somerset, Archaeological and Natural History Society.

The redemptive meaning of this inscription is reminiscent of the interpretations occasionally applied to genuine megalithic sites by writers and artists. The characterisation of the Druids as blood-thirsty pagans whose superstitious rites were overthrown by the might of Christianity was, as we have seen, a commonplace idea. It is likely that many of these garden follies triggered such associations in the minds of visitors, although only a divine perhaps felt it necessary to be so specific. Elsewhere in Law's garden the visitor might take a woodland walk to the obelisk (later replaced by a tower) crowning the summit of the ridge on which the garden is situated. At 50 yard intervals this path was flanked by pairs of standing stones, leading to a stone circle at the summit (Plate 126). It is worth considering that the presence of authentic prehistoric remains in the area helped inspire the bishop to make a feature of Druidic devices. Banwell is only a few miles from the well-known stone circles at Stanton Drew, whose function had been an object of speculation since at least Stukeley's time. More generally, it seems true to say that some of the imitation megaliths discussed in this chapter were planned for situations such as Bierley, Wilton and Pocklington's Island which were not too far distant from a genuine prehistoric site. This indicates that at least a few of these structures are not as whimsical as they may at first sight appear and that what looks like extreme Celtomania was kept within bounds by some notion of appropriateness, a check that manifestly did not apply to the more indulgent building of grottoes and hermitages.

More incidental uses of megalithic features can be found in a number of other gardens of this period. The so-called Druid's Sideboard at Alton Towers in Stafford-

127　Druid's Sideboard (Stonehenge) at Alton Towers, Staffordshire, *c.* 1814–27.

shire (Plate 127) was constructed between 1814 and 1827 for Charles Talbot, the 15th Earl of Shrewsbury. This double-decker approach may perhaps have been modelled on the ruin of the Temple of Poseidon at Paestum, where two classical storeys of columns and entablature are superimposed. Certainly, there was no antiquarian rationale for this treatment of megaliths and the nickname is well deserved. The garden at Alton Towers may be seen as almost a revival of that mid eighteenth-century tendency to include Druidical structures within an overall scheme of many diverse features. The earl was a Fellow of the Society of Antiquaries, which indicates something of his intellectual tastes, but the rationale behind the megalithic structure at Alton Towers is unfortunately lost to us.[46] J.C. Loudon visited the spot in 1826 and 1831 and published an account in the 1833 edition of his *Encyclopedia of Cottage, Farm and Villa Architecture.*

> The scenery of the Valley of Alton Towers is not here presented as a model for imitation. On the contrary, we consider the greater part of it in excessively bad taste, or rather, perhaps, as the work of a morbid imagination joined to the command of unlimited resources. Still, however, there are many excellent things in it . . . Indeed we know no place in Britain . . . capable of affording, both by faults and beauties, so much instruction.[47]

Loudon's reservations are consistent with his own aesthetic of garden design, with its debt to Humphrey Repton manifest in his adherence to a picturesque philosophy of landscape. As early as the 1822 edition of his *Encyclopedia of Gardening* he had attacked gardens which he considered to be over-cluttered with artificial structures.

> Considered, however, in the light of natural expression, the meaness of root-houses and grottos, the absurdity of hermits' cells, heathen temples, triumphal arches, mock chapels, etc. and the inutility of all of them, render them positive deformities in scenes of natural or picturesque beauty. They break in upon repose, simplicity, and all allusion to natural scenery by their frequency, and suggest ideas of ostentatious vanity in the owner, rather than of propriety and elegance of taste.[48]

Loudon's comments here together with his strictures on the taste of Alton Towers champion a planned garden either in the tradition of Rousham or Hagley, or in accordance with Repton's belief in providing self-consistent thematic environments within an overall design. At Alton Towers we seem to witness a return to the taste of a hundred years earlier, with the garden functioning as a pleasure ground of discrete experiences rather than an organised structuring of one dominant meaning or mood. Programmatic gardens like Stourhead and Stowe function rather like poems, with an unfolding discourse articulated by the prescribed route to be followed and a metaphorical meaning achieved through the associative stimulus of buildings and sculpture. Repton's use of concordant features was less ambitious in its orchestration of a large space but aimed nevertheless to use the full range of gardening and horticultural techniques to present a unified experience. Alton Towers, however, like Kent's work at Richmond Park or Sir Richard Hill's at Hawkstone Hall, invites the spectator to a discontinuous experience; to follow the analogy of a text, one 'reads' Alton Towers as one might an encyclopedia or catalogue. (It is thus somewhat ironic that Loudon should criticise the garden in an encyclopedia of his own.)

Loudon's travels throughout England took him to Stonehenge itself in September 1833 and prompted some thoughts on how primitive structures might be used as garden ornaments; but it is noteworthy that he seems to have debarred prehistoric antiquities from any role more significant than that of eyecatchers, to be seen at a distance.

> This ruin of what may be considered a primeval temple of philosophy, of religion, of devotion, or of instruction (for all these we consider to be essentially the same), affords some good hints for garden buildings on a large scale. A circle of pillars, whether square or round, on a large scale, joined by massive architraves, either with or without cornices, is a noble and imposing object, and would be so even if the pillars were built of brick, and covered with Roman cement. Such an ornament might form a fine termination to a wooded hill; and we do not believe there are any which would produce so grand an effect for so small a sum. The ruins of Stonehenge, though exceedingly interesting in an antiquarian point of view, are very deficient in architectural interest.[49]

The vogue for prehistoric structures in gardens, such as it was, declined after the 1820s. In reality, few of the nineteenth-century gardens to include megalithic features are memorable outside of a certain whimsical charm. The sublime moment had passed and with it the chances of an integrated approach to prehistoric motifs in garden design.[50] Certainly, as the nineteenth century wears on it becomes clear that the motives for employing Druidic monuments within gardens rarely match those deployed for Gothic and Classical features and that the ambitious schemes at Swinton and Banwell were not developed elsewhere. A curious tail-piece to this occurs in 1875 when the botanical artist Worthington G. Smith suggested in *The Gardener's Chronicle* that gardens could be used as a means of preserving prehistoric remains threatened by land improvement. Cromlechs 'could easily be moulded and reproduced in concrete . . . and set up in our better rock-gardens and parks before all traces of the original are utterly lost.' In reply to Smith's letter, S.P. Oliver of the Royal Artillery proposed the construction of a stone circle at Alexandra Palace and Druidical Stones were later erected at Buxton Pavilion Gardens.[51]

One crucial exception to this overall picture is Wales which had become the home to a number of sham stone circles in the nineteenth century as a result of the activities of Iolo Morganwg, the inventor of the Gorsedd.[52] The first Gorsedd of the Bards was held on Primrose Hill in London on 22 September 1792, and included a circle of stones surrounding the *Maen Gorsedd* (or throne).[53] After this inaugural meeting Iolo conducted Gorsedd ceremonies in Wales but made little headway until 1819 when he successfully incorporated the Gorsedd as part of the Eisteddfod being held in Camarthen. By grafting the Gorsedd on to the legitimate stock of the Eisteddfod Iolo ensured its survival as part of a living ceremonial. Since then stone circles have been built as part of the Eisteddfod and can be found all over Wales. The stone circle in Cardiff, erected at the turn of the century is the most accessible and best known of these Eisteddfod circles. It is somehow fitting that this sham monument is visible from the revivalist windows of William Burges's Cardiff Castle, allowing mediaeval fantasy to hold a silent communion with bardic myth-making. Iolo, like a number of other enthusiasts, believed that the bards had maintained a tradition that dated back to prehistoric times and thus the erection of new stone circles was part of a living ceremonial rather than mere antiquarian revivalism. Coupled with a keen sense of national pride, the Gorsedd and its circle could be seen as the tangible expression of an authentic tradition antedating all other ceremonial occasions in Britain. The Gorsedd was thus an active participant within debates on Welsh nationality and history and managed to articulate through symbolism, ceremonial and public presentation something that had been the preserve of scholarly study hitherto. Its survival to this day, despite any number of scholarly disproofs and exposés, is a witness to its success in manipulating a particular view of the past.[54]

This linking of stone circles with national pride and a selective reading of the past should allow us to think in wider terms when reviewing the place of mega-lithic structures in gardens as a whole. As we have seen in earlier chapters, a variety of readings may have been occasioned by these emblems of the archaic past and in most cases it is difficult to be sure which of them is sanctioned. Druids may be associated with bloody sacrificial rites, with contemplative wisdom or with patri-otic resistance to Roman invaders and one and the same monument might trigger any or all of these reactions. In general, though, it would be fair to say that the Druid hut or its hermitage equivalent would have been seen as a reminder of the solitude and learning of primitive philosophers, while its architectural form adopted the most primitive configuration as part of the eighteenth-century's fascination with the origins of architecture.[55] The Druid grotto is a less easily defined category, sometimes taking over the connotations of the Druid hut but also being heavily involved with those aspects of the horrible and the otherworldly that surrounded the image of the Druid as necromancer and sacrificial priest. Cromlechs, standing stones and other megalithic arrangements share this ambiguity; while current thinking was still unclear as to the purposes of Druidical temples so their revived forms would have inherited this uncertainty. It is only when we are in possession of an explanatory text for a particular structure that more specific readings can be offered. Bishop Law's garden at Banwell and Iolo Morganwg's Gorsedd circles are at least explicit in their meanings, but examples such as those at Swinton and Alton Towers seem to escape definite analysis.

It seems likely that many of these Druidic structures, rather than merely being an exercise in Gothick terror, functioned mainly as picturesque historical examples, reminders of the remotest past in these islands. To stumble across a relic of Britain's archaic history in the security of an estate was to encounter in miniature some of the reactions we have already noted with regard to Stonehenge and other authentic monuments. Swinton and Park Place especially may be said to have achieved this through careful positioning and the avoidance of distracting alternatives close at hand. Others, including the structures on Pocklington's Island and at Alton Towers and Cobham Park have in their relationship to the whole something of the same effect as the trophy plates in Bowyer's edition of Hume's *History of England* (Plate 128). Their function is essentially metonymic and rhetorical and as a result the staginess of their presentation cannot detract from their meaning.

If in general the use of prehistoric remains was sanctioned by an enthusiasm for the unusual in garden ornament and an interest in British prehistory, on one occasion, at least, the identification of prehistoric remains with a quite specific meaning can be documented. In 1768 Philip Thicknesse wrote to John Wilkes, imprisoned in the King's Bench Prison, with a message of support and the following suggestion.

> Upon a piece of land belonging to me in the side of a mountain, and on which are stones of an immense size and which can be seen from every part of the County and many parts of Gloucestershire, I am about to make a little *Stone-*Henge, very *rude you may be sure* in workmanship, but it shall be lasting, on one of which I intend to put an inscription, and inscribe it to *Liberty*. This I cannot do without the name of a man who has suffered much in the cause. Leaving *the name* therefore to me, will you give me a few *strong words*, which future ages may understand and the present admire?[56]

If Thicknesse saw the immediate relevance of Stonehenge to Liberty in the 1760s, it might very well be the case that other designers thought on similar lines when including megalithic structures in their gardens. With reference to archaic Britain we have already traced the eighteenth-century connection between the British resistance to Roman invasion and contemporary patriotism, such that an interpretation of megalithic structures as emblematic of freedom should cause no surprise.

William Collins, for one, was prepared to view Druidic temples as shrines of Liberty in his *Ode to Liberty* of 1746.

> Then too, 'tis said, an hoary pile
> Midst the green navel of our isle,
> Thy shrine in some religious wood,
> O soul-enforcing goddess stood!
> There oft the painted native's feet
> Were wont thy form celestial meet:
> Though now with hopeless toil we trace
> Time's backward rolls to find its place.[57]

That native structures could be interpreted in this way is made clear by the example of Gothic architecture and its associations. Certainly, there were some in the eighteenth century who were prepared to associate Whig promotion of popular government with the irregularity and ancestral allure of Gothic architecture. Samuel Kliger quotes an anonymous essayist in 1739 making precisely that connection:

> I entered [those old hospitable Gothick halls] with a Constitutional Sort of Reverence . . . Our old Gothick Constitution had a noble strength and simplicity in it, which was well enough represented by the bold Arches and the solid Pillars of the Edifices of those Days.[58]

Gothic sturdiness, irregularity and lack of restraint were compared to classical refinement, regularity and control; and if the former could be glossed as emblems of constitutional liberty so the latter might be seen as redolent of Tory and monarchical ideology. Thus, at Stowe a crude altar surrounded by statues of Saxon gods, set amidst a woodland glade, was apostrophised as a temple of liberty by Lord Cobham's nephew, Gilbert West, in his descriptive poem on the gardens, published in 1732.

> Forsaking now the Covert of the Maze,
> Along the broader Walk's more open Space,
> Pass we to where a sylvan Temple spreads
> Around the *Saxon Gods*, its hallow'd Shades.
> Hail! Gods of our renown'd Fore-Fathers, hail!
> Ador'd Protectors once of *England*'s weal.
> Gods, of a Nation, valiant, wise, and free,
> Who conquer'd to establish *Liberty*!
> To whose auspicious care *Britannia* owes
> Those Laws, on which she stands, by which she rose.
> Still may your Sons that noble Plan pursue,
> Of equal Government prescrib'd by you.
> Nor e'er indignant may you blush to see,
> The Shame of your corrupted Progeny![59]

Although it must be stressed that such readings were not necessarily widely shared and that they might alter over time (Gothic architecture would also be seen in subsequent generations as symbolic of feudalism in its secular guise and of spiritu-ality in its ecclesiastical one) they nevertheless indicate that it was possible to view architectural style in political terms at this date. We need to be careful, however, in assuming too glibly that prehistoric remains were always associated with liberty as easily as Thicknesse proposed. As we have already noted with respect to arguments about historiography and the cultural status of Celtic Britain, the histori-cal and constitutional resonance of Saxon architecture would have provided a clear political symbolism almost wholly lacking in prehistoric remains. If prehistoric structures were ever regarded as symbols of liberty they would surely have been so regarded at the height of the 'free-born Briton' enthusiasm in the second half of the eighteenth-century, just when Thicknesse wrote to Wilkes, but not necessarily, if at all, before or after that period. Bearing this in mind, it is probably reasonable to claim that megalithic structures in at least late eighteenth-century garden design might be open to receiving the same patriotic interpretation as were examples of Gothic architecture in certain Whig circles. And if this is true, then it is conceivable that the free-born Briton could have received emblematic representation in the fantastic Druidical structures of certain country estates and that some of these sham megaliths are not quite as whimsical as they seem.

If so, the speaker of the envoi to this chapter can only be Stephen Duck. In the 1730s he had inhabited Merlin's Cave in Richmond Park as a sort of poet-in-residence for Queen Caroline. Twenty years later he wrote his ambitious poem *Caesar's Camp* for Joseph Spence, busy planting and improving his estate at St George's Hill. In it a Druid, captured by the Romans and angry at their despoliation of the land, prophesises the future of Britain and speaks of the improvements made by Spence and his contemporaries.

Is't not sufficient that your eagles soar
From Asia's empire to Iberia's shore?
But must you shake *our* island with alarms?
Must Britain *too* submit to Roman arms?
Must all our crops be ravish'd from the land?
Must all our forests fall beneath your hand?
Yet tho' they fall by thy ambitious crimes,
Again restor'd, they rise in future times –
I see those future times – I see, with joy,
Those who can faster plant than thou destroy.
Thy Camp, where now embattled legions shine,
Shall bear the spreading beech and tow'ring pine.[60]

When even a plantation could be celebrated as a token of liberty and historical continuity, might not a megalith as well?

Chapter Ten
CONCLUSION

De Loutherbourg's trophy plate, *The Britons*, was engraved by John Landseer and published on 13 November 1793 (Plate 128). It is part of a series of similar plates showing *Antiquaries*, *British Coins* and the like which were contributed by Robert Smirke and de Loutherbourg to ornament Bowyer's edition of Hume's *History of England*. Let us itemise its contents. Discarded war-gear litters the foreground and a scythe-wheeled chariot, containing a British target, is parked to one side of a menhir. This standing stone has become a stele, on which appears a shallow relief carving of the profile heads of a male and female Briton, while on its top can be discerned a crudely made pot, a sickle and a sprig of mistletoe. A fire emits a billowing cloud of smoke from behind the menhir, rising up to obscure part of the lintel of an enormous trilithon encrusted with moss and lichen. Looking at the profile heads in more detail it is plain that the woman wears a diadem and the man may possibly have a laurel garland on his brow. Their regular features and noble demeanour suggest that we are, in fact, looking at Boadicea and Caractacus.

There can be little doubt that this carefully constructed image is a highly compressed summation of received opinion on the Celtic Britons as manifested at the end of the eighteenth century. Produced as it was in the middle of the period surveyed by this book it may stand as the epitome of the phenomenon we have been examining in the preceding nine chapters. All the important features of the Ancient Britons are represented here, their architecture, their leaders, their method of warfare, even their religion, though the Druids and their mysteries are indicated by synecdoche (the sickle, mistletoe, fire and trilithon) as opposed to appearing in their own right. The inscription 'The Britons' is (deliberately?) placed in such a way as to encroach on the relief, cutting across its surround as though to emphasise that we are witnessing the later imposition of a civilised, literate graffito on the physical remains of a pre-literate culture. This clash of representations could happen with respect to other epochs in British history, with late eighteenth-century typography sitting ill amidst Saxon or mediaeval relics, say, but only here is the contrast so absolute because only here is literacy itself part of the distinction between them and us. The inscription 'The Britons' is in all other respects a redundant addition to the plate, for what else could this concatenation of clichés signify?

What can we make of this engraving? Perhaps the first thing to say is that it is coherent, that the investigation of prehistoric Britain had produced something of a consensus in the public mind by the close of the eighteenth century which

128   John Landseer after Philippe Jacques de Loutherbourg, *The Britons*, 1793, engraving, in Robert Bowyer's edition of David Hume's *History of England*, London, 1806. The British Library.

enabled this sort of iconic compression to make sense not just to antiquaries but to the public at large. We are, if you like, examining the irreducible essence of what 'Ancient Britain' meant in 1793. Iconographically there are elements here which are derivative – for example, de Loutherbourg borrows the targe and chariot from Edward Barnard's *History of England*, published three years previously, and the moustachioed Caractacus may perhaps owe a debt to Hayman – but this 'plagiarism' is no more than an acknowledgement that the image of the Ancient Briton had set, that the identity of Celtic Britain was to this extent pre-fabricated, ready for assembly on any imaginative site.

But equally, this satisfaction with established iconic devices is indicative of the procedures immanent within the antiquarian approach to archaic Britain and its own reliance on authorities. For all their debates and disagreements, at bottom antiquarians were typically involved in the elaboration of their predecessors' theories, reliant on classical reports and the scholarship which had accumulated around them. Caught in a labyrinthine world of exegetical speculation, with no new data or methodologies to show them the way out, antiquarians were involved in research which had lost touch with the brute facts of empirical study. Scholarship, in other words, had become a sort of performance, like art, where success or truth lies not in the relationship between the representation and what it represents but in the conviction of the performer and the skill of the operation. As already mentioned, Bowyer included a number of these trophy plates in his edition of Hume but my contention is that de Loutherbourg's *Britons* is the only one of them which operates so successfully purely as an emblem, and the reason for this is primarily because the imaging of ancient Britain operated without an empirical check; there was no discursive alternative rich enough to threaten imaginative approaches to the archaic past. De Loutherbourg's emblematic representation stands, therefore, as a symbol not just of artists' approaches to prehistoric Britain but of the antiquarian endeavour itself.

De Loutherbourg's image is, finally, elegiac in tone. Everything here is past, we know this culture only by its relics. The plate does not show us, as contemporary history paintings did, the Britons as living, active agents desperate to secure their liberty against Roman aggression; nor does it detail the foul rites or, alternatively, the patriotic exhortation of the Druids. All is abandoned here, the protagonists gone, leaving behind them only signs that they were here at all. The menhir, with its carved portraits and inscription is also a tombstone, to be encountered centuries later by the discerning eye of the scholar or the amateur. If there is a sort of dying fall, a plaintive tone, to the whole image it is because a whole era has been reduced to an elaborate funerary monument.

If prehistoric Britain, in all its complexity, has become for us today more than an assemblage of grave goods, menhirs and idle speculation we have archaeology to thank. But how far has this change in understanding actually reached? Without wishing to decry the enormous contributions to knowledge made by archaeology in the twentieth century, there are some grounds for thinking that outside specialist circles the image de Loutherbourg designed in 1793 is in many respects an appropriate model for the one still in circulation two hundred years later. What images inhabit our minds when we are asked to envisage the prehistory of these islands? We may acknowledge in the 1990s that the builders of Stonehenge and the

Iron Age Celts belong to different cultural circumstances but are archaeological distinctions urgent, are they real to us? Popular guides to prehistoric Britain tend to treat the whole pre-Roman period within the confines of one volume and unless we are professionally involved in making the necessary effort my guess is that most of us jog along with a fairly hazy view of prehistory. Stonehenge and one or two other spectacular sites may be threatened by mass tourism but how much of that interest is being satisfied beyond the physical experience of simply being in the presence of something ancient and enigmatic? How far have we really travelled from the sublime encounters of antiquarian enthusiasm? We read the information made available to us at the sites, we buy guide-books and popular archaeology books, but how much of this activity changes that deeper, romantic approach to dolmens, stone circles and the like elaborated in the eighteenth century?

It seems to me that the study of prehistoric and Iron Age Britain faces a pretty similar task to the one faced by antiquarianism in a polite age, how to make current research attractive to a wide audience who would profit from a more informed engagement with the relics of the remote past.[1] As we have seen, there was a moment in the late eighteenth and early nineteenth centuries when enthusiasm for ancient Britain was manifested right the way across the arts and academe, when it was woven into the fabric of British culture. As it developed into a discipline professional archaeology, like all academic endeavour in the West, increasingly distanced itself from amateur enthusiasm; to do it properly requires sound training in method, the most exacting techniques of detection, description, analysis and historical awareness. It would be unreasonable to expect the general public to take that heavy burden on, but what is the acceptable substitute for it, if the public is not to be left to the vagaries of romantic effusions regarding Celtic Britain, the Druids and the mystery of the megaliths? A promiscuous mixture of ancestor worship, the defence of liberty and other manifestations of interest appropriate to the eighteenth and nineteenth centuries cannot be deployed any longer; we inhabit a different, multi-cultural world today and denial of that world in the interests of empathetic engagement with prehistory is at best emptily nostalgic and at worst deeply worrying. Equally, however, the resurgence of at times angry feelings that these monuments belong to the public, not just the archaeologists, is indicative of the fact that prehistoric Britain matters in a wider cultural sense than the academic desire to set the historical record straight. At the beginning of this book I indicated that the poetics of prehistory should be distinguished from progressivist histories of archaeology. The question for us, therefore, is what are the poetics of prehistory in a post-modern world? New archaeological thinking will, of course, filter through and continue to determine many of our views on prehistory just as antiquarianism affected its own era, but what kind of knowledge this is and how we use it will itself reveal wider, deeper aspects of British culture at the close of the twentieth century.

NOTES

Chapter One

1 For an introduction to the achievements of early excavators see Barry M. Marsden, *The Early Barrow-Diggers*, Princes Risborough, 1974.

2 Robert Henry, *The History of Great Britain* (second edition), 1788, II, pp. 375–6.

3 Charles Darwin, *The Descent of Man* (second edition), 1891, II, p. 440, cited in Keith Thomas, *Man and the Natural World; Changing Attitudes in England 1500–1800*, Harmondsworth, 1989, p. 188.

4 The ideological power of archaeological illustration, its iconic authority, has recently begun to receive attention. Stuart Piggott, *Antiquity Depicted: Aspects of Archaeological Illustration*, London, 1978, is the most relevant study for Ancient British history; Martin Rudwick, *Scenes from Deep Time, Early Pictorial Representations of the Prehistoric World*, Chicago 1992, chiefly examines archaeological illustration of extinct species, but includes some telling examples of the pictorial treatment of Stone Age man. A concise review of the recent literature on archaeological illustration is contained in Stephanie Moser, 'The visual language of archaeology: a case study of Neanderthals', *Antiquity*, LXVI, no. 253, December 1992, pp. 831–44.

5 For a critique of empirical archaeology and suggestions for other approaches to the past see Michael Shanks, *Experiencing the Past – on the Character of Archaeology*, London, 1992.

6 By Daniel Wilson in his *The Archaeology and Prehistoric Annals of Scotland*. See Glyn Daniel, *The Idea of Prehistory*, Harmondsworth, 1971, p. 9.

7 James Ussher, *Annals of the Ancient and New Testaments*, 1650. See also Stuart Piggott, *Ancient Britons and the Antiquarian Imagination – Ideas from the Renaissance to the Regency*, London, 1989, pp. 38–43.

8 Joan Evans, *A History of the Society of Antiquaries*, Oxford, 1956, p. 121.

9 William Stukeley, *Abury, A Temple of the British Druids*, London, 1743, p. 53; Henry Browne, *An Illustration of Abury and Stonehenge*, 1823.

10 Sharon Turner, *The History of the Anglo-Saxons* (third edition), London, 1820, p. 6.

11 See Donald K. Grayson, *The Establishment of Human Antiquity*, New York, 1983, pp. 31–6.

12 See A. Hallam, *Great Geological Controversies*, Oxford, 1983, pp. 3–25; Roy Porter, *The Making of Geology – Earth Science in Britain 1660–1815*, Cambridge, 1977, pp. 189–98.

13 Hallam, *Great Geological Controversies*, pp. 29–45. It is important to note that Lyell himself believed that the appearance of human beings on earth was a relatively recent phenomenon, obeying a different biological imperative to all other species. See Grayson, *Human Antiquity*, pp. 78–84.

14 *Archaeologia* XIII, pp. 204–5. Frere had found the stone implements in 1790.

15 For general background on these developments see Grayson, *Human Antiquity*, Hallam, *Great Geological Controversies*, Porter, *Geology* and Daniel, *Prehistory*; also Robert Heizer, *Man's Discovery of his Past*, Tunbridge Wells, 1980; André Senet, *Man in Search of his Ancestors*, London, 1955; Ole Klindt-Jensen, *A History of Scandanavian Archaeology*, London, 1975.

16 Letter dated 24 May 1851. Quoted in James Hamilton Buckley, *The Triumph of Time – A Study of the Victorian Concepts of Time, History, Progress and Decadence*, Cambridge, Mass., 1967, p. 28.

17 pp. 12–13. Of course, for some commentators the realisation of a long prehistory was uncomfortable. As Julia Wedgwood, Darwin's niece, wrote in 1863, 'There is something dreary in the indefinite lengthening of a savage and blood-stained past'. *Macmillan's Magazine*, p. 486; quoted in Grayson, *Human Antiquity*, p. 217.

Chapter Two

1 Letter I, *The Gentleman's Magazine*, LVIII, February 1788, p. 127.

2 Letter II, *ibid.*, March 1788, p. 196.

3 See T.D. Kendrick, *British Antiquity*, London, 1950, especially chapter VI 'The Battle over the British History'.

4 Letter VI, *Gentleman's Magazine*, LVIII, July 1788, p. 591. Pinkerton is at pains to distinguish such

credulity from Ireland's older tradition of well-founded historiography.

5 pp. 1-2.

6 For British historiography in this period see J.R. Hale (ed), *The Evolution of British Historiography*, London, 1967, especially pp. 21-36, Thomas Preston Peardon, *The Transition in English Historical Writing, 1760-1830*, New York, 1966, passim.

7 Hale, *British Historiography*, p. 30. See also Hugh A. Macdougall, *Racial Myth in English History - Trojans, Teutons and Anglo-Saxons*, Montreal, Hanover and London, 1982, especially pp. 79-86.

8 *History of England*, revised edition ed. Hewson Clarke, 1813, p. 3. 'The History of England from the Invasion of Julius Caesar to the accession of Henry VII' was one of four volumes in the original edition, but the last to be written and published. Hume's 'Memoranda for my History of England, written July, 1745 or 1746' show, however, that he had always intended to begin his History in the Roman era. See Victor G. Wexter, *David Hume and the 'History of England'*, Philadelphia, 1979, p. 108.

9 I, p. 1.

10 Quoted by G.F. Mitchell, 'Antiquities' in T.Ó. Raifeartaigh (ed), *The Royal Irish Academy - A Bicentennial History, 1785-1985*, Dublin, 1985, p. 95.

11 See Clare O'Halloran 'Irish Re-Creations of the Gaelic Past: The Challenge of Macpherson's Ossian', *Past and Present*, no. 124, August 1989, p. 75. For recent scholarship in Irish historiography see Ned Lebow, 'British Historians and Irish History', *Eire-Ireland*, VIII: 4, 1973, especially pp. 27-31; Ann De Valera, *Antiquarian and Historical Investigations in Ireland in the Eighteenth Century*, unpublished MA Thesis, University College, Dublin, 1978; Jacqueline R. Hill, 'Popery and Protestantism, Civil and Religious Liberty: the Disputed Lessons of Irish History 1690-1812', *Past and Present*, no. 118, February 1988, pp. 97-129.

12 Quoted in R.A. Breatnach, 'Two Eighteenth-Century Irish Scholars: J.C. Walker and Charlotte Brooke', *Studia Hibernica*, V, 1965, pp. 88-9.

13 Given the novelty of this exercise much of the information needed to be initially collected by means of questionnaires, on which see Gwyn Walters, 'The Antiquary and the Map', *Word and Image*, IV, no. 2, April-June 1988, pp. 529-44.

14 *History of Scotland*, p. 5. The development of 'text-free' accounts of pre-Roman Britain had developed from the late seventeenth century in antiquarian study, but it was not until the mid eighteenth century that these researches began to vie with 'philosophical' historiography. See Stuart Piggott, *Ancient Britons and the Antiquarian Imagination; Ideas from the Renaissance to the Regency*, London, 1989, pp. 21-8; A. Momigliano, 'Ancient History and the Antiquarian' in *Studies in Historiography*, London, 1966, pp. 1-39.

15 p. xviii.

16 *Gentleman's Magazine*, LVIII, Letter XI, December 1788, p. 1057.

17 See Peardon, *Historical Writing*, p. 293.

18 *Gentleman's Magazine*, LVIII, Letter IV, May 1788, p. 405.

19 Quoted in Joan Evans, *A History of the Society of Antiquaries*, Oxford, 1956, p. 118.

20 James Douglas, *Nenia Britannica or the Sepulchral History of Great Britain* (London, 1786), quoted in Glyn Daniel *The Idea of Prehistory*, Harmondsworth, 1971, p. 17.

21 Preface to *Antiquities of Cornwall* (1754), quoted in P.A.S. Pool, *William Borlase*, Truro, 1986, pp. 148-9.

22 See John Frew, 'An Aspect of the Early Gothic Revival: The Transformation of Medievalist Research, 1770-1800', *Journal of the Warburg and Courtauld Institutes*, XLIII, 1980, pp. 174-85.

23 Quoted in Evans, *Society of Antiquaries*, p. 155.

24 There is a vast literature on the subject of Primitivism. My own research is obviously indebted to the following scholarly treatments: Hoxie Neale Fairchild, *The Noble Savage - a Study in Romantic Nationalism*, New York, 1928; Gladys Bryson, *Man and Society: the Scottish Enlightenment of the Eighteenth century*, Princeton, 1945; Samuel Kliger, *The Goths in England; a Study in Seventeenth and Eighteenth Century Thought*, Cambridge, Mass., 1952; Ronald L. Meek, *Social Science and the Ignoble Savage*, Cambridge, 1976. As this project was nearing completion I caught belated sight of Sharon McFarlan Kahin, *Eighteenth Century British Primitivism*, unpublished PhD dissertation, Cornell University, 1981, whose treatment of the topic is the most recent study. Although my focus is different from Dr Kahin's, many of our conclusions coincide.

25 In saying this I am adopting a much more positive interpretation than that of Stuart Piggott who has rightly pointed out that antiquarian learning, as it had developed in the seventeenth century, collapsed in the 1730s and did not reach the same heights of exacting scholarship generally until the later nineteenth century (see for example his 'Antiquarian Thought in the Sixteenth and Seventeenth centuries' in *Ruins in a Landscape*, Edinburgh, 1976). Taking up a point made by Roy Porter regarding geological understanding in this period (*The Making of Geology - Earth Sciences in Britain 1660-1815*, Cambridge, 1977, pp. 92-3), I would suggest that while it is undoubtedly true that prehistoric investigation hardly advanced in archaeological understanding until the 1850s or even later, the growth of academic, institutional and institutional structures, the increased participation of the general public and the consequent potential for a wider range of contributions to the field all played their part in preparing for the growth and maturity of archaeology proper and its related disciplines.

26 See Evans, *Society of Antiquaries*, chapter VII, 'The Charter 1748-53'.

27 See R.T. Jenkins and Helen M. Ramage, *A History of the Honourable Society of Cymmrodorion*, London, 1951, pp. 10-15.

28 See Stuart Piggott, 'The Ancestors of Jonathon Oldbuck' in *Ruins in a Landscape*, Edinburgh, 1976, especially pp. 146ff.

29 See De Valera, *Investigations*, pp. 133-50; R.B. McDowell, 'The Main Narrative' in Raifeartaigh, *Academy*, pp. 1-21.

30 Snyder notes that Lewis Morris, founder of the Cymmrodorion Society, was responsible for the 'Historical Account of the Rise of British Music' which was included in Parry's book. See Edward D. Snyder, *The Celtic Revival in English Literatre 1760-1800*, Cambridge, Mass., 1923, p. 20, n. 4.

31 See Stuart Piggott, 'William Camden and the "Britannia"' in *Ruins in a Landscape*, Edinburgh, 1976, pp. 33-53.

32 William Stukeley and James Douglas, for example, were reasonably proficient draughtsmen and Borlase, skilled in drawing from his youth, took up landscape painting in 1747. See Stuart Piggott, *Antiquity Depicted; Aspects of Archaeological Illustration*, London, 1978; Pool, *Borlase*, pp. 101 and 272; and Ann Payne, *Views of the Past - Topographical Drawings in the British Library*, London, 1987.

33 Richard Gough, *Topographical Antiquities*, quoted in Evans, *Society of Antiquaries*, p. 136.

34 These included Benjamin West, Joseph Farington, George Stubbs, Richard Cosway, Robert Smirke, Thomas Lawrence, Osias Humphrey, William Beechey, Richard Westmacott, Francis Chantrey, Charles Alfred Stothard, Samuel Prout and Charles Lock Eastlake. See Evans, *Society of Antiquaries*, pp. 201, 237-8.

35 *Ibid.*, p. 176.

36 See Roy Strong, *And When did you Last see your Father? The Victorian Painter and British History*, London, 1978, pp. 50-6.

37 See Malcolm Andrews, *The Search for the Picturesque*, Aldershot, 1989; Esther Moir, *The Discovery of Britain*, London, 1964; Payne, *Views of The Past*.

38 Thomas Love Peacock, *The Four Ages of Poetry*, 1820, quoted in Neale Fairchild, *Noble Sarage*, p. 496.

39 Philippa Levine, *The Amateur and the Professional - Antiquarians, Historians and Archaeologists in Victorian England, 1838-1886*, Cambridge, 1986.

40 See Stuart Piggott, 'The Origins of the English County Archaeological Societies' in *Ruins in a Landscape*, Edinburgh, 1976; Levine, *The Amateur*, pp. 59-69, 182-3.

41 Henry Thomas Buckle, *History of Civilization in England*, London, 1857, I, pp. 121-2.

Chapter Three

1 See Benedict Anderson, *Imagined Communities*, London, 1983; Ernest Gellner, *Nations and Nationalism*, Oxford, 1983. Anthony D. Smith, however, in *National Identity*, Harmondsworth, 1991, argues for a concept of 'ethnie' which predates capitalist formations. Of specific interest for this study, Linda Colley, 'Whose Nation? Class and National Consciousness in Britain, 1750-1830', *Past and Present*, no. 113, November 1986, pp. 96-117, argues for a more nuanced investigation of national identity than traditional and over-reductive accounts of British national sentiment have allowed.

2 See Ole Klindt-Jensen, *A History of Scandinavian Archaeology*, London, 1975, pp. 14-24.

3 See Ulla Houkjaer, 'Dutch Artists in the Service of Danish History - The Kronborg Series', *Apollo*, August 1988, CXXVIII, no. 318 (New Series) pp. 99-103; H.D. Schepelern and Ulla Houkjaer, *The Kronborg Series. King Christian IV and his Pictures of Early Danish History*, Copenhagen, 1988.

4 See S. Bruce and S. Yearley, 'The Social Construction of Tradition: The Restoration Portraits and the Kings of Scotland' in David McCrone, Stephen Kendrick and Pat Straw (eds), *The Making of Scotland: Nation, Culture and Social Change*, Edinburgh, 1989, pp. 175-88.

5 See Thomas Preston Peardon, *The Transition in English Historical Writing 1760-1830*, New York, 1966, p. 104.

6 See Thor J. Beck, *Northern Antiquities in French Learning and Literature (1755-1855), A Study in Pre-romantic Ideas*, Publications of the Institute of French Studies, Columbia University, New York, 1934-5.

7 Klindt-Jensen, *Scandinavian Archaeology*, pp. 41-5.

8 *Ibid.*, p. 70. Worsaae's text might be compared with the contemporary paintings of megaliths by J.C. Dahl and J.T. Lundbye.

9 Jacques Gury, 'Nos ancetres les Gaulois dans le décor pittoresque dans le dernier tiers du XVIIIe siècle' in Paul Viallaneix and Jean Ehrard, *Nos ancêtres les Gaulois*, Actes du Colloque International de Clermont-Ferrand, 1982, pp. 119-26.

10 Noël Hallé's *Druidical Ceremony* (c.1737-44) now in the National Gallery of Scotland seems to be a unique example of earlier French artistic interest in Gaulish subject matter. See also Jean-Pierre Mouilleseaux, 'A propos d'Eponine et Sabinus: un épisode de la résistance gauloise au Salon de 1789' in Viallaneix and Ehrard, *Nos Ancêtres*, p. 298; also Anthony D. Smith *Patriotism and Neo-Classicism: The "historical revival" in French and English painting and sculpture, 1746-1800*, unpublished PhD dissertation, University College, London, 1987, pp. 299-305, 452-6. Earlier French interest in their primaeval origins is discussed in R.E. Asher *National Myths in Renaissance France - Francus, Samothes and the Druids*, Edinburgh, 1993.

11 Norman Hampson, *The Enlightenment*, Harmondsworth, 1968, p. 177.

12 Quoted in Gerald Newman, *The Rise of English*

Nationalism: A Cultural History 1740-1830, London, 1987, p. 116.

13 See Elisabeth Roudinesco (transl. Martin Thom), *Théroigne de Méricourt - a Melancholic Woman during the French Revolution*, London, 1991, pp. 95-7.

14 See Stuart Woolf, 'French Civilization and Ethnicity in the Napoleonic Empire', *Past and Present*, no. 124, August 1989, pp. 96-120.

15 I, p. 165, quoted in Remi Mallet 'Henri Martin et les Gaulois: histoire et mythe' in Viallaneix and Ehrard, *Nos Ancêtres*, p. 235.

16 Suzanne G. Lindsay, Anne Pingeot, Joseph Rishel, *The Second Empire - Art in France under Napoloeon III*, Philadelphia, 1978, p. 204.

17 See Anne Pingeot, 'Les Gaulois sculptés (1850-1914)' in Villaneix and Ehrard, *Nos Ancêtres*, pp. 255-75.

18 For Préault see *ibid.* and David Mower, 'Antoine Auguste Préault (1809-1879)', *Art Bulletin*, June 1981, LXIII, no. 2, pp. 288-307.

19 This painting was later in the Kunsthistorisches Museum but is now destroyed. See *Angelika Kauffmann und ihre zeit. Graphik und Zeichnungen von 1760-1810*, Dusseldorf, 1979, p. 68.

20 See M. Snodin (ed), *Karl Friedrich Schinkel: A Universal Man,* New Haven and London, 1991, pp. 105-6, cat. no. 24, 'Hermann of the Cherusii'.

21 Fittingly, the sword brandished high above Hermann's head was forged by Krupp.

22 'The Ommegang of Brussels', *The Art Journal*, 1849, p. 149.

23 See Linda Colley, *Britons - Forging the Nation 1701-1837*, New Haven and London, 1992. Colley insists, rightly, that Protestant religion, aristocratic intermarriage, good communications and urbanisation throughout England and lowland Scotland were all crucial factors in knitting the kingdom together; but she acknowledges at the same time that 'Welshness, Scottishness and Englishness also remained powerful divides - though not perhaps as powerful as regionalism and localism . . . It would be wrong, then, to interpret the growth of British national consciousness in this period in terms of a new cultural and political uniformity being resolutely imposed on the peripheries of the island by its centre. For many poorer and less literate Britons, Scotland, Wales and England remained more potent rallying calls than Great Britain, except in times of danger from abroad.' (p. 373). While I agree with Colley's overall thesis, I would maintain that Welsh, Scottish and Irish celebration of cultural difference in antiquarian and historical writing indicates that the affluent and highly literate, too, might find potent rallying calls in their own Celtic culture.

24 See Colley, *ibid.*; Newman, *Nationalism*, John Lucas, *England and Englishness, Ideas of Nationhood in English Poetry 1688-1900*, London, 1990.

25 Poliakov has made a strong case for 'double-ancestry' in other European states, such that the British situation might seem less special than I argue here. Yet, in terms of the debate, there is a consistency, volume and vigour on this side of the Channel which contrasts markedly, as far as I am able to judge, with the nature of the debate in France, for example. See Leon Poliakov, *The Aryan Myth: A History of Racist and Nationalist Ideas in Europe*, London, 1974.

26 See Prys Morgan, 'From a Death to a View: The Hunt for the Welsh Past in the Romantic Period' in Eric Hobsbawm and Terence Ranger (eds), *The Invention of Tradition*, Cambridge, 1983, pp. 43-100. Prys Morgan's full-length study, *The Eighteenth Century Renaissance*, Llandybie, 1981, is definitive. Chapters Two, Three and Four are especially recommended.

27 Quoted in Morgan, *Eighteenth Century Renaissance*, p. 96. See also Jocelyn Hackforth-Jones 'Views of Wales *c.* 1770-1820' unpublished PhD dissertation, University of Sydney, 1988, pp. 99-103, 116-119.

28 Morgan, *Eighteenth Century Renaissance*, p. 99.

29 Rev. Richard Warner, *Excursions from Bath*, Bath, 1801, p. 227.

30 For the politics of the London Welsh see R.T. Jenkins and Helen Ramage, *A History of the Honourable Society of Cymmrodorion*, London, 1951, pp. 11-12, 122-8.

31 *Ibid.*, pp. 128-9.

32 Dynval Moelmud is, of course the 'Molmutius Dunvallo' whose tradition Warner had mocked two years earlier. See note 27 above.

33 See Hugh Trevor-Roper, 'The Invention of Tradition: The Highland Tradition of Scotland' in Hobsbawm and Ranger, *Tradition*, pp. 15-41.

34 From a sermon entitled 'The Situation of the World at the Time of Christ's Appearance', Edinburgh, 1755, p. 45.

35 Quoted in Stuart Piggott, 'The Ancestors of Jonathon Oldbuck', *Ruins in a Landscape*, Edinburgh, 1976, p. 142; see also Joseph M. Levine, *Dr. Woodward's Shield - History, Science, and Satire in Augustan England*, Berkeley, California, 1977, pp. 261-3.

36 A passage from Buchan's treatise on the topography of Roman Scotland (1786) quoted in Iain Gordon Brown, *The Hobby-Horsical Antiquary - A Scottish Character 1640-1830*, Edinburgh, 1980, p. 45.

37 See Chapter Four. Malcolm Chapman, *The Celts - The Construction of a Myth*, Basingstoke, 1992, has recently attempted a wholesale refutation of this set of assumptions as they apply to contemporary thinking on the Celts.

38 Though J.C. Walker's *Outlines of a Plan for Promoting the Art of Painting in Ireland*, 1790, which recommended subjects from Irish history, is an exception and a fore-runner of Davis' similar exhortations in the 1840s. See Ann De Valera, 'Antiquarian and Historical Investigations in Ireland in the Eighteenth Century', unpublished MA

thesis, University College, Dublin, 1978, p. 248.

39 See Jeanne Sheehy, *The Rediscovery of Ireland's Past: the Celtic Revival 1830-1930*, London, 1980, p. 13.

40 See Thomas Davis, 'National Art', 'Illustrations of Ireland' and 'Hints for Irish Historical Paintings' in *Literary and Historical Essays*, Dublin, 1846, pp. 153-62, 165-8, 169-72. Further discussion of Irish nationalism and art can be found in Cyril Barrett, 'Irish Nationalism and Art 1800-1921', *Studies*, Winter 1975, pp. 393-409; Sheehy, *Ireland's Past*.

41 Letter dated 13 November 1781. W.S. Lewis (ed), *The Correspondence of Horace Walpole*, New Haven and London, 1937-83, XXIX, p. 165.

42 See John Sunderland, 'Samuel Johnson and History Painting' in D.G.C. Allan and John L. Abbott, *The Virtuoso Tribe of Arts and Sciences - Studies in the Eighteenth-Century Work and Membership of the London Society of Arts*, Athens (Georgia) and London, 1992, pp. 183-94. Smith 'Patriotism' is the fullest study to date of the historical revival. Some of his more significant findings were originally published in his 'The "Historical Revival" in late Eighteenth Century England and France', *Art History*, II, 2, June 1979, pp. 156-78.

43 See Chapter Seven.

44 The subjects are listed in F. Knight Hunt (ed), *The Book of Art - Cartoons, Frescoes, Sculpture and Decorative Art as Applied to the New Houses of Parliament*, London, 1846.

Chapter Four

1 Appended to *The Poems of Ossian*, New York, 1807, pp. 96-7.

2 Walter Scott (ed), *The Poetical Works of Anna Seward*, Edinburgh, 1810, I, p. lvii.

3 A good example of an entirely derivative use of Gray is Act 3, Scene 5 of James Boaden's *Cambo-Britons*, London, 1798, which re-enacts the poem as a dramatic incident. The play was first performed at the Theatre Royal, Haymarket, on 21 July 1798, when 'M. Marinari, the painter, very ably aided [Boaden] in providing the splendid effects of the spectacle', p. vi.

4 See Henry Okun, 'Ossian in Painting', *Journal of the Warburg and Courtauld Institutes*, XXX, 1967, pp. 327-56; Werner Hofmann, Hannah Hohl and Daniel Ternois, *Ossian*, Editions des musées nationaux, Paris, 1974.

5 Edward D. Snyder, *The Celtic Revival in English Literature, 1760-1800*, Cambridge, Mass., 1923, reprinted 1965, p. 4. For scholarly treatment of the parallel development of interest in Scandinavian heroic literature see Frank Edgar Farley, *Scandinavian Influences in the English Romantic Movement*, Studies and Notes in Philology and Literature, IX, Modern Languages Department, Harvard University, Boston, 1903.

6 Annotations to 'Poems' by William Wordsworth (1825), pp. 364-5, written in 1826. Geoffrey Keynes (ed), *Blake - Complete Writings*, Oxford, 1966, p. 783.

7 Keynes, *Blake*, p. 578.

8 See Snyder, *Celtic Revival*, pp. 42-4; F.I. McCarthy, 'The Bard of Thomas Gray, its composition and its use by painters', *The National Library of Wales Journal*, XIV, no. 1, Summer 1965, pp. 105-6.

9 McCarthy, 'The Bard', p. 106.

10 Charles H. Hinnant, 'Changing Perspectives on the Past: The Reception of Thomas Gray's *The Bard*', *Clio* III/3, June 1974, pp. 315-29.

11 *The Gentleman's Magazine*, January 1796, pp. 63-4.

12 I.2, 15-26; Arthur Johnston (ed), *Selected Poems of Thomas Gray and William Collins*, London, 1967, pp. 78-9.

13 McCarthy, 'The Bard', p. 106.

14 Letter dated 18 September 1755, in W.S. Lewis (ed), *The Yale Edition of Horace Walpole's Correspondence*, New Haven and London, 1937-83, XXXV, pp. 251-2.

15 The designs are most recently and fully discussed in Loftus Jestin, *The Answer to the Lyre - Richard Bentley's Illustrations to Thomas Gray's Poems*, Philadelphia, 1990, pp. 218-21; see also John Dixon Hunt, *The Figure in the Landscape: Poetry, Painting, and Gardening during the Eighteenth Century*, Baltimore, 1976, pp. 145-9.

16 Quoted in McCarthy, 'The Bard', p. 110.

17 *Ibid*.

18 Paul Oppé (ed), 'Memoirs of Thomas Jones Penkerrig Radnorshire 1803', *Walpole Society*, XXXII (1946-8), 1951, p. 21.

19 *The Gentleman's Magazine*, October 1792, pp. 956-7.

20 See Prys Morgan, *The Eighteenth Century Renaissance*, Llandybie, 1981, pp. 41-3.

21 See Arthur S. Marks, 'The Source of John Martin's "The Bard" ', Supplement: Notes on British Art 6, *Apollo*, August 1966, pp. 1-2.

22 William Godwin, *Essay on Sepulchres*, London, 1809, p. 69.

23 'The Voice of the Ancient Bard' is included as one of the *Songs of Innocence* (1789).

24 Keynes, *Blake*, p. 576.

25 Howard Gaskill, ' "Ossian" Macpherson: towards a rehabilitation', *Comparative Criticism - An annual journal*, No. 8, Cambridge, 1986, pp. 113-46.

26 Quoted in Gaskill, *ibid.*, p. 131.

27 *c.* 20 June 1760. Letter 313 in Paget Toynbee and Leonard Whibley (eds), *Correspondence of Thomas Gray*, Oxford, 1935, p. 680.

28 7 August 1760. Letter 317 in *ibid.*, p. 690.

29 See above, note 1.

30 See Chapter Six for a fuller discussion of theories of human progress.

31 pp. 16-17, quoted in Ronald L. Meek, *Social Science and the Ignoble Savage*, Cambridge, 1976, p. 180.

32 See Margaret Mary Rubel, *Savage and Barbarian - Historical Attitudes in the Criticism of Homer and Ossian, 1760-1800*, Amsterdam, Oxford and New York, 1978, especially pp. 46-69; Snyder, *Celtic Revival*, pp. 78-85.

33 Quoted in Susan Booth, 'The Early Career of Alexander Runciman and his Relations with Sir James Clerk of Penicuik', *Journal of the Warburg and Courtauld Institutes*, XXXII, 1969, p. 339.

34 John L. Greenway, 'The Gateway to Innocence: Ossian and the Nordic Bard as Myth', *Studies in Eighteenth Century Culture*, IV, 1975, pp.161-70.

35 See Richard B. Sher, ' "Those Scotch Imposters and their Cabal": Ossian and the Scottish Enlightenment', in *Man and Nature - proceedings of the Canadian Society for Eighteenth Century Studies*, University of Western Ontario, 1982, pp. 55-63.

36 Rubel, *Savage and Barbarian*, p. 51, n. 28.

37 See William L. Pressly, *The Life and Art of James Barry*, New Haven and London, 1981, p. 297. For Irish interest in Ossian see Clare O'Halloran, 'Irish Re-Creations of the Gaelic Past: the Challenge of Macpherson's Ossian', *Past and Present*, no. 124, August 1989, pp. 69-95.

38 Quoted in Rubel, *Savage and Barbarian*, p. 49.

39 Quoted in Thomas Preston Peardon, *The Transition in English Historical Writing 1760-1830*, New York, 1966, p. 110.

40 *Ibid.*, pp. 248-9.

41 Graham, *Essay*, pp. 27-28.

42 Hugh Blair, *Lectures on Rhetoric and Belles Lettres*, Edinburgh, 1783, 1811 edition, I, Lecture iv, p. 74 quoted in Rubel, *Savage and Barbarian*, p. 92.

43 William Gilpin, *Observations, relative chiefly to Picturesque Beauty, Made in the Year 1776, On several parts of Great Britain; particularly the High-Lands of Scotland*, London, 1789, II, p. 138.

44 Booth, 'Alexander Runciman', pp. 332-43.

45 Forty years later Robert Smirke was commissioned to produce an Ossian cycle for another Scottish house, Kinmount in Dumfriesshire, the seat of the fifth Marquis of Queensbury. The house was designed in 1812 by Sir Robert Smirke, the artist's son, and it is likely that he commissioned his father to design the frieze around the entrance hall and staircase landing. The decision to celebrate Ossian in the aftermath of Macpherson's exposure is, like Chalmers's *Caledonia*, a testament to the patriotic hold the bard had within Scottish circles, even at this late date. The mixture of classical and 'Highland' grab is a notable feature of Smirke's designs and, as with Barralet's work of the 1780s, this miscellany of picturesque elements at times teeters on the edge of the absurd. Smirke's drawings for these scenes are illustrated and briefly discussed by Michael Bellamy in Peter Cannon-Brookes (ed), *The Painted Word - British History Painting: 1750-1830*, London, 1991, pp. 124-5. See also Susan Manning, 'Ossian, Scott, and Nineteenth-Century Scottish Literary Nationalism', *Studies in Scottish Literature*, XVII, 1982, pp. 39-54.

46 Letter dated 6 September 1799. Dawson Turner (ed), *The Literary Correspondence of John Pinkerton*, London, 1830, II, p. 92.

47 pp. 3-4.

48 See Pressly, *James Barry*, pp. 129-32, 266, 280.

49 *Ibid.*, pp. 55-8, 231, 234-5. Jones's view that Stonehenge 'is mingled of *Greek* and *Tuscane* work' is in his, *The most notable Antiquity of Great Britain vulgarly called Stone-Heng on Salisbury plain. Restored*, London, 1655, pp. 67-8, 76, 102.

50 See Robert Rosenblum, *Transformations in Late Eighteenth Century Art*, Princeton, 1969, pp. 46-9; Hans Naef, 'Henrietta Harvey and Elizabeth Norton: Two English Artists', *Burlington Magazine*, CXIII, no. 815, February 1971, pp. 79-89.

51 David Bindman, 'Blake's "Gothicised Imagination" and the History of England' in Morton D. Paley and Michael Phillips (eds), *William Blake - Essays in honour of Sir Geoffrey Keynes*, Oxford, 1973, pp. 29-49. A drawing entitled *Joseph of Arimathea Preaching to the Inhabitants of Britain* (c.1780), now in the Rosenbach Museum and Library, Philadelphia, and the two coloured relief etchings of the same title derived from it, now in the British Museum and the National Gallery of Art, Washington, D.C. (c.1794-6), should perhaps be associated with this early interest in archaic British history.

52 Keynes, *Blake*, p. 577.

53 *Ibid.*, p. 578.

54 Quoted in Morton D. Paley, 'William Blake, The Prince of the Hebrews, and The Woman Clothed with the Sun' in Paley and Phillips (eds), *William Blake*, p. 283.

55 *Ibid.*

56 See Prys Morgan, *Iolo Morganwg*, Aberystwyth, 1975.

57 Edith J. Morley (ed), *Blake, Coleridge, Wordsworth, Lamb, Etc. being Selections from the Remains of Henry Crabb Robinson*, Manchester, 1922, p. 20.

58 Keynes, *Blake*, pp. 580-1.

59 Quoted in A.G. Swinburne, *William Blake - a critical essay*, London, 1868, p. 81.

60 See Martin Butlin, *The Paintings and Drawings of William Blake*, New Haven and London, 1981, pp. 477-8.

61 Keynes, *Blake*, pp. 577-8.

Chapter Five

1 John Horsley's *Britannia Romana*, London, 1732, for example, was an annotated collection of the relevant classical texts. The bulk of these classical reports are gathered together in translation in Thomas Kendrick's, *The Druids: A Study in Keltic Prehistory*, London, 1927, reprinted 1966, pp. 73ff.

2 William Gilpin, *Observations, relative chiefly to*

Picturesque Beauty, Made in the Year 1772, On several Parts of England; particularly the Mountains, and Lakes of Cumberland and Westmoreland, II, 1786, p. 28.

3 As examples of bearings, medals and tokens the following are representative. The 1787 penny trade token of Thomas Williams' Parys Mines Company, Anglesey, bears a Druid's head on its obverse; the original plaster model by Richard Cockle Lucas (*c*.1850) for Colt Hoare's tomb, now displayed in the library at Stourhead, is flanked by Druid supporters; from 1807 the Clerk coat of arms included 'on the sinister side a Druid priest with a flowing beard proper vested and hooded argent holding in his exterior hand a branch of Oak acorned proper' (see John M. Gray, *Memoirs of the Life of Sir John Clerk of Penicuik*, Edinburgh, 1892, p. 5, n. 3); the Cymmrodorion armorial bearings, designed by Richard and William Morris, had a Druid supporter and members of Council of the Gwyneddigion Society wore silver badges with Druids' heads (see R.T. Jenkins and Helen M. Ramage, *A History of the Honourable Society of Cymmrodorion*, London, 1951, pp. 52 and 112).

4 *The Druids*, pp. 22–3.

5 See Stephen Orgel and Roy Strong, *Inigo Jones. The Theatre of the Stuart Court*, Sotheby Parke Bernet, London, 1973, II, pp. 724–5.

6 For a discussion of this series see Pamela M. Jones, 'Two newly-discovered hermit landscapes by Paul Bril' *The Burlington Magazine*, CXXX, no. 1018, January 1988, pp. 32–4.

7 The two most authoritative studies on Aubrey and Stukeley are respectively Michael Hunter, *John Aubrey and the Realm of Learning*, London, 1975 and Stuart Piggott, *William Stukeley, an Eighteenth Century Antiquary*, Oxford, 1950.

8 Part IV 'Britain', 626–46 in James Sambrook (ed), *James Thomson Liberty, The Castle of Indolence and other poems*, Oxford, 1986, pp. 107–8.

9 See A.L. Owen, *The Famous Druids - a survey of three centuries of English literature on the Druids*, Oxford, 1962, pp. 28–35, 59–60.

10 K.M. Burton (ed), *Milton's Prose Writings*, London, 1958, p. 176.

11 Unpaginated.

12 Quoted in Howard C. Levis, *Bladud of Bath, The British King who tried to fly*, 1919, reprinted 1973, p. 95.

13 Stuart Piggott, *The Druids*, Harmondsworth, 1968, pp. 129–31. See also Tim Mowl and Brian Earnshaw, *John Wood - Architect of Obsession*, Huddersfield, 1988, especially pp. 179–94; Eileen Harris, 'John Wood's system of architecture', *The Burlington Magazine*, CXXXI, no. 1031, February 1989, pp. 101–7.

14 Second edition, London, 1788, II, pp. 3ff. Henry was, however, critical of their pretensions to magic and divination, although he believed they were no more guilty in this than any similar priesthood in the ancient world. *Ibid.*, pp. 66–7.

15 p. 119.

16 p. 102.

17 Quoted in Edward D. Snyder, *The Celtic Revival in English Literature, 1760-1800*, Cambridge, Mass., 1923, p. 144.

18 See Aileen Elizabeth Ribeiro, *The Dress Worn at Masquerades in England, 1730-1790, and its Relation to Fancy Dress in Portraiture*, PhD dissertation, University of London (Courtauld Institute of Art), 1975, Garland reprint, 1984, pp. 67, 94, 98–9. Fisher's *Masque of the Druids*, staged at Covent Garden in 1774 and 1775, should be seen as part of this same enthusiasm.

19 Snyder, *Celtic Revival*, p. 157.

20 p. 2.

21 See Margaret Candee Jacob, 'John Toland and the Newtonian Ideology', *Journal of the Warburg and Courtauld Institutes*, XXXII, 1969, pp. 307–31.

22 John Toland, *A Critical History of the Celtic Religion and Learning: Containing an account of the Druids*, London, n.d. (?1740), pp. 50–1.

23 Owen, *Famous Druids*, p. 121.

24 p. 9.

25 Quoted in Snyder, *Celtic Revival*, p. 168.

26 Quoted in Owen, *Famous Druids*, pp. 130–1.

27 Edmund Burke, *An Enquiry into the Origin of our Ideas of the Sublime and Beautiful*, second edition, London, 1759, p. 100.

28 *Archaeologia*, VII, pp. 304–5.

29 *Ibid.*, p. 313.

30 p. 10.

31 Stephen Gill (ed), *The Salisbury Plain Poems of William Wordsworth*, New York, 1975, p. 24.

32 1805 text, Book 12, lines 315–353. For a discussion of the Druids, liberty and Wordsworth's development as a poet see Laurence Goldstein, *Ruins and Empire; The Evolution of a Theme in Augustan and Romantic Literature*, Pittsburgh 1977, pp. 126–80 passim.; Anne Janowitz, *England's Ruins - Poetic Purpose and the National Landscape*, Oxford, 1990, pp. 92–144.

33 Henry, *History*, pp. 63–7.

34 pp. 17–18.

35 *Ibid.*, p. 16, n. 32.

36 *Ibid.*, p. 15.

37 *Jerusalem*, plate 80, 48–50, Geoffrey Keynes (ed), *Blake - Complete Writings*, Oxford, 1990, p. 723.

38 On Blake and Druidism see Peter F. Fisher, 'Blake and the Druids', *Journal of English and Germanic Philology*, 1959, LVIII, pp. 589–612; Denis Saurat *Blake and Modern Thought*, London, 1929, pp. 51–85; Ruthven Todd, *Tracks in the Snow*, London, 1946, pp. 46–56; Owen, *Famous Druids*, pp. 224–36; Janowitz, *England's Ruins*, pp. 145–76.

39 *History of Great Britain*, I, p. 137.

40 p. 161.

41 Plate 11, 15–16, Keynes, *Blake*, p. 153.

42 Several of Blake's contemporary illustrations to the *Book of Job* (*c*.1805-26) also show megalithic

architecture in the background. This is entirely consistent, of course, with Blake's identification of Druidism with the patriarchs.

43 Lines 2-19, Keynes, *Blake*, p. 649.

44 Plate 6 in copy D, 20-6, *ibid.*, pp. 485-6.

45 Plate 4 in copy D, 11 and 27, *ibid.*, pp. 483-4.

46 Lines 15-16, *ibid.*, p. 708.

47 Plate 66, 1-15, *ibid.*, pp. 701-2.

48 Plate 24, 10, *ibid.*, p. 647.

49 Third edition, 1977, especially pp. 201-25, 462-87.

50 Geller is almost irredeemably obscure, but this engraving is illustrated and discussed by Richard Burnett in Michael Campbell, *John Martin, Visionary Printmaker*, Campbell Fine Art in association with York City Art Gallery, 1992, p. 195.

51 Gilpin, *Observations*, pp. 29 31.

52 See Brian Allen, *Francis Hayman*, New Haven and London, 1987, pp. 146-8; Brian Allen, *Francis Hayman and the English Rococo*, University of London (Courtauld Institute of Art) Phd dissertation, 1984, pp. 335-48.

53 Book XVI, 249, quoted in Kendrick, *The Druids*, pp. 88-9.

54 See John Sunderland, 'John Hamilton Mortimer; his life and works' *Walpole Society*, LII, 1986, pp. 19-22, cat. nos 13-13d, pp. 123-4, cat. no. 221, p. 211. It seems plausible to speculate that Mortimer's *Homer repeating his Verses to the Greeks*, etched by Robert Blyth in 1781 from a 1774 drawing (*ibid.*, cat. no. 99, p. 166) is a reprise of the *Saint Paul* etching and may even be its pendant.

55 *Ibid.*, p. 20.

56 *Ibid.*, cat. no. 163, p. 198.

57 *Cymbeline*, Act 5, Scene IV, in *A Collection of the Pieces formerly published by Henry Brooke Esq.*, 1778, p. 244. It is not clear whether the play was performed before 1778.

58 See John Gilmartin, 'Vincent Waldré's ceiling paintings in Dublin Castle', *Apollo*, XCV, no. 119 (new series), January 1972, pp. 42-7; Edward McParland, 'A Note on Vincent Waldré', *Apollo*, XCVI, no. 129 (new series) November 1972, p. 467.

59 William L. Pressly, 'James Barry's "The Baptism of the King of Cashel by St Patrick"', *The Burlington Magazine*, CXVIII, September 1976, pp. 643-7; William L Pressly, *The Life and Art of James Barry*, New Haven and London, 1981, pp. 2, 228 and 235.

60 Pressly, 'Baptism', 1976, pp. 645-6 and *Barry*, 1981, pp. 143-4, 175-6, 228, 235-6.

61 *The Illustrated London News*, no. 62, III, 8 July 1843, p. 18. See also T.S.R. Boase 'The Decoration of the New Palace of Westminster, 1841-1863', *Journal of the Warburg and Courtauld Institutes*, XVII, 1954, pp. 319-58.

62 The linking of Stonehenge with Druidism and hence with all pagan religion in these islands sanctioned its entirely anachronistic appearance, even according to nineteenth-century thinking on

its purpose, in the 1843 and 1844 fresco competitions when W.C. Thomas and J.C. Horsley both included its trilithons as a sign of Saxon paganism in their cartoons of *St Augustine Preaching to Ethelbert*. See Boase, *New Palace*, p. 337.

63 Owen, *Famous Druids*, pp. 59-61.

64 Lindsay Errington, *Social and Religious Themes in English Art, 1840-1860*, Garland reprint of Courtauld Institute of Art PhD dissertation, London, 1984, pp. 275-88.

65 Herbert Weinstock, *Vincenzo Bellini - His Life and His Operas*, London, 1972, pp. 275-6.

66 Leslie Orrey, *Bellini*, London, 1969, pp. 42-6.

67 See J.R. Planché, *Recollections and Reflections*, London, 1872, I, pp. 272-4. *Bonduca* was revived retitled as *Caractacus*.

68 Weinstock, *Bellini*, pp. 149-52, 268-72; Harold Rosenthal, *Two Centuries of Opera at Covent Garden*, London, 1958, pp. 45-61, 73-89, 679ff.

69 Davies, *Celtic Researches*, pp. 141, 172-3.

70 George Chalmers, *Caledonia: or, An Account of North Britain from the Most Ancient to the Present Times*, London, 1807, p. 70.

71 *The Annals of Tacitus*, transl. George Gilbert Ramsay, London, 1909, Book XIV, Chapters 29 and 30, p. 207.

72 pp. 38-9.

73 Those that are listed in Ernest A. Baker, *Guide to Historical Fiction*, London, 1914, are described as juvenile in the main and are typically produced no earlier than the last quarter of the nineteenth century. The most distinguished exception to this tendency is Sir Samuel Ferguson's historical poem *Congal*, Dublin and London, 1872, which relates the contest between paganism and Christianity in Ireland in the mid seventh century AD.

74 J.G. Lockhart, *Valerius: a Roman Story*, London 1821, III, pp. 297-8.

Chapter Six

1 See Reginald Horsman, 'Origins of Racial Anglo-Saxonism in Great Britain before 1850', *Journal of the History of Ideas*, XXXVII, July–September 1976, no. 3, pp. 387-410; J.W. Burrow, *Evolution and Society; A Study in Victorian Social Theory*, Cambridge, 1966, and *A Liberal Descent; Victorian Historians and the English Past*, Cambridge, 1981, especially pp. 108-19; Hugh A. MacDougall, *Racial Myth in English History; Trojans, Teutons and Anglo-Saxons*, Montreal, Hanover and London, 1982, pp. 89-130. My account draws heavily on Horsman and MacDougall's analyses. The present study concentrates on the image of ancient Britain alone and I have not attempted to pursue the constructions of Saxon England in the eighteenth and nineteenth centuries which would have at least doubled the length of this book and perhaps weakened its focus.

2 For an examination of cultural bias in the art history of this period see William Vaughan, 'The

Englishness of British Art', *The Oxford Art Journal*, XIII, no. 2, 1990, pp. 11-23.

3 For eighteenth-century theories of social development see Ronald L. Meek, *Social Science and the Ignoble Savage*, Cambridge, 1976.

4 '. . . all nations, even the most polished and civilized, of which we read in history, were originally barbarians . . . man himself was originally a wild savage animal, till he was tamed, and, as I may say, humanized, by civility and arts.' I, p. 144, quoted in J.S. Slotkin (ed), *Readings in Early Anthropology*, London, 1965, p. 447. Monboddo's stages of development progressed from the quadraped feral man to the orang-outan to wild savages and thence to herding and gathering. See E.L. Cloyd, *James Burnett, Lord Monboddo*, Oxford, 1972, especially pp. 40-4.

5 1800 edition, pp. 146-7, quoted in Slotkin, *Readings*, p. 436.

6 My understanding of the Four Stages theory of human progress and its development is heavily indebted to Meek's thorough study of the topic in *Social Science and the Ignoble Savage*.

7 Third edition, London, 1873, p. 79.

8 *Ibid.*, p. 59.

9 Keith Thomas, *Man and the Natural World; Changing Attitudes in England 1500-1800*, Harmondsworth, 1987, p. 94.

10 Cited in Edward D. Snyder, 'The Wild Irish: A Study of Some English Satires against the Irish, Scots, and Welsh', *Modern Philology*, April 1920, p. 149.

11 I part company here with Linda Colley, who has stressed the process of national integration between England, Wales and Scotland in this period. Colley emphasises, rightly, that ethnic difference was submerged by a growth in patriotic and British nationalist feeling. My point is that such a trans-national patriotism overlay older, deeper distinctions and that the image of the Celts presented in this period is testament to the preservation of these distinctions. As from some *cathédrale engloutie* the Celtic bell tolled beneath the sea of an essentially Anglo-Saxon 'British' patriotism. See Linda Colley 'Whose Nation? Class and National Consciousness in Britain 1750-1830', *Past and Present*, no. 113, November 1986, pp. 97-117 and *Britons; Forging the Nation 1707-1837*, New Haven and London, 1992.

12 Quoted in Ned Lebow, 'British Historians and Irish History', *Eire-Ireland*, VIII: 4, 1973, pp. 17-18.

13 pp. i-ii and xvi. See also Nicholas Canny 'The Formation of the Irish Mind: Religion, Politics and Gaelic Irish literature 1580-1750', *Past and Present*, no. 95, May 1982, pp. 91-116.

14 See Snyder, 'The Wild Irish', pp. 147-85; W.R. Jones, 'England against the Celtic Fringe: A Study in Cultural Stereotypes', *Journal of World History*, XIII - I - 1971, pp. 155-71; Lebow, 'British Historians', pp. 3-38.

15 [William Richards] *The Briton Describ'd; or, A Journey through WALES*, 1749 edition, pp. 34-54. It should be noted, however, that the first 34 pages of Richards' account are pretty disparaging about English country life too.

16 Snyder, 'The Wild Irish', p. 183.

17 Quoted in *ibid.*, p. 179, n. 2.

18 Thomas Carte, *A General History of England*, London, 1750, II, p. 196; see also Carte, pp. 186-96 on the Welsh and Edward I's conquest of Wales, which contains many similar statements.

19 See Gwyn A. Williams, 'Druids and Democrats: organic intellectuals and the first Welsh radicalism' in Raphael Samuel and Gareth Stedman Jones (eds), *Culture, Ideology and Politics*, History Workshop Series, London, 1982, pp. 247-76; D.J.V. Jones, *Before Rebecca: Popular Protest in Wales 1793-1835*, London, 1973.

20 pp. 67-8.

21 Walpole's letter to Pinkerton is dated 31 July 1789. Amidst a number of remarks critical of antiquarian research and supporting Pinkerton's attacks on the Celtomaniacs Walpole adds, 'Objection I have but one; I think you make yourself too much a party against the Celts - I do not think they were or are worthy of hatred.' W.S. Lewis (ed), *The Yale Edition of Horace Walpole's Correspondence*, New Haven and London, 1937-83, XVI, pp. 302-5. See also Pinkerton's letter of 10 November 1789, to the Earl of Buchan concerning his work's reception in Scotland in Dawson Turner (ed), *The Literary Correspondence of John Pinkerton*, London, 1830, I, pp. 236-7. Two lengthy replies to Pinkerton were John Lanne Buchanan's *A Defence of the Scots Highlanders*, London, 1794 and Edward Williams's *A Vindication of the Celts*, London, 1803.

22 p. 26.

23 *Ibid.*, p. 379.

24 David Hume, *The History of England*, revised edition, London, 1802, I, p. 425; quoted in Lebow, 'British Historians', p. 19.

25 Peter Levi (ed), Samuel Johnson, *A Journey to the Western Islands of Scotland*, London, 1775, Harmondsworth, 1984, p. 51.

26 The distinctions I draw here between eighteenth- and nineteenth-century understanding of race are derived from Michael Banton *The Idea of Race*, London, 1977, especially Chapter Two 'The racializing of the West', pp. 13-26.

27 Second edition 1788, II, p. 1.

28 See Thomas Preston Peardon, *The Transition in English Historical Writing 1760-1830*, New York, 1966, pp. 34-7; 'Robert Henry' in *Dictionary of National Biography*.

29 p. 92.

30 See Horsman, 'Origins', pp. 396-8.

31 See Mary Cowling, *The Artist as Anthropologist - The representation of type and character in Victorian Art*, Cambridge, 1989, pp. 17-60.

32 *Ibid.*, pp. 40-54.

33 'The Great and Comprehensive Measure',

Fraser's Magazine for Town and Country, XXV, no. 207, March 1847, p. 373.

34 pp. 6-8. Despite Pearson's use of archaeological data here it is noteworthy that archaeology itself did not fall prey to the Teutonic enthusiasms of other disciplines in this period. Even so, as Pearson's example demonstrates, the context in which archaeology's findings were received, the epistemic matrix of the age, would have affected the uses to which archaeology might be put.

35 Thomas Carlyle, *Chartism*, London, 1858 edition, pp. 18-19. Carlyle's conclusion is devestating: 'The time has come when the Irish population must either be improved a little, or else exterminated' (*ibid.*, p. 19). As is well known, Engels quoted from this passage in 'Irish Immigration', part of his *Condition of the Working Class in England* (1845) and endorsed Carlyle's account of the impact of Irish immigration on English labourers' pay and conditions. See also V.G. Kiernan, 'Britons Old and New' and Sheridan Gilley, 'English Attitudes to the Irish in England, 1780-1900' in Colin Holmes (ed), *Immigrants and Minorities in British Society*, London, 1978, pp. 23-59 and 81-110.

36 The work of L. Perry Curtis has done most to draw attention to racist depiction of the Irish; despite more recent studies (e.g. Gilley, 'English Attitudes') challenging his thesis that the Irish were simianised as part of a virulent racist stereotyping by hostile English commentators, Curtis' work is still important. See L. Perry Curtis, Jr. *Anglo-Saxons and Celts: A Study of Anti-Irish Prejudice in Victorian England*, Conference on British Studies, Bridgeport, Connecticut, 1968 and *Apes and Angels - The Irishman in Victorian Caricature*, Washington, 1971.

37 Frederic G. Stephens, *A Memoir of George Cruikshank*, London, 1891, p. 55. Stephens goes on to explain the disappearance of Irish casual labourers with reference to the increased mechanisation of agriculture. Cruikshank's veracity in his depiction of the Irish is vindicated, for Stephens, by the fact that 'Mr. Tenniel still delineates their baboon-like faces with muzzles and the eyes of sullen beasts of prey' (*Ibid.*).

38 See Samuel Kliger, *The Goths in England - a study in seventeenth and eighteenth century thought*, Cambridge, Mass., 1952, pp. 115-43; T.D. Kendrick *British Antiquity*, London, 1955, pp. 34-64; MacDougall, *Racial Myth*, pp. 31-63.

39 See MacDougall, *Racial Myth*, p. 56; David C. Douglas, *English Scholars, 1660-1730*, revised edition, London, 1951, p. 119.

40 Quoted in Kliger, *The Goths*, pp. 190-1. Sydney's *Works* were republished in 1772.

41 Paul Rapin de Thoyras, *The History of England*, second edition, London, 1732, p. vi; Carte, *A General History of England*, London, 1747, I, p. 27; for Blackstone see Burrow, *A Liberal Descent*, p. 111.

42 For Whitaker see Peardon, *Transition*, pp. 135-8;

Henry, *History*, I, pp. 293-330.

43 See Peardon, *Transition*, p. 101.

44 Luke Owen Pike, *The English and their Origin*, London, 1866, pp. 15-16, quoted in Banton, *The Idea of Race*, p. 26.

45 pp. xii-xiii.

46 p. 32.

47 See Horsman, 'Origins', p. 394; 'Sharon Turner' in *Dictionary of National Biography*.

48 Sharon Turner, *The History of the Anglo-Saxons*, third edition, London, 1820, p. 101.

49 Robert Southey, *Colloquies on Society*, 1887 edition, pp. 48-55, 61-7.

50 p. 4.

51 Huxley's article appeared in the *Pall Mall Gazette*, 10 January 1870, pp. 8-9; Allen's in the *Fortnightly Review*, XXVIII, 1880, pp. 472-87. Both of these articles are reprinted in the excellent anthology edited by Michael D. Biddis, *Images of Race*, Leicester, 1979, pp. 157-69 and 237-56 respectively.

52 Allen, 'Are We Englishmen?', p. 487, quoted in Biddis, *Images of Race*, p. 255.

Chapter Seven

1 See Paul Hulton, *America 1585; The Complete Drawings of John White*, North Carolina and London, 1984. De Heere is discussed in Christopher Chippindale, *Stonehenge Complete*, London, 1983, pp. 33-6.

2 John Edward Jackson (ed), *Wiltshire. The Topographical Collections of John Aubrey F.R.S. A.D. 1659-70 with illustrations*, Wiltshire Archaeological Society, Devizes, 1862, pp. 4-5.

3 The classic account of primitivism is A.O. Lovejoy and G. Boas, *Primitivism and Related Ideas in Antiquity*, Baltimore, 1935, who first differentiated 'hard' from 'soft' primitivism. See also Lois Whitney, 'English Primitivistic Theories of Epic origins', *Modern Philology*, XXI, no. 4, May 1924, pp. 337-78; Hoxie Neale Fairchild, *The Noble Savage - a study in Romantic naturalism*, New York, 1961.

4 p. 11.

5 Stephen Bann, *The Clothing of Clio*, Cambridge, 1984.

6 Blakey's work for the Knaptons and Dodsley is discussed in Brian Allen, *Francis Hayman and the English Rococo*, University of London (Courtauld Institute of Art) PhD dissertation, 1984, pp. 335-40.

7 Twas on those downs, by Roman hosts annoy'd
  Fought our bold fathers, rustic, unrefin'd.
  Freedom's plain sons, in martial cares employ'd!
  They tinged their bodies, but unmask'd their mind
'Elegy XV', in *Works in Verse and Prose*, London, 1764, I, p. 52; quoted in Samuel Kliger, *The Goths in England*, Harvard, 1952, p. 89.

8 Edward D. Snyder, *The Celtic Revival in English*

Literature 1760-1800, Harvard, 1923, p. 88.

9 William Hay, *Mount Caburn - a poem*, London, 1730, pp. 12-13.

10 Second epode of William Collins 'Ode to Liberty', from *Odes on Several Descriptive and Allegorical Subjects*, 1746, in Arthur Johnston (ed), *Selected Poems of Thomas Gray and William Collins*, London, 1967, p. 180.

11 Walpole saw the play that December and gave it a mixed review. 'There is a new play of Glover's, in which Boadicea the heroine rants as much as Visconti screams; but happily you hear no more of her after the third act, till in the last scene somebody brings a card with her compliments and she is very sorry she can't wait upon you, but she is dead. Then there is a scene between *Lord Sussex* and *Lord Cathcart*, two captives, which is most incredibly absurd; but yet the parts are so well acted, the dresses so fine, and two or three scenes pleasing enough, that it is worth seeing.' Letter dated 6 December 1753 in W.S. Lewis (ed), *The Yale Edition of Horace Walpole's Correspondence*, New Haven and London, 1937-83, IX, pp.157-8.

12 William Mason, *Caractacus; a Dramatic Poem*, Dublin, 1764, p. 28.

13 In Thomas Pennant, *Tours in Wales*, III, London, 1810, p. 275.

14 Edward Davies, *Aphtharte, or the Genius of Britain*, Bath, 1784, pp. 17-18. The advertisement to the poem says that it was written chiefly in 1774.

15 Abraham Portal, *Vortimer, or the True Patriot*, London, 1796, p. 8.

16 *Ibid.*, p. 60.

17 pp. 5-6. The play was never performed.

18 Barbara Jones, *Follies and Grottoes*, revised edition, London, 1974, p. 54.

19 See John W. Draper, *William Mason - a Study in eighteenth century Culture*, New York, 1924, pp. 177-8; on Mason's politics see Bernard Barr and John Ingamells, *A Candidate for Praise; William Mason 1725-97 Precentor of York*, York Festival, 1973, pp. 75-6.

20 The stories of Caractacus and Boadicea are as follows. Caratacus (the correct spelling) son of Cunobelinus (the Cymbeline of Shakespeare) incited the Trinovantes to oppose the Roman invasion in AD 43 but was defeated by Plautius and fled to the Silures, at whose head he resisted Roman domination until defeated by Ostorius in AD 50. He then fled to the Brigantes but was betrayed by their queen Cartimandua and handed over to Ostorius, taken to Rome and eventually pardoned by Claudius. The story is chiefly related in Tacitus' *Annals*, books xi-xii and Dio's *Roman History*, book lx. Boadicea (correctly known as Boudicca) the widow of king Prasutagus had been intended to rule the Iceni in partnership with her two daughters and Rome. The Romans reneged on the agreement, plundered the kingdom, flogged Boudicca and violated her daughters. She led a major revolt in AD 61 at the head of a confederacy of eastern tribes, sacked Colchester and London but was defeated by Suetonius Paulinus and poisoned herself. The story is related in Tacitus' *Annals*, books xiii-xiv and his *Agricola*, chapters 15-16 and in Dio's *Roman History*, book lxii.

21 Quoted in Stuart Piggott, *The Druids*, Harmondsworth, 1974, p. 184. As Briggs had painted Samuel Rush Meyrick's portrait in 1829 it is perhaps reasonable to associate this picture with that antiquarian's influence.

22 A further example is William Holman Hunt's *Roman Soldier reading the New Testament to a British Family*, engraved by W.J. Linton as the frontispiece for *Days of Old. Three Stories from Old English History. For the Young* by the author of *Ruth and her Friends*, Macmillan, London, 1858. Hunt's image illustrated the story *Caradoc and Deva*, set in AD 43.

23 T.S. Eliot (ed), *A Choice of Kipling's Verse*, London, 1963, p. 287.

24 See Victor Kiernan, 'Tennyson, King Arthur and imperialism' in Raphael Samuel and Gareth Stedman Jones (eds), *Culture, Ideology and Politics*, History Workshop Series, London, 1982, pp. 126-48.

25 pp. 40 and 49, quoted in Philippa Levine, *The Amateur and the Professional; Antiquarians, Historians and Archaeologists in Victorian England, 1838-1886*, Cambridge, 1986, p. 82.

26 The Trevelyans' patronage of Scott and Woolner is described in Raleigh Trevelyan, *A Pre-Raphaelite Circle*, London, 1978.

27 From a review in the *Athenaeum*, quoted in Amy Woolner *Thomas Woolner, R.A., Sculptor and Poet - his Life in Letters*, London, 1917, p. 3.

28 See Mary Cowling, *The Artist as Anthropologist - the Representation of Type and Character in Victorian Art*, Cambridge, 1989.

29 *Ibid.*, pp. 123-30.

30 In this connection it is noteworthy that Scott's use of his friends as models for the protagonists in the Wallington series did not include these Celtic tribespeople.

31 Second edition, London, 1849, I, p. 4. It is likely that Macaulay's views were received sympathetically at Wallington given that Macaulay was related by marriage to the Trevelyan family. In 1834 his sister, Hannah, married Walter Calverley Trevelyan's cousin Sir Charles Trevelyan, who inherited Wallington Hall from Calverley on his death in 1876. Lady Trevelyan edited volume V of Macaulay's *History of England* (1861) and George Otto Trevelyan, his nephew, wrote his biography in 1876.

32 G.M. Young (ed), *Macaulay - Prose and Poetry*, London, 1952, p. 718.

33 Quoted in T.S.R. Boase, 'The Decoration of the New Palace of Westminster, 1841-1863', *Journal of the Warburg and Courtauld Institutes*, XVII, 1954, p. 341.

34 I, 'Revolutions of Race', p. 14.

35 Each of the six sculptors was to receive £700 for his commission to illustrate 'the creations of the poets of Great Britain', which means that Mason, presumably, as author of *Caractacus* would be rubbing shoulders with Gray (William Theed's *Bard*), Spenser (Wyon's *Britomart*), Shakespeare (Durham's *Hermione*), Milton (Baily's *Spirit of the Woods*) and Byron (Weekes' *Sardanapalus*). Given the otherwise reputable choice of poets I suspect that *Caractacus*, uniquely in this group, represented *himself* rather than Mason's interpretation of him, whose critical fortunes did not survive the eighteenth century. See the *Art Journal*, 1856, p. 126 and 1860, p. 86.

36 W. Cosmo Monkhouse, *The Works of John Henry Foley RA Sculptor*, London, 1875, pp. 30-1.

37 *Ibid.*, p. 31.

38 Quoted in Brian Allen, *Francis Hayman* (1984), p. 336.

39 *Ibid.*, p. 337.

40 No page number.

41 *Elucidation of Mr Bowyer's Plan for a magnificent edition of Hume's History of England*, London, 1795. See also T.S.R. Boase 'Macklin and Bowyer', *Journal of the Warburg and Courtauld Institutes*, XXVI, 1963, pp. 148-77.

42 See T.P. Hudson, 'Moor Park, Leoni and Sir James Thornhill', *Burlington Magazine*, CXIII, November 1971, pp. 657-61; *English Baroque Sketches - the painted Interior in the Age of Thornhill*, London, 1974, nos 55-60.

43 '*The noble Behaviour of* Caractacus *the* Briton, *before the Emperor* Claudius *at* Rome'. The print and its accompanying letterpress are in the collection of the Yale Center for British Art, New Haven (B. 1977.14. 11716/21). For a further discussion see Allen, *Francis Hayman*, pp. 335-44.

44 Sammes, *Britannia Antiqua Illustrata*, 1676, p. 130.

45 See Draper, *William Mason*, pp. 89-90.

46 The most explicitly Christ-like Caractacus known to me is Howard Dudley's engraving 'Caractacus before Ostorius, the Roman General' in John Lingard's, *History of England*, sixth edition, 1854, opposite page 23.

47 See C.F. Bell (ed), *Annals of Thomas Banks*, Cambridge, 1938, pp. 43-5.

48 R.T. Jenkins and Helen M. Ramage, *A History of the Honourable Society of Cymmrodorion*, London, 1951, p. 128.

49 Quoted in M.S. Watts, *George Frederick Watts - The Annals of an Artist's Life*, London, 1912, I, p. 44.

50 'Exhibition of Cartoons in Westminster Hall', *The Illustrated London News*, III, no. 62, 8 July 1843, p. 18.

51 Quoted in Ronald Chapman, *The Laurel and the Thorn - a study of G F Watts*, London, 1945, p. 19.

52 Third edition, London, 1873, pp. 89-90.

53 Glover's play may have been performed much earlier, if Thomas Gray's letter of Spring 1742 is reliable. See Draper, *William Mason*, p. 176.

54 See John Sunderland 'Samuel Johnson and History Painting' in D.G.C. Allan and John L. Abbott (eds), *The Virtuoso Tribe of Arts and Sciences - Studies in the Eighteenth-Century Work and Membership of the London Society of Arts*, Athens (Georgia) and London, 1992, pp. 183-94.

55 *Britannia Antiqua Illustrata*, p. 228, engraved W. Faithorne.

56 Stanzas 1 and 5 , in *Tennyson Poems and Plays*, Oxford, 1965, pp. 224-5. See also Kiernan, 'Tennyson', p. 138, who suggests that Tennyson may have modelled his Boadicea on the Rani of Jhansi.

57 Quoted in Elfrida Manning, *Marble and Bronze - the Art and Life of Hamo Thornycroft*, London, 1982, p. 38.

Chapter Eight

1 See Leslie V. Grinsell, *Folklore of Prehistoric Sites in Britain*, Newton Abbot, 1976.

2 Christopher Chippindale, *Stonehenge Complete*, London, 1983. This book is not only the fundamental guide to Stonehenge itself and its representations, but also provides in one volume the most accessible authoritative introduction to antiquarian thought in this period.

3 Louis Hawes, *Constable's Stonehenge*, HMSO, 1975, p. 11.

4 See Arthur Lambert Flett, *Ruins: The Development of a Theme in Eighteenth Century British Landscape Painting c.1760-1800*, unpublished PhD dissertation, Indiana University, 1981, pp. 93-5.

5 One thinks, for example, of Paul Nash, Henry Moore, Barbara Hepworth and Richard Long in this country, of Carl André and 1970s Land Art in the U.S.A., of Yves Tanguy in France. For information on the more recent manifestations of this phenomenon see Lucy Lippard, *Overlay: Contemporary Art and the Art of Prehistory*, New York, 1983 and Elizabeth Jaeger, *Neolithic Stone Circles and Contemporary Art in the Landscape*, New York, 1984.

6 See Ian Ousby, *The Englishman's England - Taste, travel and the rise of tourism*, Cambridge, 1990; Malcolm Andrews, *The Search for the Picturesque*, Aldershot, 1989; Esther Moir, *The Discovery of Britain*, London, 1964.

7 The three most extensive treatments known to me of ruins in the romantic imagination are Flett; Laurence Goldstein, *Ruins and Empire. The Evolution of a Theme in Augustan and Romantic Literature*, Pittsburgh, 1977; and Anne Janowitz, *England's Ruins - Poetic Purpose and the National Landscape*, Oxford, 1990.

8 Quoted in William Long, 'Stonehenge and its Bar-

rows', *The Wiltshire Magazine*, XVI , no. 46, 1876, p. 89.

9 A.G. Bradley, *Round about Wiltshire*, London, 1907, p. 174.

10 Garland Greever (ed) *A Wiltshire Parson and his Friends - The Correspondence of William Lisle Bowles*, London, 1926, p. 78. Letter dated 2 May 1828.

11 p. 160.

12 VII, 1818.

13 Henry Fuseli, 'Lecture IV - On Invention, Part II' in John Knowles (ed), *The Life and Writings of J.H. Fuseli Esq., MA, RA*, II, London, 1831, p. 217.

14 Peter Levi (ed), James Boswell, *The Journal of a Tour to the Hebrides with Samuel Johnson, LL. D.* (1786), Harmondsworth, 1984. Journal entry for Monday, 30 August 1773.

15 p. 139.

16 Robert Latham and William Matthews (eds) *The Diary of Samuel Pepys*, London. 1976, IX, p. 228. Entry for 10 June 1668.

17 pp. 77, 80-1.

18 William Gilpin, 'On Picturesque Beauty', *Three Essays*, London, 1792, p. 19.

19 1810 edition, I, pp. 51-2.

20 Revd. Richard Warner, *A Tour through Cornwall in the Autumn of 1808*, Bath, 1809, pp. 120-2. Warner's first quotation is from William Mason's dramatic poem *Caractacus* (1759).

21 Wilkie Collins, *Rambles beyond Railways or notes in Cornwall taken a-foot*, London, 1851, p. 26.

22 1835 edition. This *Guide* was the fifth version of a description of the Lakes which had first appeared anonymously in 1810. The Long Meg poem occurs as part of a lengthy footnote on the second page of 'Section Second. Aspect of the Country as affected by its Inhabitants'.

23 Paul Oppé (ed), 'Memoirs of Thomas Jones, Penkerrig Radnorshire, 1803', *Walpole Society*, XXXII, 1946-8, p. 21.

24 Edward Daniel Clarke, *A Tour through the South of England, Wales, and part of Ireland made during the summer of 1791*, London, 1793, p. 33.

25 [Richard Fenton] *A Tour in Quest of Genealogy through several parts of Wales, Somersetshire and Wiltshire in a series of letters to a friend in Dublin*, London, 1811, pp. 268-9.

26 This watercolour is probably based on a drawing by George Robertson. See Hawes, *Constable's Stonehenge*, p. 22, n. 49.

27 John Hassell, *Tour of the Isle of Wight*, London, 1790, II, pp. 227-8, 235-7.

28 In *Poetical Essays on Several Occasions*, London, 1733, I, p. 111.

29 See Allen M. Samuels, 'Rudolph Ackermann and *The English Dance of Death*', *The Book Collector*, XXIII, no. 3, Autumn 1974, pp. 371-80. The artist is usually presumed to be Thomas Rowlandson but Samuels attributes this design to Richard Cosway on the basis of a letter from

Ackermann to Cosway concerning the design of the plate.

30 Quoted in Hawes, *Constable's Stonehenge*, p. 9.

31 *Ibid.*, p. 5.

32 As is well known, Constable was critical of Ruisdael's attempts to produce explicitly allegorical meanings in his 'Cemetery'; nevertheless, while we may not be justified in thinking Constable a symbolic painter, a case can certainly be made for his use of allusive and poetically suggestive combinations of motif in much of his mature work of the 1830s.

33 See Chapter One.

34 Archibald Geikie, *Life of Sir Roderick I Murchison*, London, 1875, I, pp. 227-8.

35 Roy Porter, *The Making of Geology - Earth sciences in Britain 1660-1815*, Cambridge, 1977, p. 103.

36 John Ruskin, *Modern Painters*, London, 1888, V, pp. 147-8.

37 Hawes, *Constable's Stonehenge*, p. 10.

38 John Macpherson, *Critical dissertations on the origin, antiquities, language, government, manners, and religion, of the antient Caledonians, their posterity the Picts, and the British and Irish Scots*, Dubin, 1768, p. 288.

39 John Britton, *A Topographical and Historical Description of the County of Wilts* (c. 1819) [reissue of *Beauties of Wiltshire*, 1813], pp. 357-8.

40 For this drawing see Adele M. Holcomb, 'Devil's Den: An Early Drawing by John Sell Cotman', *Master Drawings*, XI, no. 4, Winter 1973, pp. 393-8. My thanks to Michael Pidgley for drawing my attention to this article. Two drawings, dated 1824 and attributed to Cotman, of Plas Newydd, Anglesey, and Winterbourne Abbas, Dorset are to be found among the eleven watercolours of prehistoric antiquities on the front of John Britton's "Celtic Cabinet" in Devizes Museum. I am advised, however, by Michael Pidgley that these attributions to Cotman are probably erroneous. See Christopher Chippindale, 'John Britton's "Celtic Cabinet" in Devizes Museum and its context', *The Antiquaries Journal*, LXV, part 1, 1985, pp. 121-37.

41 These boulders are usually referred to as the Ponty-Cromlech Boulders and lie below the cliff of Dinas Cromlech in Llanberis Pass, close to Cromlech Bridge. See *Country Life*, 10 April 1986, p. 944 and 22 May 1986, p. 1447. Hilarie Faberman (personal communication) suggests that 'The House of the Three Stones' may be a dealer's title. See Hilarie Faberman, *Modern Master Drawings; Forty Years of Collecting at the University of Michigan Museum of Art*, Ann Arbor, 1986, p. 40.

42 Both drawings are briefly discussed in Sydney Kitson, *The Life of John Sell Cotman*, London, 1937, pp. 29-38. For Cotman and the Sketching Society generally see Jean Hamilton, *The Sketching Society 1799-1851*, HMSO, 1971.

234

Chapter Nine

1 See David Watkin, *The English Vision*, London, 1982, pp. 22-3; David Jacques, *Georgian Gardens - The Reign of Nature*, London, 1983, p. 50.

2 See Michel Baridon, 'Ruins as a mental construct', *Journal of Garden History*, V, no. 1, January-March 1985, pp. 84-96; John Dixon Hunt and Peter Willis (eds), *The Genius of the Place - The English Landscape Garden, 1620-1820*, London, 1975, pp. 33-41.

3 Recognition of prehistoric garden motifs as a romantic phenomenon stems from Barbara Jones, *Follies and Grottoes*, London, 1953, revised edition 1974; see also Glyn Daniel, *Megaliths in History*, London, 1972, pp. 39-52.

4 Inigo Jones, *The most notable Antiquity of Great Britain, vulgarly called Stone-Heng on Salisbury plain. Restored.*, London, 1655, p. 4. Jones' insistence on the Druids' lack of architecture was a preliminary to his attempted demonstration that Stonehenge was a Roman temple. This sparked a contoversy; Dr Walter Charleton attacked Jones's thesis in *Chorea Gigantum*, 1663, and John Webb defended Jones in *A Vindication of Stone-Heng Restored*, 1665. A second edition of Jones's work was published in 1725 so prolonging the debate into the eighteenth century.

5 I am indebted to David Jacques for this point.

6 Hunt and Willis, *The Genius of the Place*, p. 291.

7 *Ibid.*, p. 305.

8 *The World*, no. 76, 13 June 1754, quoted in Jacques *Georgian Gardens*, p. 64.

9 For hermitages in early garden design see John Dixon Hunt, *The Figure in the Landscape: Poetry, Painting, and Gardening during the Eighteenth Century*, Baltimore, 1976, pp. 2ff.

10 Quoted in David Irwin, 'A "Picturesque" experience: The Hermitage at Dunkeld', *The Connoisseur*, CLXXXVII, no. 753, November 1974, p. 201.

11 Thomas Wright, *Universal Architecture Book II, Six Original Designs of Grottos*, London, 1758, Plate I and Ip.

12 Thomas Wright, *Universal Architecture Book I, Six Original Designs of Arbours*, London, 1755, Plate E and Ep.

13 For Wright's career see Eileen Harris (ed), *Thomas Wright- Arbours and Grottos - a facsimile of the two parts of Universal Architecture (1755 and 1758) with a catalogue of Wright's works in architecture and garden design*, Aldershot, 1979.

14 *Kemys-Tynte papers*, Somerset Record Office, DD/S/WH 320, diary entry for Wednesday, 25 August 1756.

15 Quoted in Revd. John Collinson *The History and Antiquities of the County of Somerset*, Bath, 1791, p. 83.

16 Barbara Jones, *Follies and Grottoes*, London, 1974, pp. 100-5.

17 Letter dated 30 November 1771, quoted in Kenneth Woodbridge, *The Stourhead Landscape*, The National Trust, 1989, p. 27; for an extensive treatment of Henry Hoare's development of Stourhead see also Kenneth Woodbridge, *Landscape and Antiquity*, Oxford, 1970.

18 See Arthur Oswald, 'Beauties and Wonders of Hawkstone', *Country Life*, CXXIV, no. 3207, 3 July 1958, pp. 18-21 and no. 3208, 10 July 1958, pp. 72-5.

19 Richard Warner, *A Tour through the Northern Counties of England and the Borders of Scotland*, Bath, 1802, II, p. 178.

20 See Jones, *Follies*, p. 142; I have followed Luke Hermann, *Paul and Thomas Sandby*, Victoria and Albert Museum, 1986, pp. 146-50, who makes the case for the date and patron.

21 See Christopher Thacker, *Masters of the Grotto - Joseph and Josiah Lane*, Tisbury, 1976; Geoffrey Grigson *Gardenage, or the plants of Ninhursaga*, London, 1952, pp. 150-65.

22 Richard Warner, *Excursions from Bath*, Bath, 1801, p. 210.

23 Daniel, *Megaliths*, pp. 39-40.

24 Unpaginated.

25 See Kimerly Rorschach, *The Early Georgian Landscape Garden*, Yale Center for British Art, 1983, pp. 48-9.

26 See James Holloway and Lindsay Errington, *The Discovery of Scotland; The Appreciation of Scottish Scenery through Two Centuries of Painting*, National Gallery of Scotland, 1978, p. 57.

27 See Peter Bicknell, 'The Picturesque Scenery of the Lake District, 1752-1855', *The Book Collector*, Summer 1987, pp. 186-9.

28 Warner, *Northern Counties* p. 99.

29 Quoted in Malcolm Andrews, *The Search for the Picturesque*, Aldershot, 1989, pp. 182-3.

30 pp. 10-11.

31 See Caroline Kerkham, 'Hafod: paradise lost', *Journal of Garden History*, 1991, XI, no. 4, pp. 207-16. The fullest account of Johnes and the development of Hafod is Elisabeth Inglis-Jones, *Peacocks in Paradise*, London, 1950.

32 Andrews, *Search for the Picturesque*, pp. 145-8.

33 Quoted in Herbert M. Vaughan, 'Some Letters of Thomas Johnes of Hafod (1794-1807)', *Y Cymmrodor*, 1925, p. 203.

34 See Aubrey Burl, *The Stone Circles of the British Isles*, New Haven and London, 1976, p. 11.

35 See George Sheeran, 'The Richardsons and their garden at Bierley Hall', *Bradford Antiquary*, 3 series, no. 4, 1988/89, pp. 3-10.

36 This is suggested by G. Bernard Wood, 'Bierley Hall', *Yorkshire Life Illustrated*, October 1956, p. 43.

37 Book 4, 414-28. As Mason notes, Villario refers to the disappointed landscape improver of Pope's *Epistle to Lord Burlington*, 79-88.

38 *Ibid.*, 407-12.

39 See Ursula Powys 'Recreations of a Georgian Family', *Country Life*, CXXVII, no. 3290, 24 March 1960, pp. 640-2. Further relocations of megaliths, in addition to those discussed in this chapter,

include the 1830 removal of 'Poind's Man' from Shaftoe Crags to Wallington Hall, Northumberland; see Michael Shanks, *Experiencing the Past – on the Character of Archaeology*, London, 1992, p. 121.

40 Letter dated 12 September 1788 in W.S. Lewis (ed), *The Yale Edition of Horace Walpole's Correspondence*, New Haven and London, 1937–83, XXXV, p. 396; see also XI, p. 75, XXXIV, pp. 14–15, 21, XXXV, p. 395, XXXIX, pp. 460–1. Walpole kept a model of the temple in the Small Closet at Strawberry Hill.

41 See Nigel Temple, *John Nash & the Village Picturesque*, Gloucester, 1979, pp. 61–3.

42 See John Meehan 'Lady Darnley's Flower Garden: History, Survey and Restoration', (Special Study submitted for the Landscape Ecology, Design and Maintainance MSc, Wye College 1987), pp. 22–8. The evidence is ambiguous, however, and a date of 1830 for the cromlech and standing stones is suggested in Kedrun Laurie, *Cobham Hall Kent – Historical Survey of the Park* (Survey for Cobham Hall Heritage Trust), 1984, pp. 79–81. My thanks to Pauline King, the Cobham Hall archivist for bringing these sources to my attention.

43 Studies of Masham include John Cornforth 'Swinton, Yorkshire – III', *Country Life*, CXXXIX, no. 3607, 21 April 1966, pp. 944–8; Stewart F. Sanderson 'Druids-As-Wished-For' in J.V.S. Megaw (ed), *To Illustrate the Monuments-Essays in Archaeology presented to Stuart Piggott*, London, 1976, pp. 24–6. Cornforth states that the temple was in existence by 1803, Sanderson that it was built in the 1820s. Susan Cunliffe-Lister dates it to about 1800, modelled on an example Danby had seen on a continental tour; see her *Days of Yore: a History of Masham*, 1978, p. 120.

44 'Viator' 'Banwell Cottage, Somersetshire. The seat of the Bishop of Bath and Wells', *The Gentleman's Magazine*, VIII, New Series, November 1837, p. 467.

45 Jones, *Follies* p. 126.

46 Nor is the designer identified from among those who worked for Talbot.

47 Quoted in Christopher Hussey, 'Alton Towers, Staffordshire – the valley garden and its buildings', *Country Life*, CXXVII, no. 3300, 2 June 1960, p. 1246. Loudon provided a less explicitly critical description of Alton Towers in the following year in the 1834 edition of his *Encyclopedia of Gardening*, pp. 327–33.

48 J.C. Loudon, *An Encyclopaedia of Gardening*, London, 1822, p. 1172.

49 Note dated 2 September 1833 in 'Notes on Gardens and Country seats . . . by the CONDUCTOR' *The Gardener's Magazine*, October 1836, p. 508. My thanks to Howard Leathlean for finding the original source. Some of this material has been republished in Priscilla Boniface (ed), *In Search of English Gardens – The Travels of John Claudius Loudon and his wife Jane*, Harpenden, 1987.

50 Late eighteenth and nineteenth century prehistoric follies of various sizes can be found at Busbridge Lakes, Surrey; The Quinta, Weston Rhyn, Shropshire; West Meon Hut, Hampshire; Kingston Deverill, Wiltshire; Tracey Park, Doynton, Avon; Reynoldston, Gower; Hagley Hall, Worcestershire; Stancombe Park, Gloucestershire; Piercefield Park, Chepstow, Monmouthshire and Blarney Castle, Co. Cork. Most of them are discussed in Jones, *Follies*.

51 The correspondence is discussed in Brent Elliott, *Victorian Gardens*, London, 1986, pp. 178–9. My thanks to Howard Leathlean for bringing this to my attention.

52 Edward Williams, a self-educated stone-mason, adopted this name (Ned of Glamorgan) sometime in 1788, prompted by his researches into mediaeval Welsh literature and his elaboration of a Druid/bardic tradition for Wales. See Prys Morgan, *Iolo Morganwg*, Aberystwith, 1975.

53 *The Gentleman's Magazine*, October 1792, pp. 956–7. Some sources give 21 June 1792 as the date (the summer solstice as opposed to the autumnal equinox of 22 September) but I can find no record of a June meeting. Dillwyn Miles, *The Royal National Eisteddfod of Wales*, Swansea, 1977, p. 45, for example quotes extracts from the *Gentleman's Magazine* report but relates them to the putative June meeting and concludes that a second meeting was held on 22 September. I suspect that this confusion stems from reliance on the authority of R.T. Jenkins and Helen M. Ramage, *A History of the Honourable Society of Cymmrodorion*, London, 1951, p. 127, which also gives 21 June but without a source.

54 See Miles, *Eisteddfod*, pp. 57, 81–5, 146–52.

55 Cf. Wright, *Universal Architecture*, 1755, 'In general, great Precaution will be necessary with Regard to the Situation of these Designs that no one of them appear in Sight of another or of any regular Piece of Architecture, being imagined to please most, where they may be naturally supposed the only Productions of the Age, before Building became a Science.'

56 Undated letter reprinted in Philip Gosse *Dr Viper. The Querulous Life of Philip Thicknesse*, London, 1952, p. 146.

57 Second Epode, 89–96. Arthur Johnston (ed), *Selected Poems of Thomas Gray and William Collins*, London, 1967, p. 180.

58 *Common Sense*, no. 150, 15 December 1739, quoted in Samuel Kliger, *The Goths in England- a Study in Seventeenth and Eighteenth Century Thought*, Cambridge, Mass., 1952, p. 27.

59 For a discussion of the garden's politics see George Clarke, 'Grecian Taste and Gothic Virtue: Lord Cobham's gardening programme and its iconography', *Apollo*, XCVII (new series) no. 136, June 1973, pp. 566–71. The seven sculptures executed by Michael Rysbrack are discussed in Susan Moore 'Hail! Gods of our Fore-Fathers – Rysbrack's "lost" Saxon Deities at Stowe', *Coun-*

try Life, CLXXVII, no. 4563, 31 January 1985, pp. 250-1 and in John Kenworthy-Browne, 'Rysbrack's Saxon Deities', *Apollo*, CXXII, September 1985, pp. 220-7. See also Gervase Jackson-Stops, 'John Michael Rysbrack; A Saxon Goddess Saved' *National Art Collections Fund Review*, 1992, pp. 64-6. Sometime before 1744 the statues were moved from their original situation to surround the Gothic temple. Stowe's impact on contemporary taste is evidenced by a heptagonal 'Altar of the Saxon Gods' shown as number 26 on an itemised plan of Boringdon House, Devon, dated *c.* 1735, now in the Morley Collection, Saltram House (National Trust).

60 *Caesar's Camp - or St George's Hill*, London, 1755, p. 15.

Chapter Ten

1 The use of television programmes and computer imaging is a manifestly successful strategy in terms of transmitting new research. The question remains, however; of what should be transmitted, whether this research should come over as objective and disinterested or engaged and problematic. The 1985 exhibition *Symbols of Power at the time of Stonehenge*, mounted by the National Museum of Antiquities of Scotland, is in my view an exemplary instance of what can be achieved.

SELECT BIBLIOGRAPHY

Alison, Archibald *Essays on the Nature and Principles of Taste*, Edinburgh, 1790.

Allan, D.G.C. and Abbott, John L (eds) *The Virtuoso Tribe of Arts and Sciences–Studies in the Eighteenth-Century Work and Membership of the London Society of Arts*, Athens (Georgia) and London 1992

Allen, Brian *Francis Hayman and the English Rococo*, University of London (Courtauld Institute of Art) PhD dissertation, 1984

Allen, Brian *Francis Hayman*, New Haven and London, 1987

Anderson, Benedict *Imagined Communities*, London, 1983

Andrews, Malcolm *The Search for the Picturesque*, Aldershot, 1989

Bann, Stephen *The Clothing of Clio*, Cambridge, 1984

Banton, Michael *The Idea of Race*, London, 1977

Baridon, Michel 'Ruins as a mental construct', *Journal of Garden History*, v, no. 1, January–March 1985, pp. 84–96

Barr, Bernard and Ingamells, John *A Candidate for Praise; William Mason 1725–97 Precentor of York*, York 1973

Barrett, Cyril 'Irish Nationalism and Art 1800–1921, *Studies*, Winter 1975, pp. 393–409

Beck, Thor J. *Northern Antiquities in French Learning and Literature (1755–1855), A Study in Preromantic Ideas*, Publications of the Institute of French Studies, Columbia University, New York, 1934–1935

Bell, C.F. (ed) *Annals of Thomas Banks*, Cambridge, 1938

Biddis, Michael D. *Images of Race*, Leicester, 1979

Blair, Hugh *Lectures on Rhetoric and Belles Lettres*, Edinburgh, 1783, 1811 edition

Blair, Hugh *A Critical Dissertation on the Poems of Ossian*, New York, 1807

Boaden, James *Cambo-Britons*, London, 1798

Boase, T.S.R. 'Macklin and Bowyer', *Journal of the Warburg and Courtauld Institutes*, XXVI, 1963, pp. 148–77

Boase T.S.R. 'The Decoration of the New Palace of Westminster, 1841–1863', *Journal of the Warburg and Courtauld Institutes*, XVII, 1954, pp. 319–58

Boniface, Priscilla (ed) *In Search of English Gardens – The Travels of John Claudius Loudon and his wife Jane*, Harpenden, 1987

Booth, Susan 'The Early Career of Alexander Runciman and his Relations with Sir James Clerk of Penicuik', *Journal of the Warburg and Courtauld Institutes*, XXXII, 1969, pp. 332–43

Bowden, Samuel *Poetical Essays on Several Occasions*, London, 1733

Breatnach, R.A. 'Two Eighteenth-Century Irish Scholars: J.C. Walker and Charlotte Brooke', *Studia Hibernica*, v, 1965, pp. 88–9

Britton, John *A Topographical and Historical Description of the County of Wilts*, London (c. 1819)

Brooke, Henry *A Collection of the Pieces formerly published by Henry Brooke, esq.* London, 1778

Brown, Iain Gordon *The Hobby-Horsical Antiquary – A Scottish Character 1640–1830*, Edinburgh, 1980

Bryson, Gladys   *Man and Society: the Scottish Enlightenment of the Eighteenth century*, Princeton, 1945

Buchanan, John Lanne   *A Defence of the Scots Highlanders*, London, 1794

Buckle, Henry Thomas   *The History of Civilization in England*, London, 1857

Buckley, James Hamilton   *The Triumph of Time – A Study of the Victorian Concepts of Time, History, Progress and Decadence*, Cambridge, Mass, 1967

Burke, Edmund   *A Philosophical Enquiry into the Origins of our Ideas of the Sublime and Beautiful*, second edition, London, 1759

Burl, Aubrey   *The Stone Circles of the British Isles*, New Haven and London, 1976

Burrow, J.W.   *Evolution and Society; A Study in Victorian Social Theory*, Cambridge, 1966

Burrow, J.W.   *A Liberal Descent; Victorian Historians and the English Past*, Cambridge, 1981

Butlin, Martin   *The Paintings and Drawings of William Blake*, New Haven and London, 1981

Campbell, Michael   *John Martin, Visionary Printmaker*, Campbell Fine Art in association with York City Art Gallery, 1992

Cannon-Brookes, Peter (ed)   *The Painted Word; British History Painting: 1750–1830*, London, 1991

Canny, Nicholas   'The Formation of the Irish Mind: Religion, Politics and Gaelic Irish literature 1580–1750', *Past and Present*, 95, May 1982, pp. 91–116

Carlyle, Thomas   *Chartism*, London, 1858 edition

Carte, Thomas   *A General History of England*, I, II London, 1747, 1750

Chalmers George   *Caledonia: or, An Account of North Britain from the Most Ancient to the Present Times*, London, 1807

Chapman, Ronald   *The Laurel and the Thorn – a study of G F Watts*, London, 1945

Charleton, Walter   *Chorea Gigantum*, London, 1663

Chippindale, Christopher   *Stonehenge Complete*, London, 1983

Chippindale, Christopher   'John Britton's "Celtic Cabinet" in Devizes Museum and its context', *The Antiquaries Journal*, LXV, part 1, 1985, pp. 121–37

Clarke, Edward Daniel   *A Tour through the South of England, Wales, and Part of Ireland made During the Summer of 1791*, London 1793

Clarke, George   'Grecian Taste and Gothic Virtue: Lord Cobham's gardening programme and its iconography', *Apollo*, XCVII (new series) no. 136, June 1973, pp. 566–71

Clarke, William   *The Antiquarian Itinerary*, London, 1815–18

Cloyd, E.L.   *James Burnett, Lord Monboddo*, Oxford, 1972

Colley, Linda   'Whose Nation? Class and National Consciousness in Britain, 1750–1830', *Past and Present*, 113, November 1986, pp. 96–117

Colley Linda   *Britons – Forging the Nation 1701–1837*, New Haven and London, 1992

Collins Wilkie   *Rambles beyond Railways or notes in Cornwall taken a-foot*, London, 1851

Collinson, John rev.   *The History and Antiquities of the County of Somerset*, Bath 1791

Cooke, William   *An Enquiry into the Patriarchal and Druidical Religion, Temples, etc.*, London, 1754

Cornforth, John   'Swinton, Yorkshire – III', *Country Life*, CXXXIX, no. 3607, 21 April 1966, pp. 944–8

Cowling Mary   *The Artist as Anthropologist – the representation of Type and Character in Victorian art*, Cambridge, 1989

Craik, George and Macfarlane, Charles   *The Pictorial History of England*, London, 1837–41

Cumberland, George   *An Attempt to Describe Hafod*, London, 1796

Curtis, L. Perry Jr   *Anglo-Saxons and Celts: A Study of Anti-Irish Prejudice in Victorian England*, Bridgeport, Connecticut, 1968

Curtis, L. Perry Jr   *Apes and Angels – The Irishman in Victorian Caricature*, Washington, 1971

Daniel, Glyn   *The Idea of Prehistory*, Harmondsworth, 1971

Daniel, Glyn   *Megaliths in History*, London, 1972

Davies, Edward   *Aphtharte, or the Genius of Britain*, Bath, 1784

Davies, Edward   *Celtic Researches*, London, 1804

Davis, Thomas   *Literary and Historical Essays*, Dublin, 1846

De Valera, Ann   *Antiquarian and Historical Investigations in Ireland in the Eighteenth Century*, unpublished MA Thesis, University College, Dublin, 1978

Dictionary of National Biography

Dixon Hunt, John and Willis, Peter (eds)   *The Genius of the Place - The English Landscape Garden, 1620-1820*, London, 1975

Dixon Hunt, John   *The Figure in the Landscape: Poetry, Painting, and Gardening during the Eighteenth Century*, Baltimore, 1976

Douglas, David C.   *English Scholars, 1660-1730*, revised edition, London, 1951

Draper, John W.   *William Mason - a Study in Eighteenth Century Culture*, New York, 1924

Duck, Stephen *Caesar's Camp - or St George's Hill*, London, 1755

Elliott, Brent   *Victorian Gardens*, London, 1986

Elucidation of Mr Bowyer's Plan for a Magnificent Edition of Hume's History of England, London, 1795

Erdman, David   *Blake: Prophet against Empire*, London, 1977

Errington, Lindsay   *Social and Religious Themes in English Art, 1840-1860*, Garland reprint of Courtauld Institute of Art PhD dissertation, London, 1984

Evans, Evan   *Some Specimens of the Poetry of the Antient Welsh Bards*, London, 1764

Evans, Joan   *A History of the Society of Antiquaries*, Oxford, 1956

Fairchild, Hoxie Neale   *The Noble Savage - a study in Romantic Naturalism*, New York, 1928, reprinted 1961

Farley, Frank Edgar   *Scandinavian Influences in the English Romantic Movement*, Boston, 1903

Fenton, Richard   *A Tour in Quest of Genealogy through Several Parts of Wales, Somersetshire and Wiltshire in a Series of Letters to a Friend in Dublin*, London, 1811

Fisher, Peter F.   'Blake and the Druids', *Journal of English and Germanic Philology*, 1959, LVIII, pp. 589-612

Flett, Arthur Lambert   *Ruins: The Development of a Theme in Eighteenth Century British Landscape Painting c.1760-1800*, unpublished PhD dissertation, Indiana University, 1981

Frere, John   'An Account of Flint Weapons discovered at Hoxne in Suffolk', *Archaeologia*, XIII, 1800, pp. 204-5

Frew, John   'An Aspect of the Early Gothic Revival: The Transformation of Medievalist Research, 1770-1800', *Journal of the Warburg and Courtauld Institutes*, XLIII, 1980, pp. 174-85

Gaskill, Howard   '"Ossian" Macpherson: towards a rehabilitation', *Comparative Criticism - An Annual Journal*, No. 8, Cambridge, 1986, pp. 113-46

Gellner, Ernest   *Nations and Nationalism*, Oxford, 1983

Gill, Stephen (ed)   *The Salisbury Plain Poems of William Wordsworth*, New York, 1975

Gilmartin, John   'Vincent Waldré's ceiling paintings in Dublin Castle, *Apollo*, XCV, no. 119 (new series), January 1972, pp. 42-7

Gilpin William   *Observations, relative chiefly to Picturesque Beauty, Made in the Year 1772, On several Parts of England; particularly the Mountains, and Lakes of Cumberland, and Westmoreland*, London, 1786

Gilpin, William   *Observations, relative chiefly to Picturesque Beauty, Made in the Year 1776, On several parts of Great Britain; particularly the High-Lands of Scotland*, London, 1789

Gilpin William   *Three Essays: On Picturesque Beauty; On Picturesque Travel; and On Sketching Landscape*, London, 1792

Gilpin, William   *Observations on the Western Parts of England relative chiefly to Picturesque Beauty*, London, 1798

Godwin, William   *Essay on Sepulchres*, London, 1809

Goldstein, Laurence   *Ruins and Empire. The Evolution of a Theme in Augustan and Romantic Literature*, Pittsburgh, 1977

Gosse, Philip   *Dr. Viper. The Querulous Life of Philip Thicknesse*, London, 1952

Graham, Patrick   *Essay on the Authenticity of the Poems of Ossian*, Edinburgh, 1807

Grayson, Donald K.   *The Establishment of Human Antiquity*, New York, 1983

Greater London Council   *English Baroque Sketches - the Painted Interior in the Age of Thornhill*, London, 1974

Greenway, John L.   'The Gateway to Innocence: Ossian and the Nordic Bard as Myth', *Studies in Eighteenth Century Culture*, IV, 1975, pp. 161–70

Greever, Garland (ed)   *A Wiltshire Parson and his Friends - The Correspondence of William Lisle Bowles*, London, 1926

Grigson, Geoffrey   *Gardenage, or the plants of Ninhursaga*, London, 1952

Grinsell, Leslie V.   *Folklore of Prehistoric Sites in Britain*, Newton Abbot, 1976

Hale, J.R. (ed)   *The Evolution of British Historiography*, London, 1967

Hallam, A   *Great Geological Controversies*, Oxford, 1983

Hamilton Jean   *The Sketching Society 1799-1851*, London, 1971

Hampson, Norman   *The Enlightenment*, Harmondsworth, 1968

Harris, Eileen (ed)   *Thomas Wright- Arbours and Grottos - a Facsimile of the Two Parts of Universal Architecture (1755 and 1758) with a Catalogue of Wright's Works in Architecture and Garden Design*, Aldershot, 1979

Harris, Eileen   'John Wood's system of architecture', *The Burlington Magazine*, CXXXI, no. 1031, February 1989, pp. 101–7

Hassell, John   *Tour of the Isle of Wight*, London, 1790

Hawes, Louis   *Constable's Stonehenge*, London, 1975

Hay, William   *Mount Caburn - a poem*, London, 1730

Heizer, Robert   *Man's Discovery of his Past*, Tunbridge Wells, 1980

Henry, Robert   *The History of Great Britain* (second edition), London, 1788

Hermann, Luke   *Paul and Thomas Sandby*, London, 1986

Hill, Jacqueline R.   'Popery and Protestantism, Civil and Religious Liberty: the Disputed Lessons of Irish History 1690–1812', *Past and Present*, 118, February 1988, pp. 97–129

Hinnant, Charles H.   'Changing Perspectives on the Past: The Reception of Thomas Gray's *The Bard*', *Clio* III/3, June 1974, pp. 315–29

Hobsbawm, Eric and Ranger, Terence (eds)   *The Invention of Tradition*, Cambridge, 1983

Hofmann, Werner, Hohl, Hannah and Ternois, Daniel   *Ossian*, Paris, 1974

Holcomb, Adele M.   'Devil's Den: An Early Drawing by John Sell Cotman', *Master Drawings*, XI, no. 4, Winter 1973, pp. 393–8

Holloway, James and Errington, Lindsay   *The Discovery of Scotland; The Appreciation of Scottish Scenery through Two Centuries of Painting*, Edinburgh, 1978

Holmes, Colin (ed)   *Immigrants and Minorities in British Society*, London, 1978

Horsley, John   *Britannia Romana*, London, 1732

Horsman, Reginald   'Origins of Racial Anglo-Saxonism in Great Britain before 1850', *Journal of the History of Ideas*, XXXVII, July–September 1976, number 3, pp. 387–410

Houkjaer, Ulla   'Dutch Artists in the Service of Danish History - The Kronborg Series', *Apollo*, August 1988, CXXVIII, no. 318 (New Series) pp. 99–103

Hudson, T.P.   'Moor Park, Leoni and Sir James Thornhill', *Burlington Magazine*, CXIII, November 1971, pp. 657–61

Hulme, Obadiah   *An Historical Essay on the English Constitution*, Dublin, 1771

Hulton, Paul   *America 1585: The Complete Drawings of John White*, North Carolina and London, 1984

Hume, David   *The History of England*, London, 1754–62; revised edition 1813

Hunt, F. Knight (ed)   *The Book of Art - Cartoons, Frescoes, Sculpture and Decorative Art as Applied to the New Houses of Parliament*, London, 1846

Hunter, Michael *John Aubrey and the Realm of Learning*, London, 1975

Hussey, Christopher 'Alton Towers, Staffordshire – the valley garden and its buildings', *Country Life*, CXXVII, no. 3300, 2 June 1960, pp. 1246–9

Inglis-Jones, Elisabeth *Peacocks in Paradise*, London, 1950

Irwin, David 'A "Picturesque" experience: The Hermitage at Dunkeld', *The Connoisseur*, CLXXXVII, no. 753, November 1974, pp. 196–201

Jackson, John Edward (ed) *Wiltshire. The Topographical Collections of John Aubrey F.R.S. A.D. 1659–70 with Illustrations*, Devizes, 1862

Jackson-Stops, Gervase 'John Michael Rysbrack; A Saxon Goddess Saved' *National Art Collections Fund Review*, 1992, pp. 64–66

Jacob, Margaret Candee 'John Toland and the Newtonian Ideology', *Journal of the Warburg and Courtauld Institutes*, XXXII, 1969, pp. 307–31

Jacques, David *Georgian Gardens – The Reign of Nature*, Batsford, London, 1983

Janowitz, Anne *England's Ruins – Poetic Purpose and the National Landscape*, Oxford, 1990

Jefferys, Thomas *A Collection of the Dresses of Different Nations*, London, 1757 and 1772

Jenkins, R.T. and Ramage, Helen M., *A History of the Honourable Society of Cymmrodorion*, London, 1951

Jestin, Loftus *The Answer to the Lyre – Richard Bentley's Illustrations to Thomas Gray's Poems*, Philadelphia, 1990

Johnston, Arthur (ed) *Selected Poems of Thomas Gray and William Collins*, London, 1967

Jones, Barbara *Follies and Grottoes*, London, 1974

Jones, D.J.V. *Before Rebecca: Popular Protest in Wales 1793–1835*, London, 1973

Jones, Edward *Musical and Poetical Relicks of the Welsh Bards*, London, 1784

Jones, Edward *The Bardic Museum*, London, 1802

Jones, Inigo *The Most Notable Antiquity of Great Britain, Vulgarly called Stone-Heng on Salisbury Plain. Restored.*, London, 1655

Jones, W.R. 'England against the Celtic Fringe: A Study in Cultural Stereotypes', *Journal of World History*, XIII-I-1971, pp. 155–71

Kahin, Sharon McFarlan *Eighteenth Century British Primitivism*, unpublished PhD dissertation, Cornell University, 1981

Keating, Geoffrey *The General History of Ireland*, Dublin, 1723

Kemys-Tynte Papers, Somerset Record Office, DD/S/WH 320

Kendrick, T.D. *The Druids: A Study in Keltic Prehistory*, London, 1927

Kendrick T.D. *British Antiquity*, London, 1950

Kenworthy-Browne, John 'Rysbrack's Saxon Deities', *Apollo*, CXXII, September 1985, pp. 220–7

Kerkham, Caroline 'Hafod: paradise lost', *Journal of Garden History*, 1991, XI, no. 4, pp. 207–16

Keynes, Geoffrey (ed) *Blake – Complete Writings*, Oxford, 1990

King, Edward *Munimenta Antiqua*, London, 1799

Kitson, Sydney *The Life of John Sell Cotman*, London, 1937

Kliger, Samuel *The Goths in England – a Study in Seventeenth and Eighteenth Century Thought*, Harvard, 1952

Klindt-Jensen, Ole *A History of Scandinavian Archaeology*, London, 1975

Knowles, John (ed) *The Life and Writings of J.H. Fuseli Esq., MA, RA*, London, 1831

Knox, Robert *The Races of Men*, London, 1850

Lebow, Ned 'British Historians and Irish History', *Eire-Ireland*, VIII: 4, 1973, pp. 3–38

Ledwich, Edward 'Dissertation on the Religion of the Druids', *Archaeologia*, VII, 1785, pp. 303–22

Levi, Peter (ed) *Samuel Johnson and James Boswell: A Journey to the Western Islands of Scotland, and The Journal of a Tour to the Hebrides* Harmondsworth, 1984

Levine, Joseph M.   *Dr. Woodward's Shield - History, Science, and Satire in Augustan England*, Berkeley. California, 1977

Levine, Philippa   *The Amateur and the Professional; Antiquarians, Historians and Archaeologists in Victorian England, 1838-1886*, Cambridge, 1986

Levis, Howard C.   *Bladud of Bath, The British King who Tried to Fly*, 1919, reprinted 1973

Lewis. W.S. (ed)   *The Yale Edition of Horace Walpole's Correspondence*, New Haven and London, 1937-83

Lindsay, Suzanne G., Pingeot, Anne and Rishel, Joseph   *The Second Empire - Art in France under Napoloeon III*, Philadelphia, 1978

Lingard, John   *History of England*, 1819, 6th edition, London, 1854

Lockhart, J.G.   *Valerius: a Roman Story*, London, 1821

Loudon, J.C.   *An Encyclopaedia of Gardening*, London, 1822, 1834

Loudon, J.C.   *Encyclopedia of Cottage, Farm and Villa Architecture*, London, 1833

Lovejoy, A.O. and Boas, G.   *Primitivism and Related Ideas in Antiquity*, Baltimore, 1935

Lucas, John   *England and Englishness, Ideas of Nationhood in English Poetry 1688-1900*, London, 1990

Macaulay, Thomas Babington   *History of England* second edition, London, 1849

MacDougall, Hugh A.   *Racial Myth in English History; Trojans, Teutons and Anglo-Saxons*, Montreal, Hanover and London, 1982

Macpherson, James   *The Works of Ossian*, London, 1765

Macpherson, James   *Introduction to the History of Great Britain and Ireland*, London, 1771

Macpherson, John   *Critical Dissertations on the Origin, Antiquities, Language, Government, Manners, and Religion, of the Antient Caledonians, their Posterity the Picts, and the British and Irish Scots*, Dubin, 1768

Mallet, Paul-Henri (Transl. Thomas Percy)   *Northern Antiquities*, London, 1770

Manning, Elfrida   *Marble and Bronze - the Art and Life of Hamo Thornycroft*, London, 1982

Manning, Susan   'Ossian, Scott, and Nineteenth-Century Scottish Literary Nationalism', *Studies in Scottish Literature*, XVII, 1982, pp. 39-54

Marks, Arthur S.   'The Source of John Martin's "The Bard"', Supplement: Notes on British Art 6, *Apollo*, August 1966, pp. 1-2

Marsden, Barry M.   *The Early Barrow-Diggers*, Princes Risborough, 1974

Mason William   *Caractacus; a Dramatic Poem*, Dublin, 1764

Mason, William   *The English Garden*, London, 1783

McCarthy, F.I.   '*The Bard* of Thomas Gray, its composition and its use by painters', *The National Library of Wales Journal*, XIV, No. 1, Summer 1965, pp. 105-113

McCrone, David, Kendrick, Stephen and Straw Pat (eds)   *The Making of Scotland: Nation, Culture and Social Change*, Edinburgh, 1989

McParland, Edward   'A Note on Vincent Waldré', *Apollo*, XCVI, no. 129 (new series) November 1972, p. 467

Meek, Ronald L.   *Social Science and the Ignoble Savage*, Cambridge, 1976

Megaw J.V.S. (ed)   *To Illustrate the Monuments - Essays in Archaeology presented to Stuart Piggott*, London, 1976

Meyrick, Samuel Rush and Smith, Charles Hamilton   *The Costume of the Original Inhabitants of the British Islands*, London, 1815

Miles, Dillwyn   *The Royal National Eisteddfod of Wales*, Swansea, 1977

Moir, Esther   *The Discovery of Britain*, London, 1964

Momigliano, A.   *Studies in Historiography*, London, 1966

Monkhouse, W. Cosmo   *The Works of John Henry Foley RA Sculptor*, London, 1875

Moore, Susan   'Hail! Gods of our Fore-Fathers - Rysbrack's "lost" Saxon Deities at Stowe', *Country Life*, CLXXVII, no. 4563, 31 January 1985, pp. 250-1

Morgan, Prys   *Iolo Morganwg*, Aberystwyth, 1975

Morgan, Prys   *The Eighteenth Century Renaissance*, Llandybie, 1981

Morley, Edith J. (ed) *Blake, Coleridge, Wordsworth, Lamb, Etc. being Selections from the Remains of Henry Crabb Robinson*, Manchester, 1922

Moser, Stephanie 'The Visual Language of Archaeology: a Case Study of Neanderthals', *Antiquity*, LXVI, no. 253, December 1992, pp. 831–44

Mower, David 'Antoine Auguste Préault (1809-1879)', *Art Bulletin*, June 1981, LXIII, no. 2, pp. 288–307

Mowl, Tim and Earnshaw, Brian *John Wood - Architect of Obsession*, Huddersfield, 1988

Naef, Hans 'Henrietta Harvey and Elizabeth Norton: Two English Artists', *Burlington Magazine*, CXIII, no. 815, February 1971, pp. 79–89

Newman, Gerald *The Rise of English Nationalism: A Cultural History 1740–1830*, London, 1987

Nicholas, Thomas *The Pedigree of the English People*, 1868, third edition London, 1873

O'Halloran, Clare 'Irish Re-Creations of the Gaelic Past: the Challenge of Macpherson's Ossian', *Past and Present*, 124, August 1989, pp. 69–95

Okun, Henry 'Ossian in Painting', *Journal of the Warburg and Courtauld Institutes*, XXX, 1967, pp. 327-56

Oppé, Paul (ed) 'Memoirs of Thomas Jones Penkerrig Radnorshire 1803', *Walpole Society*, XXXII (1946-8), 1951

Orgel, Stephen and Strong, Roy *Inigo Jones. The Theatre of the Stuart Court*, London, 1973

Orrey, Leslie *Bellini*, London, 1969

Oswald, Arthur 'Beauties and Wonders of Hawkstone', *Country Life*, CXXIV, no. 3207, 3 July 1958, pp. 18–21 and no. 3208, 10 July 1958, pp. 72–5

Ousby, Ian *The Englishman's England - Taste, Travel and the Rise of Tourism*, Cambridge, 1990

Owen, A.L. *The Famous Druids - a Survey of Three Centuries of English Literature on the Druids*, Oxford, 1962

Paley, Morton D. and Phillips, Michael (eds), *William Blake-Essays in Honour of Sir Geoffrey Keynes*, Oxford, 1973

Payne, Ann *Views of the Past - Topographical Drawings in the British Library*, London, 1987

Peardon, Thomas Preston *The Transition in English Historical Writing 1760-1830*, New York, 1966

Pearson, Charles *The Early and Middle Ages of England*, London, 1861

Pennant, Thomas *Tours in Wales*, London, 1810

Piggott Stuart *William Stukeley, an Eighteenth Century Antiquary*, Oxford, 1950

Piggott Stuart *The Druids*, Harmondsworth, 1974

Piggott Stuart *Ruins in a Landscape*, Edinburgh, 1976

Piggott Stuart *Antiquity Depicted; Aspects of Archaeological Illustration*, London, 1978

Piggott, Stuart *Ancient Britons and the Antiquarian Imagination; Ideas from the Renaissance to the Regency*, London, 1989

Pinkerton, John 'Letters to the People of Great Britain, on the Cultivation of their National History', *The Gentleman's Magazine*, LVIII, January-December, 1788

Planché, J.R. *Recollections and Reflections*, London 1872

Poliakov, Leon *The Aryan Myth: A History of Racist and Nationalist Ideas in Europe*, London 1974

Pool, P.A.S. *William Borlase*, Truro, 1986

Portal, Abraham *Vortimer, or the True Patriot*, London, 1796

Porter, Roy *The Making of Geology - Earth sciences in Britain 1660-1815*, Cambridge, 1977

Powys, Ursula 'Recreations of a Georgian Family', *Country Life*, CXXVII, no. 3290, 24 March 1960, pp. 640–2

Pressly, William L. 'James Barry's "The Baptism of the King of Cashel by St Patrick"', *The Burlington Magazine*, CXVIII, September 1976, pp. 643–7

Pressly, William L. *The Life and Art of James Barry*, New Haven and London, 1981

Price, Uvedale *Essay on the Picturesque*, 1794, London, 1810 edition

Pughe, William Owen *The Myvyrian Archaiology of Wales*, London, 1801–7

Pughe, William Owen *The Cambrian Biography*, London, 1803

Raifeartaigh, T.Ó. (ed) *The Royal Irish Academy – a Bicentennial History, 1785-1985*, Dublin, 1985

Ramsay, George Gilbert (transl.) *The Annals of Tacitus*, London, 1909

Rapin de Thoyras, Paul *The History of England*, second edition, London, 1732

Ribeiro, Aileen Elizabeth *The Dress Worn at Masquerades in England, 1730-1790, and its Relation to Fancy Dress in Portraiture*, PhD thesis, Courtauld Institute of Art, 1975, Garland reprint, 1984

Richards, William *The Briton Describ'd; or, A Journey Through WALES*, London, 1749

Robertson, William *The History of Scotland*, London, 1759

Rorschach, Kimerly *The Early Georgian Landscape Garden*, New Haven and London, 1983

Rosenblum, Robert *Transformations in Late Eighteenth Century Art*, Princeton, 1969

Rosenthal, Harold *Two Centuries of Opera at Covent Garden*, London, 1958

Roudinesco, Elisabeth (transl. Martin Thom), *Théroigne de Méricourt - a Melancholic Woman during the French Revolution*, Verso, 1991

Rowlands, Henry *Mona Antiqua Restaurata*, Dublin, 1723

Rubel, Margaret Mary *Savage and Barbarian - Historical Attitudes in the Criticism of Homer and Ossian, 1760-1800*, Amsterdam, Oxford and New York, 1978

Rudwick, Martin *Scenes from Deep Time, Early Pictorial Representations of the Prehistoric World*, Chicago, 1992

Ruskin, John *Modern Painters*, London, 1888

Sambrook, James (ed) *James Thomson Liberty, The Castle of Indolence and other poems*, Oxford, 1986

Sammes, Aylett *Britannia Antiqua Illustrata*, London, 1676

Samuel, Raphael and Jones, Gareth Stedman (eds) *Culture, Ideology and Politics* London, 1982

Samuels, Allen M. 'Rudolph Ackermann and *The English Dance of Death', The Book Collector*, XXIII, no. 3, Autumn 1974, pp. 371–80

Saurat, Denis *Blake and Modern Thought*, London, 1929

Schepelern, H.D. and Ulla Houkjaer *The Kronborg Series. King Christian IV and his Pictures of Early Danish History*, Copenhagen, 1988

Scott, Walter (ed) *The Poetical Works of Anna Seward*, Edinburgh, 1810

Senet, André *Man in Search of his Ancestors*, London, 1955

Shanks, Michael *Experiencing the Past - on the Character of Archaeology*, London, 1992

Sheehy, Jeanne *The Rediscovery of Ireland's Past: the Celtic Revival 1830-1930*, London, 1980

Sheeran, George 'The Richardsons and their garden at Bierley Hall', *Bradford Antiquary*, 3 series, no. 4, 1988/89 pp. 3–10

Sher, Richard B '"Those Scotch Imposters and their Cabal": Ossian and the Scottish Enlightenment', in *Man and Nature - Proceedings of the Canadian Society for Eighteenth Century Studies*, University of Western Ontario, 1982, pp. 55–63

Slotkin, J.S. (ed) *Readings in Early Anthropology*, London, 1965

Smith, Anthony D *Patriotism and Neo-Classicism: The 'Historical Revival' in French and English Painting and Sculpture, 1746-1800*, PhD dissertation, University College, London, 1987

Smith, Anthony D. *National Identity*, Harmondsworth, 1991

Smith, John *Galic Antiquities*, Edinburgh, 1780

Snodin, Michael, *Karl Friedrich Schinkel, Universal Man*, New Haven and London, 1991

Snyder, Edward D. 'The Wild Irish: A Study of Some English Satires against the Irish, Scots, and Welsh', *Modern Philology*, April 1920, pp. 147–85

Snyder, Edward D. *The Celtic Revival in English Literature 1760–1800*, Harvard, 1923

Southey, Robert *Colloquies on Society*, London, 1824

Stephens, Frederic G. *A Memoir of George Cruikshank*, London, 1891

Strong, Roy *And when did you last see your father? The Victorian Painter and British History*, London, 1978

Strutt, Joseph *Honda Angel-Cynnan*, London 1774–75

Stukeley, William *Stonehenge, a Temple restor'd to the British Druids*, London, 1740

Stukeley, William *Abury, A Temple of the British Druids*, London, 1743

Sunderland, John 'John Hamilton Mortimer; his life and works' *Walpole Society*, LII, 1986

Swinburne, A.G. *William Blake – a Critical Essay*, London, 1868

Tasker, William *Arviragus, A Tragedy*, London, 1796

Temple, Nigel *John Nash & the Village Picturesque*, Gloucester, 1979

Thacker, Christopher *Masters of the Grotto – Joseph and Josiah Lane*, Tisbury, 1976

Thacker, Christopher *The Wildness Pleases*, London, 1983

Thomas, Keith *Man and the Natural World; changing attitudes in England 1500–1800*, Harmondsworth, 1987

Todd, Ruthven *Tracks in the Snow*, London, 1946

Toland, John *A Critical History of the Celtic Religion and Learning: Containing an account of the Druids*, London, n.d. (?1740)

Toynbee, Paget and Whibley, Leonard (eds) *Correspondence of Thomas Gray*, Oxford, 1935

Trevelyan, Raleigh *A Pre-Raphaelite Circle*, London, 1978

Turner, Dawson (ed) *The Literary Correspondence of John Pinkerton*, London, 1830

Turner, Sharon *The History of the Anglo-Saxons*, third edition, London, 1820

Ussher, James *Annals of the Ancient and New Testaments*, London, 1650

Vaughan, Herbert M 'Some Letters of Thomas Johnes of Hafod (1794–1807)', *Y Cymmrodor*, 1925, pp. 200–13

Vaughan, Robert *Revolutions in English History*, London, 1859

Vaughan, William 'The Englishness of British Art', *The Oxford Art Journal*, XIII, no. 2, 1990, pp. 11–23

Viallaneix, Paul and Ehrard, Jean *Nos ancêtres les Gaulois*, Clermont-Ferrand, 1982

Walters, Gwyn 'The antiquary and the map', *Word and Image*, IV, no. 2, April–June 1988, pp. 529–44

Warner, Rev. Richard *Excursions from Bath*, Bath 1801

Warner, Rev. Richard *A Tour through the Northern Counties of England and the Borders of Scotland*, Bath, 1802

Warner, Rev. Richard *A Tour through Cornwall in the Autumn of 1808*, Bath 1809

Watkin, David *The English Vision*, London, 1982

Watts, M.S. *George Frederick Watts – The Annals of an Artist's Life*, London, 1912

Webb, John *A Vindication of Stone-Heng Restored*, London, 1665

Weinstock, Herbert *Vincenzo Bellini – His Life and His Operas*, London, 1972

Wexter, Victor G. *David Hume and the 'History of England'*, Philadelphia, 1979

Whitney, Lois 'English Primitivistic Theories of Epic origins', *Modern Philology*, XXI, no. 4, May 1924, pp. 337–78

Williams, Edward *A Vindication of the Celts*, London, 1803

Woodbridge, Kenneth *Landscape and Antiquity*, Oxford, 1970

Woodbridge, Kenneth *The Stourhead Landscape*, The National Trust, 1989

Woolf, Stuart 'French Civilization and Ethnicity in the Napoleonic Empire', *Past and Present*, 124, August 1989, pp. 96–120

Woolner, Amy *Thomas Woolner, R.A., Sculptor and Poet – his Life in Letters*, London, 1917

Wordsworth, William   *Guide Through the District of the Lakes*, London, 1835

Wright, Thomas   *Universal Architecture Book I, Six Original Designs of Arbours; Book II, Six Original Designs of Grottos,* London, 1755 and 1758

Wright, Thomas   *The Celt, the Roman and the Saxon*, London, 1852

Young, G.M. (ed)   *Macaulay – Prose and Poetry*, London, 1952

INDEX

Page references in italics indicate illustrations

A'Beckett, Gilbert Abbott 151
Abildgaard, Nicolai *29*, 29
Ackermann, Rudolph 59, 182, *183*
Alexander, William *208*
Alison, Archibald 188
Allen, Grant 127
Alton Towers 211-13, *212*, 215
Ambiorix 37
Amesbury Abbey 203
Angiviller, Comte d' 30
Anglo-Saxon Magazine, The 122
Antient Britons, Honourable and Loyal Society
    of 40
Antiquaries, Society of 3, 14-16, 18-19, 212
Antiquaries of Scotland, Society of 16
Arminius (Hermann) 34-36
Armitage, Edward 135-6, *136*, 148, 157
Arne, Thomas 137
Arnot, Hugo 65
Aubrey, John 80, 85, 129-30
Auldgarth 205
Avebury 4, 7, 63, 80, 82, 84, 86, 91, 96, 203,
    210

Bacon, Nathaniel 124
Baker, J. 189-90
Bale, John 124
Bandel, Ernst von *36*, 36-7
Banks, Thomas *156*, 156
Banwell 210-11, *211*, 214-15
Bards 7, 34, 41, 46-75 *passim.*, 91, 110-11, 190,
    214
Barnard, Edward 140-1, 160, 219
Barralet, James 66, *67*
Barry, James 64, 70, *71*, 102-4, *103*
Bates, Benjamin 98, 100
Beckford, William 203
Bell, Charles 121
Bellini, Vincenzo 108
Bentley, Richard 50, *51*, 51, 52, 53
Bertin, Jules 37, *38*
Bierley Hall 205-6, *206*, 211
Blackstone, William 125
Bladud 73, 82-3, 200
Blair, Hugh 46-7, 63, 66
Blaise Hamlet 208, *209*

Blake, William 48, *60*, 60, *61*, 61, 70, 72-5, 91-6,
    94, 95, *96*,
Blakey, Nicholas 44, *134*, 134-5, 151
Blumenbach, Johann Frederick 119, 121
Boadicea 17, 26, 42-5, 72-3, 137-8, 140, 148, 153,
    158-9, 161, 163-4, 218, 232 n.20
Boccaccio 161
Boece, Hector 27, 82
Bolingbroke, Henry St John, first Viscount 10, 13,
    24
Borlase, William 13-15, 22, 224 n.32
Boscawen, William 49
Boucher de Perthes, Jacques 6
Bowden, Samuel 182
Bowles, William Lisle 170
Bowyer, Robert 45, 151-2, 160, 215, 218-19
Boydell, John 71
Brennus 31, 33
Briggs, Henry Perronet *141*, 141
Britton, John 86, *87*, 188-9, 191, 234 n.40
Brooke, Charlotte 17
Brooke, Henry 100
Brooke, W.H. 163
Brown, Ford Madox *146*, 146
Brown, Lancelot 'Capability' 195
Browne, Henry 4
Bruce, J.C. 144, 146-7
Bry, Theodor de 129, *130*, 132
Buckle, Henry Thomas 23-4
Buckler, John *211*
Buffon, Georges-Louis Leclerc, comte de 4
Bunting, Edward 17
Bure, Johan 27
Burges, William 214
Burke, Edmund 88, 173-4
Burney, Edward *134*, 135
Byrne, William 168, *169*

'CH' 186
Caesar, Julius 3, 11, 21, 33, 44, 46, 72-3, 76, 106,
    108, 115, 124, 126, 134-6, 139, 154, 157, 164
Cambrensis, Giraldus 116
Cambrian Register, The 55, 56
Cambridge, Richard Owen 197
Camden, William 18, 77, 80, 116, 165
Camper, Pieter 121

Caractacus 17, 26-7, 40, 42-5, 73, 77, 97, 137-40, 148-51, 153-4, 156-9, 164, 184, 193, 207, 218-19, 232 n.20
Caradogion Society 41, 157
Cardiff Castle 214
Carlell, Lodowick 78
Carlyle, Thomas 122-3
Carte, Thomas 49, 117, 125
Carter, John 19
Celtes, Conrad 79
Celtic Academy (Paris) 31
Celtic revival 16, 18, 47-8, 55, 75, 83, 117, 125
Chalmers, George 65, 109-10
Chateaubriand, François-René, vicomte de 31, 108
Clarke, Edward 180-1
Clarke, William 171-2, 177
Clerk, Sir James 69
Clerk, Sir John 42-3, 228 n.3
Cobham Hall 208, *209*, 215
Coke, Sir Edward 124
Colley, Linda 224 n.1, 225 n.23, 230 n.11
Collins, Wilkie 177-8, 187
Collins, William 137, 216
Combe, George 121, 146
Condorcet, Jean Antoine Nicolas Caritat, marquis de 114
Constable, John *183*, 183-5, 234 n.32
Cooke, William 85
Corbould, Edward Henry *109*, 109, *142*, 142, 162, 163
Corbould, Henry *133*, 133
Corbould, Richard *55*, 56, *57*, 57
Cosway, Richard *59*, 59, 224 n.34, 234 n.29
Cotman, John Sell *190*, *191*, *192*, 190-3, 234 n.40
Cowper, William 17, 159, 163-4
Cox, Richard 116
Crabbe, George 170-1, 189
Craik, George 45
Cruikshank, George *123*, 123-4
Cumberland, George 205
Cymmrodorion, Honourable Society of 16, 40-1, 55, 228 n.3

Darwin, Charles 2, 5
Dashwood, Francis 98, 200
Davies, Edward 83, 91, 109, 138
Davis, Sneyd 137-8
Davis, Thomas 44
Decker, Thomas *198*, 198-200
Deepdene, The 196
Diggle, Elizabeth 204-5
Dilettanti, Society of 18
Dodsley, James 51
Dodsley, Robert 98, 135, 151-3
Douglas, James 14, 224 n.32
Downman, John 58, *59*, 59
Drayton, Michael 77
Druids 3, 7, 14-15, 30, 33-4, 40, 46-8, 53, 55, 63, 72-112 *passim.*, 113, 127, 133, 141, 148, 160, 174-5, 185-8, 193, 195-208, 210-12, 214-18, 220-1
Dublin Society 16
Duck, Stephen 217
Dunkeld House 198

Eisteddfod 41, 214
Evans, Evan 17, 40, 48, 55
Evans, Theophilus 41

Fairholt, Frederick William 19
Fenton, Richard 69, 181
Ferguson, Adam 114, 118
Flaxman, John 60-1, 156
Fletcher, John 77, 108, 153, 159
Flitcroft, Henry 200
Fonthill 203
Foley, John Henry 149, *150*, 151, 153, 157-8, 163
Four Stages theory 63, 114-15, 119-20
Foxe, John 124
Friedrich, Caspar David 34, *35*, 36, *37*, 37
Frere, John 5
Fuseli, Henry 154, *155*, 156, 173

Galgacus 43, 44, 111, 163
Gall, Frans Joseph 121
Gandon, James 43
Geller, William Overend 96, *97*, 104
Geoffrey of Monmouth 9, 41
Gibbon, Edward 13, 48
Gibson, Edmund 18, 80
Giles, James *187*, 187
Gilpin, William 66, 77, 96-7, 174-5, 188
Girtin, Thomas *181*, 181-2, 191
Glyndŵr, Owain 40
Glover, Richard 137, 159, 232 n.11
Godwin, William 57-8
Gough, Richard 18-19
Gorsedd 55, 214-15
Graham, Patrick 65-6
Grand Lodge of the Order of Druids 84
Grattan, Henry 11-12, 43, 102-3
Gray, Thomas vii, 18, 47-51, 53, 56-63, 66, 70, 74
Grose, Francis 19
Grotius, Hugo 27
Guizot, François 31, 33
Gwyneddigion Society 41, 228 n.3

Hagley 213
Hafod 205-6, 208
Hamilton, John *140*, 140-1
Hamilton, William 154-6, *155*
Hardiman, James 17
Harford, John 208
Harrison, Thomas 205
Harvey, Elizabeth *72*, 72
Hassell, John 4, 187
Haswell, House 200
Havell, Robert *20*, 21, *87*, *132*, *162*
Hawkstone Hall 201, 205, 213
Hay, William 136-7
Hayman, Francis 44, 97-8, *98*, 100, 107, 151, 153-4, *154*, *160*, 160, 219
Hearne, Thomas 168, *169*, 191
Heere, Lucas de 129
Helmont, F.M. van 85
Henry, Robert 1-2, 64, 83, 91-2, 119-20, 125
Herbert, John Rogers 106, *106*
Herder, Johann Gottfried 34
Hermann (see Arminius)

Higden, Ranulph 116
Highland Society 16
Highland Society of Edinburgh 64
Hill, Sir Richard 201, 205, 213
Historiography 8ff., 21-5, 39-40, 48, 151-3
Hoare, Henry 200-1
Hoare, Richard Colt 24-5, 228 n.3
Holinshed, Raphael 116, 159
Holmes, Robert 89
Hopkins, Charles 159
Howard, Sir Robert 159
Hulme, Obadiah 126
Hume, David 10-14, 20-1, 24, 45, 48, 110,
    118-19, 133, 135, 149, 151, 160, 163, 215,
    218-19
Hunt, William Homan *107*, 107-8, 232 n.22
Hutton, James 4-5
Huxley, Thomas 127

Ibbetson, Julius Caesar 17, *17*, 53, *189*, 189-90
Innes, Thomas 42

Jefferys, Thomas *20*, 19-21, 129
Johnes, Thomas 205-6, 208-9, 211
Johnson, Samuel 62, 117-19, 173
Jones, David 16
Jones, Edward 17, 55
Jones, Inigo 15, 71, 78, *79*, 83, 196, 203
Jones, Rice 55
Jones, Theophilus 40-1
Jones, Thomas 53, *54*, 100, 180, 185

Kames, Henry Home, Lord 114
Kauffmann, Angelica *34*, 34
Keating, Geoffrey 103-4, 116
Kemys-Tynte, Sir Charles 200
Kent, William 198, 213
King, Edward 92, 171
Kipling, Rudyard 142
Kirkup, Seymour 74
Kleist, Heinrich von 34
Klopstock, Friedrich Gottlieb 34
Knapton, John and Paul 98, 134-5, 151-3
Knight, Charles 104, *105*
Knight, Richard Payne 205
Knox, Robert 118, 120, 122

Laing, Malcolm 64, 65, 69
Lane, Josiah 203
Lapworth, Charles 184
Lavater, Johann Kaspar 121
Law, George Henry 210-11, 215
Ledwich, Edward 88-9
Leland, John 18, 82, 124, 165
Lhuyd, Edward 16, 40
Lingard, John 91, 131
Lockhart, John Gibson 111
Loggan, David 166-7, *167*
Long Meg and her Daughters 104, 148
Loudon, John Claudius 212-13
Loutherbourg, Philippe Jacques de *56*, 56, 133,
    218-20, *219*
Lucas, Charles 86
Lyell, Charles 4-5

Macaulay, Thomas Babington 147
Macculloch, John 198
Macfarlane, Charles (see Craik, George)
Macpherson, James 17, 34, 42-3, 47-9, 62-6, 69,
    74, 83, 88, 136, 193
Macpherson, John 188
Maclise, Daniel 148, 163
Malcolm, David 42
Malkin, Benjamin Heath 41
Mallet, David 137
Mallet, Paul Henri 28-9, 125-6
Malton, James 168, *169*
Map, Walter 116
Martin, Henri 33
Martin, John 56, *57*, 57, 86-8, *87*, 96
Mason, William 17, 44, 48, 51, 53, 63, 97, 137,
    139, 154, 156, 193, 206, 207
Massy, Richard Tuthill 127
Méricourt, Théroigne de 30-1
Merlin's Cave, Richmond Park 198, 213, 217
Meyrick, Samuel Rush 19-21, 86, 88, 96, 132-3,
    161, 163
Millais, John Everett 142, *143*
Millar, John 115
Miller, Sanderson 139
Milles, Jeremiah 19
Millet, Aimé *32*, 33, 36-7
Milton, John 48, 82
Monboddo, James Burnett, Lord 114
Monkhouse, W. Cosmo 149-51, 153, 157-8
Montesquieu, Charles-Louis de Secondat 65
Moore, Thomas 17
Morganwg, Iolo (Edward Williams) 41, 55-6, 74,
    214-15
Morris, Lewis, Richard and William 55, 224 n.30,
    228 n.3
Mortimer, John Hamilton 69-70, 98, *99*, 100, *101*,
    106
Moyne, Jacques le 129
Murchison, Sir Roderick Impey 184

Napoleon III 33
Nash, John 208
nationalism 26-45 *passim.*, 135-6, 151, 214
Nesfield, William Andrews *179*, 179-80
Neuville, Alphonse de 31
Nicholas, Thomas 115, 127, 158-9
Norma 108, 109

O'Conor, Charles 11-12, 43
O'Halloran, Sylvester 11
Ogilvie, John 83-4
Oldfield, T.H. 125
Oliver, S.P. 214
Opie, John 160, *161*
Ossian 17, 34, 42-3, 46-9, 59, 62-6, 69, 72, 77, 83,
    108, 112, 191-3, 198

Park Place 207-8, *208*
Parker, Matthew 124
Parliament, fresco competition for redecoration
    of 44, 45, 105, 135, 144-8, 152-3, 157, 163
Parmigianino 50
Parris, Edmund Thomas *105*, 105-6

Parry, John 17, 49, 55
Peacock, Thomas Love 23
Pearson, Charles 122
Pembroke, Earl of 203-4
Pengelly, William 6
Pepys, Samuel 173-4
Percy, James 17, 125-6
Pezron, Paul Yves 16, 40
Piggott, Stuart viii, 75-6, 82, 88, 223 n.25
Pike, Luke Owen 125
Pinkerton, John 8-10, 13-14, 24, 64-5, 69, 117-18,
    120-1, 126
Piper, Frederik Magnus *201*, 201
Planché, James 19
Plas Newydd 190, 203
Playfair, John 4
Pocklington, Joseph *204*, 204-5, 211, 215
Portal, Abraham 138-9
Posidonius 75-6, 86, 89, 92
Préault, Antoine 33
Price, Uvedale 175, 205
Prichard, James Cowles 120-1
primitivism 15-16, 57, 64-5, 130-3
Prout, Samuel 19
Pughe, William Owen 41-2, 56, 73, 86, 92, 109,
    126
Pyne, James Baker *179*, 179-80

race 115-28, 146-51
Raphael 50
Rapin-Thoyras, Paul de 48, 100, 125
Ravensdale Park 205
Rembrandt van Rijn 27
Repton, George 208, *209*
Repton, Humphrey 208, *209*, 212-13
Richards, George 154
Richards, William 117
Richardson, Richard 205-6
Robertson, William 10, 12, 14, 16, 21, 24, 42, 65
Robinson, Henry Crabb 74
Rosa, Salvator 50, 53, *54*
Rousham 197, 213
Rousseau, Jean-Jacques 16, 126
Rowlands, Henry 79-80, *81*, 88, 110, *159*, 159-60
Rowlandson, Thomas 182, *183*
Royal Irish Academy 16
Royal Society 6, 18
Rude, François *31*, 31
Runciman, Alexander *68*, 69-70
Ruskin, John 6, 185-6
Ryley, Charles Reuben 69, *70*, 70

Sadeler, Jan and Raphael 79, *80*
Salmon, T.S. 183
Sammes, Aylett *79*, 79-80, 129, 154, 159
Sandby, Paul 51, 53
Sandby, Thomas *202*, 202-3
Schinkel, Karl Friedrich *35*, 35-6
Scott, William Bell *143*, *144*, 143-4, 146-7
Sedgwick, Adam 184
Selden, John 77, 79
Selous, Humphrey Courtney 148, *162*, 163
Sergel, Johan T. 29
Seward, Anna 47

Shaw, William 64
Shelley, Percy Bysshe 184
Shenstone, William 63, 136, 196
Sieyès, Abbé 30
Smirke, Robert 110, *111*, *135*, 135, 218, 224 n.34,
    227 n.45
Smith, Adam 114-15
Smith, Charles Hamilton (see also Meyrick,
    S.R.) *20*, 87, *132*, *162*
Smith, John (of Edinburgh) 62, 83
Smith, John (of Salisbury) 83
Smith, Worthington G. 214
Smollett, Tobias 160
Society for the Encouragement of Arts 44, 64, 98,
    159
Sotheby, William 110
Southey, Robert 73, 126, 170
Spurzheim, J.C. 121
Speed, John 21, 100, 129, *131*, 159
Stanton Drew 82, 167, 200, 211
Stephens, Frederic 123-4
Steuart, George 198
Stonehenge 3-4, 7, 53, 63, 73, 75, 80, 82-4, 86,
    88-91, 96, 127, 165, 168, 171, 173-6, 178,
    180-90, 200, 203, 205, 207, 213, 215, 220,
    235 n.4
Stonor 203
Stothard, Charles Alfred 19
Stothard, Thomas 160-1, *161*, *162*
Stourhead 200-1, 213
Stowe 101, 156, 197, 213, 216
Strichen House 203
Strutt, Joseph 11-12, 19-20
Stuart, Gilbert 119
Stukeley, William 3-4, 63, 79-80, 82, 84-6, 91-2,
    96, *167*, 167, 203, 210, 224 n.32
Swinburne, Algernon Charles 74
Swinton Hall *210*, 210, 214-15
Sydney, Algernon 124

Tacitus 3, 30, 46, 65, 76, 110, 115, 159
Tasker, William 139
Taymouth Castle 203
Temple Druid 203
Tennyson, Alfred 159, 163
Thicknesse, Philip 215, 217
Thierry, Amédée 33
Thomson, Henry *176*, 176
Thomson, James 80-2, 86, 137
Thompson, Jacob 104, *104*
Thomsen, C.J. 5
Thornhill, Sir James 153
Thornycroft, Thomas 36, 163-4, *164*
Three Age system 5-6
Three Shires Stone 203
time, changing understanding of 3-6, 184-5
Toland, John 85, 88, 92
Tone, Wolfe 102
Torbuck, John 117
Trevelyan family 143, 232 n.31
Turgot, Anne-Robert-Jacques 114
Turner, J.M.W. vii, 185-6, *186*
Turner, Sharon 4, 126-7
Turner, William (of Oxford) 168, *169*

251

Ubaldini, Petruccio 159
Ussher, James 3

Vallancey, Charles 11, 16
Vaughan, Robert 6, 148
Velleda 31, 33, 108
Vercingetorix 31–4, 36, 139
Vergil, Polydore 9, 41
Verstegen, Richard 124
Viollet-le-Duc, Eugène-Emmanuel 33
Virginia Water 202–3
Vos, Marten de 79

Waldré, Vincent 101–3, *102*
Wale, Samuel 66, *68*
Walker, Joseph Cooper 11, 17, 19
Walpole, Horace 15, 44–5, 50–1, 53, 117–18, 156, 207
Ward, E.M. 163
Wardour Castle 203
Warner, Richard 41, 177, 201–4
Watts, George Frederick 148, *157*, 157-8
West, Benjamin *58*, 58, 224 n.34

West, Francis Robert *160*, 160
West, Gilbert 216
West, Raphael Lamar 77, *78*
West Wycombe 200
Wet, Jacob de 27, *28*
Wharton, Thomas 51, 62
Whately, Thomas 196
Whitaker, John 125
White, John 95, 129, *130*
Wilkes, John 117, 215, 217
Williams, Evan 17
Wilton House 203, 211
Wood, John 82–3
Woolner, Thomas 144–5, *145*, 148
Wordsworth, William 89–91, 178
Worm, Ole 27
Worsaae, J.J.A. 5, 29–30, 36–7
Wright, Thomas (architect) *199*, 199–200, 236 n.55
Wright, Thomas 126

Young, Arthur 200